Changing Landscapes in the Atlantic World

Cultures, Societies, Exchanges, and Conflict from 1492 to 1877

First Edition

EDITED BY

Marlin Barber

SAN DIEGO

Bassim Hamadeh, CEO and Publisher

Angela Schultz, Senior Field Acquisitions Editor

Alisa Munoz, Project Editor

Casey Hands, Production Editor

Jess Estrella, Senior Graphic Designer

Greg Isales, Licensing Associate

Natalie Piccotti, Director of Marketing

Kassie Graves, Vice President of Editorial

Jamie Giganti, Director of Academic Publishing

Cover image cover: Copyright © 2013 iStockphoto LP/baona.

Printed in the United States of America.

cognella® | ACADEMIC PUBLISHING

3970 Sorrento Valley Blvd., Ste. 500, San Diego, CA 92121

Contents

iii

Chapter 1

Exploration and the Struggle for Liberty

Readings in Western Atlantic World Political
Changes from 1492 to 1877

Introduction

In this chapter we will explore the early political aspirations in the Americas and how they factored substantially into the development of the identity of the United States. Students should pay close attention to efforts by groups such as indigenous Americans, Europeans, and Africans to establish a physical place where individuals and groups maintained their own systems of rules and regulations. Although these systems have been largely dominated by Eurocentric customs and philosophies, recent scholars have identified efforts of various groups who came together in the Americas beginning in the fifteenth century to assert their own political influence within the larger political framework that came to dominate what would become the United States. It was a system that came to revolve around more representative democratic principles in which those whom the political structure initially marginalized could secure greater rights under the law. Students should look at how race, class, gender, and nationality factored into an Anglocentric political structure that came to serve as the blueprint for the United States.

This chapter includes selected titles that examine the shifting politics of the United States from the colonial period through Reconstruction, while also exploring the overlap of nationality, race, class, region, and gender. This is critical in learning how democratic principles were not the initial aim of European and English colonizers. However, because of multiculturalism, regional distinctions, emerging class differences, and shifting gender roles, the United States would embrace those principles. Readings in this section look at subjects such as pre-Columbian American civilizations that were independent societies wrought with cultural, political, and economic systems and that the Italian explorer Christopher Columbus was not in fact a discoverer of the Americas during his fifteenth-century voyages. Also included are topics such as connections between ideas of the Enlightenment and race, the nullification crisis of the 1830s, the political turmoil of the Republican Party and secession, and female activism in the years following the Civil War.

The selections in this section also seek to prompt questions regarding the following concepts.

1. How do the readings shape your understanding of the United States' development of democratic republican political ideas?
2. Why do you think it was a struggle to arrive at the acceptance of egalitarian ideas, even though the Americas were multicultural?

Reading 1.1

The Myth of Columbus

Alice Beck Kehoe

"I N FOURTEEN HUNDRED AND NINETY-TWO, COLUMBUS sailed the ocean blue." This is true. It is not true that he discovered a new world, and it is not even true that he was the first documented European to see the Americas. Bjarni Herjólfsson earned that notice when his ship was blown off course to Greenland in 986.

Bjarni, a merchant working between Norway and Iceland, was traveling to see his parents who had recently moved from Iceland to the new Norse settlement in Greenland. When storm and fog lifted, Bjarni and his crew saw a forested land they knew was not Greenland. Anxious to find his parents, Bjarni refused his crew's appeals to go ashore during the several days they coasted along Labrador. At the Greenland Norse settlement and then at the Norwegian royal court, Bjarni described the unknown land he had seen, inspiring Leif, son of the Greenland colony's leader, Eirik the Red. Leif organized a settler party to explore the Canadian coast west of Greenland, from northern Labrador to the Gulf of St. Lawrence. L'Anse aux Meadows, a Norse settlement on the northern end of Newfoundland that has been radiocarbon dated to around 1000 CE, may be Leif's short-lived colony (Kolodny 2012:51–57). Two Icelandic family epics, the *Groenlendinga saga* (Greenlanders' Saga) and *Eiríks saga rauða* (Saga of Erik the Red), describe these explorations and colonizing efforts.

How could textbooks generally ignore this credible, documented history of European colonization of the western side of the North Atlantic, Greenland, and its Norse farmers' use of the Canadian Maritimes? Why is the Italian mariner sailing five hundred years after Leif Eiriksson lauded as the discoverer of an unknown new world? Why, to delve deeper, is any European credited with discovering a new world teeming with the millions descended from real discoverers coming from Asia near the end of the Ice Age, fifteen thousand years ago? Racism? Propaganda? The politics of capitalist competition?

Columbus's "discovery of America" is a myth, the kind of myth that anthropologists have studied for more than a century. Bronislaw Malinowski, a prominent British-resident anthropologist, termed myths like the one crediting Columbus *social charters*. Such myths profess to tell, in the form of a story, the origin of a community or nation. Once upon a time, says the story, a hero (or heroine) transformed a people into the community we know. Because the hero was super intelligent or magically powerful, perhaps divine or divinely blessed, the community has prospered up to today. Moral of the story: What we do, and have done, is right. Like a charter for a school or business, a social charter myth prescribes a community's basic organization and operations.

Columbus, in the myth, "opened a New World" for exploitation by the major European powers of his day.[1] At that time, 1492, Scandinavian nations were not yet strong enough to contend with the more southern European nations. Greenland's climate had worsened for farmers and the Norse Greenlanders had abandoned their two settlements. The myth of Columbus is a story of an Italian working for Spain, dealing with Portuguese, and challenged by other Italians working for England. It is a story with a clear, exciting plot. The well-told story has no space for sidebars about Columbus's predecessors. They are relegated to "prehistory," thereby excluded from history. Critical thinking demands they be discussed.

Roots of the Columbus Myth

Cristoforo Colombo, born 1451 in Genoa, Italy, died 1506, was an ambitious seaman determined to forge a place in the forefront of his peers in a time of fervid efforts to find seaways between Atlantic Europe and fabled riches of the Orient. Conquest of Constantinople (modern Istanbul, Turkey) by the Ottoman Turks in 1453 had chopped off Europe's accustomed source of Chinese silks, Southeast Asian spices, and other luxury goods from Asia. European entrepreneurs, often supported by their monarchs, searched for new shipping routes out of their Atlantic ports, sailing along western Africa and finding a route to the Indian Ocean around the Cape of Good Hope at the south end of Africa, or sailing into the Atlantic hoping to reach China and Japan by circling the globe westward. Colombo calculated this distance, using figures from the classical Greek scientist Aristotle. Because he didn't realize that Aristotle's "league" measurement wasn't the same as the "league" of medieval Europe, Colombo's result was much shorter than the correct distance.[2] He insisted to possible patrons, in Portugal and Spain, that he had skills and knowledge for a successful voyage, if they would give him ships and men.

At first denied, in part because a Spanish committee decided, correctly, that his projected sailing distance was erroneous, in 1492 Spain's king and queen decided to risk sponsoring him. Their conquest of Muslim-ruled Granada early in 1492 ended ten years' expense of war,

FIGURE 1.1.1 European depiction of heroic Columbus encountering New World savages; engraving by Theodor de Bry (1528–1598). Courtesy the Library of Congress, via Wikimedia Commons.

bringing them new wealth that they augmented by decreeing that all Jews who refused to convert to Christianity must emigrate, forfeiting to the Crown the possessions they could not carry away. With the three ships the monarchs provided to him out of this confiscation, Colombo sailed into the Atlantic on the morning after the last of the ships laden with Jews left the Spanish port. Two-and-a-half months later, Colombo's ships encountered Caribbean island outliers of America.

Surprisingly, Columbus wasn't hailed as Discoverer of America until America, that is, the United States, was born. A patriotic young Princeton graduate, Philip Freneu, wrote an epic poem "The Pictures of Columbus" in 1774, published in 1788. His Columbus displays "every sentiment that sways the brave," seeking royal patrons who share his "daring aims and persevering soul" (Bauer 2011:15, 18). During the same period, shortly after the American Revolution, a second patriot, Joel Barlow, published in 1787 a poem tying the new nation to Biblical themes: Columbus is the new Moses traveling through "dreary wastes" to the Promised Land (Bauer 2011:28). The new nation that won its heroic struggles against nefarious

King George across the ocean praised the non-British Genoese who claimed America for Britain's enemy, Spain. "It is not a conquered, but a discovered country. It came not to the king by descent, but was explored by the settlers," wrote John Adams, second president of the United States (Usner 2013:636). In 1791, dictionary maker Noah Webster, who had established an American English, also published "The Story of Columbus" in a reader for American children, praising the hero's "courage and coolness in the hour of danger" (Bauer 2011:23).

A generation later, in 1828, popular writer Washington Irving published a thick biography of the hero Columbus, enhancing it by embroidering what he found in archives. Founding Fathers Jefferson and John Adams had recently died, both on July 4, 1826. Populist General Andrew Jackson was elected president in 1828, forcibly cleansing the United States of its First Nations east of the Mississippi. Strong-willed, manly, vigorous Columbus matched Jackson's forceful personality and determination to seize the lands of the feckless natives. Soon after Pearl Harbor in 1941, Columbus was hailed a naval hero, with U.S. Admiral and Harvard historian Samuel Eliot Morison publishing in 1942 another popular biography, *Admiral of the Ocean Sea*. Scholars point out how cannily Christoforo Colombo composed his public letters to the Spanish rulers Ferdinand and Isabella, providing plenty of self-praise that easily rendered him the hero Americans sought.

For the fourth centenary of Columbus's discovery in 1892, the rapidly growing city of Chicago hosted an awesome exposition of America's glories and power. Building a "White City" at the shore of its inland sea, Lake Michigan, Chicago constructed imposing stone exhibition halls filled with scientific, technical, and luxury marvels. Outside, a midway stretched westward, offering fairgoers the sight of exotic "primitive" people in native costumes beside their huts, interspersed with hootchie-cootchie dancers and carnival games. At the lakefront, the SS *Christopher Columbus*, largest ship on the Great Lakes, provided excursion sails to better view the magnificent vista. So ambitious it couldn't be completed in time for 1892, the World Columbian Exposition of 1893 epitomized Columbus opening the New World in the West. Columbus Day, October 12, was celebrated in towns and schools in the calendar of American civil religion, calling up patriotic exhortations to emulate the daring vision, the steadfast courage, of this first civilized man to broach the wilderness.

One century later, the fifth centenary provoked a radically opposite commemoration ("commemoration," many insisted, not "celebration"). America in 1992 had increasing First Nations[3] populations and burgeoning Latin American and Asian numbers. The First Nations objected to initial expectations that this quincentenary would be marked by parades honoring the heroic Genoese, with pretty White girls draped and crowned as Columbia. Fourteen hundred and ninety-two marked, for First Nations, inauguration of five hundred years of slaughter, horrible new diseases, destruction of homes, seizure of lands, ethnocidal denial of their heritages, imposed poverty, and tearing children from parents' arms to incarcerate them in cold, distant boarding schools. October 12 was a day of mourning for them. Significantly, when a national Jubilee Commission was appointed in 1985, no American Indian was included. Backlash from a range of First Nations leaders calling attention to the devastation unleashed by Columbus's invasions of Caribbean islands upset the Commission's planning. The "Quincentenary ... had become a battleground for our entire view of Western culture" (Summerhill and Williams 2000:119).

Postcolonialism is the label for this perspective on Western culture. After five centuries of aggrandizement, European powers rocking from the ravages of World War II decided that administering far-flung colonies was too costly. Global companies undergirded by international banking could better exploit Third World countries. Although economic independence was a chimera for most of the new nations, their intelligentsia, freed of the colonizer's yoke, developed subaltern literatures challenging foreign conquerors' versions of their histories (Kolodny 2015). American First Nations' views were voiced by scholars and writers chronicling true American heroes, from Popé who led the Pueblos' revolt against Spanish domination in 1680, through Tecumseh's alliance of Indian troops with Britain in the War of 1812, to the 28 American Indian soldiers awarded the highest honor given by the United States, the Congressional Medal of Honor. Civilian heroes, too, are celebrated, including Pocahontas, whose diplomatic marriage to John Rolfe stabilized the Jamestown settlement; Sacajawea, the captive young concubine bravely guiding Lewis and Clark; Hinmaton-yalatkit (Chief Joseph), desperately seeking safety in Canada for his Nimipu in 1877; and twentieth-century stalwarts like David Sohappy, a Wanapum protecting his people's salmon fishery. From a postcolonial standpoint, Columbus is the poster boy for European imperialists' self-serving lies.

The Myth of Columbus and the Myth of Progress

While the expanding United States was creating Columbus the model hero, it similarly beatified Progress. Pictured like a Greek goddess, Progress much resembled Columbia, both depicted treading in the air above American pioneers in covered wagon trains heading west. The goddess's outstretched right arm pointed to the farther sea. She might be labeled Destiny, referring to the popular slogan coined in 1845 to launch the Mexican War, *America's Manifest Destiny is to stretch from sea to sea.*

War-mongering for empire was justified by racism, alleging all darker-skinned people to be inferior to fair Northwest Europeans. Scales of progress to civilization were constructed, with American Indians and Africans on the bottom, China, Japan, and India in the middle, and the imperial European powers at the top. Lewis Henry Morgan, a lawyer in Rochester, New York, did fieldwork among Iroquois near his home and on month-long trips to see Indians along the Missouri River. Climaxing his studies, in 1877 he published *Ancient Society,* setting up three stages of human progress, from Savagery through Barbarism (simple agricultural villages) to Civilization. Accusing Cortés and the other Spanish conquistadors of exaggerating Mexican cities and pomp, he declared no native American nations had achieved Civilization, not even the Aztecs.

Morgan's scheme found favor with the founder of the Smithsonian's Bureau of American Ethnology, the intrepid explorer of the Colorado River, Major John Wesley Powell, and also with English aristocrat John Lubbock, whose own popular books, *Pre-historic Times* (1865) and *The Origin of Civilisation and the Primitive Condition of Man: Mental and Social Condition of Savages* (1870), illustrated the "lowest stage of savagery" with photos of South American Indians beggared by commercial seal hunters killing off their principal food. Morgan's and Lubbock's idea of native America goes back to John Locke's 1689 statement that "in the beginning all the World was America" (Locke 1689: Chapter 5, par. 49). This rendered native America the exemplar of the primitive stage beyond which Europeans developed their superior societies. Serving as spinmeister to the politician Earl of Shaftesbury, Locke persuasively justified his patron's taking of Carolina from its inhabitants (Kehoe 2009). Columbus's discovery of a New World becomes discovery of a benighted world separated from fulfilling God's command to improve the earth.

"Progress" may seem obvious. See how computers progressed from huge rooms of vacuum tubes in stacks, to the powerful little device that fits in a hand. See how aircraft progressed from flimsy one-man contraptions to airships carrying hundreds across oceans. Mechanization of work has certainly progressed to relieve men and women and children of backbreaking labor. "Progress" is often equated with technological development[4], belatedly acknowledging downsides in pollution and destruction. The nineteenth-century idea, promulgated by English popular philosopher Herbert Spencer, that there is a vital force propelling us in progress toward a perfect world, was blasted by the bestiality of World War I. That horror fit the medieval belief that, far from progressing toward utopia, the world was degenerating, damned by sin. Progress isn't obvious unless an observer is primed to see it and to ignore degeneration such as despoiling forests and waterways. It is a myth that "every day in every way we get better and better."[5]

Bolstering the idea of progress in the era of Western imperialism was the assumption that those technologically powerful nations had evolved farther from primate ancestors and savages, compared to the countries they conquered. Colonies were peopled by inferior, less evolved "races"—"living fossils" exemplifying stages in the evolution of civilization. It was "natural" that enlightened, literate, progressed White men should rule over darker-skinned natives, and over European peasants browned by laboring outdoors. Those enlightened, schooled White men expounded the social-charter myth of progress, legitimating their domination.

During the nineteenth century, technical progress in mechanizing work tied into professionalization of science in Western nations. Dropping the label "natural philosophy," the sciences as we know them were separated. Standards of research were formulated. A basic idea was that science consists in experiments that may be replicated to check whether their conclusions are valid. How can a geologist, a paleontologist, a biological taxonomist, or an archaeologist replicate nature's experiments that produced observed data? Nature's time scale can be enormous, far beyond human lifetimes. Scientists who cannot replicate an inferred process, as physicists and chemists might in a laboratory, look for "natural experiments"—situations that differ from each other in one, likely significant, factor. For example, was a drying climate the stimulus for developing agriculture? Compare the situations of early agricultural societies, and see whether or not most evidence a drying climate. (The answer here is that the hypothesis was rejected; data demonstrated agriculture and its early situations are extremely varied.)

The method of seeking natural experiments for what cannot be manipulated experimentally led archaeologists to seize the idea that the Americas were totally isolated from Eurasia and Africa until 1492; American cultural developments would show whether Progress, as Europeans knew it, is natural to human societies, or instead perhaps due to circumstances unique to the White race of Europe. America, isolated, was a natural experiment for the science of culture.

The myth of Columbus's discovery of a new world enabled the science-minded to put forth the Americas as a natural experiment, where the varied degrees of progress seen among American First Nations replicated similar differing stages of progress observed in Africa, Asia, Australia, and rural Europe. In Europe, Asia, and Africa, the natural experiment was compromised by millennia of intercourse between the more and the less evolved peoples. In isolated Australia, the experiment was incomplete because its natives apparently never evolved beyond "savagery." The Americas, then, by virtue of postulated complete isolation since the Ice Age and because they did show stages of progress up to "archaic" kingdoms, could serve as the scientific test of the validity of progressive cultural evolution inherent in human societies. America's capitulation to European White men proved that such men, indeed, were the most progressed, evolved to lead those others their superiority had colonized.

Postcolonial anthropology cannot accept either the myth of Columbus the discoverer of a hidden new world, nor the myth of progress. Both myths are social charters perpetrating injustice and exploitation. We don't deny that often "might makes right," yet, neither should we complacently accept its consequences. Critically examining premises and political outcomes of these two myths frees us, as citizens, to more intelligently deal with contemporary problems. Biological anthropology refutes the idea of less-evolved races of people, and cultural ecology shows how populations adapted to environments, often with sophisticated techniques that made deserts bloom and icy wastes produce food and shelter. In this book, we will look at the world before 1492, a world in which humans have always lived in global networks, moving and mixing. The myth of Columbus and the myth of progress came from an era of slavery, of the subjugation of women, of voting limited to men of property, of inhuman working conditions in mines and mills and plantations. They don't belong in today's world.

Critical Thinking can be discomforting. Demanding as many data as may be relevant, thoroughly checking their authenticity, alert for discrepancies and contradictions, critical thinkers come up to "popular knowledge" handed down by political parties to get votes and legislation serving their interests. Denying non-Western societies' achievements in seafaring to justify taking over their "newly discovered" territories, like denying their achievements in "civilization," has been part of the ideology of Manifest Destiny. In this book, we see how archaeology and genetics have amassed data that make untenable the notion that oceans cut the Americas out of the global world until 1492.

Notes

1. Linguist Johanna Nichols suggests the myth of unknown, uninhabited wilderness discovered by progenitors of a present nation may be common among Indo-European speakers (Nichols 1997:262, note 5).

2. In the early eleventh century, the Arabic scientist al-Biruni had correctly calculated the circumference of the earth, using geometry and his own measurements of longitude at a number of sites. Realizing there is a huge area on the globe not recorded in the geographies of his day, al-Biruni suggested there is likely a large land mass in the ocean between Asia and Europe. This postulation of inhabited lands should earn al-Biruni the title of discoverer of America, one historian urges, even though the Central Asian scholar never sailed to find it (Starr 2013:375–377).

3. First Nations refers to the indigenous nations invaded by Europeans following Columbus's voyage. Canada officially uses this term for its indigenous peoples. The United States still officially uses "tribe," a term associated since the Roman empire with smaller nations invaded by empires. Most First Nations citizens say they are American Indians, or Indian people, rather than Native Americans, a term contested by some European-descended U. S.-born citizens.

4. Early in the "modern" period in Europe, so labeled by many self-confident writers in the sixteenth century there, three inventions were singled out as the key innovations launching "modern" progress: firearms, printing, and the nautical compass (Boruchoff 2012). Ironically, all three were Chinese inventions used there for centuries before diffused to Europe (Needham 2004:20, 53, 204).

5. Originally a phrase taught as a placebo by French pharmacist Émile Coué (1857–1926).

References

Bauer, Marta Louise. 2011. "Christopher Columbus: An Analysis of Myth Creation and Longevity in Early America." Honors thesis, Oakland University. Online pdf, accessed March, 2014.

Boruchoff, David A. "The Three Greatest Inventions of Modern Times: An Idea and Its Public." *Entangled Knowledge: Scientific Discourses and Cultural Difference*. Klaus Hock and Gesa Mackenthun, eds. Münster: Waxmann, 2012, pp. 133–163.

———— "Deconstructing John Locke." *Postcolonial Perspectives in Archaeology*. Peter Bikouis, Dominic Lacroix, and Meaghan M. Peuramaki-Brown, eds. Calgary: University of Calgary Archaeological Association, 2009, pp. 125–132.

Kolodny, Annette 2012 *Search of First Contact: The Vikings of Vinland, the Peoples of the Dawnland, and the Anglo-American Anxiety of Discovery*. Durham NC: Duke University Press.

Locke, John. "Two Treatises of Government." *Two Treatises of Government and A Letter Concerning Toleration*. Ian Shapiro, ed. New Haven: Yale University Press 2003[1689], pp. 3–209.

Needham, Joseph. "General Conclusions and Reflections." *Science and Civilisation in China*, vol. 7, pt. II. Kenneth Girdwood Robinson, ed. Cambridge: Cambridge University Press, 2004.

Nichols, Johanna. "The Eurasian Spread Zone and the Indo-European Dispersal." *Archaeology and Language I: Theoretical and Methodological Orientations*. Roger Blench and Matthew Spriggs, eds. New York: Routledge, 1997, pp. 220–266.

Starr, S. Frederick. *Lost Enlightenment: Central Asia's Golden Age from the Arab Conquest to Tamerlane*. Princeton: Princeton University Press, 2013.

Summerhill, Stephen J., and John Alexander Williams. *Sinking Columbus: Contested History, Cultural Politics, and Mythmaking during the Quincentenary*. Gainesville: University Press of Florida, 2000.

Usner, Daniel H. 2013. "'A Savage Feast They Made of It:' John Adams and the Paradoxical Origins of Federal Indian Policy." *Journal of the Early Republic* 33:607–641.

Reading 1.2

Enlightenment

Ibram X. Kendi

NOTHING FAZED HIM. HE CARRIED TIRED mules. He pressed on while companions fainted. He cut down predators as calmly as he rested in trees at night. Peter Jefferson had a job to do in 1747: he was surveying land never before seen by White settlers, in order to continue the boundary-line between Virginia and North Carolina across the dangerous Blue Ridge Mountains. He had been commissioned to certify that colonial America's westernmost point had not become like Jamaica's Blue Mountains, a haven for runaways.[1]

In time, Peter Jefferson's mesmerizing stamina, strength, and courage on surveying trips became transfixed in family lore. Among the first to hear the stories was four-year-old Thomas, overjoyed when his father finally came home at the end of 1747. Thomas was Peter's oldest son, born on April 13 during the memorable year of 1743. Cotton Mather's missionary counterpart in Virginia, James Blair, died sixteen days after Thomas's birth, marking the end of an era when theologians almost completely dominated the racial discourse in America. The year also marked the birth of a new intellectual era. "Enlightened" thinkers started secularizing and expanding the racist discourse throughout the colonies, tutoring future antislavery, anti-abolitionist, and anti-royal revolutionaries in Thomas Jefferson's generation. And Cotton Mather's greatest secular disciple led the way.

"The first drudgery of settling new colonies is now pretty well over," Benjamin Franklin observed in 1743, "and there are many in every province in circumstances that set them at ease, and afford leisure to cultivate the finer arts, and improve the common stock of knowledge." At thirty-seven, Franklin's circumstances certainly set him at ease. Since fleeing Boston, he had built an empire of stores, almanacs, and newspapers in Philadelphia. For men like him, who leisured about as their capital literally or figuratively worked for them, his observations about living at

Ibram X. Kendi, "Enlightenment," *Stamped from the Beginning: The Definitive History of Racist Ideas in America*, pp. 79-91, 522-524. Copyright © 2017 by Perseus Books Group. Reprinted with permission.

ease were no doubt true. Franklin founded the American Philosophical Society (APS) in 1743 in Philadelphia. Modeled after the Royal Society, the APS became the colonies' first formal association of scholars since the Mathers' Boston Society in the 1680s. Franklin's scholarly baby died in infancy, but it was revived in 1767 with a commitment to "all philosophical Experiments that let Light into the Nature of Things."[2]

The scientific revolution of the 1600s had given way to a greater intellectual movement in the 1700s. Secular knowledge, and notions of the propensity for universal human progress, had long been distrusted in Christian Europe. That changed with the dawn of an age that came to be known as *les Lumières* in France, *Aufklärung* in Germany, *Illuminismo* in Italy, and the *Enlightenment* in Great Britain and America.

For Enlightenment intellectuals, the metaphor of light typically had a double meaning. Europeans had rediscovered learning after a thousand years in religious darkness, and their bright continental beacon of insight existed in the midst of a "dark" world not yet touched by light. Light, then, became a metaphor for Europeanness, and therefore Whiteness, a notion that Benjamin Franklin and his philosophical society eagerly embraced and imported to the colonies. White colonists, Franklin alleged in *Observations Concerning the Increase of Mankind* (1751), were "making this side of our Globe reflect a brighter Light." Let us bar uneconomical slavery and Black people, Franklin suggested. "But perhaps," he thought, "I am partial to the complexion of my Country, for such kind of partiality is natural to Mankind." Enlightenment ideas gave legitimacy to this long-held racist "partiality," the connection between lightness and Whiteness and reason, on the one hand, and between darkness and Blackness and ignorance, on the other.[3]

These Enlightenment counterpoints arose, conveniently, at a time when Western Europe's triangular transatlantic trade was flourishing. Great Britain, France, and colonial America principally furnished ships and manufactured goods. The ships sailed to West Africa, and traders exchanged these goods, at a profit, for human merchandise. Manufactured cloth became the most sought-after item in eighteenth-century Africa for the same reason that cloth was coveted in Europe—nearly everyone in Africa (as in Europe) wore clothes, and nearly everyone in Africa (as in Europe) desired better clothes. Only the poorest of African people did not wear an upper garment, but this small number became representative in the European mind. It was the irony of the age: slave traders knew that cloth was the most desired commodity in both places, but at the same time some of them were producing the racist idea that Africans walked around naked like animals. Producers of this racist idea had to know their tales were false. But they went on producing them anyway to justify their lucrative commerce in human beings.[4]

The slave ships traveled from Africa to the Americas, where dealers exchanged at another profit the newly enslaved Africans for raw materials that had been produced by the long-enslaved Africans. The ships and traders returned home and began the process anew, providing a "triple stimulus" for European commerce (and a triple exploitation of African people). Practically all the coastal manufacturing and trading towns in the Western world developed an enriching connection to the transatlantic trade during the eighteenth century. Profits exploded with the growth and prosperity of the slave trade in Britain's principal port, Richard Mather's old preaching ground, Liverpool. The principal American slave-trading port was Newport, Rhode Island, and the proceeds produced mammoth fortunes that can be seen in the mansions still dotting the town's historic waterfront.

In his 1745 book endorsing the slave-trading Royal African Company, famous economics writer Malachy Postlethwayt defined the British Empire as "a magnificent superstructure of American commerce and naval power, on an African foundation." But another foundation lay beneath that foundation: those all-important producers of racist ideas, who ensured that this magnificent superstructure would continue to seem normal to potential resisters. Enlightenment intellectuals produced the racist idea that the growing socioeconomic inequities between England and Senegambia, Europe and Africa, the enslavers and enslaved, had to be God's or nature's or nurture's will. Racist ideas clouded the discrimination, rationalized the racial disparities, defined the enslaved, as opposed to the enslavers, as the problem people. Antiracist ideas hardly made the dictionary of racial thought during the Enlightenment.[5]

Carl Linnaeus, the progenitor of Sweden's Enlightenment, followed in the footsteps of François Bernier and took the lead classifying humanity into a racial hierarchy for the new intellectual and commercial age. In *Systema Naturae*, first published in 1735, Linnaeus placed humans at the pinnacle of the animal kingdom. He sliced the genus *Homo* into *Homo sapiens* (humans) and *Homo troglodytes* (ape), and so on, and further divided the single *Homo sapiens* species into four varieties. At the pinnacle of his human kingdom reigned *H. sapiens europaeus*: "Very smart, inventive. Covered by tight clothing. Ruled by law." Then came *H. sapiens americanus* ("Ruled by custom") and *H. sapiens asiaticus* ("Ruled by opinion"). He relegated humanity's nadir, *H. sapiens afer*, to the bottom, calling this group "sluggish, lazy ... [c]rafty, slow, careless. Covered by grease. Ruled by caprice," describing, in particular, the "females with genital flap and elongated breasts."[6]

Carl Linnaeus created a hierarchy within the animal kingdom and a hierarchy within the human kingdom, and this human hierarchy was based on race. His "enlightened" peers were also creating human hierarchies; within the European kingdom, they placed Irish people, Jews, Romani, and southern and eastern Europeans at the bottom. Enslavers and slave traders were creating similar ethnic hierarchies within the African kingdom. Enslaved Africans in North America were coming mainly from seven cultural-geopolitical regions: Angola (26 percent), Senegambia (20 percent), Nigeria (17 percent), Sierra Leone (11 percent), Ghana (11 percent), Ivory Coast (6 percent), and Benin (3 percent). Since the hierarchies were usually based on which ancestral groups were thought to make the best slaves, or whose ways most resembled those of Europeans, different enslavers with different needs and different cultures had different hierarchies. Generally, Angolans were classed as the most inferior Africans, since they were priced so cheaply in slave markets (due to their greater supply). Linnaeus classed the Khoi (or Hottentot) of South Africa as a divergent branch of humanity, *Homo monstrosis monorchidei*. Since the late seventeenth century, the Khoi people had been deemed "the missing link between human and ape species."[7]

Making hierarchies of Black ethnic groups within the African kingdom can be termed *ethnic racism*, because it is at the intersection of ethnocentric and racist ideas, while making hierarchies pitting all Europeans over all Africans was simply racism. In the end, both classified a Black ethnic group as inferior. Standards of measurement for the ethnic groups within the African hierarchies were based on European cultural values and traits, and hierarchy-making was wielded in the service of a political project: enslavement. Senegambians were deemed superior to Angolans because they supposedly made better slaves, and because supposedly their ways were closer to European ways. Imported Africans in the Americas no doubt recognized the hierarchy of African peoples as quickly as imported White servants recognized the broader racial hierarchy. When and if Senegambians cast themselves as superior to Angolans to justify any relative privileges they received, Senegambians were espousing ethnically racist ideas, just like those Whites who used racist ideas to justify their White privileges. Whenever a Black person or group used White people as a standard of measurement, and cast another Black person or group as inferior, it was another instance of racism. Carl Linnaeus and company crafted one massive hierarchy of races and of ethnic groups within the races. The entire ladder and all of its steps—from the Greeks or Brits at the very top down to the Angolans and Hottentots at the bottom—everything bespoke ethnic racism. Some "superior" Africans agreed with the collection of ethnocentric steps for Africans, but rejected the racist ladder that deemed them inferior to White people. They smacked the racist chicken and enjoyed its racist eggs.[8]

Every traded African ethnic group was like a product, and slave traders seemed to be valuing and devaluing these ethnic products based on the laws of supply and demand. Linnaeus did not seem to be part of a grandiose scheme to force-feed ethnic racism to enslaved peoples to divide and conquer them. But whenever ethnic racism did set the natural allies on American plantations apart, in the manner that racism set the natural allies in American poverty apart, enslavers hardly minded. They were usually willing to deploy any tool—intellectual or otherwise—to suppress slave resistance and ensure returns on their investments.

Voltaire, France's enlightenment guru, used Linnaeus's racist ladder in the book of additions that supplemented his half-million-word *Essay on Universal History* in 1756. He agreed there was a permanent natural order of the species. He asked, "Were the flowers, fruits, trees, and animals with which nature covers the face of the earth, planted by her at first only in one spot, in order that they might be spread over the rest of the world?" No, he boldly declared. "The negro race is a species of men as different from ours as the breed of spaniels is from that of greyhound. ... If their understanding is not of a different nature from ours it is at least greatly inferior." The African people were like animals, he added, merely living to satisfy "bodily wants." However, as a "warlike, hardy, and cruel people," they were "superior" soldiers.[9]

With the publication of *Essay on Universal History*, Voltaire became the first prominent writer in almost a century daring enough to suggest polygenesis. The theory of separately created races was a contrast to the assimilationist idea of monogenesis, that is, of all humans as descendants of a White Adam and Eve. Voltaire emerged as the eighteenth century's chief arbiter of segregationist thought, promoting the idea that the races were fundamentally separate, that the separation was immutable, and that the inferior Black race had no capability to assimilate, to be normal, or to be civilized and White. The Enlightenment shift to secular thought had thus opened the door to the production of more segregationist ideas. And segregationist ideas of permanent Black inferiority appealed to enslavers, because they bolstered their defense of the permanent enslavement of Black people.

Voltaire was intellectually at odds with naturalist Georges Louis Leclerc, who adopted the name Buffon. Buffon headed the moderate mainstream of the French Enlightenment through his encyclopedic *Histoire naturelle* (Natural history), which appeared in forty-five volumes over fifty-five years beginning in 1749. Nearly every European intellectual read them. And while Voltaire promoted segregationist thinking, Buffon remained committed to assimilationist ideas.

The argument over Voltaire's multiple human species versus Buffon's single human species was one aspect of a larger scientific divide during the Enlightenment era. Their beloved Sir Isaac Newton envisioned the natural world as an assembled machine running on "natural laws." Newton did not explain how it was assembled. That was fine for Voltaire, who believed the natural world—including the races—to be unchangeable, even from God's power. Buffon instead beheld an ever-changing world. Buffon and Voltaire did agree on one thing: they both opposed slavery. Actually, most of the leading Enlightenment intellectuals were producers of racist ideas *and* abolitionist thought.[10]

Buffon defined a species as "a constant succession of similar individuals that can reproduce together." And since different races could reproduce together, they must be of the same species, he argued. Buffon was responding to some of the first segregationist denigrations of biracial people. Polygenesists were questioning or rejecting the reproductive capability of biracial people in order to substantiate their arguments for racial groups being separate species. If Blacks and Whites were separate species, then their offspring would be infertile. And so the word *mulatto*, which came from "mule," came into being, because mules were the infertile offspring of horses and donkeys. In the eighteenth century, the adage "black as the devil" battled for popularity in the English-speaking world with "God made the white man, the devil made the mulatto."[11]

Buffon distinguished six races or varieties of a single human species (and the Khoi people of South Africa he placed with monkeys). He positioned Africans "between the extremes of barbarism and of civilization." They had "little knowledge" of the "arts and sciences," and their language was "without rules," said Buffon. As a climate theorist and monogenesist, Buffon did not believe these qualities were fixed in stone. If Africans were imported to Europe, then their color would gradually change and become "perhaps as white as the natives" of Europe. It was in Europe where "we behold the human form in its greatest perfection," and where "we ought to form our ideas of the real and natural colour of man." Buffon sounded like the foundational thinker of modern European art history, Johann Joachim Winckelmann of Germany. "A beautiful body will be all the more beautiful the whiter it is," Winckelmann said in his disciplinary classic, *Geschichte der Kunst des Alterthums* (*History of the Art of Antiquity*) in 1764. These were the "enlightened" ideas on race that Benjamin Franklin's American Philosophical Society and a young Thomas Jefferson were consuming and importing to America on the eve of the American Revolution.[12]

Peter Jefferson acquired around twelve hundred acres in Virginia's Albemarle County and went on to represent the county in the House of Burgesses, Virginia's legislative body. Shadwell, his tobacco plantation, sat about five miles east of the current center of Charlottesville. The Jefferson home was a popular rest stop for nearby Cherokees and Catawbas on their regular diplomatic journeys to Williamsburg. The young Thomas Jefferson "acquired impressions of attachment and commiseration for them which have never been obliterated," he reminisced years later.[13]

While Thomas was raised on the common sight of distinguished Native American visitors, he commonly saw African people as house workers tending to his every need as well as field workers tending to tobacco. In 1745, someone brought a two-year-old Thomas Jefferson out of Shadwell's big house. Thomas was held up to a woman on horseback who placed him on a pillow secured to the horse. The rider, who was a slave, took the boy for a ride to a relative's plantation. This was Thomas Jefferson's earliest childhood memory. It associated slavery with comfort. The slave was entrusted with looking after him, and on his soft saddle he felt safe and secure, later recalling the woman as "kind and gentle."[14]

When he played with African boys years later, Thomas learned more about slaveholding. As he recalled, "The parent storms, the child looks on, catches the lineaments of wrath, puts on the same airs in the circle of smaller slaves, gives a loose to his worst passions, and thus nursed, educated, and daily exercised in tyranny, cannot but be stamped by it with odious peculiarities."[15]

In his home, no one around him saw anything wrong with the tyranny. Slavery was as customary as prisons are today. Few could imagine an ordered world without them. Peter Jefferson had accumulated almost sixty captives by the 1750s, which made him the second-largest slaveholder in Albemarle County. Peter preached to his children the importance of self-reliance—oblivious of the contradiction—to which he credited his own success.

Peter did not, however, preach to his son the importance of religion. In fact, when Virginia's First Great Awakening reached the area, it bypassed the Shadwell plantation. Peter did not allow Samuel Davies, who almost single-handedly brought the Awakening to Virginia, to minister to his children or his captives. It is likely that Peter believed—like many of his slaveholding peers—"that Christianizing the Negroes makes them proud and saucy, and tempts them to imagine themselves upon an equality with the white people," as Davies reported in his most celebrated sermon in 1757. Some American planters had been sold on Davies's viewpoint that "some should be Masters and some Servants," and more were open to converting their captives than ever before. But not enough of them to satisfy Cotton Mather's likeminded missionaries, who agreed with Davies that "a *good Christian* will always be a *good Servant*." Enslavers commonly "let [slaves] live on in their Pagan darkness," fearing Christianity would incite their resistance, observed a visiting Swede, Peter Kalm, in the late 1740s. Twenty years later, irritable Virginia planter Landon Carter fumed about Blacks being "devils," adding, "to make them otherwise than slaves will be to set devils free."[16]

Not all Christian missionaries were protecting slavery by preaching Christian submission in the mid-eighteenth century. In 1742, New Jersey native John Woolman, a store clerk, was asked to write a bill of sale for an unnamed African woman. He began to question the institution and soon kicked off what became a legendary traveling ministry, spreading Quakerism and antislavery. After his first Quaker mission in the harrowing slaveholding South in 1746, Woolman jotted down *Some Considerations on the Keeping of Negroes*.[17]

"We are in a high Station, and enjoy greater Favours than they," Woolman theorized. God had endowed White Christians with "distinguished Gifts." By sanctioning slavery, America was "misusing his Gifts." Woolman planted his groundbreaking abolitionist tree in the same racist soil that proslavery theologians like Cotton Mather—preaching divine slavery—had used a century ago. Their divergences over slavery itself obscured their parallel political racism that denied Black people self-determination. Mather's proslavery theological treatises proclaimed masters divinely charged to care for the degraded race of natural servants. Woolman's antislavery treatise proclaimed Christians to be divinely charged with "greater Favours" to emancipate, Christianize, and care for the degraded slaves. But whether they were to be given eternal slavery or eventual emancipation, enslaved Africans would be acted upon as dependent children reliant on White enslavers or abolitionists for their fate.[18]

John Woolman bided his time before submitting his essay to the press of the Philadelphia Yearly Meeting. Woolman knew the history of Quakers quarreling over slavery, of abolitionists disrupting meetings and being banished. He cared just as much about his Quaker ministry and Quaker unity as he did antislavery. In 1752, when abolitionist Anthony Benezet was elected to the press's editorial board, Woolman knew the time was right to publish his eight-year-old essay. By early 1754, Benjamin Franklin's *Pennsylvania Gazette* was advertising the new publication of *Some Considerations on the Keeping of Negroes.*

By the end of the year, some Quakers had started to move like never before against slavery, pushed by Benezet and Woolman and the contradictions of Christian slavery. Benezet had edited Woolman's essay. If Woolman thrived in privacy, Benezet thrived in public, and the two reformers made a dynamic duo of antislavery activists. In September 1754, the Philadelphia Yearly Meeting approved for publication the *Epistle of Caution and Advice Concerning the Buying and Keeping of Slaves.* In the *Epistle*, antislavery reformers struck a compromise, urging Quakers to buy no more slaves. The writers evoked the Golden Law on the sixty-sixth uncelebrated anniversary of the Germantown Petition. Benezet initiated the writing of the *Epistle* and incorporated input from Woolman. Hundreds of copies were shipped to the quarterly meetings in the Delaware Valley. The front door of American Quakerism had officially been opened to antislavery. But Quaker masters quickly slammed the doors to their separate rooms. Seventy percent refused to free their captives. Woolman learned firsthand of their dogged refusal when he ventured into Maryland, Virginia, and North Carolina in 1757.[19]

Slavery's defenders spewed many racist ideas, ranging from Blacks being a backward people, to them living better in America than in Africa, to the curse of Ham. It "troubled" Woolman "to perceive the darkness of their imagination." He never faltered in shooting back, in his calm, compassionate way. No one is inferior in God's eyes, he stressed. They had not imported Africans for their own good, as demonstrated by their constant abuse, overwork, starvation, and scarce clothing.[20]

In 1760, Woolman traveled to the Rhode Island homes of some of colonial America's wealthiest slave-traders. Their "smooth conduct" and "superficial friendship" nearly lured him away from antislavery. He ventured back home to New Jersey as he had done from the South years earlier—dragging a heavy bag of thoughts. In arguing against slavery over the years, he found himself arguing against African inferiority, and thus arguing against himself.

He had to rethink whether White people were in fact bestowed a "high Station." In 1762, he updated *Considerations on Keeping Negroes*.[21]

We must speak out against slavery "from a love of equity," Woolman avowed in the second part of the pamphlet. He dropped the rhetoric of greater "Favours" in a racial sense, although it remained in a religious sense. His antiracism shined. "Placing on Men the ignominious Title SLAVE, dressing them in uncomely Garments, keeping them to servile Labour ... tends gradually to fix a Nation in the mind, that they are a Sort of People below us in Nature," stated Woolman. But Whites should not connect slavery "with the Black Colour, and Liberty with the White," because "where false Ideas are twisted into our Minds, it is with Difficulty we get fair disentangled." In matters of right and equity, "the Colour of a Man avails nothing."[22]

Woolman's antiracism was ahead of its time, like his passionate sermons against poverty, animal cruelty, military conscription, and war. But Woolman's antislavery in the 1750s and 1760s was right on time for the American Revolution, a political upheaval that forced freedom fighters of Thomas Jefferson's generation to address their relationships with slavery.[23]

Dr. Thomas Walker's remedies did not work, and when his patient, the forty-nine-year-old father of Thomas Jefferson, died on August 17, 1757, it was an unbelievable sight for all who had heard the family lore of Peter Jefferson's strength. The fourteen-year-old Thomas had to run his own life. As the oldest male, he now headed the household, according to Virginia's patriarchal creed. But by all accounts, the thirty-seven-year-old Jane Randolph Jefferson did not look to her fourteen-year-old son for guidance, or to Dr. Walker, the estate's overseer. She became the manager of eight children, sixty-six enslaved people, and at least 2,750 acres. Jane Jefferson was sociable, fond of luxury, and meticulous about keeping the plantation's records—traits she bestowed upon Thomas.[24]

In 1760, Thomas Jefferson enrolled in the College of William & Mary, where he thoroughly immersed himself in Enlightenment thought, including its antislavery ideas. He studied under the newly hired twenty-six-year-old Enlightenment intellectual William Small of Scotland, who taught that reason, not religion, should command human affairs, a lesson that would inform Jefferson's views about government. Jefferson also read Buffon's *Natural History*, and he studied Francis Bacon, John Locke, and Isaac Newton, a trio he later called "the three greatest men the world has ever produced."

When Jefferson graduated in 1762, he entered the informal law school of Virginia's leading lawyer, George Wythe, well known for his legal mind and taste for luxury. Admitted to the bar at twenty-four years old in 1767, Jefferson stepped into the political whirlwind of the House of Burgesses, representing Albemarle County like his father had. The Burgesses protested England's latest imposition of taxes, prompting Virginia's royal governor to close their doors on May 17, 1769. Jefferson had been seated all of ten days.[25]

Even after he lost his seat, Jefferson actively participated in the growing hostilities to England and to slavery. He took the freedom suit of twenty-seven-year-old fugitive Samuel Howell. Virginia law prescribed thirty years of servitude for first-generation biracial children of free parents "to prevent that abominable mixture of white man or women with negroes or mulattoes." Howell was second generation, and Jefferson told the court that it was wicked to extend slavery, because "under the law of nature, all men are born free." Wythe, the opposing attorney, stood up to start his rejoinder. The judge ordered Wythe back down and ruled against Jefferson. The law in the colonies was still staunchly proslavery, and racial laws were becoming staunchly segregationist. But then, suddenly, a Boston panel of judges reversed the ideological trend.[26]

Notes

1.   Parent, *Foul Means*, 169–170.
2.   Benjamin Franklin, "A Proposal for Promoting Useful Knowledge Among the British Plantations in America," *Transactions of the Literary and Philosophical Society of New York* 1, no. 1 (1815): 89–90.
3.   Benjamin Franklin, *Observations Concerning the Increase of Mankind, Peopling of Countries* (Tarrytown, NY: W. Abbatt, 1918), 10.
4.   Thomas, *Slave Trade*, 319, 325–327.
5.   Malachy Postlethwayt, *The African Trade, the Great Pillar* (London, 1745), 4.
6.   Dorothy E. Roberts, *Fatal Invention: How Science, Politics, and Big Business Re-Create Race in the Twenty-First Century* (New York: New Press, 2011), 29–30; Bethencourt, *Racisms*, 252–253.
7.   Harriet A. Washington, *Medical Apartheid: The Dark History of Medical Experimentation on Black Americans from Colonial Times to the Present* (New York: Harlem Moon, 2006), 83; Thomas C. Holt, *Children of Fire: A History of African Americans* (New York: Hill and Wang, 2010), 21.
8.   Holt, *Children of Fire*, 19–21; Thomas, *Slave Trade*, 399–402.
9.   Voltaire, *Additions to the Essay on General History*, trans. T. Franklin et al., vol. 22, *The Works of M. De Voltaire* (London: Crowder et al., 1763), 227–228, 234.
10. Thomas, *Slave Trade*, 464–465.
11. Bethencourt, *Racisms*, 165–166, 172–173, 178; Roberts, *Fatal Invention*, 31–32.
12. Georges Louis Leclerc Buffon, *Natural History of Man*, new ed., vol. 1 (London: J. Annereau, 1801), 78–79, 83–94; Georges Louis Leclerc Buffon, *Natural History, General and Particular*, trans. William Smellie, 20 vols., vol. 3 (London: T. Cadell et al., 1812), 440–441; Johann Joachim Winckelmann, *History of the Art of Antiquity*, trans. Harry Francis Mallgrave (Los Angeles: Getty Research Institute, 2006), 192–195.

13. Thomas Jefferson, "To John Adams," in *The Writings of Thomas Jefferson*, ed. H. A. Washington (Washington, DC: Taylor and Maury, 1854), 61.

14. Silvio A. Bedini, *Thomas Jefferson: Statesman of Science* (New York: Macmillan, 1990), 12–13.

15. Thomas Jefferson, *Notes on the State of Virginia* (London: J. Stockdale, 1787), 271.

16. Samuel Davies, "The Duty of Christians to Propagate Their Religion Among the Heathens," in *Proslavery and Sectional Thought in the Early South, 1740–1829: An Anthology*, ed. Jeffrey Robert Young (Columbia: University of South Carolina Press, 2006), 113; Peter Kalm, "Travels into North America," in *A General Collection of the Best and Most Interesting Voyages and Travels in All Parts of the World*, ed. John Pinkerton (London: Longman, Hurst, Rees, and Orme, 1812), 503; Landon Carter, *The Diary of Colonel Landon Carter of Sabine Hall, 1752–1778*, 2 vols., vol. 2 (Charlottesville: University Press of Virginia, 1965), 1149.

17. Thomas P. Slaughter, *The Beautiful Soul of John Woolman, Apostle of Abolition* (New York: Hill and Wang, 2008), 94–133.

18. John Woolman, *Some Considerations on the Keeping of Negroes* (Philadelphia: Tract Association of Friends, 1754), 4.

19. Geoffrey Gilbert Plank, *John Woolman's Path to the Peaceable Kingdom: A Quaker in the British Empire* (Philadelphia: University of Pennsylvania Press, 2012), 105–109.

20. Ibid., 110; Slaughter, *Beautiful Soul*, 194–196; John Woolman, "The Journal of John Woolman," in *The Journal and Major Essays of John Woolman*, ed. Phillips P. Moulton (New York: Oxford University Press, 1971), 63.

21. Slaughter, *Beautiful Soul*, 231–236; Plank, *John Woolman's Path*, 175–177.

22. John Woolman, *Considerations on Keeping Negroes: Part Second* (Philadelphia: B. Franklin and D. Hall, 1762), 24, 30.

23. Slaughter, *Beautiful Soul*, 173; Plank, *John Woolman's Path*, 133, 149–153; Woolman, *Journal and Major Essays*, 53–57, 75–78.

24. Jon Meacham, *Thomas Jefferson: The Art of Power* (New York: Random House, 2012), 11–12.

25. Ibid., 39, 44–45; Bedini, *Thomas Jefferson*, 34, 39, 49.

26. Henry Wiencek, *Master of the Mountain: Thomas Jefferson and His Slaves* (New York: Farrar, Straus, and Giroux, 2012), 24–26; Meacham, *Thomas Jefferson*, 47–49.

Reading 1.3

Rhetoric of Fear
South Carolina Newspapers and the State and
National Politics of 1830

Erika J. Pribanic-Smith

*South Carolinians declared protective tariffs Congress passed in 1824 and 1828 uncon-
stitutional and unfair for placing undue burden on the South while benefiting the North.
A political faction formed that saw the rights of the state as paramount and sought to
protect them, to the point of rebelling against the federal government through nullification of its laws. In response, two additional groups arose: one that aimed to preserve
the Union above all and one that upheld the state's rights and Union equally, urging a
moderate course. Each of these three groups had newspapers to advance its views. This
article studies those newspapers during the seminal year of 1830, which encompassed
four key events in state and national politics that heightened the nullification debate and
realigned the state's political parties. It concludes that rhetoric from all sides preyed on
readers' fear.*

T HE WORDS OF CONGRESSMAN ROBERT BARNWELL RHETT reverberated through the hall
in Columbia, South Carolina, where Rhett and his fellow State Rights activists met on
September 29, 1830. His stirring oration included the revelation that George Washington, Samuel
Adams, Patrick Henry, and Thomas Jefferson all were disunionists and traitors in their time,
"and they broke the British Empire and redrew the map of the world with the sword." Rhett
continued that under the current administration of Andrew Jackson, the Union had no choice
but to dissolve. "It goes down with the inevitable weight of its own gravitation, into that dark
abyss of anarchy and ruin, where all tyrannies have fallen," he proclaimed. To end his speech,
Rhett asserted that if his sentiments constituted him as a disunionist and a traitor, then, "I am
a disunionist! I am a traitor!"[1]

Rhett's words during the heated nullification crisis in South Carolina represented the sentiments of a radical sect in the early years of the antebellum period—men who felt that actions perceived as threatening to the southern states required drastic actions to protect their rights, much as the colonies had against the British. These sentiments sparked tension not only between the northern and southern states but also among southerners, as a war of words exploded over issues concerning the rights of the states versus the value of the Union. Tension between factions characterized South Carolina during the antebellum period, and their debates—many of which played out in the state's newspapers—originated the ideology behind southern secession.

Historians have demonstrated the importance of southern newspapers during the decades preceding the Civil War. Because the southern press remained fiercely partisan throughout the antebellum era, political issues of the day became editorial issues. Slavery and state rights rhetoric largely consumed the southern newspapers' pages, mirroring and in some cases amplifying what occurred in other political forums as reactions to activities in the various branches of national government tore at the threads of the Union.[2]

The first state to secede in December 1860, South Carolina was anomalous in many ways. Its unique geography and demographics created an economic dependence on agriculture exceeding that of other southern states, and its aristocratic origins created a ruling planter class intent on preserving its slave-driven way of life as well as its political and social dominance of the state. These attributes created a radical element that advocated disunion earlier and with more vigor than in any other southern state.[3] In the nineteenth century, South Carolinians clung to their agrarian ideals and became agitated by the industrialist North's growing power. Most of the state's representatives in Congress turned sectionalist by the Missouri statehood debates of the early 1820s, and a rift between South Carolina and Union began to form.[4]

This chasm widened as Congress engaged in a series of actions lumped together as the "American System." Primarily the brainchild of Kentucky Senator Henry Clay, the American System featured policies that many southerners perceived as consolidating power under the federal head while ignoring the states' rights to govern themselves. Some of the most contentious acts distributed federal funds to build roads and canals within individual states with the goal of creating a nationwide transportation infrastructure. Critics in the South argued that the federal government had no right to meddle in state affairs, but they also complained that a majority of internal improvement funds went to northern states.[5]

Protective tariffs to encourage domestic manufacturing were even more controversial. Americans nationwide had supported a tariff passed in 1816 due to an atmosphere of rampant nationalism in the wake of the War of 1812. Sectionalist accusations arose when an 1824 tariff added imports that the prior act had not included, which were perceived as specifically

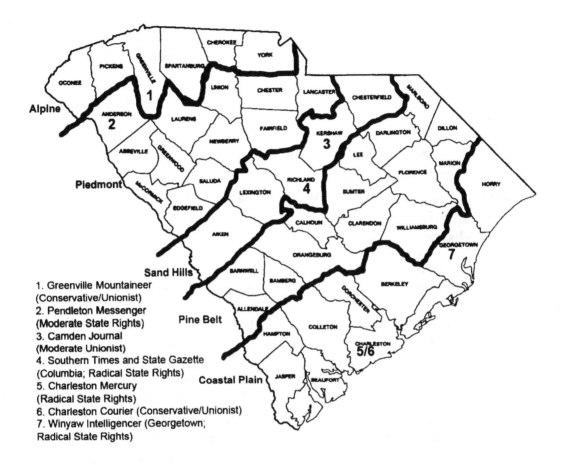

1. Greenville Mountaineer
(Conservative/Unionist)
2. Pendleton Messenger
(Moderate State Rights)
3. Camden Journal
(Moderate Unionist)
4. Southern Times and State Gazette
(Columbia; Radical State Rights)
5. Charleston Mercury
(Radical State Rights)
6. Charleston Courier (Conservative/Unionist)
7. Winyaw Intelligencer (Georgetown;
Radical State Rights)

protecting western and northern interests. The act also raised existing taxes to as much as 37 percent of the goods' value, making them prohibitively expensive for a state that had been hit particularly hard by a depression beginning in 1819. Rather than heeding South Carolinians' complaints and reducing the taxes, Congress passed in 1828 what became known as the "Tariff of Abominations," raising rates to as much as 50 percent of the goods' value.[6]

South Carolinians declared the 1824 and 1828 tariffs unconstitutional, in that they believed Congress overstepped the authority granted by the federal compact, and unfair for placing undue burden on the South while benefiting other regions. Not only did the duties excessively inflate the cost of European imports, but South Carolina consumers also complained that northern manufactures cost more than what they had been paying for goods from overseas. Adding insult to injury, the state's planters complained that they lost income when Great Britain decreased its importation of raw cotton.[7]

Hearing the cries of his fellow South Carolinians, then-Vice President John C. Calhoun drafted the *South Carolina Exposition and Protest* at the end of 1828, declaring that the states had the right to void offending federal laws within their borders by calling nullification conventions.[8] Whereas the tariffs and their sister issue of internal improvements had drawn a fairly uniform response from southerners who feared a government of unlimited power and unequal benevolence, the idea of nullification sparked passionate debate. Not only did other southern states denounce nullification, but the concept also created friction among political groups within South Carolina, which held varying allegiances to the state and nation.[9]

Three factions formed: those who saw the rights of the state as paramount and sought to protect them, to the point of rebelling against the federal government; those who aimed to preserve the Union above all, at risk of subjecting the state to measures they admitted were unjust; and those who upheld the state's rights and Union equally, urging a moderate course until federal usurpations became so intolerable as to warrant drastic action. Each of these groups had newspapers to advance its views.[10]

> *"Rhetoric from all sides preyed on fear. The nullifiers asserted that if the state submitted quietly, the people could be oppressed forever, and the federal government could be allowed to pervert the sacred Constitution at will. Unionists proclaimed that if South Carolina rebelled, the state could be engulfed in a bloody war with the nation the people loved."*

South Carolina thus entered the year 1830 in the throes of heated political and editorial debate with potentially dangerous consequences. Following in the footsteps of "year study" pioneer W. Joseph Campbell,[11] this article offers a close examination of South Carolina newspapers during twelve months that encompassed events crucial to shaping the state's response to national politics. Four events of this seminal year brought the nullification dispute to a head in South Carolina's newspapers and altered the state's party system: key tariff reductions the Twenty-First United States Congress passed during its first session;[12] President Jackson's veto of a major internal improvement appropriation;[13] debates in Congress over a public lands bill;[14] and the state's city and legislative elections.[15]

Historians of the era's politics have recognized the importance of the state's newspapers during this time and used them as sources in their work. Some scholars have investigated South Carolina's antebellum press history, either in sweeping general accounts of the state's media or focused studies of Charleston publications.[16] From this scholarship, it is clear that the state's political parties had strong networks of partisan papers publishing daily in Charleston and Columbia, weekly in other towns statewide. No prior work, however, has focused on South Carolina partisan newspapers—the foremost rhetorical tool of the era— during the crucial nullification crisis, let alone the pivotal year of 1830. It is important to do so in order to understand how South Carolina came to be the only state that nullified the tariffs in the short term, and the first state to secede a few decades later. With a nod toward Bernard Bailyn, whose Pulitzer Prize-winning study of Colonial American pamphlets revealed the origins of Revolutionary War ideology,[17] this article examines editorial-column content originating throughout South Carolina from January to December of 1830 to illuminate the burgeoning beliefs that ultimately resulted in the state's secession.

Histories of South Carolina demarcate five regions based on topographical features and types of crops historically planted. Selected for study were the highest-circulating partisan newspapers for which extant copies exist for the entire year's run from four of those regions: *Greenville Mountaineer* from the Alpine region; *Pendleton Messenger* from the Piedmont region; *Camden Journal* and *Southern Times and State Gazette* (Columbia) from the Sand Hills region; and the *Winyaw Intelligencer* (Georgetown), *Charleston Mercury*, and *Charleston Courier* from the Coastal Plain. No newspapers met the researcher's selection criteria from the Pine Belt region.

For every issue of these seven newspapers, the researcher conducted a qualitative historical analysis of items in the editorial columns that addressed American System policy and potential means of redress. This primarily included unsigned and often untitled editorials written by newspaper staff, although some letters submitted by readers and politicians appeared as well. In addition to representing a geographical cross-section of the state, the selected newspapers encompass an even spread of conservative, moderate, and radical political stances.

Rhetoric from all sides preyed on fear. The nullifiers asserted that if the state submitted quietly, the people could be oppressed forever, and the federal government could be allowed to pervert the sacred Constitution at will. Unionists proclaimed that if South Carolina rebelled, the state could be engulfed in a bloody war with the nation the people loved.

South Carolina's newspaper editors began 1830 with a watchful eye on Congress. Lacking agreement on whether or how to resist the American System, South Carolinians only could hope that the federal government would hear their pleas and alleviate their suffering through repeal of the hated import duties. Their hopes were dashed in January, when the House's Committee on Manufactures presented a report declaring any alteration to the existing tariff law inexpedient.[18]

Although the *Greenville Mountaineer's* editor perceived from the report's wording that the friends of the American System were "evidently alarmed" and the system was "beginning to totter," other writers responded less positively. A January 13 editorial in the *Charleston Mercury* called the report "a death blow to all hopes of modification of the system" and predicted the "system of consolidation will be fixed upon us, under which the southern states, taxed and oppressed for the benefit of the manufacturers, can not fail to sink into a deplorable state of poverty and degradation." The report's true aim even may have been to increase the tariffs at a later date, according to the *Camden Journal*. The editor accused tariff supporters on the committee of quashing debate to avoid replying to "some of the unanswerable abominations of the present tariff" and posited that the tariffites "may probably get more plunder hereafter, if they will just 'hush' for a little while."[19]

Editors' ire increased in February, when the House immediately and decisively tabled a bill South Carolina Rep. George McDuffie proposed to reduce the tariff. The *Pendleton Messenger's* editor believed Congress simply wanted to avoid a "long and stormy" debate, which would not come to much because of majority support for the duties. Columbia's *Southern Times* and the *Charleston Mercury* pinned more sinister motives on congressmen who "shamefully gagged" discussion on the proposed tariff modification, and both editors called South Carolinians to action. "No man, not wilfully [sic] blind, can longer look to congress for redress," the *Times* proclaimed on February 25. The *Mercury* concurred, offering the "gag law" as proof that "the longer oppression is submitted to, the more rigorously will it continue to be extended and enforced." Its editor called for the South to rise up "as sovereign members of a violated league."[20]

Despite what the *Pendleton Messenger* perceived as attempts of the congressional majority to dispose of all efforts at tariff discussion, the *Camden Journal* declared that Vermont Rep. Rollin Mallary's proposed antismuggling resolution provided an opportunity for the anti-tariff members to "cudgel the monster in his own den." As part of the debate surrounding the bill, the Carolinian McDuffie proposed a substitute resolution that would gradually reduce the duties to the innocuous level passed in 1816. The *Charleston Mercury* proclaimed the ensuing debate to be "a struggle for life or death" and insisted that the continuance of the Union depended on the outcome. When Congress defeated McDuffie's measure, the *Southern Times* asserted, "If anything had yet been wanting to convince us of the idiotic folly of reposing a hope for relief of the South, elsewhere than in her own State Sovereignties—here it would be amply supplied." A correspondent to the *Mercury* invited those who hoped for "the returning sense of justice of our Northern brethren" to visit Washington for "a radical cure of the delusion."[21]

> "Not all South Carolina newspapers met the veto with
> gloom. The conservative Greenville Mountaineer *called the*
> *proscription 'a mighty triumph for the South' in that it spelled*
> *the downfall of internal improvements and provided evidence*
> *that the good sense of the American people was returning."*

Even when Congress voted to reduce duties on several items, the newspapers responded pessimistically. According to the newspaper editors, reductions of duties on tea, coffee, cocoa, salt, and molasses were a triumph for the tariff party, not the South. Editorials appearing during May and early June in the *Winyaw Intelligencer, Charleston Mercury, Southern Times, Camden Journal,* and *Greenville Mountaineer* unanimously proclaimed that the decreases were for the benefit of northern consumers and New England shipping interests who found those duties inconvenient. Furthermore, the editors averred that the tariffites' goal was to diminish the national revenue, thus extending the time required to pay off the national debt and providing a pretext for continuing the American System. The *Mountaineer* later decided that Congress's actions late in the session augured "very strongly the downfall of that system of high protecting duties," while the *Times* and *Mercury* remained vigilant in their call for South Carolinians to resist the tariffs entirely, lest the systemizers view their forbearance as submission and justification for oppressive actions.[22]

Editors had little hope of Congress reversing its policy on internal improvements, either. Their complaints about the appropriation of funds for infrastructure projects in the states were similar to those lodged against the tariffs: it was unfair and unconstitutional. The *Pendleton Messenger* asserted that the people of the South might not complain as much about the tariffs if the funds collected from them benefited the entire nation, rather than being distributed for internal improvements on a sectional basis. April editorials in the *Charleston Mercury* warned that if "instead of respecting the sovereignty of the States," Congress continued to "invade their soil, and carry on works of this kind within them against their consent," there would be only one mode of redress by which the southern states could "save themselves from perpetual plunder and extortion"—becoming separate, distinct and independent sovereignties.[23]

Much as the reduction of various duties failed to calm South Carolina editors' attacks against the tariff, President Jacksons veto of the Maysville Road bill did little to diminish the editors' hatred of internal improvements. In the June 12 issue, the *Camden Journal* praised the president for recognizing that the road linking Lexington to the Ohio River was a local work that affected Kentucky alone, not the nation, and that the depleted state of the treasury precluded appropriating such an enormous amount of funds. The *Journal's* editor wished, however, that the president had acknowledged the general government did not have the constitutional right to "pursue these wild schemes of money spending." Therefore, editors in Charleston, Columbia, Georgetown, Pendleton, and Cheraw claimed that Jackson fell short of arresting "the tide of extravagance and corruption." A June 7 editorial in the *Southern Times* noted that the president had affirmed the practice of appropriating for internal improvements of a national nature within the states. The *Cheraw Republican* cited outcry in response to the veto as proof that systemizers would not stop pushing for such expenditures, filled as they were with "the inflexible determination ... to enforce their opinions even at the hazard of the Union; to be discouraged by no defeat—to despair at no reverse." The *Winyaw Intelligencers* editor called the act a "temporary obstruction to a mountain torrent," while the *Times* averred, "The veto has lopped off but a single twig from the tree, from which innumerable sprouts will shoot forth." According to the *Mercury*, southerners needed to adhere to their principles and "struggle for their rights with redoubled zeal" because complete abolition of the protective system depended on their firmness and perseverance.[24]

Not all South Carolina newspapers met the veto with gloom. The conservative *Greenville Mountaineer* called the proscription "a mighty triumph for the South" in that it spelled the downfall of internal improvements and provided evidence that the good sense of the American people was returning. The editor declared that "the clouds and tempests have blown away, leaving our political horizon fairer and brighter than ever," and urged patience and forbearance until the tariff party's delusion had time to pass. Writers in both the *Mountaineer* and *Charleston Courier* pleaded with influential citizens to restore peace and contentment in the state. A common argument was that the southern states were not enduring the great and unequal burden that the people were led to believe, and even if they were, the suffering was not enough to warrant the excitement that existed. A writer called "R" in the *Mountaineer* and a *Courier* correspondent with the pseudonym "Moultrie" accused certain newspapers of spreading what they knew to be fallacies in order to maintain the ferment. Moultrie declared that all the prosperous state of South Carolina needed to be peaceful and happy was to "get rid of about one dozen of hot headed, ambitious, weak, turbulent and reckless men; who, by repeating Ruin, Northern monopoly, Plunder, and such hard words, actually have contrived to fright the state from its propriety."[25]

Another congressional act fueled debate between South Carolina's factional newspapers. A resolution Connecticut Senator Samuel Augustus Foot proposed in December of 1829 to restrict the sale of public lands set off a conflict regarding state sovereignty among several senators. Most notably, Robert Y. Hayne of South Carolina and Daniel Webster of Massachusetts debated the issue January 19–27, 1830. Although Webster agreed that unconstitutional laws should be resisted, he argued that the federal judiciary alone had the power to decide on the constitutionality of federal laws. Furthermore, he posited that if a state declared a law void, it would have to resort to military power to prevent the nation from enforcing the law within its limits, and civil war must follow. Webster famously proclaimed that the survival of the Union was more important than individual liberties. On the other hand, Hayne contended that the general government should not have the power to determine the extent of its own powers with no check but the revolutionary right of the people. Hayne did not think it insurrectionary for a state to nullify a law within its own borders only; such a power was necessary for the protection of the state, and sovereign states were worthy to be trusted with such a power.[26]

> *"The Courier's editor asked, 'Shall we be deemed opposed to Southern rights and interests, because we would not apply a torch to the temple of our Liberty, and destroy by one incendiary act, the last*

*refuge of human freedom?' He proclaimed, 'Southern rights and
interests need no such sacrifice.' The editor declared perpetuity of
the Union to be essential to the future prosperity of the state but feared
that the disunion forces controlling some of the state's presses ...
would prevent the people from hearing Unionist arguments."*

Most South Carolina editors perceived Webster's speeches to be an attack on their state and defended against it for months. Like Hayne, the *Winyaw Intelligencer, Southern Times,* and *Charleston Mercury* declared the "Carolina doctrine" to be far more moderate than Webster and some of their fellow South Carolina editors asserted. Despite the forceful language they used to call readers to action, the editors argued that nullification merely declares a law unconstitutional and void within the state's borders; it does not pronounce the state separate from the Union. In the June 24 issue, the *Mercury's* editor asked, "Is there no alternative between unqualified submission to unconstitutional oppression, and a separation of the Union? Can we not assert our rights, or redress our grievances, and yet remain within the Confederacy?" Editorials in the *Intelligencer* accused Webster of attempting to frighten the people into submission through false accusations of revolution and argued that submitting would destroy the Union more than nullification would, because "there is small friendship between subdued provinces and their despotic masters." The *Times* editor posited that the people had hesitated to nullify in the past because they were alarmed at the prospect of disunion and convinced by the Unionist presses that secession was the nullifiers' aim. If the people could be convinced that nullification was a peaceful measure, the Columbia and Georgetown editors believed the state would adopt it.[27]

Editors in Georgetown, Columbia, and Charleston also asserted their belief that the state has paramount authority. "Our allegiance is to her, and we know nothing of the General Government, except from the adhesion to it of South Carolina," declared the *Intelligencer's* editor. If Webster was right and South Carolina yielded up her sovereignty when entering the confederacy, the *Southern Times* avowed, "she has made a desperately bad bargain, and the sooner she can get rid of it, upon fair terms, the better." Its editor believed the only way to hold the Union together was to fully acknowledge the right of the states to protect themselves from unjust and oppressive legislation "before all the ancient love between Northern and Southern brethren (*by courtesy*) has expired." Against arguments that the federal judiciary can arbitrate between states and the nation, the *Times* declared that the Supreme Court possesses supremacy only over the other courts of government. Appealing to readers' reverence for the nation's founding fathers, the *Winyaw Intelligencer* and *Charleston Mercury* cited the Declaration of Independence and Constitution as well as resolutions Thomas Jefferson and James Madison penned in the late 1790s as sources for the belief that the states had the right to judge infractions of the Constitution and interpose for maintaining their liberties. The editors asserted that these documents offered nullification specifically as a rightful remedy.[28]

On the other hand, the *Charleston Courier* lauded Webster's speeches as an unanswerable defense of the Constitution against destruction by the state legislatures and an exhibit of "the fatal consequences of the contemplated State usurpation." Writers in both the *Courier* and the *Camden Journal* expressed disbelief that the nullification papers intended anything less than disunion. Editorials in the *Journal* called nullification absurd and proclaimed there to be no difference between it and rebellion. The editor affirmed the state's right to secede, but he questioned whether the oppressions heaped upon her citizens had become sufficiently intolerable to warrant such a step. If they had, he declared, then the state should secede outright and not mask it with nullification. "Let not the citizens of South Carolina be drawn into a bloody collision with her sister States, by any pitiful indirection—by pursuing measures ostensibly peaceful, but in their nature necessarily and inevitably warlike," he proclaimed.[29]

Letters poured into the *Courier* blaming the state's excitement not on Webster but on the state's nullification papers. A March 25 letter signed "Washington" lamented that a few men of the state had so long and loudly cried about state rights and the tariffs that they had worked themselves into a frenzy and made themselves erroneously believe that South Carolina depended on the power of the state to nullify the acts of Congress. Washington cautioned readers that "wisdom shrinks from extremes, and fixes on a medium as her choice." Several writers responded to nullification papers' claims that resistance was the true Carolina doctrine and that anyone against the measure was against the state. The *Courier's* editor asked, "Shall we be deemed opposed to Southern rights and interests, because we would not apply a torch to the temple of our Liberty, and destroy by one incendiary act, the last refuge of human freedom?" He proclaimed, "Southern rights and interests need no such sacrifice." The editor declared perpetuity of the Union to be essential to the future prosperity of the state but feared that the disunion forces controlling some of the state's presses, particularly in Columbia, would prevent the people from hearing Unionist arguments. Correspondents called on the state's citizens to "shake off those wild delusions which are circulated to madden her passions, and precipitate her into errors from which it will be painful to recede and ruinous to prosecute." Although against the tariff, these Charleston writers supported only peaceful and constitutional measures to set it right, and they asserted that nullification was neither.[30]

> "It was no compromise, though. Editors who saw the American System
> with all its oppressions as less harmful than disunion assigned the
> same dangers to a convention that they did to nullification. Just as
> the Camden Journal's editor had argued that nullification was but
> a mask for secession, he assigned the same ruse to a convention."

The *Greenville Mountaineer's* editor latched onto Webster's idea of arbitration by the federal judiciary and penned several editorials advocating it as a peaceful alternative to nullification. He claimed the federal convention made the judiciary the interpreter and guardian of the Constitution in order to prevent tyranny, revolutions and civil wars. Furthermore, he posited that states are not independent sovereignties because they do not have the authority to do anything and everything they please; they could be considered sovereign only in the exercise of their reserved rights, and declaring laws unconstitutional was not one of them. The editor argued that the Constitution makes it "utterly impossible for such a power to exist in the States" and noted that James Madison denied writing anything akin to South Carolina's doctrine of nullification. Like the Camden editor, the *Mountaineer's* chief averred that the state had a right to secede "peacefully if we can, forcibly if we must" if it became clear that the government had adopted a fixed and settled policy "which must inevitably ruin and crush us to the earth if we continue members of this Union." He did not think that time had come, though. The proper course, he proclaimed, was to join with other southern states to decide on a peaceful and constitutional means of redress.[31]

As the state's citizens celebrated Independence Day, toasts throughout the state harped on the oppressions many South Carolinians perceived the government had heaped upon them as well as those they saw coming in the future. The *Southern Times*, now merged with another Columbia paper to become the *Southern Times and State Gazette*, rejoiced that the state's celebrations from seaboard to mountaintop rang out with the near unanimous cry, "Some way or other we must resist!" As newspaper columns following the Webster-Hayne debates foretold, however, the need for resistance was by no means undisputed. Whereas some toasters advocated secession or nullification, others vehemently spoke out in favor of preserving the Union from such fanatical doctrines. Some advocated a third option that they saw as a compromise between the Unionists and nullifiers: a convention of the state's most upstanding citizens to decide the course to be pursued.[32]

It was no compromise, though. Editors who saw the American System with all its oppressions as less harmful than disunion assigned the same dangers to a convention that they did to nullification. Just as the *Camden Journal's* editor had argued that nullification was but a mask for secession, he assigned the same ruse to a convention. In a September 11 editorial, he called "those who would push this people to the very verge of Revolution" delusional and pronounced, "Well may the patriot tremble upon the brink of such a precipice." Editorials in the *Charleston Courier* and *Greenville Mountaineer* advanced the same arguments, declaring that a convention in fact would result in nullification, which would lead to war against the federal government. The *Courier's* editor proclaimed that even the odious tariff did not justify such measures. The *Mountaineer's* chief and one of his correspondents agreed;

they reiterated the good that had been accomplished during the last session of Congress and emphasized that the American System was tottering. If it didn't, the Greenville editor concurred with his Camden counterpart that the state should throw off the mask of nullification and go straight to its inevitable result of secession.[33]

The most outspoken advocates of nullification proved to be the most ardent supporters of a convention as well. When the *Southern Times* and *State Gazette* merged in July, the *Timess* editor told his new readers of his distinct object: "to advocate a convention, to be called by the next Legislature, and gifted by the people with full powers to devise ways and means to free them from their present enormous burdens." He considered a convention to be the best remedy because it would express the will of the people on the subject. If the people chose nullification or submission, the editor believed the extremists on each end would be more likely to accept the decision than if it came from the legislature. On the other hand, he answered fears that a convention necessarily would result in forcible resistance by saying that merely calling a convention pledged the state to nothing in particular. The editor also questioned why the anti-convention editors could not trust their fellow citizens with convening to express their desires under the weight of oppression. He argued that if they could not do so, "we cannot see that there is any longer a hope of self government, or of elevating a republic above a tyranny of demagogues." The Columbia editor called the anti-conventioners "weak and timid" and accused them of shrinking "from the responsibility involved in a firm defence [sic] of our rights." He declared that any action short of calling a convention would amount to submission, which would fix the oppressive system upon the South for good.[34]

Though not as vehement in their arguments, editors in Pendleton and Georgetown promoted the convention with much of the same reasoning as their Columbia brother, proclaiming a convention to be the only way to leave the matter to the people. Editorials in both papers explained that a convention was nothing more than a meeting of citizens who would, through reasoned deliberation, decide on the best course. No course was set, they averred. The editors declared the government a failure if the people were not allowed the opportunity to govern themselves. They also proclaimed undiminished attachment to the Union and the belief that a convention would preserve it by finding a peaceable means to instigate repeal of the American System.[35]

> *"Throughout the state, newspapers called on the candidates of their respective districts to express their opinions on the constitutionality and oppressiveness of the American System, whether South Carolina should take action against it, the propriety of submitting the matter to a convention of the people, and the ability of states to nullify or secede."*

Regardless of his stance, each editor pointed to the next session of the state legislature as an important one for deciding South Carolina's fate. The *Southern Times* averred that South Carolinians could not stand with dignity or honor beyond the legislative session; to refuse action then was to submit. Another Columbia paper, the *Telescope,* concurred, noting that the people of the state should be prepared for the legislature to throw off the current "system of plunder and robbery" via means that could lead to bloodshed. The Unionist *Charleston Courier* responded that the people needed to be aware of what their legislature intended and "rise in the majesty of their strength to prostrate the evil disposed." According to the *Greenville Mountaineer,* this responsibility of resolving the conflicting dangers of "dissolution of the Union by hastiness and violence" and "loss of liberties by an absolute submission to the tyranny under which we groan" made the session "the most important certainly of any since the Revolution."[36]

Such weight placed upon the legislative session elevated the significance of the October 1830 election for state legislators. Writers in the *Pendleton Messenger* implored the paper's readers to take their suffrage seriously and select "men of intelligence and firmness, who will dare to think for themselves." A correspondent to the *Columbia Telescope* instructed voters to select moderate candidates, excluding both the overly conservative and the overly hostile members that had "paralyzed our legislative efforts, dishonored the State, and by a want of moral course, degraded the character of South-Carolina."[37]

As support for and opposition to a convention both gained momentum, editorials and correspondence on both sides of the issue noted that the elections would turn upon the question of whether the people wanted their legislators to call one. Whereas convention advocates called for readers to vote for legislators who would protect the state's rights and fight for the citizens' liberty, convention opponents implored voters to choose representatives dedicated to preserving peace and the Union.[38]

Throughout the state, newspapers called on the candidates of their respective districts to express their opinions on the constitutionality and oppressiveness of the American System, whether South Carolina should take action against it, the propriety of submitting the matter to a convention of the people, and the ability of states to nullify or secede. Editors emphasized the importance of this particular election and that the people needed to be well-informed about the men for whom they were voting.[39] As the candidates complied, their answers served as additional fodder for convention debate, both in the press and political meetings.

The *Pendleton Messenger* reported tremendous excitement over the issue in the upcountry, where the candidates universally opposed the American System but differed regarding how the state should respond. In Pendleton, most candidates supported referring the issue to a convention, though they generally hoped the result would not be disunion. Those in Edgefield all supported the call of a convention but differed as to the ultimate course the convention should pursue. Abbeville candidates were split on the issue of a convention, although on July 30, a *Greenville Mountaineer* writer named "Union" proclaimed so many of them to be in favor it was clear the "nullifiers there have commenced their work." The *Messengers* editor proclaimed the Abbeville, Pendleton, and Edgefield candidates to generally reflect the sentiments of their potential constituents, but such was not the case in Greenville. Citizens there so echoed their *Mountaineer's* feelings against a convention that several legislative candidates who voiced opinions in favor of one were forced to withdraw from the race.[40]

Greenville and other communities throughout the state made their anti-convention stance clear in political meetings during September. In addition to expressing their views in speeches, the citizens at these gatherings passed resolutions opposing the convention and announcing which candidates best represented their views. The *Mountaineer* reported one such meeting in the upcountry town of Laurens, at which attendees spoke out against pro-convention forces that were "deaf to every voice of reason." They resolved that South Carolina should pursue "a temperate, firm and unwavering opposition to the Tariff ... in concert with the rest of the Southern States," rather than taking rash action on her own that inevitably would lead to her downfall. Meetings in the coastal cities of Charleston and Beaufort and the midstate town of Sumter similarly lambasted the pro-convention party for threatening the Union and generating unwarranted excitement among the state's people. They called for a moderate approach, using constitutional means to resist the tariff. Some citizens in Edgefield resolved to instruct their legislators that if they called a convention, they should limit it to the purpose of sending a remonstrance to Congress. An unlimited convention, Edgefield's people declared, would result in "nothing but *disunion*, united with *civil war, misery and death!*"[41]

Meetings also took place statewide in which citizens presented speeches and passed resolutions in favor of a convention and candidates sympathetic to their cause. Speakers at two such meetings in the upcountry towns of Lancaster and Pickens claimed that a convention was the only alternative left to alleviate the burdens borne by the state and its people. The coastal city of Georgetown resolved that through a convention, the people of South Carolina "in their sovereign capacity" could take the necessary actions to provide relief. In the state capital, more than 2,000 men gathered and passed nearly unanimously a resolution supporting the call for a convention. Although the *Charleston Mercury's* editor lamented that his own city had abandoned the proper course, he declared on September 24 that "the flood of light that will be poured out from the centre of the State cannot fail to reach and illumine every corner of it."[42]

"Commentary throughout the state after Charleston's city election
noted the breaking down of old parties and the formation of
new ones. On September 15, the Charleston Courier *thanked*

*the level-headed press of the state for working to convince people
that South Carolina had suffered no more than any other state,
'thus escaping the delusion that allowed the [nullification] party's
former success and exposing the party's treasonous designs.'"*

Charleston's pro-convention faction faced greater difficulties than a definitively anti-convention meeting. The convention controversy spilled over into the September 1830 election for Charleston city intendant (the equivalent of a mayor), which pitted the incumbent, *Charleston Mercury* editor and nullification leader Henry L. Pinckney, against James Pringle, the customs collector for the Port of Charleston. Leading up to the polling date, writers in the *Charleston Courier* promoted Pringle and aimed to convince readers of Pinckney's goals "to separate Carolina from the Union, and bring upon her disgrace and ruin." Meanwhile, writers in the *Mercury* accused Pringle's supporters of aiming to put down Pinckney because they saw him as too zealous. Pringle's party aimed to defeat the incumbent "by endeavoring, fellow citizens, to excite your apprehensions, by raising cries of *Disunion and Rebellion and War and Bloodshed*" A record number of voters selected Pringle, drawing cheers from the anti-convention *Greenville Mountaineer*. The *Southern Times and State Gazette,* on the other hand, mourned the "loss of Charleston" and labeled Pringle's victory as ominous due to his position as collector of tariffs.[43]

Commentary throughout the state after Charlestons city election noted the breaking down of old parties and the formation of new ones. On September 15, the *Charleston Courier* thanked the level-headed press of the state for working to convince people that South Carolina had suffered no more than any other state, "thus escaping the delusion that allowed the [nullification] party's former success and exposing the party's treasonous designs." Consequently, "the honest men of all parties of the state" joined together in "a new great party to overthrow the nullifiers." In a September 11 report on a rally after the election, the *Mercury* noted that the new party had formed when "timid" members of the State Rights party defected over the issues of state sovereignty and convention, which allowed the formerly weak Unionist camp to draw new allies from their ranks. The *Mercury* encouraged convention supporters to persevere despite the defeat and make it obvious via the legislative election that Charleston still sympathized with the rest of the State.[44]

Perhaps sensing their cause slipping away, pro-convention writers throughout South Carolina engaged in what appeared to be a frantic last-ditch effort to sway voters on the eve of the state election. A correspondent with the pseudonym "Hampden" addressed the anti-convention readers of the Unionist *Greenville Mountaineer* on October 8 with a plea not to submit patiently and quietly while the rights of the state were trampled. He called for voters to "ignore the demagogues who would frighten you into support of themselves or friends by the cry of disunion and civil war." The *Pendleton Messenger's* editor similarly insisted that many men who were interested in continuing the American System had preyed upon the fears of the state's patriotic citizens to convince them of the dangers of a convention. He labeled those fears absurd and declared that the legislature had gone as far as it could; the people needed to take the next step. An October 12 editorial in the *Charleston Mercury* asked voters to stand firmly and united in support of not only the state's rights but also the Constitution and Union. If they did not, the *Southern Times and State Gazette* warned, "then may the people of the South look at once to the means of wearing their chains in the most comfortable manner—then may they prepare to yield every right which is worth invading." The Columbia editor sought to stir readers' patriotism by reminding them that brave men from Boston to Savannah had rallied when cries of oppression rang out before the Revolution. It should be even easier for South Carolinians to do so now, because there was no call to arms but to "a *peaceful* method of resistance." He asked, "Shall we refuse to do our duty, until the hour of actual conflict comes?"[45]

During the middle weeks of October, each newspaper contained results from its own and other districts as they trickled in. Although some districts elected a full pro-convention or anti-convention ticket, most districts sent representatives from both parties to the capital. Contrary to indications before the election, the anti-conventioners carried Columbia, whereas the pro-convention men took Charleston. In the end, the convention party controlled the legislature by a slim margin (even electing the *Mercury's* Pinckney as speaker of the House), but their numbers did not form a constitutional majority, and the convention issue failed.[46]

This marked the end of the controversy for the *Greenville Mountaineer's* editor, who declared that the excitement which "the great question" produced was dying away, "and minds of our readers are now prepared to receive other food." Other editors, however, announced plans to remain vigilant to the anti-tariff cause. Although fewer than fifty out of 800 voters had gone for the convention ticket in Camden, the *Journal's* editor noted that not one submission man could be found in that district. He called for the state legislature to give Congress another solemn warning that the time was fast approaching when its current system of national legislation would be looked upon as insupportable. He believed that "reason and sound feeling [would] march through" the next session of Congress, and the states worries would be at an end.[47]

State Rights party editors were not so optimistic about the government relieving the state of its burdens, but they were pleased with the numbers they had gained in the state legislature. Editorials in the *Southern Times and State Gazette* and the *Winyaw Intelligencer* cited not only Pinckney's election as speaker but also the legislature's passage of a resolution recognizing the right of the state to interpose and arrest the usurpations of the federal government as evidence that the State Rights party triumphantly had sustained its principles.

The *Intelligencer* avowed that the state would maintain those political doctrines, "which are considered to be as expedient in securing the integrity of the 'Union,' as they will be effectual in protecting the 'States' in the enjoyment of their just and equal rights." Furthermore, the *Times and Gazette* predicted that the elaborate discussion of the fundamental principles of government undertaken over the course of the year would leave an impression in the people's minds, forming "a new era in the constitutional history of this country."[48]

> *"Although the nullification implications of a convention and the overzealous language of some of its supporters may have kept the State Rights party from achieving the constitutional majority required to call a convention, they still convinced enough voters of the dangers of federalism that they took control of the state legislature and subsequently elected one of their most outspoken leaders as speaker of the House."*

South Carolina newspaper editors and correspondents generally found the tariffs and internal improvements unjust and unconstitutional. They disagreed, however, as to whether nullification was the appropriate mode of redress. Disagreement heightened as the first session of the Twenty-First Congress progressed, and many editors saw no hope of relief from the oppressive system. Although some preached continued forbearance and patience in wake of tariff reductions and the Maysville Road veto, others saw those actions as proof that the American System would be fixed upon South Carolina forever if the state did not resist.

The Webster-Hayne debates surrounding Foot's public lands resolution instigated discussion among South Carolina's writers about whether the state had the authority to void offending laws of Congress, and a sect fiercely loyal to the Union arose in the wake of rampant nullification and disunion talk. Sensing the unpopularity of their ideas during these debates, nullification proponents turned their attention toward advocating the call of a convention of South Carolina's citizens to decide upon the best course. Although the nullifiers believed a convention would be more palatable to the Unionist faction, opponents saw the convention as thinly veiled nullification doctrine. The debate over nullification/convention versus patient forbearance reached fever pitch as candidates stumped for state legislative offices. Each side accused the other of raising disunion excitement within the state and insisted its own method of redress was the only peaceable option. Meanwhile, the State Rights party fractured over the issues of state sovereignty and convention, and a new party developed that encompassed the more conservative State Rights men as well as moderates and conservatives from other parties.[49]

This split proved to be an important turning point in the partisan newspapers as well. Before the 1830 fall elections, editorial writers could be categorized into three camps: those who were willing to rebel against the federal government to protect the rights of the sovereign state; those willing to submit to oppression in order to preserve the Union; and those who advocated drastic action only under circumstances of unbearable tyranny, which they argued were absent. Editorials and correspondence in the fall reveal a melding of the latter two sects, coinciding with the development of the state's new political party.

The new party not only sealed the victory of tariff collector Pringle over the nullifier Pinckney for the office of Charleston city intendant, but it likely also played a role in the outcome of the election for state legislators in districts throughout the state. In the newspapers as in the political arena, the goal of the combined moderate and conservative forces appeared to be quieting the radicals. Although the nullification papers tried their best throughout the campaign season to emphasize that their proposed modes of redress were peaceful, the damage already was done. If the words published in conservative/moderate newspapers such as the *Charleston Courier, Greenville Mountaineer,* and *Camden Journal* are any indication, forceful language in nullification prints such as the *Winyaw Intelligencer, Southern Times,* and *Charleston Mercury* during the congressional session likely struck fear into the hearts of the people. In some, they provoked alarm of the government assuming unlimited control, just as their editors clearly had hoped. In others, however, they instigated panic that war and bloodshed were forthcoming. Unionist papers helped fuel that terror with their own rhetoric, to the point of winning Charleston votes for a man who enforced the very laws that the people had been disputing.

The State Rights party's assumption that the new Unionist party saw Pinckney as overzealous was true, and editorials in newspapers statewide advanced the same claim regarding State Rights candidates for legislature. The *Camden Journal* called the toasts at a proconvention dinner "rather too bellicose for our taste," and an editorial in the *Edgefield Carolinian* declared that South Carolinians would rather see the state's rights restored by its juries than its men of war. A correspondent told the *Charleston Courier's* readers that the people had become frightened by the revolutionaries and begun to speak out in "a milder tone of language in reference to grievances and oppression."[50]

Although the nullification implications of a convention and the overzealous language of some of its supporters may have kept the State Rights party from achieving the constitutional majority required to call a convention, they still convinced enough voters of the dangers of federalism that they took control of the state legislature and subsequently elected one of their most outspoken leaders as speaker of the House. Their influence would continue to grow during the next two years, as would their rhetorical conflict with those who held the Union in higher esteem, until finally the State Rights party won out and nullified the tariff acts in 1832.[51]

This struggle between South Carolina's parties and their mouthpieces in print had widespread ramifications beyond the nullification controversy of the 1830s as well. Radical

South Carolinians continued to rebel against federal laws, starting the Bluffton Movement toward nullification of additional tariffs in the 1840s. They also pushed for outright secession in 1849 and 1850, in the wake of statehood debates that threatened the balance of power between slaveholding states and non-slaveholding states after the Mexican War. During those episodes, moderates and conservatives from within South Carolina as well as other southern states prevented disunion. However, the radicals skillfully used their rhetoric—in print and otherwise—to grow their power and influence as the antebellum era wore on. The result was South Carolina's secession in 1860, and at that time, other southern states followed suit.[52]

Notes

1. Speech in Columbia, S.C., Sept. 29, 1830, in *Charleston Mercury*, Oct. 19, 1830.

2. Hodding Carter, *Their Words Were Bullets: The Southern Press in War, Reconstruction, and Peace* (Athens: University of Georgia Press, 1969): Dwight Lowell Dumond, ed., *Southern Editorials on Secession* (New York: Century, 1931); Carl R. Osthaus, *Partisans of the Southern Press* (Knoxville: University Press of Kentucky, 1994); Lorman A. Ratner and Dwight L. Teeter, Jr., *Fanatics and Fire-eaters: Newspapers and the Coming of the Civil War* (Urbana: University of Illinois Press. 2003); and Donald E. Reynolds, *Editors Make War: Southern Newspapers in the Secession Crisis* (Nashville: Vanderbilt University Press, 1966).

3. James M. Banner Jr., "The Problem of South Carolina," in eds. Eric McKitrick and Stanley Elkins, The Hofstadter Aegis: A Memorial (New York: Knopf, 1974); Charles Edward Cauthen, *South Carolina Goes to War. 1860–1865* (Chapel Hill: University of North Carolina Press, 1950); Peter A. Coclanis, "Bitter Harvest: The South Carolina Low Country in Historical Perspective," *Journal of Economic History* 45 (June 1985): 251–59; Peter A. Coclanis, "The Rise and Fall of the South Carolina Low Country: An Essay in Economic Interpretation." *Southern Studies* 24 (Summer 1985): 143–66; William J. Cooper, Jr., *Liberty and Slavery: Southern Politics to 1860* (New York: Knopf, 1983); William W. Freehling, *Prelude to Civil War: The Nullification Controversy in South Carolina, 1816–1836* (New York: Harper & Row, 1966); Manisha Sinha, "Revolution or Counterrevolution? The Political Ideology of Secession in Antebellum South Carolina," *Civil War History* 46 (September 2000): 205–26; Rebecca Starr, *A School for Politics: Commercial Lobbying and Political Culture in Early South Carolina* (Baltimore: Johns Hopkins Press, 1998); Rosser H. Taylor, *Ante-bellum South Carolina: A Social and Cultural History* (Chapel Hill: The University of North Carolina Press, 1942); and John Harold Wolfe, "The Roots of Jeffersonian Democracy: With Special Emphasis on South Carolina," in ed. Fletcher Melvin Green, *Essays in Southern History Presented to Joseph DeRoulhac Hamilton by His Former Students at the University of North Carolina* (Chapel Hill: University of North Carolina Press, 1949).

4. Kenneth S. Greenberg, "Representation and the Isolation of South Carolina, 1776–1860," *Journal of American History* 64 (December 1977): 723–43; A. V. Huff, Jr., "The Eagle and the Vulture: Changing Attitudes Toward Nationalism in Fourth of July Orations Delivered in Charleston, 1778–1860," *South Atlantic Quarterly* 73 (Winter 1974): 10–22; Ernest McPherson Lander and Robert Kilgo Ackerman, *Perspectives in South Carolina History, the First 300 Years* (Columbia: University of South Carolina Press, 1973); and George C. Rogers Jr., "South Carolina Federalists and the Origins of the Nullification Movement," *South Carolina Historical Magazine* 101 (January 2000): 53–67.

5. Carter Goodrich, "American Development Policy: The Case of Internal Improvements," *Journal of Economic History* 16 (December 1956): 449–60; Carter Goodrich, *Government Promotion of American Canals and Railroads, 1800–1890* (New York: Columbia University Press, 1960); Carter Goodrich, "National Planning of Internal Improvements," *Political Science Quarterly* 63 (March 1948): 16–44; John Lauritz Larson, *Internal Improvement.: National Public Works and the Promise of Popular Government in the Early United States* (Chapel Hill: The University of North Carolina Press, 2000); Robert A. Lively, "The American System: A Review Article," *Business History Review* 29 (Spring 1955): 81–96; Stephen Minicucci, "The 'Cement of Interest': Interest-Based Models of Nation-Building in the Early Republic," *Social Science History* 25 (Summer 2001): 247–74; Frederick Jackson Turner, *Rise of the New West, 1819–1829* (New York: Harper & Brothers, 1909); John R. Van Atta, "Western Lands and the Political Economy of Henry Clay s American System, 1819–1832," *Journal of the Early Republic* 21 (Winter 2001): 633–65; and Naomi Wiulf, "'The Greatest General Good': Road Construction, National Interest, and Federal Funding in Jacksonian America," *European Contributions to American Studies* 47 (June 2001): 53–72.

6. William G. Carleton, "Tariffs and the Rise of Sectionalism," *Current History* 42 (May 1962): 333–38, 363; John L. Conger, "South Carolina and the Early Tariffs," *Mississippi Valley Historical Review* 5 (March 1919): 415–33; Dali W. Forsythe, *Taxation and Political Change in the Young Nation, 1781–1833* (New York: Columbia University Press, 1977); James L. Huston, "Virtue Besieged: Virtue, Equality, and the General Welfare in the Tariff Debates of the 1820s," *Journal of the Early Republic* 14 (Winter 1994): 523–47; Douglas A. Irwin, *Antebellum Tariff Politics: Coalition Formation and Shifting Regional Interests* (Cambridge, Mass.: National Bureau of Economic Research, 2006); Douglas A. Irwin, "Antebellum Tariff Politics: Regional Coalitions and Shifting Economic Interests," *Journal of Law & Economics* 51 (November 2008): 715–41; Eugene C. Lewis, *A History of the American Tariff 1789–1860* (Chicago: C.H. Kerr and Co., 1896); Lars Magnusson, *Free Trade & Protection in America: 1822–1890* (London: Routledge, 2000); William McKinley, *The Tariff in the Days of Henry Clay, and Since: An Exhaustive Review of Our Tariff Legislation from 1812 to 1896* (New York: Henry Clay Pub. Co., 1896); Broadus Mitchell, "The Abominable Tariff-Making, 1789–1828," *Current History* 42 (May 1962): 327–32, 362–63; J.J. Pincus. *Pressure Groups and Politics in Antebellum Tariffs* (New York: Columbia University Press, 1977); Edward Stanwood, *American Tariff Controversies in the Nineteenth Century* (Boston: Houghton Mifflin, 1903); George Rogers

Taylor, *The Great Tariff Debate, 1820–1830* (Boston: Heath, 1953); and John George Van Deusen, *Economic Bases of Disunion in South Carolina* (New York: Columbia University Press, 1928).

7. Carleton, "Tariffs and the Rise of Sectionalism"; Conger, "South Carolina and the Early Tariffs"; Freehling, *Prelude to Civil War,* Donald W. Livingston, "The Southern Tradition and Limited Government," *Modern Age* 49 (Fall 2007): 452–62; and Van Deusen, *Economic Bases of Disunion in South Carolina.*

8. Frederic Bancroft, *Calhoun and the South Carolina Nullification Movement* (Baltimore: The Johns Hopkins Press, 1925); Gerald M. Capers, "A Reconsideration of John C. Calhoun's Transition from Nationalism to Nullification," *Journal of Southern History* 14 (February 1948): 34–48; Pauline Maier, "The Road not Taken: Nullification, John C. Calhoun, and the Revolutionary Tradition in South Carolina," *South Carolina Historical Magazine* 82 (January 1981): 1–19; J. P. Ochenkowski, "The Origins of Nullification in South Carolina," *South Carolina Historical Magazine* 83 (April 1982): 121–53; and W. Kirk Wood, "In Defense of the Republic: John C. Calhoun and State Interposition in South Carolina, 1776–1833," *Southern Studies* (Spring/Summer 2003): 9–48.

9. Chauncey Samuel Boucher, *The Nullification Controversy in South Carolina* (Chicago, Ill.: University of Chicago Press, 1916); Richard E. Ellis, *The Union at Risk: Jacksonian Democracy, States' Rights, and the Nullification Crisis* (New York: Oxford University Press, 1987); Freehling, *Prelude to Civil War,* David Franklin Houston, *A Critical Study of Nullification in South Carolina* (New York; Longmans, Green, and Co., 1896); and Van Deusen, *Economic Bases of Disunion in South Carolina.*

10. Boucher, *The Nullification Controversy in South Carolina,* Ellis, *The Union at Risk,* David F. Ericson, *The Shaping of American Liberalism: The Debates over Ratification, Nullification, and Slavery* (Chicago: University of Chicago Press, 1993); Freehling, *Prelude to Civil War,* Houston, *A Critical Study of Nullification in South Carolina,* Gaillard Hunt, "South Carolina during the Nullification Struggle," *Political Science Quarterly* 6 (June 1891): 232–47; Livingston, "The Southern Tradition and Limited Government"; Jane H. Pease and William H. Pease, "The Economics and Politics of Charleston's Nullification Crisis," *Journal of Southern History* 47 (August 1981): 335–62; Donald J. Ratcliffe, "The Nullification Crisis, Southern Discontents, and the American Political Process," *American Nineteenth Century History* [Great Britain] 1, 2 (Summer 2000): 1–30; and David Schroeder, "Nullification in South Carolina: A Revisitation," (Ph.D. diss., University of Alabama, 1999).

11. W. Joseph Campbell, *The Year That Defined American Journalism; 1897 and the Clash of Paradigms* (New York: Routledge, 2006).

12. Forsythe, *Taxation and Political Change in the Young Nation;* Irwin, *Antebellum Tariff Politics;* Lewis, *A History of the American Tariff, 1789–1860;* McKinley, *The Tariff in the Days of Henry Clay;* Pincus, *Pressure Groups and Politics in Antebellum Tariffs;* and Van Deusen, *Economic Bases of Disunion in South Carolina.*

13. Carlton Jackson, "The Internal Improvement Vetoes of Andrew Jackson," *Tennessee Historical Quarterly* 25 (September 1966): 261–80; Daniel Mark Jansen, "Andrew Jackson's Maysville Road

Veto: A Reappraisal" (master's thesis, University of Tennessee, 1992); and Wulf, "The Greatest General Good."

14. Christopher Apap, "The Genius of Latitude: Daniel Webster and the Geographical Imagination in Early America," *Journal of the Early Republic* 30 (Summer 2010): 201–23; Stefan Marc Brooks, *The Webster-Hayne Debate: An Inquiry into the Nature of the Union* (Lanham, Md.: University Press of America, 2009); Wayne Fields, "The Reply to Hayne: Daniel Webster and the Rhetoric of Stewardship," *Political Theory* 11 (February 1983): 5–28; Ruth Armstrong Graheme, "An Investigation of the Historical Significance of Foot's Resolution" (master's thesis, University of Maine, 1916); Peter C. Hoffer, "Sectionalism and National History: American History in the Debate over Foote's Resolution, December 1829–May 1830," *Missouri Historical Quarterly* 66 (July 1972): 520–38; Edward Connery Lathem, *Daniel Webster: The Noblest Effort of His Career* (Lunenburg, Vt.: Stinehour Press, 1960); Caleb William Loring, *Nullification, Secession, Webster's Argument, and the Kentucky and Virginia Resolutions, Considered in Reference to the Constitution and Historically* (New York: G.P. Putnam's Sons, 1893); and Lane Patterson, "The Battle of the Giants: Webster and Hayne: Orators at Odds," *American History Illustrated* 18, 6 (October 1983): 18–22.

15. Boucher, *The Nullification Controversy in South Carolina*; Freehling, *Prelude to Civil War*.

16. Gerald Baldasty, "The Charleston, South Carolina Press and National News, 1808–47," *Journalism Quarterly* 55 (Autumn 1978): 519–526; John Stanford Coussons, "Thirty Years with Calhoun, Rhett, and the Charleston *Mercury*: A Chapter in South Carolina Politics" (Ph.D. diss., Louisiana State University, 1971); Maurice R. Cullen Jr., "William Gilmore Simms, Southern Journalist," *Journalism Quarterly* 38 (September 1961): 298–302, 412; William C. Davis, *Rhett: The Turbulent Life and Times of a Fire-eater* (Columbia: University of South Carolina Press, 2001); William L. King, *The Newspaper Press of Charleston, S.C.* (1872; reprint ed., New York: Arno, 1970); Patricia G. McNeely, *Fighting Words: The History of the Media in South Carolina* (Columbia: South Carolina Press Association, 1998); James B. Meriwether, ed., *South Carolina Journals and Journalists* (Spartanburg, S.C.: The Reprint Co., 1975); Osthaus, "The Triumph of Sectional Journalism: The *Charleston Daily Courier* and *Charleston Mercury* on the Eve of Secession," in *Partisans of the Southern Press*, 69–94; Granville Torrey Prior, "A History of the Charleston *Mercury*, 1822–1852" (Ph.D. diss., Harvard University, 1946); Herbert Ravenel Sass, *Outspoken: 150 Years of the News and Courier* (Columbia: University of South Carolina Press, 1953); and Ernest B. Segars, "A Study of the Charleston (S.C.) *Mercury* during Robert Barnwell Rhett, Senior's Tenure as an Editorial Writer" (master's thesis, University of South Carolina, 1974).

17. Bernard Bailyn, *The Ideological Origins of the American Revolution* (1967; enlarged ed., Cambridge, Mass.: The Belknap Press of Harvard University Press, 1992).

18. *House Journal*, 21st Cong., 1st Sess., Jan. 5, 1830, 130.

19. *Greenville Mountaineer,* Jan. 23, 1830; "The Tariff," *Charleston Mercury,* Jan. 13, 1830; *Camden Journal,* Jan. 23, 1830. See also "The Tariff," *Greenville Mountaineer,* Jan. 16, 1830, and *Charleston Mercury,* Jan. 29, 1830.

20. 6 *Cong. Deb.* 555, 556 (1830); *Pendleton Messenger,* Feb. 10, 1830, and Feb. 24, 1830; *Southern Times,* Feb. 25, 1830; *Charleston Mercury,* Feb. 16, 1830, and Feb. 19, 1830. See also *Greenville Mountaineer,* Feb. 13, 1830.

21. H.R. 164, 21st Cong. (1830); *Pendleton Messenger,* March 31, 1830; *Camden Journal,* May 8, 1830,; *Charleston Mercury,* May 8, 1830; *Southern Times,* May 20, 1830; and "Extract of a letter to the Editor, dated WASHINGTON, May 6, 1830," *Charleston Mercury,* May 13, 1830.

22. H.R. 207, 21st Cong. (1830); 6 *Cong. Deb.* 807 (1830); Act of May 29, 1830, Ch. 185, 4 *Stat.* 419; Act of May 29, 1830, Ch. 189, 4 *Stat.* 419; "The Tariff," *Greenville Mountaineer,* May 7, 1830; *Winyaw Intelligencer,* May 19, 1830, May 22, 1830, and June 16, 1830; *Charleston Mercury,* May 29, 1830, and June 3, 1830; *Southern Times,* May 27, 1830; "The Tariff," *Camden Journal,* May 15, 1830; and "Congress," *Greenville Mountaineer,* June 11, 1830.

23. *Pendleton Messenger,* Aug. 4, 1830; *Charleston Mercury,* April 9, 1830, and April 17, 1830.

24. 6 *Cong. Deb.* 133–42 (1830); *Camden Journal,* June 12, 1830; *Charleston Mercury,* June 3, 1830, and June 19, 1830; *Southern Times,* June 7, 1830; "Twenty-First Congress," *Southern Times,* June 10, 1830; *Winyaw Intelligencer,* June 9, 1830, and June 12, 1830; "The Veto," *Cheraw Republican,* reprinted in *Winyaw Intelligencer,* June 16, 1830; and *Pendleton Messenger,* Aug. 25, 1830.

25. "The Maysville Road," *Greenville Mountaineer,* June 11, 1830; *Greenville Mountaineer,* July 2, 1830; "The 4th of July," *Greenville Mountaineer,* July 2, 1830, and July 9,1830; *Greenville Mountaineer,* Aug. 27, 1830; R, "For the Mountaineer," *Greenville Mountaineer,* July 9, 1830; R, "For the Mountaineer," *Greenville Mountaineer,* July 23, 1830; "From our Correspondent," *Charleston Courier,* May 20, 1830; and Moultrie, "The Times," *Charleston Courier,* June 10, 1830.

26. "Debate in the Senate," *Niles' Weekly Register,* Feb. 13, 1830, 415–18; "Debate in the Senate," *Niles' Weekly Register,* Feb. 20, 1830, 435–40; "Debate in the Senate," *Niles' Weekly Register,* Feb. 27, 1830, 10–24; and "Debate in the Senate," *Niles' Weekly Register,* March 6, 1830, 25–47.

27. *Charleston Mercury,* June 24, 1830; *Winyaw Intelligencer,* March 6, 1830; "Nullifying Law," *Winyaw Intelligencer,* March 13, 1830; "Disunion," *Winyaw Intelligencer,* July 17, 1830; *Winyaw Intelligencer,* Aug. 25, 1830; "Nullification and Its Effects," *Southern Times,* May 10 , 1830; and *Southern Times,* Feb. 22, 1830.

28. "Mr. Hayne and Mr. Webster," *Southern Times,* March 15, 1830; "State Rights," *Southern Times,* April 1, 1830; *Southern Times,* June 3, 1830; *Winyaw Intelligencer,* March 24, 1830, and April 28, 1830; "Nullification," *Charleston Mercury,* March 25, 1830; *Charleston Mercury,* April 2, 1830. See also "Nullification," *Winyaw Intelligencer,* June 2, 1830; and *Charleston Mercury,* Feb. 10, 1830, and March 25, 1830. Italics are in the original.

29. "Mr. Webster's Speech," *Charleston Courier*, March 9, 1830; "Nullification," *Camden Journal*, July 3, 1830; and *Camden Journal*, Sept. 4, 1830.

30. Washington, "Mr. Editor," *Charleston Courier*, March 25, 1830; "Mr. Editor," *Charleston Courier*, Feb. 16, 1830; *Charleston Courier*, May 17, 1830, June 18, 1830, and July 21, 1830; South Carolina, "For the Courier," *Charleston Courier*, June 15, 1830; Carolina, "For the Courier," *Charleston Courier*, June 18, 1830; The Democrats of Charleston, "To the Honest Old State Rights Party Throughout the Union," *Charleston Courier*, Aug. 25, 1830; A Man, "They Are Against Carolina," *Charleston Courier*, July 30, 1830; and Another of the People, "For the Courier," *Charleston Courier.*, Aug. 25, 1830.

31. "The Federal Judiciary," *Greenville Mountaineer*, Feb. 27, 1830; *Greenville Mountaineer*, April 3, 1830; "State Sovereignty," *Greenville Mountaineer*, April 23, 1830; "Livingston's Speech," *Greenville Mountaineer*, May 28, 1830; "The Power of Nullification," *Greenville Mountaineer*, April 3, 1830; *Greenville Mountaineer*, Sept. 17, 1830, Sept. 10, 1830, Oct. 22, 1830, and Oct. 29, 1830; and "This Is the Correct View of the Whole Matter," *Greenville Mountaineer*, July 16, 1830.

32. "The Prospect Before Us," *Southern Times and State Gazette*, July 19, 1830; *Pendleton Messenger*, July 7, 1830; and *Greenville Mountaineer*, July 16, 1830.

33. "What We Believe and What We Disbelieve," *Camden Journal*, Sept. 11, 1830; *Camden Journal*, Aug. 21, 1830; *Charleston Courier*, Aug. 28, 1830; *Greenville Mountaineer*, Aug. 27, 1830; "The Present Crisis," *Greenville Mountaineer*, May 21, 1830; *Greenville Mountaineer*, July 23, 1830, and July 30, 1830; and John H. Harrison, "To the People of Greenville District," *Greenville Mountaineer*, Aug. 6, 1830.

34. *Southern Times and State Gazette*, July 8, 1830; "Convention," *Southern Times and State Gazette*, August 16, 1830; *Southern Times and State Gazette*, Aug. 26, 1830; "The Prospect Before Us," *Southern Times and State Gazette*, July 19, 1830; "Union and Disunion," *Southern Times*, June 17, 1830; "Who is a Disunionist?" *Southern Times*, June 28, 1830; and "Convention," *Southern Times and State Gazette*, Aug. 12, 1830.

35. *Winyaw Intelligencer*, June 26, 1830; "Convention," *Winyaw Intelligencer*, Sept. 1, 1830; "The Minority in Edgefield," *Winyaw Intelligencer*, Oct 2, 1830; and *Pendleton Messenger*, Aug. 18, 1830, and Sept. 8, 1830.

36. *Southern Times*, June 14, 1830; *Columbia Telescope*, reprinted in the *Charleston Courier*, Feb. 16, 1830; *Charleston Courier*, Feb. 16, 1830; and Public Spirit, "The Next Legislature," *Greenville Mountaineer*, July 23, 1830.

37. *Pendleton Messenger*, June 9, 1830; One of the People, "For the Messenger," *Pendleton Messenger*, June 16, 1830; and South-Carolina, "To the Editor," *Columbia Telescope*, reprinted in *Winyaw Intelligencer*, Feb. 6, 1830.

38. "Convention," *Southern Times and State Gazette*, Aug. 12, 1830; "The Present Crisis," *Greenville Mountaineer*, May 21, 1830; *Greenville Mountaineer*, July 23, 1830; *Southern Times and State Gazette*,

Aug. 5, 1830; A Native Carolinian, "For the Courier," *Charleston Courier*, July 10, 1830; Father Paul, "For the Courier," *Charleston Courier*, July 10, 1830; *Pendleton Messenger*, Aug. 25, 1830; "Convention," *Camden Journal*, Sept. 11, 1830; and A Native of Chesterfield District, "To the People of South Carolina," *Charleston Courier*, Sept. 7, 1830.

39. *Greenville Mountaineer*, July 23, 1830, and July 30, 1830; *Pendleton Messenger*, July 28, 1830; *Camden Journal*, Aug. 7, 1830; and *Southern Times and State Gazette*, Aug. 9, 1830.

40. *Pendleton Messenger*, Aug. 11, 1830, and Aug. 18, 1830; John Maxwell, "To the Electors of the Pendleton District," *Pendleton Messenger*, Aug. 11, 1830; Bailey Barton, "To the Voters of Pendleton District," *Pendleton Messenger*, Aug. 18, 1830; Union, "Nullification," *Greenville Mountaineer*, July 30, 1830; *Edgefield Carolinian*, reprinted in *Charleston Mercury*, Aug. 13, 1830; "Politics of Greenville," *Greenville Mountaineer*, Aug. 6, 1830; *Greenville Mountaineer*, Aug. 20, 1830; and "The Non Convention Party," *Greenville Mountaineer*, Aug. 6, 1830.

41. *Greenville Mountaineer*, Sept. 24. 1830; "Meeting of Citizens," *Charleston Courier*, Aug. 30, 1830; "To the Editor of the Mercury," *Charleston Mercury*, Sept. 13, 1830; "Edgefield," *Southern Times and State Gazette*, Sept. 9, 1830; and *Charleston Courier*, Sept. 28, 1830.

42. *Charleston Courier*, Sept. 28, 1830; *Lancaster Beacon*, reprinted in the *Pendleton Messenger*, Oct. 6, 1830; "Good News from Lancaster," *Southern Times and State Gazette*, Sept. 27, 1830; *Pendleton Messenger*, Sept. 15, 1830; *Winyaw Intelligencer*, Sept. 1, 1830; *Charleston Mercury*, Sept. 13, 1830; and "Great State Rights Meeting at Columbia," *Charleston Mercury*, Sept. 24, 1830.

43. Q, "For the Courier," *Charleston Courier*, July 21, 1830; A Looker On, "Communication," *Charleston Courier*, July 22, 1830; Aristides, "Fellow Citizens," *Charleston Mercury*, Aug. 26, 1830; "City Election," *Charleston Mercury*, Sept. 8, 1830; *Greenville Mountaineer*, Sept. 17, 1830; and "Charleston," *Southern Times and State Gazette*, Sept. 13, 1830.

44. *Pendleton Messenger*, Sept. 15, 1830; "Charleston," *Southern Times and State Gazette*, Sept. 13, 1830; State Rights and Union, "Circular," *Charleston Courier*, Sept. 15, 1830; and "Rally of the State Rights' Party," *Charleston Mercury*, Sept. 11, 1830.

45. Hampden, "For the Mountaineer," *Greenville Mountaineer*, Oct. 8, 1830; *Pendleton Messenger*, Oct. 6, 1830; "To the State Rights and Jackson Party," *Charleston Mercury*, Oct. 12, 1830; and "The Election," *Southern Times and State Gazette*, Oct. 4, 1830.

46. *Pendleton Messenger*, Oct. 14, 1830, and Oct. 20, 1830; *Greenville Mountaineer*, Oct. 15, 1830, and Oct. 22, 1830; *Southern Times and State Gazette*, Oct. 18, 1830; "The Election," *Charleston Mercury*, Oct. 15, 1830; and *Charleston Mercury*, Oct. 28, 1830.

47. *Greenville Mountaineer*, Oct. 22, 1830; *Camden Journal*, reprinted in the *Pendleton Messenger*, Oct. 20, 1830.; and *Camden Journal*, reprinted in the *Southern Times and State Gazette*, Oct. 21, 1830.

48. "Legislature," *Southern Times and State Gazette*, Dec. 18, 1830; "South Carolina Politics," *Southern Times and State Gazette*, Dec. 23, 1830; and *Winyaw Intelligencer*, Dec. 1, 1830, and Dec. 8, 1830.

49. For discussions of the state's shifting party structure during the tariff and nullification debates, see Boucher, *The Nullification Controversy in South Carolina*, and Freehling, *Prelude to Civil War*.

50. *Camden Journal*, Aug. 28, 1830; *Edgefield Carolinian*, quoted in *Camden Journal*, Sept. 4, 1830; and A Native Carolinian, "For the Courier," *Charleston Courier*, July 10, 1830. See also Greenville, "A Voice from the Mountains," *Charleston Courier*, Aug. 20, 1830.

51. Boucher, *The Nullification Controversy in South Carolina*; Ellis, *The Union at Risk*; Freehling, *Prelude to Civil War*, Houston, *A Critical Study of Nullification in South Carolina*; Hunt, "South Carolina during the Nullification Struggle"; Livingston, "The Southern Tradition and Limited Government"; and Schroeder, "Nullification in South Carolina."

52. Huff, "The Eagle and the Vulture"; Lander & Ackerman, *Perspectives in South Carolina History*; Sinha, "Revolution or Counterrevolution?"; Van Deusen, *Economic Bases of Disunion in South Carolina*; and Laura A. White, *Robert Barnwell Rhett: Father of Secession* (1931; repr., Gloucester. Mass: Peter Smith, 1965).

Reading 1.4

Secession

Paul D. Escott

THERE WAS LITTLE TIME FOR CELEBRATION. Surely Lincoln and the "little short woman" who was interested in his success shared some quiet moments of wonder. After all, they had reached the highest goal of their dreams. But there was no opportunity to relax. Friends, allies, and office seekers demanded attention. The cabinet had to be selected, various appointments made, and an inaugural address written. On top of the many customary and important duties, a greater question imposed itself. What would the president-elect do to save the Union?

It was immediately clear that the Republican victory heightened the danger of secession. Frederick Douglass had predicted that "[t]he slaveholders know that ... their power is over when a Republican President is elected."[1] Now those Southern leaders warned that they would not live under "Black Republicans." They saw little difference between Lincoln's party and the abolitionists and feared any change in racial arrangements. Before Christmas arrived, South Carolina would decide its future, and that action would probably influence other states. Time to save the Union, many believed, was short.

The pressure on Lincoln came from all sides. Northern Democrats, moderate Southerners, newspaper editors, all wanted him to act, and act quickly. Even within the Republican Party there were powerful elements, mainly eastern business interests, that urged some measure of compromise to avert a disaster.[2] All these groups looked anxiously to Lincoln for some statement or plan.

Congressman John A. Gilmer of North Carolina was one of those who wrote, pleading "the present perilous condition of the Country." Gilmer admitted that he and his constituents had done "all we could" to defeat Lincoln, but now he appealed to the president-elect to save the Union. "[A]pprehensions of real danger and harm to them and their peculiar institution ...

have seized the people of my section," Gilmer wrote. He hoped that "the dangers of the crisis" would excuse his urgent request that Lincoln give assurances about his intentions toward slavery.[3]

From the beginning Lincoln resisted such pleas and arguments. He wanted to stand by the positions he had so painstakingly defined. Beyond that, he discounted the reality of Southern threats. Told by a fellow Republican that there were "men honestly alarmed" in the South who feared he would attack slavery, he immediately objected: "There are no such men." Such claims were merely "the trick by which the South breaks down every Northern man." Lincoln felt his "first duty to the Country would be to stand by the men who elected me." If he betrayed them he would arrive in Washington "as powerless as a block of buckeye wood."[4]

Judge Daniel Breck of Kentucky was another visitor to Springfield. Breck was both a member of the Kentucky Supreme Court and a distant in-law of Lincoln's. He urged the president-elect to appoint conservatives to his cabinet, including some non-Republicans from the South. Lincoln replied that no "prominent public Republican had justly made himself obnoxious to the South." Breck wanted Republicans to "surrender the Government into the hands of the men they had just conquered." Efforts to placate the South meant "that the cause should take to its bosom the enemy who had always fought it and who would still continue to fight and oppose it."[5]

Lincoln took a similar tone with John Gilmer (who was offered a cabinet seat, which he declined). "Is it desired that I shall shift the ground on which I have been elected?" Lincoln pointedly asked. "I can not do it." Besides, he told Gilmer, to relieve Southern fears "[y]ou need only to acquaint yourself with that ground, and press it upon the attention of the South." Lincoln believed he had taken no positions contrary to the South's constitutional rights. Repeating his views now would allow his enemies to claim that he repented "for the crime of being elected." He asked if Gilmer had even read his speeches or the Republican Party platform. He referred Gilmer to the Republican platform and to specific pages in a published version of his debates with Douglas.[6]

After making his point, Lincoln privately assured Gilmer on several issues. He had "no thought" of recommending abolition either of slavery in the District of Columbia or of the slave trade among the states. Nor did he plan to give patronage jobs to Republicans throughout the slave states or put slaves to work in arsenals or dockyards. Lincoln could not imagine himself ever being in "a mood of harassing the people, either North or South." But he added, "On the territorial question, I am inflexible." That issue revealed "the only substantial difference" between white Southerners and Republicans. "You think slavery is right and ought to be extended; we think it is wrong and ought to be restricted. For this, neither has any just occasion to be angry with the other."[7]

Lincoln's instinct for firmness troubled Republicans like Henry Raymond, editor of the *New York Times*. But it received strong support from the Blair family. Both Frank Blair and his father, Francis Preston Blair, visited Springfield and conferred with Lincoln. For reasons of history and temperament, the Blairs believed in a tough line against threats to the Union. Andrew Jackson was their exemplar, and they admired his determination to enforce the tariff against South Carolina's nullification in 1832. The domination of the federal government by Southern aristocrats, they believed, had to end. Lincoln shared their unwillingness to give in to what seemed an unending series of Southern threats.[8]

But nationwide anxiety over the destruction of the Union continued to build. In Washington both houses of Congress struggled to draft a compromise. The House formed a special Committee of Thirty-three; the Senate created its own blue-ribbon Committee of Thirteen. In both committees attention soon focused on a proposal by Kentucky's John J. Crittenden. The key element of Crittenden's compromise was to divide all U.S. territories, "now held or hereafter acquired," at 36 degrees, 30 minutes (the Missouri Compromise line). Slavery would be permitted south of that line but prohibited above it. Public opinion seemed to favor Crittenden's proposal. Massive petitions and letters favoring it poured into Congress.[9]

On the territorial question, however, Lincoln was unshakable. Illinois's William Kellogg served on the Committee of Thirty-three, which was considering Crittenden's idea. On December 11 Lincoln wrote to him in unequivocal terms. "Entertain no proposition for a compromise in regard to the *extension* of slavery. The instant you do, they have us under again; all our labor is lost. ... The tug has to come & better now than later."[10]

Nor would Lincoln bend before Southerners on the Senate's Committee of Thirteen. Jefferson Davis of Mississippi and Robert Toombs of Georgia were among the committee's most influential members, along with Northerners Stephen Douglas and William H. Seward. In December Jefferson Davis made it known that he and Toombs would support Crittenden's compromise, *if* the committee's Republicans would agree to it.[11] This went further than senators from the Deep South had previously been willing to go. The possibility of reaching a compromise now depended on the Republicans.

To learn Lincoln's views, they sent a veteran New York editor and strategist, Thurlow Weed, to Springfield. Lincoln and Weed spent almost an entire day together. At the end of their meeting Lincoln drafted some resolutions to be shared with Seward and the Republican senators.[12] Lincoln made sure that "they do not touch the territorial question." Instead, he offered three proposals. First, the fugitive slave law should be enforced by a law of Congress "not obliging private persons to assist in its execution, but punishing all who resist it" and with "safeguards" against a free man being wrongly sent into slavery. Second, state laws in conflict with that law should be repealed. Third, "the Federal Union must be preserved." By the time Republicans on the committee discussed these proposals, Seward had already offered slightly different proposals, without winning agreement.[13] The efforts of the Committee of Thirteen came to nothing.

On the very day that Thurlow Weed conferred with Lincoln, South Carolina seceded from the Union. In a proclamation explaining its action, the Palmetto State's secession convention complained of the North's failure to enforce the fugitive slave law. Then it enumerated its fears for the future of slavery. The entire North was guilty of "increasing hostility ... to the institution of slavery," which it "denounced as sinful." A "sectional party" possessed "the means of subverting the Constitution." A man "hostile to slavery" had won the office of president. Moreover, some Northern states had "elevat[ed] to citizenship, persons who, by the supreme law of the land, are incapable of becoming citizens." Charging that Republicans had announced "that a war must be waged against slavery until it shall cease throughout the United States," South Carolina declared the Union "dissolved."[14]

Though unwelcome, this action did not change Lincoln's course. Two days later, on December 22, 1860, he replied to a note from Alexander Stephens of Georgia. From his term in Congress Lincoln remembered Stephens as "a friend." For that reason he offered some reassurance, but it was "for your own eye only" and was concise, even terse. "Do the people of the South really entertain fears that a Republican administration would, *directly,* or *indirectly,* interfere with their slaves, or with them, about their slaves?" Lincoln asked. There was "no cause for such fears." Then he added the words he had used with John Gilmer: "You think slavery is *right* and ought to be extended; while we think it is *wrong* and ought to be restricted. That I suppose is the rub. It certainly is the only substantial difference between us."[15]

As the new year began, Lincoln remained in Springfield, but hardly in isolation from national events. Letters and visitors arrived as frequently as news of important events. The mail brought many threats of "assassination, mayhem, fire and brimstone." John Nicolay said that Lincoln's "mail is infested with brutal and vulgar menace." One man who actually signed his name wrote "God damn you" over and over, while "A young creole" told Lincoln, "You will be shot on the 4th of March ... we are decided and our aim is sure." Lincoln tried to ignore these threats, but when Major David Hunter repeatedly sent warnings, Lincoln took him more seriously.[16] Hunter would accompany the president-elect on his route to Washington.

Letters with a friendly tone came from the Blair family. Francis Preston Blair Sr. wrote from Washington and offered to send reports on the developing situation in the nation's capital. Looking ahead to February, Montgomery Blair invited Mr. and Mrs. Lincoln to stay with him, rather than in a hotel, before the inauguration. Blair House contained the room that "General Jackson intended to occupy after leaving the White house," and Lincoln could "begin where he left."[17] From various quarters, advice on appointments poured in. Work on the staffing of the new administration continued, but little about the situation was normal.

The dismantling of the Union gathered speed. On January 9 Mississippi adopted an ordinance of secession. Florida followed the next day, and Alabama the day after that. At intervals of about a week, Georgia and then Louisiana seceded, and on February 1 Texas began its process of leaving the Union. Lincoln saw that before he could take the oath of office on March 4, the states of the Deep South would have left the Union.

Most of these states chose to issue declarations about their actions. Like South Carolina, they named slavery and race as their central concerns. "Our position," proclaimed Mississippi's convention, "is thoroughly identified with the institution of slavery." "None but the black race can bear exposure to the tropical sun," claimed the convention, which saw no choice but "submission to the mandates of abolition, or a dissolution of the Union." Alabama complained that the victory of "a sectional party, avowedly hostile" to slavery was "insulting and menacing." Georgia insisted on "the political and social inequality of the African race" and condemned the Republican Party as "antislavery in its mission and its purpose." Georgia was seceding "to avoid the desolation of our homes, our altars, and our firesides." Texans declared "as undeniable truths" that the nation was "established exclusively by the white race," that African Americans "were rightfully held and regarded as an inferior and dependent race," and that slavery was "justified" by "the revealed will of the Almighty Creator."[18]

Still a private citizen with no governmental authority, Lincoln could do little except to comment or advise. The deteriorating situation softened his stance only a little. On maintaining the Union and arresting the spread of slavery Lincoln remained adamant. When Francis Preston Blair sent information about General Winfield Scott's view of the military situation, Lincoln gratefully replied. It gave him an opportunity to stiffen military thinking. If forts were "given up before the inaugeration [sic]," Lincoln wrote, "the General must retake them afterwards." On February 1 he told Seward that the territories were key. He was inflexible on the territories but cared comparatively little about such issues as fugitive slaves, the District of Columbia, the slave trade in the slave states, "and whatever springs of necessity from the fact that the institution is amongst us." Consequently, he was exasperated when Congress, just days before the inauguration, organized the Colorado, Nevada, and Dakota territories with no provision excluding slavery. "I only wish I could have got there," said Lincoln, "to lock the door before the horse was stolen."[19]

His work on cabinet appointments continued. Sensitive egos and the demands of various states and party factions turned this task into a delicate and protracted minuet. Lincoln was determined from the outset to bring major Republican figures into his cabinet. A balance of former Democrats and former Whigs also seemed essential in such a new, diverse, and compound political organization. From December into the first days of March, Lincoln consulted, planned, flattered, and balanced interests to get the cabinet he wanted.

A rival for the Republican nomination, **Edward Bates** was one of many Republicans who could not imagine a nation in which the races were equal.

Seward was so prominent that from the start Lincoln thought of him for secretary of state. He also wanted Salmon Chase, whose record Lincoln admired though he had never actually met the vain and ambitious Ohioan. As secretary of the treasury Chase would handle a difficult task rather well while scheming for higher office. Edward Bates of Missouri agreed to be attorney general, and Gideon Welles of Connecticut accepted the post of secretary of the navy. Indiana's Caleb Smith agreed to be interior secretary, but naming the Pennsylvania political boss Simon Cameron to the War Department proved contentious (and soon unwise).[20]

The many who recommended Montgomery Blair for a position in the cabinet noted the importance of melding the diverse elements of the Republican Party. As early as November 20, Ohio's Benjamin Wade joined with New York's Preston King in urging that Blair should have an appointment. "The zeal and ability with which that whole family" had promoted the Republican Party weighed heavily in their favor. "An additional and powerful reason why the appointment should be made" was "the fact that they live in a Slave State [Maryland] and are from the old Democratic party." In the middle of December Lyman Trumbull argued that "besides his personal fitness," Montgomery Blair came "from the South" and had "Democratic antecedents." Others pointed out that he "represent[ed] the views of the old Jackson portion of the Republican party," and Maryland Republicans stressed the race issue. "He has the addition[al] qualification of having studied the great social question of slavery more thoroughly than almost any man in America, always excepting Mr. Jefferson." Like Jefferson, Montgomery Blair recognized "the importance of providing homes for the emancipated as an essential and indispensable counterpoint to emancipation."[21] Blair became postmaster general, a post from which he would give Lincoln staunch support.

Before the cabinet was fully set, the Lincolns set out for Washington. Their trip consumed twelve days, and everything Lincoln said or did went under a microscope. Cheering crowds in Springfield, Indianapolis, Indiana, and Columbus, Ohio, buoyed his spirits. At most stops he tried to say little and be optimistic in what he did say. But in Philadelphia, at Independence Hall, he grew more serious. He identified the Declaration of Independence as the source of all his political feelings. The Declaration gave "hope to the world for all future time ... [and] promise that in due time the weights should be lifted from the shoulders of all men, and that *all* should have an equal chance." Immediately a Democratic newspaper charged that this meant emancipation and enfranchisement for African Americans.[22]

Such extreme charges did not trouble Lincoln, who said he would "rather be assassinated" than surrender that principle of the Declaration. Talk of assassination had loomed up as the presidential party planned its route to Baltimore, where pro-Southern sentiment was strong. The detective Allan Pinkerton sent undercover agents to the city. There he found reason to doubt the loyalty of the police force and soon learned of a serious plot. Pinkerton himself heard the group's leader declare, "If I alone must do it, I shall. Lincoln shall die in this city."[23]

Warnings of violence from Pinkerton and others convinced Lincoln to travel quietly by night through the city, arriving in Washington one day earlier than planned. This change of plans succeeded without incident, except for the anger and belligerent noncooperation of Mary Todd Lincoln. Enraged that she was to stay behind on the original schedule, she argued loudly and publicly, compromising the secrecy of the arrangements. The Pennsylvania editor and politician Alexander K. McClure decided she was "a hopeless fool" and never spoke to her again.[24]

The atmosphere in Washington was little better than Baltimore. The nation's capital had always been a Southern city, and now the crisis had heightened pro-Southern sentiment. Democrats had dominated the city's social life through the 1850s. The "Black Republicans" were not welcome with the "resident elite," many of whom "were Secessionists or in sympathy with Secessionists." Secretary of the Navy Gideon Welles described the atmosphere as "thick with treason." The *New York Tribune* would praise Lincoln for ignoring "villains who had threatened to shoot him." Even as Southern Democrats left Congress, some Northern Democrats sympathized with the rebels and wanted Lincoln's administration to fail.[25]

It was in this climate that Lincoln put the finishing touches on his Inaugural Address. In the Union's crisis, with secession well under way, it was sure to be an unusually important statement. His words could foster unity or further division. Lincoln needed to defend and uphold the Union, but could he do it in a way that would not precipitate war? How far should he go to calm Southern fears and allay discontent in the upper South?

A misperception shaped part of Lincoln's approach and colored many of his later actions. Knowing border state Southerners as he did and feeling some connection to them, Lincoln believed that there was a deep vein of Unionism in the South. He hoped that Virginia and other border states would remain in the Union. If they did, sentiment then might shift in the states that had already seceded, as Unionism and sober second thoughts emerged.[26]

Lincoln showed his text to only three men. Francis Blair Sr. counseled him on content and tone, along with Secretary of State Seward and Illinois Republican Orville Browning. A key word of advice that Lincoln received from these advisers was that if conflict were to occur, "it is very important that the traitors shall be the aggressors." For that reason the president said, "The government will not assail you. You can have no conflict, without being yourselves the aggressors." To this he added, "*You* have no oath registered in Heaven to destroy the government, while *I* shall have the most solemn one to 'preserve, protect and defend' it."[27]

Lincoln used the very beginning of his address to offer reassurance to the people of the South. "Nearly all" his published speeches contained "ample evidence" that Southerners had no reason to fear that "their property, and their peace, and personal security" would be endangered. He quoted one of these earlier statements: "I have no purpose, directly or indirectly, to interfere with the institution of slavery in the States where it exists. I believe I have no lawful right to do so, and I have no inclination to do so." In addition, he cited the Republican Party's platform, which stated that "the right of each State to order and control its own domestic institutions according to its own judgment exclusively" was "essential to that balance of power on which the perfection and endurance of our political fabric depend." This platform, Lincoln added, was "a law" to Republicans "and to me."

Later in his speech he went even further. Congress had proposed a constitutional amendment providing "that the federal government, shall never interfere with the domestic institutions of the States, including that of persons held to service." This proposed amendment would now go before the states for rejection or ratification. The president had no constitutional role in this process. Yet Lincoln went "so far as to say that, holding such a provision to now be implied constitutional law, I have no objection to its being made express, and irrevocable."

On the most controversial issues, he appealed to reason and to reasonable men. Southerners had no need to fear his administration, as the Founders had limited the power of the central government. Elected officials had "but little power for mischief," and the people had the power to change that government "at very short intervals." Surely a fugitive slave law could be drawn that would safeguard liberty and respect the rights of citizens of all the states. Slavery in the territories was one of those questions on which the Constitution gave no "express" and clear statement. Discussion, even of Supreme Court decisions, would necessarily continue in a government controlled by the people. Again he acknowledged that Northerners and Southerners disagreed over the morality of slavery. Such differences over slavery "cannot be perfectly cured," but they would "be *worse* ... after the separation of the sections than before."

Lincoln's words on the Union were strong and unequivocal. "[T]he Union of these States is perpetual," he declared. Not only did the Founders and the Constitution intend for the government to "endure forever," but "the central idea of secession, is the essence of anarchy." Majority rule was "the only true sovereign of a free people." Secession, by contrast, would breed further secession by any dissatisfied minority. Lincoln's oath required him to "take care ... that the laws of the Union be faithfully executed in all the States." And his duty was not only to administer the government but also "to transmit it, unimpaired" to his successor.

Lincoln promised "to hold, occupy, and possess the property, and places belonging to the government, and to collect the duties and imposts." But he sought to avoid collision and offered conciliatory words. There would be "no invasion—no using of force against ... the people anywhere" and no forcing of "obnoxious strangers among the people." He would try to promote "a peaceful solution of the national troubles, and a restoration of fraternal sympathies and affections." His closing words about the "mystic chords of memory" that might "yet swell the chorus of the Union" testified to his hope for peace.

The fate of that hope depended on events in the days ahead. Lincoln knew that they would be trying days, days that would spell the difference between peace in a slaveholding nation and a civil war of untold consequences. The inauguration was over and the responsibilities of office had begun.

Notes

1.   Blight, *Frederick Douglass' Civil War*, 57–58.

2.   See Potter, *Lincoln and His Party in the Secession Crisis*.

3.   John A. Gilmer to Abraham Lincoln, December 10, 1860, Abraham Lincoln Papers.

4.   Nicolay, *With Lincoln in the White House*, 7 (entry for November 5, 1860).

5.   Ibid., 10 (November 16, 1860).

6.   Lincoln to Gilmer, December 15, 1860, Abraham Lincoln Papers.

7.   Ibid.

8.   W. E. Smith, *The Francis Preston Blair Family*, 1:514.

9.   Potter, *The Impending Crisis*, 549–50.

10.   Nicolay, *With Lincoln in the White House*, 15.

11.   This is the testimony of Stephen Douglas, quoted in Rhodes, *History of the United States*, 3:151–55. See also Current, *The Lincoln Nobody Knows*, 88–90.

12.   Lincoln, *Collected Works*, 4:158–59.

13.   Letter to Lyman Trumbull, ibid., 4:158, and Resolutions, 4:156–57, especially the note on 157.

14. Declarations of Causes of Seceding States: Civil War South Carolina.

15. Lincoln, *Collected Works*, 4:160.

16. Stashower, *The Hour of Peril*, 82–85.

17. Francis Preston Blair Sr. to Lincoln, January 12, 1861, and Montgomery Blair to Lincoln, December 8, 1860, both in Abraham Lincoln Papers; Goodwin, *Team of Rivals*, 312.

18. Escott, *"What Shall We Do with the Negro?,"* 3–4.

19. Lincoln to Francis P. Blair Sr., December 21, 1860, in Lincoln, *Collected Works*, 4:157; Burlingame, *Abraham Lincoln*, 1:749, 758.

20. See Burlingame, *Abraham Lincoln*, 1: chaps. 18 and 19; and Goodwin, *Team of Rivals*, 283–319.

21. Benjamin Wade to Preston King, November 20, 1860; Lyman Trumbull to Lincoln, December 18, 1860; William Pinckney Ewing to Lincoln, February 2, 1861; and Francis S. Corkran and John C. Underwood to Lincoln, February 26, 1861, all in Abraham Lincoln Papers.

22. Burlingame, *Abraham Lincoln*, 2:35; Goodwin, *Team of Rivals*, 310.

23. Stashower, *The Hour of Peril*, 157.

24. Goodwin, *Team of Rivals*, 310–11; Burlingame, *Abraham Lincoln*, 2:36.

25. Welles, *Diary*, 1:55, 10; Stashower, *The Hour of Peril*, 15.

26. Welles, *Diary*, 1:39.

27. Burlingame, *Abraham Lincoln*, 2:46; Lincoln, *This Fiery Trial*, 96. It is known that more than one of the three advisers recommended that the seceded states should be and appear the aggressors.

    All quotations in the remaining paragraphs of this chapter come from the Inaugural Address, as found in Lincoln, *This Fiery Trial*, 88–97.

Selected Bibliography

Blight, David W. *Frederick Douglass' Civil War: Keeping Faith in Jubilee.* Baton Rouge: Louisiana State University Press, 1989.

Burlingame, Michael. *Abraham Lincoln: A Life.* 2 vols. Baltimore: Johns Hopkins University Press, 2008.

Declarations of Causes of Seceding States: Civil War South Carolina. http://www.AmericanCivilWar. com/documents/causes_south_carolina.html.

———. *"What Shall We Do with the Negro?": Lincoln, White Racism, and Civil War America.* Charlottesville: University of Virginia Press, 2009.

Goodwin, Doris Kearns. *Team of Rivals: The Political Genius of Abraham Lincoln.* New York: Simon and Schuster, 2005.

Lincoln, Abraham. Abraham Lincoln Papers, Library of Congress. Available on American Memory website, http://memory.loc.gov.

———. *The Collected Works of Abraham Lincoln*. Edited by Roy Basler. 9 vols. New Brunswick, NJ: Rutgers University Press, 1953.

———. *This Fiery Trial: The Speeches and Writings of Abraham Lincoln*. Edited by William E. Gienapp. New York: Oxford University Press, 2002.

Nicolay, John G. *With Lincoln in the White House: Letters, Memoranda, and Other Writings of John G. Nicolay, 1860–1865*. Edited by Michael Burlingame. Carbondale: Southern Illinois University Press, 2000.

Potter, David M. *The Impending Crisis, 1848–1861*. New York: Harper & Row, 1976.

———. *Lincoln and His Party in the Secession Crisis*. New Haven: Yale University Press, 1962.

Rhodes, James Ford. *History of the United States from the Compromise of 1850*. 9 vols. New York: Harper and Brothers, 1913–22.

Smith, William Earnest. *The Francis Preston Blair Family in Politics*. 2 vols. New York: Macmillan, 1933.

Stashower, Daniel. *The Hour of Peril: The Secret Plot to Murder Lincoln before the Civil War*. New York: Minotaur Books, 2013.

Welles, Gideon. *Diary of Gideon Welles, Secretary of the Navy under Lincoln and Johnson*. Introduction by John T. Morse Jr. 3 vols. Boston: Houghton Mifflin, 1909, 1910, 1911.

Reading 1.5

"A New Field of Labor"

Antislavery Women, Freedmen's Aid, and Political Power

Carol Faulkner

T HE HUMANITARIAN CRISIS FOLLOWING EMANCIPATION PROVIDED many Northern women, white and black, with a new opportunity to advise government officials and implement federal policy.[1] Responding to the demand for missionaries and teachers in Union-controlled areas of the South, women explained their participation in the freedmen's aid movement by citing their gender's presumed role as caretakers of the young, sick, and poor. As the war developed, female activists, most of them seasoned abolitionists and women's rights advocates, argued that their work in behalf of former slaves justified access to real political power. Like many Radical Republican politicians, they envisioned a federal government with power to protect the rights of citizens. But female reformers saw their own benevolent presence in the halls of government—as employees, lobbyists, teachers, entrepreneurs, and potentially voters—as central to their vision of a reconstructed nation. Women's physical and ideological movement into the world of national policy did not go unchallenged. Beginning during the war and intensifying after 1865, military officials and male reformers set limits upon both activist women and their gendered vision for Reconstruction.

Historians frequently describe the Civil War as a watershed in the public lives of Northern women, but few trace the continuation of women's wartime activities after Appomattox. Historians of Civil War women usually end their analysis at the Confederate Army's surrender and demobilization. Between 1861 and 1865, women's role as nurses, writers, freedmen's teachers, and organizers of the U.S. Sanitary Commission gave them a new, if fleeting, visibility. As Lyde Cullen Sizer concludes, "The rule remained: women in the mid-nineteenth century had few options for employment or for public or political power."[2] Studies of women's reform during Reconstruction focus on freedmen's teachers or suffragists, disguising the true extent of women's postwar activities.[3] In fact, women's participation accelerated when government and Northern voluntary associations took on the burdens of aiding former slaves. The Bureau of Refugees, Freedmen, and Abandoned Lands (Freedmen's Bureau), a temporary division of the War Department established in 1865, and freedmen's aid societies cooperated to reorganize labor, establish schools, distribute aid, and protect the basic rights of former slaves in the South. Abolitionist women viewed the Freedmen's Bureau as their own, an official arena for freedmen's relief and a vehicle for the political and economic rights of women and African Americans.

Despite women's hopes for the Freedmen's Bureau, the end of the war heightened anxieties about both freedmen's aid and women's public labors. An expanding federal government, which placed women in positions of authority and created a newly entitled citizenry composed of African Americans, threatened commonly held assumptions about male privilege, white supremacy, and limited federal power.[4] During the war, the military only half-heartedly endorsed the efforts of female reformers, viewing them as an unfortunate necessity in helping impoverished slave refugees. The officers who staffed the Freedmen's Bureau voiced a similar disapproval of women's assumed authority over the distribution of clothes and food to former slaves.[5] Though gender did not divide freedmen's aid associations during the war, the new alliance between male abolitionists and the Republican Party isolated female coworkers after 1865. Only by extending the boundaries of the war into Reconstruction can we understand the gendered battles over emancipation, charity, and women's work.

Women's interest in freedmen's aid grew not only from their antislavery convictions but also from their self-proclaimed empathy for former slaves. In 1863, for example, the Rochester Ladies' Anti-Slavery Society (RLASS) noted that "a new field of labor has opened to us" in "comforting, cheering, advising, educating the *freed* men, women and children."[6] The society hired its own freedmen's agent, former member Julia A. Wilbur, to go to Washington, D.C., and Alexandria, Virginia, to investigate and respond to the needs of former slaves. Welcomed by the male leaders of the National Freedmen's Relief Association of Washington, in October 1862 she headed to Alexandria, where large numbers of refugees from slavery had gathered. When she arrived, she informed the RLASS that "there are none but white men to care for [freed-women] & minister to their most delicate necessities. I was sick. I was disgusted." She believed that former slaves desperately needed female agents, writing, "There are women here that need woman's care & counsel & kind words." Though the nation's middle-class and elite women had long devoted themselves to benevolent enterprises, Wilbur and the RLASS nonetheless described their plan to work with former slaves as a "new field of labor." Abolitionist women assumed the guardianship and care of recently freed women and children, hoping for a broader social and political transformation.[7]

The Ladies' Contraband Relief Society of St. Louis, Missouri, also viewed the care of freedwomen and children as their special province. Located at an urban crossroads between North and South, the Contraband Relief Society served a large number of former slaves displaced by the war. They reported, "There were at least 100,000 on the river between St. Louis and Vicksburg who were in suffering condition. These sufferers were mostly women and children whose husbands and fathers had in many cases entered the Union Army."[8] As freedwomen and children lacked the protection of male relatives, the women of St. Louis concluded that someone must care for them. As in the antislavery movement, women lamented the effects of slavery and war on African American families. Their language was often paternalistic, imagining former slaves as a population of needy women and children. Still, female reformers called the nation's attention to the problems of former slaves, highlighting their own initiatives to assist the government.[9]

In 1864, Ohio abolitionist and women's rights activist Josephine Griffing petitioned Congress to commission women to visit camps, raise funds for freedmen's relief, hire teachers, and "in short, to look after, and secure the general welfare of these women and children." She explained that women "fully understood" the "wants and necessities" of freedwomen and their children, establishing an interracial connection on the basis of motherhood. Though her argument relied on a traditional gendered division of labor, she asked for something far more radical. At the 1850 women's rights convention held in Salem, Griffing and other participants had urged the women of Ohio "to assert their rights as independent human beings; to demand their true position as equally responsible co-workers with their brethren." Now Griffing asked Congress to appoint women as official representatives of the Union government, with full legal authority to distribute aid to former slaves.[10]

As Griffing and other women worked with former slaves, they realized they needed more power to remedy the careless treatment of freedpeople by the military and even other missionaries. Emily Howland, a New Yorker who worked in freedmen's camps around Washington, resisted pressure to affiliate with the New York National Freedmen's Relief Association, noting that she could use any donations she received more effectively than if they "were put into the treasury of a society." Her comments expressed skepticism of the society's allocation of funds, particularly in the high salaries of its male leaders.[11] Julia Wilbur wrote to Secretary of War Edwin Stanton to protest the injustices she witnessed in Alexandria. She informed Stanton that the Provost Marshal, Lieutenant Colonel H. H. Wells, was a person of "little experience." Wilbur had conducted an intense lobbying campaign for the government to build barracks in Alexandria to house African American families while they looked for work and permanent homes. Instead, Wells instituted a policy to rent rooms to freedpeople, a policy Wilbur adamantly rejected. She wrote Stanton that she had "not thought for a moment that either yourself or the President intended to extort from the Contrabands in Alex $17 00 a year as rent for these rude barracks." She also opposed the appointment of her fellow reformer, the Rev. Albert Gladwin, as Superintendent of Freedmen, calling him "altogether unfit" for the position. Although she did not presume that she could become the superintendent, she wrote, "I did think of asking for the position of *Assistant Superintendent*." She went on to describe the importance of women's efforts in Alexandria, concluding that women also deserved to get paid for their work: "I could do still more were I invested with a little more authority. Although a *woman* I would like an appointment with a fair salary attached to it, & I would expect to deserve a salary."[12] Wilbur wanted official recognition of her contributions by the government. Already paid for her work by the RLASS, she knew a government salary would carry more weight as she negotiated with Wells and other officials in Alexandria.

Wilbur faced strong resistance from military officials and male reformers in Alexandria. Even with broad social acceptance of women's benevolent activities, their incursion into military areas violated the boundaries between private and public, home front and war zone. The Rev. Gladwin, the future Superintendent of Freedmen, expressed his outrage at Wilbur's presence, informing her that she was out of her sphere and he did "not like to see a woman wear men's clothes."[13] Wells complained that Wilbur wanted "the control, the management of the contrabands." He dismissed her goals for the barracks, saying the plan to rent them was "calculated to benefit the colored people, and not render them more dependent and indolent than they now are." Further, he informed his superior officer that he did not intend to be directed by a woman.[14] Both the Rev. Gladwin and Wells had a visceral reaction to a female freedmen's agent in the male world of occupied Alexandria, but they also characterized her proposals as misguided charity. Instead, they wanted refugee women and children to become self-sufficient—and thus leave the army's care—as soon as possible. Such views reflected the army's frustration at their unexpected responsibility for freed families as well as a political aversion to dependency in any form. In their minds, the dependency of slave refugees was linked to the presence of benevolent women.[15]

Yet government officials also recognized the value of women's contributions to the relief effort. After her 1864 petition to Congress, Josephine Griffing moved to Washington to work with the National Freedmen's Relief Association. Like other women, she saw the need for an independent government agency to oversee freedmen's relief. In a letter to abolitionist William Lloyd Garrison, Griffing articulated her ideas for the future Freedmen's Bureau. In Griffing's view, the agency would be the basis for a "new & purer system of Politics," which would include the participation of women. She acknowledged that a man would head the bureau, but believed he should be "fully committed to give us *women* what we do so much need in the *Gov.*—in *Commissions* to carry forward the work of Relief to the Freedmen which he sees to be *our* work *legitimately*." Griffing saw freedmen's relief as women's work and "of great importance to the Freedmen, Women, and the country."[16] From the care of freedwomen and children, Griffing extended women's sphere of influence to all former slaves and suggested that women's labors were essential to Reconstruction. She lobbied politicians in Washington vigorously for the Freedmen's Bureau. Suffragists later described her as the originator of the Freedmen's Bureau: "Few cared to listen to the details of the necessity, and it was only through Mrs. Griffing's brave and unwearied efforts that the plan was accepted."[17] In appreciation, General Oliver Otis Howard, commissioner of the Freedmen's Bureau, appointed Griffing assistant to the assistant commissioner for Washington in 1865. Her appointment was a victory for women in the freedmen's aid movement as it acknowledged their important role in aiding former slaves.

Abolitionist women hoped the establishment of the Freedmen's Bureau would inaugurate a new era of equal rights in American politics. The Freedmen's Bureau did indeed expand the female presence in the federal government, especially in the nation's capital, as women took jobs as visitors, matrons, and teachers. Despite her negative experience with the army in Alexandria, Wilbur had enormous faith in the military officers who staffed the Freedmen's Bureau. "I hope and believe Gen. Howard is equal to the task he has assumed," she wrote the Rochester Ladies' Anti-Slavery Society. "Since the Freedmen's Bureau went into operation, many wrongs have been remedied."[18] On a visit to Richmond shortly after the end of the war, Wilbur found forty soldiers guarding the almshouse who "were rough, ignorant, and prejudiced; they took to negro driving naturally. Such men should never be out where they can wield any power over others, especially the weak and helpless." Wilbur saw the soldiers stand over freedwomen with a whip, "and in several instances women were beaten and otherwise abused."[19] In addition, small children were hired out, or apprenticed, under the army's watch. Wilbur saw women's presence as the only remedy to these injustices. But after Colonel Orlando Brown, the Freedmen's Bureau superintendent, informed Wilbur he would return the apprenticed children to their mothers, she expressed her confidence in him: "I felt that he could be trusted with the interests of the Freed-people, and then, and not till then, did I feel at liberty to leave Richmond."[20] In Wilbur's view, this male Freedmen's Bureau agent and military officer was an effective substitute for a female reformer. She and other antislavery women viewed the Freedmen's Bureau as both an extension of women's charitable activities and an official endorsement of their efforts. Emma Brown, a native of Washington, D.C., and one of the first teachers in its segregated "colored" public school system, wrote, "I don't think women have ever before had so glorious an opportunity to do something—They have always been such insignificant creatures—so dependent." She noted that she and a female colleague had "a little Freedmen's Bureau of our own."[21] As Brown and her friend distributed clothes and other goods from their schoolroom, they associated the bureau with their own version of Reconstruction, combining female benevolence with a national program to ease former slaves' transition to freedom.

Though now agents of the federal government, and thus representatives of the general public, female reformers continued to advocate for freedwomen and children. In 1865, Josephine Griffing published an appeal in Garrison's antislavery newspaper the *Liberator* that described the impoverished condition of "twenty thousand" freedpeople in Washington. She claimed these former slaves, "miserable women, with large families of children, besides old, crippled, blind and sick persons" were the "mothers and sons, and wives and children, of soldiers still in Government service as Regular U.S. Troops." According to Griffing, they needed housing, fuel, beds, blankets, food, and clothing.[22] She earnestly solicited donations from friends and sympathizers, emphasizing the nation's debt to black soldiers and their families.

Despite her emphasis on these deserving groups of former slaves, Griffing's appeal was unusual and controversial for its emphasis on direct relief to destitute freedpeople. Since the beginnings of the freedmen's aid movement, women had stressed the need for donations of money, clothing, and other items to ameliorate the poverty of former slaves. By the end of the war, the tone of the freedmen's aid movement, spurred by the demands of Republican politicians, the military, and the public, had evolved to focus on education and free labor rather than charity. Such pleas for donations of necessities embarrassed officials because they highlighted the failures rather than the successes of emancipation. But women still viewed their principal duty to be benevolent in nature. They did not see the poverty of former slaves as a racial characteristic, but a result of the specific circumstances of war and the abolition of slavery. Female activists believed that neither women nor slaves could gain independence without short-term assistance.

Griffing's appeal for the "twenty thousand" also redirected the attention of Northerners to the capital, an antebellum symbol of slavery's corrupting influence on the republic. After the abolition of the peculiar institution in the District of Columbia in 1862, female abolitionists, nurses, and visitors noticed the city's growing population of freedpeople, many of whom migrated to the city seeking shelter from slavery and the ravages of war. Though Griffing may have exaggerated the number of destitute, she accurately assessed the change in the city's black population, which grew by more than twenty thousand between 1860 and 1870. Griffing and other antislavery women, such as Rachel Moore of the Philadelphia Female Anti-Slavery Society, flocked to the district to aid impoverished former slaves, creating a population of politically active female reformers. They alerted Northerners to the continued suffering of district freed-people and the inability or unwillingness of government officials to cope with the problem. But many Freedmen's Bureau officers, uncomfortable with direct charity or the national focus on their headquarters, preferred education, employment, migration, and other solutions to those advocated by the benevolent women at their doorstep.[23]

As politicians began demanding freedpeople's adaptation to a free labor system, women's activism began to focus on work. Aid rolls swelled in Washington, D.C., between 1866 and 1868, and the Freedmen's Bureau strongly encouraged underemployed freedpeople to leave the overcrowded district for work on Southern plantations or Northern farms. Though Griffing continued to urge the government and private individuals to donate generously to freedmen's relief, she and Sojourner Truth also worked as employment agents for the Bureau, ultimately aiding the Northern migration of almost seven thousand former slaves.[24]

To find occupations for former slaves, Truth and Griffing used their antislavery connections throughout the Northeast and Midwest. Truth asked Rochester, New York, abolitionist Amy Post if she could find "some good places for women that have children."[25] After advertising in the Rochester *Democrat* and the Rochester *Express*, Truth received approximately three thousand requests. As one advertisement for their services read, "We exhort everyone in want of farm hands or household service to write to Mrs. Griffing, No. 394 No. Capitol St., Washington City, enclosing two postage stamps. It would be better still to inclose $5 at once, and ask her to send such help as you need. Our women are overworked, our farms not half tilled for want of help."[26]

While well intentioned, their efforts ultimately pitted against one another the interests of white and freed women as well as abolitionists and former slaves. Former slaves came to the North only to find themselves working as domestic servants and farmhands, which, as the advertisement suggested, eased the labors of white farm families.[27] Though the Freedmen's Bureau paid to transport freedpeople to the North, Truth and Griffing sought additional compensation for their efforts, a practice some attacked as slave trading. Since neither woman was independently wealthy, each depended on the money they could raise for their survival. Sojourner Truth justified her fee: "The people come and are willing to pay what I ask 5 cts. or 1 dollar for the sake of having help and they think it is no more than right for me to have it."[28] Both women struggled for economic security even as they assisted former slaves to achieve a measure of financial independence.

Although northern migration fulfilled the hopes of Truth and Griffing by offering former slaves new employment opportunities, the program was often paternalistic and sometimes exploitative. For example, Anna Lowell of the Howard Industrial School for Colored Women and Girls in Cambridge, Massachusetts, helped freedwomen and children resettle in the North. Her school was a branch of the Freedmen's Bureau's migration network, and she regularly received freedwomen from Washington, D.C., trained them, and found them employment in Massachusetts. The goal of her home, she explained to C. H. Howard, the assistant commissioner of the Freedmen's Bureau for the district, was "to take girls and women and teach them and then get them good places."[29] She believed that the women in her school were thus saved from "evils which can only be realized and appreciated by those who have been familiar with it," presumably referring to enslaved women's sexual vulnerability in Southern homes. "Instead of living in poverty and dependence they are all supporting themselves by honest labor," she claimed, "and their children will be more benefited than they." But Lowell's perspective on the employment of freedwomen presumed their inferiority to whites and the wholesomeness of the North; she trained African American women for jobs as domestic servants only. Though she found her pupils "good places" removed from the sexualized atmosphere of the Southern household, she offered them positions that were often isolating, demeaning, and abusive—one reason why elite white women like Lowell faced servant shortages throughout the nineteenth century. Lowell's school gave freedwomen the chance to exchange one white mistress for another.[30]

Migration limited the newfound freedoms of former slave women in even more important ways. To protect "the moral good of the next generation," Lowell created a self-consciously female environment and requested that the Freedmen's Bureau send her young girls, preferably orphans, though she also accepted women with small children because "it is not difficult to get a place for a woman with a child over 18 months—when younger than that they will meet with much that is disappointing." Lowell told C. H. Howard that she did not want men or boys, however, "as it interferes with all our arrangements."[31] Such strictures broke up married couples, including one preacher and his wife, and probably separated mothers and sons.[32] In the zeal of the Freedmen's Bureau and its agents to transfer thousands of freedpeople from Washington, these problems were inevitable, but from the perspective of some abolitionists this practice displayed eerie similarities to the slave market. In 1867, Worcester abolitionist Anna Earle complained to the Freedmen's Bureau that Griffing and her colleague Sarah Tilmon, an employment agent with the nationalist African Civilization Society, had taken a girl named Kitty Brooks to New York City without the permission or knowledge of her mother. Since then, Griffing, Tilmon, and the Freedmen's Bureau had been unable to locate Kitty. Earle wrote, "I refrain from expressing my feeling in regard to Mrs. Griffing, who it seems to me as clearly kidnapped little Kitty as if she had been a slave trader."[33]

Frederick Douglass expressed a more general skepticism of the freedmen's aid movement. Concerned that charity encouraged white Americans to view blacks as dependents, he urged abolitionists instead to work for equality: "My mission for the present is to ask equal citizenship in the state and equal fellowship for the Negro in the church. Equal rights in the street cars and equal admission in the state schools ... this is what we count and must not lose sight of in all our schemes of benevolence with special reference to the Negro." Douglass noticed the similarities of such "schemes of benevolence" to the paternalistic ideal of plantation slavery, but his reluctance to wholeheartedly endorse freedmen's aid also represented practical politics.[34] Few Americans supported a national system of charity for former slaves, especially one that relied on the labors of politically active women. Women in the freedmen's aid movement found their vision for Reconstruction severely circumscribed. Many former slaves undoubtedly agreed with Douglass that they would rather be left alone, but other impoverished freedpeople temporarily needed the assistance of the government and freedmen's aid associations.

The story of Diana Williams shows how one former slave used the assistance of female reformers and the Freedmen's Bureau to forge a new life in freedom. In 1868, Williams visited Griffing's employment office, hoping to secure a job and transportation to Hartford, Connecticut, where she had relatives. Other bureau agents frequently challenged Griffing's judgment, but she justified the use of government transportation by noting that Williams was "a constant applicant for help and employment" and that her husband approved of the move. Nevertheless, Williams's husband hid their children, forcing a change of plans. Clearly intent on leaving, Williams departed for Philadelphia several days later. The Freedmen's Bureau fielded complaints from the husband about the disappearance of his wife, demanding action from Griffing. She responded that Mr. Williams "was a worthless overbearing man" and counseled him to find work.[35] Griffing believed that she had helped Diana Williams flee an unhappy marriage while also giving her a chance at economic independence. She urged the Freedmen's Bureau to recognize Williams as an individual, independent of her husband. Juggling the demands of free labor with interrelated concerns about appropriate gender roles, Freedmen's Bureau officials sought to restore the traditional relationship between Diana Williams and her husband.

What had changed since Griffing, Wilbur, and other women expressed their hope for a new "system of Politics" embodied by the Freedmen's Bureau? The end of the war transformed the relationship of the freedmen's aid movement to former slaves. Responding to the concerns of citizens, soldiers, and politicians, the staff of the Freedmen's Bureau began to distance themselves from direct relief of freedpeople almost immediately. General Oliver Otis Howard assured the public he would not support former slaves "in idleness." As a result, the agency cut back on its charitable operations, preferring to spend its budget on transportation rather than fuel and food whenever possible. In the case of Diana Williams, Howard's subordinates linked African American self-sufficiency with the nuclear family structure, reinforcing women's status as dependents rather than economic actors in their own right.[36] As with Julia Wilbur's experience in Alexandria, fear of African American dependency coexisted with anxieties about women's new public presence. Griffing fell victim to this political reality. During and after the war, she toured the North raising funds and awareness of freedpeople's condition. But Griffing's speeches, published appeals, and her official appointment as assistant to the assistant commissioner raised questions about the Freedmen's Bureau. Was the agency funded by taxpayer money or private contributions? Was the Bureau a government charity for former slaves? What was the nature of Griffing's position in the Bureau? As a result, Griffing lost her position in the fall of 1865, less than six months after her initial appointment. Fielding inquiries from the public, Lieutenant S. N. Clark, a staff member in the district office, informed one E. Carpenter of Colchester, Connecticut, of Griffing's dismissal: "That connection has ceased. She has no authority to solicit funds for the Freedmen's Bureau and no official information to sustain her statements of the suffering among the Freedmen."[37] Explaining that Griffing had no authority or official information, the Freedmen's Bureau thus reassured the American people that the social upheaval and economic exigencies of the war were not permanent.

Male abolitionists also undermined Griffing's status at the Freedmen's Bureau. After emancipation, antislavery men like J. Miller McKim, Jacob Shipherd, and others celebrated their victory by joining the Republican Party and forming organizations with close ties to political power. McKim, former agent of the Pennsylvania Anti-Slavery Society and publisher of its paper the *Pennsylvania Freeman*, left the American Anti-Slavery Society in 1865 to found the American Freedmen's Union Commission (AFUC), an umbrella organization for freedmen's aid societies that assisted and supplemented the Freedmen's Bureau's efforts. Many Garrisonian abolitionists found such a close connection to the government disturbing, but abolitionist women found the lack of women in the commission hierarchy even more problematic. As Lucretia Mott wrote, "I told him [McKim] it was objected, that Woman was ignored in their organizn., & if really a reconstructn. for the Nation she ought not so to be—and it wd. be rather 'a come down' for our Anti Slavery women & Quaker women to consent to be thus overlooked."[38] Though McKim denied any deliberate exclusion of women, the commission helped undermine Griffing's position at the Bureau, ostensibly because she presented a threat to its political existence. Jacob R. Shipherd, the commission's secretary, wrote to General Howard that "Mrs. Griffing is simply irrepressible: & yet she must be repressed, so far as you and I have to do with her, or else we must bear the odium of her folly. She still represents the '20,000 utterly destitute' as needing *outright support* from northern charity."[39] Shipherd believed that Griffing's appeals for impoverished former slaves hurt the ability of the American Freedmen's Union Commission and the Freedmen's Bureau to sustain their educational and legal work with freed-people. Shipherd viewed charity to former slaves as harmful because it undermined free labor values and encouraged "copperheads" in their belief that African Americans were better off under slavery. Throughout his letter, Shipherd stressed Griffing's incompetence, implying that her sex disqualified her from a job meant for "sensible men."[40] By the end of 1865, the male officers and reformers in the Freedmen's Bureau and the AFUC controlled freedmen's aid, limiting the place of both women and direct relief in the movement.

Despite this transformation, abolitionist women continued to view the Freedmen's Bureau as the only government agency that embraced the political needs of women and former slaves. Griffing remained a regular at the offices of the Freedmen's Bureau because of her employment agency and industrial school. She continued to press the Bureau for greater authority, though it generally pushed back. The Freedmen's Bureau itself was fighting for its own survival throughout the 1860s, increasingly limiting operations to education starting in 1868 before finally closing in 1872. Though she acknowledged its flaws, Wilbur speculated that "if the whites behave so badly with the Freedmen's Bureau in operation, we can easily imagine what the situation of the freedpeople would be were the protection of the Bureau withdrawn."[41] In Virginia, teacher Caroline Putnam echoed this sentiment. After Putnam informed freedman Steptoe Ball of the demise of the Freedmen's Bureau, she reported "the look of being forsaken suddenly came on him, that was pitiful to see. '*Who then is going to see justice done us now?*'"[42] In 1869 Griffing wrote a desperate last appeal to General Howard for money to distribute aid to former slaves and to support herself and her daughters, writing "I feel that I am called to work in this District—and shall be greatly strengthened by your encouragement in this matter."[43] But women's plans for a true reconstruction of the nation foundered on the image of women distributing aid to thousands of destitute freedpeople in the nation's capital, an image that threatened the uneasy consensus over emancipation with sexual and racial disorder.

If the Freedmen's Bureau disappointed them in the end, many female activists hoped that the government might repay their contributions to the relief effort with political rights. Julia Wilbur witnessed the first election in Washington in which African American men voted. She wrote that she "rejoiced that I had lived to see so much progress" but admitted that she felt "a little jealous—the least bit humiliated" when she realized the male voters did not know how to read. But she concluded, "No earthquake followed these proceedings, and I presume no convulsion of nature would have occurred, had white *women* and black *women* increased that line of voters." Women in the freedmen's aid movement agitated for universal suffrage, and Wilbur attempted to register to vote with other white and black women in the district.[44] But in this, too, they were disappointed. Though African American men gained the vote during Reconstruction, women did not. In frustration, suffragist Elizabeth Cady Stanton used the example of the freedmen's aid movement to argue that women's aid to former slaves demanded equal treatment with their charges:

> Did the Negro's rough services in camp and battle outweigh the humanitarian labors of woman in all departments of government? Did his loyalty in the army count for more than her educational work in teaching the people sound principles of government? Can it be that statesmen in the nineteenth century believe that they who sacrifice human lives in bloody wars do more for the sum of human happiness and development than they who try to save the multitude and teach them how to live?[45]

Stanton's remarks also indicate the historic break between women's rights and abolition prompted by Reconstruction and the Fifteenth Amendment. Many in the women's rights movement adopted racist rhetoric to argue that white women (no longer white *and* black women) deserved the suffrage before black men.

Stanton's view was hardly universal among women's rights advocates. Many suffragists viewed the issue of freedmen's aid as a link between the rights of women and African Americans. Griffing, for example, understood the misguided policies of the federal government and the Freedmen's Bureau as a direct result of sexual inequality. She wrote Stanton, "I see the want of regulation in national affairs, that can never be accomplished, while Govmt. is administered on the *male* basis of representation."[46] Rather than seeing the sexual inequality inscribed in the Fifteenth Amendment as a reason to deride freedmen, women like Griffing saw the former slaves' cause as justifying and even necessitating women's suffrage. For such advocates, equal rights were means to an end rather than an objective in its own right.

The political opponents of women's rights and freedmen's relief also associated the two causes and discredited both. It was because military officials linked women's charity with African American dependency that they condemned the new public presence of women and free blacks. Such anxieties only increased after the war, when it seemed that women had made inroads into politics, joining with African Americans to demand full citizenship rights and economic opportunity. Reformers and government officials placed harsh limits on both populations. While former slaves learned that freedom too often meant working for their former owners with pay, women learned that in the Freedmen's Bureau and other government offices they would remain subordinate to men. In the freedmen's aid movement, women extended their sphere of influence, only to meet fierce resistance from reformers and government officials attempting to reassert sexual and racial hierarchies upset by the Civil War.

If the nation resisted women's political equality, the freedmen's aid movement nonetheless offered women significant opportunities. Women forged new connections to the government during the Civil War and Reconstruction. They forced the government to be concerned not only with the labor of former slaves but also with their education and welfare. Their testimony contributed to the establishment of the Freedmen's Bureau and ensured that its mission incorporated some provisions for the neediest populations of former slaves. Women petitioned politicians, negotiated with military officials, and frequented the halls of government as employees and concerned citizens. These changes were permanent. After Reconstruction, women continued to lobby for suffrage, temperance, and other issues. This new relationship between women and the federal government shaped women's reform into the Progressive era.

Notes

1. For a comprehensive analysis of white and black women's activism in the freedmen's aid movement, see Carol Faulkner, *Women's Radical Reconstruction: The Freedmen's Aid Movement* (Philadelphia: University of Pennsylvania Press, 2004), on which this essay is based. Copyright © 2004 University of Pennsylvania Press. Reprinted by permission of the University of Pennsylvania Press.

2. Lyde Cullen Sizer, *The Political Work of Northern Women Writers and the Civil War, 1850–1872* (Chapel Hill: University of North Carolina Press, 2000), 4. See also Wendy Hamand Venet, *Neither Ballots Nor Bullets: Women Abolitionists and the Civil War* (Charlottesville: University Press of Virginia, 1991); Elizabeth Leonard, *Yankee Women: Gender Battles in the Civil War* (New York: Norton, 1994); Jeanie Attie, *Patriotic Toil: Northern Women and the American Civil War* (Ithaca, N.Y.: Cornell University Press, 1998); Judith Ann Giesberg, *Civil War Sisterhood: The U.S. Sanitary Commission and Women's Politics in Transition* (Boston: Northeastern University Press, 2000); and Nina Silber, *Daughters of the Union: Northern Women Fight the Civil War* (Cambridge, Mass.: Harvard University Press, 2005).

3. Jacqueline Jones, *Soldiers of Light and Love: Northern Teachers and Georgia Blacks, 1865–1873* (Athens: University of Georgia Press, 1980, 1992); Julie Roy Jeffrey, *The Great Silent Army of Abolitionism: Ordinary Women in the Antislavery Movement* (Chapel Hill: University of North Carolina Press, 1998), chapter 6; Ellen Carol DuBois, *Feminism and Suffrage: The Emergence of an Independent Women's Movement in America, 1848–1869* (Ithaca, N.Y.: Cornell University Press, 1978).

4. Though the federal government expanded permanently during the Civil War, this expansion was not without tensions. Subsequently, the government scaled back as its interest in Reconstruction receded. Michael Les Benedict, "Preserving the Constitution: The Conservative Basis of Radical Reconstruction," *Journal of American History* 61 (June 1974): 65–90; Morton Keller, *Affairs of State: Public Life in the Late Nineteenth Century* (Cambridge, Mass.: Belknap Press, 1977); Richard F. Bensel, *Yankee Leviathan: The Origins of Central State Authority in America, 1859–1877* (New York: Cambridge University Press, 1991).

5. Similarly, historian Elizabeth Leonard describes the hostility to women's leadership among the male officials of the Sanitary Commission, particularly in war relief efforts. See Leonard, *Yankee Women*, 81.

6. *Twelfth Annual Report of the Rochester Ladies' Anti-Slavery Society* (Rochester, N.Y.: A. Strong, 1863), 3.

7. Julia A. Wilbur to Anna M. C. Barnes, Nov. 12, 13, 26, 1862, Rochester Ladies' Anti-Slavery Society Papers, William L. Clements Library, University of Michigan (hereinafter RLASS); Lucretia Mott, letter to Martha Coffin Wright, Dec. 27, 1862, Mott Manuscripts, Friends Historical Library, Swarthmore College. On women's voluntarism in an earlier period, see especially Anne M. Boylan, *The Origins of Women's Activism: New York and Boston, 1797–1840* (Chapel Hill: University of North Carolina Press, 2002).

8. Testimony of the Ladies' Contraband Relief Society, American Freedmen's Inquiry Commission Papers, file 7, roll 21, National Archives Microfilm Publication M69, Record Group 94, National Archives, Washington, D.C.; Leslie Schwalm, "Encountering Emancipation: Slave Migration to the Midwest During the Civil War" (paper presented at the Southern Historical Association 65th Annual Meeting, Fort Worth, Texas, Nov. 3–6, 1999).

9. For the racial and class tensions in women's benevolence, see Jones, *Soldiers of Light and Love*, 144–153; Peggy Pascoe, *Relations of Rescue: The Search for Female Moral Authority in the American West, 1874–1939* (New York: Oxford University Press, 1990); Louise Michele Newman, *White Women's Rights: The Racial Origins of Feminism in the United States* (New York: Oxford University Press, 1999).

10. Josephine Griffing, petition presented May 9, 1864, Records of the House of Representatives, HR38A-G10.5, National Archives, Washington, D.C.; Elizabeth Cady Stanton, Susan B. Anthony, and Matilda Joslyn Gage, eds., *History of Woman Suffrage* (1881; repr., New York: Source Book, 1970), 1:110.

11. Emily Howland to Slocum Howland, Apr. 29, 1866, Emily Howland Papers, Friends Historical Library, Swarthmore College, read on microfilm at the Rare Books and Manuscripts Division, Kroch Library, Cornell University, Ithaca, New York. For similar views, see Hannah Stevenson to J. Miller McKim, July 16, 1866, July 20, 1866, Samuel J. May Anti-Slavery Collection, Cornell University.

12. Wilbur to Edwin M. Stanton, Mar. 24, 1863, quoted in Ira Berlin et al., eds., *Freedom: A Documentary History of Emancipation, 1861–1867*, series 1, vol. 2: *The Wartime Genesis of Free Labor: The Upper South* (New York: Cambridge University Press, 1993), 280–82.

13. Wilbur to Anna M. C. Barnes, Feb. 27, 1863, RLASS.

14. Lt. Col. H. H. Wells to Brig. Gen. J. P. Slough, Apr. 23, 1863, quoted in Berlin et al., eds., *Freedom*, 286.

15. Amy Dru Stanley, *From Bondage to Contract: Wage Labor, Marriage, and the Market in the Age of Emancipation* (New York: Cambridge University Press, 1998), chapter 3; Nancy Fraser and Linda Gordon, "A Genealogy of Dependency: Tracing a Keyword of the U.S. Welfare State," *Signs* 19 (Winter 1994): 309–36.

16. Josephine Griffing to William Lloyd Garrison, Mar. 24, 1864, Ms.A.1.2.v.33 p. 32b, Boston Public Library. See also Henrietta S. Jacquette, ed., *South after Gettysburg: Letters from Cornelia Hancock of the Army of the Potomac, 1863–65* (Philadelphia: University of Pennsylvania Press, 1937), 42–43. During the Civil War, government agencies offered new employment opportunities for middle-class women. See Cindy Sondik Aron, *Ladies and Gentlemen of the Civil Service: Middle-Class Workers in Victorian America* (New York: Oxford University Press, 1987).

17. Elizabeth C. Stanton, Susan B. Anthony, and Matilda J. Gage, eds., *History of Woman Suffrage*, 6 vols. (New York: Arno Press, 1969), 2:37, 29. See also Griffing to Gen. Oliver Otis Howard, May

8, 1865, Officer of the Commissioner, Letters Received, National Archives Microfilm Publication M752, Bureau of Refugees, Freedmen, and Abandoned Lands (BRFAL), Record Group 105, National Archives, Washington, D.C.

18. *Fourteenth Annual Report of the Rochester Ladies' Anti-Slavery Society* (Rochester, N.Y.: Wm. S. Falls, 1865), 13; *Fifteenth Annual Report of the Rochester Ladies' Anti-Slavery Society* (Rochester, N.Y.: Wm. S. Falls, 1866), 17.

19. *Fourteenth Annual Report*, 16–17.

20. *Fourteenth Annual Report*, 25–26; Mary J. Farmer, "'Because They Are Women': Gender and the Virginia Freedmen's Bureau's 'War on Dependency,'" in *The Freedmen's Bureau and Reconstruction: Reconsiderations*, ed., Paul A. Cimbala and Randall M. Miller (New York: Fordham University Press, 1999), 161–92. For freedwomen's struggle against the apprenticeship of their children, see Karin L. Zipf, "Reconstructing 'Free Woman': African-American Women, Apprenticeship, and Custody Rights during Reconstruction," *Journal of Women's History* 12 (Spring 2000): 8–31.

21. Emma V. Brown to Emily Howland, Jan. 20, no year, Box 10, Emily Howland Papers.

22. *Liberator*, Nov. 3, 1865.

23. On Rachel Moore, see Minutes, Oct. 9, 1862, Philadelphia Female Anti-Slavery Society, Reel 30, Pennsylvania Abolition Society Papers, Historical Society of Pennsylvania; *Revolution*, Apr. 7, 1870. Mary Farmer argues that local officials of the Freedmen's Bureau were often willing to extend material aid to women and children, but women's labors in Washington provoked a different response from officials. Farmer, "'Because They Are Women,'" 161–192. See also Mary Farmer-Kaiser, *Freedwomen and the Freedmen's Bureau: Race, Gender, and Public Policy in the Age of Emancipation* (New York: Fordham University Press, 2010).

24. James M. McPherson, *Struggle for Equality: Abolitionists and the Negro in the Civil War and Reconstruction* (Princeton: Princeton University Press, 1964), 389–92; Keith Melder, "Angel of Mercy in Washington: Josephine Griffing and the Freedmen, 1864–1872," *Records of the Columbia Historical Society of the District of Columbia* 45 (1965), 259.

25. Sojourner Truth to Amy Post, July 3, 1866, Isaac and Amy Post Papers, Rush Rhees Library, University of Rochester (N.Y.).

26. J. C. Thayer to Truth, Mar. 15, 1867; Theodore Backus to Truth, Feb. 22, 1867; Davis Carpenter to Isaac Post, Mar. 14, 1867; Mrs. James Annin to Truth, Mar. 15, 1867; Griffing to Truth and Post, Mar. 26, 1867, all in Post Papers. See also Nell Irvin Painter, *Sojourner Truth: A Life, A Symbol* (New York: Norton, 1996), 217–19; Carleton Mabee, "Sojourner Truth Fights Dependence on Government: Moves Freed Slaves Off Welfare in Washington to Jobs in Upstate New York," *Afro-Americans in New York Life and History* 14 (Jan. 1990): 7–26; and "A Noble Charity," newspaper clipping with letter of A. F. Williams to S. N. Clark, Feb. 13, 1867, Letters Received, Assistant Commissioner for the District of Columbia, National Archives Microfilm Publication M1055 (ACDC), BRFAL, National Archives Building, Washington, D.C.

27. Stephanie McCurry discusses gender and race relations in yeomen farm families in the antebellum South in *Masters of Small Worlds: Yeomen Households, Gender Relations, and the Political Culture of the Antebellum South Carolina Low Country* (New York: Oxford University Press, 1997).

28. Griffing to Truth and Post, Mar. 26, 1867; Truth to Griffing, Mar. 30, 1867, both in Post Papers.

29. Anna Lowell to Gen. C. H. Howard, Dec. 4, 1866, Letters Received, ACDC, BRFAL. Anna Lowell did not identify with radical abolitionists but rather with moderate antislavery Republicans. *Reports of the Soldiers' Memorial Society Presented at its Third Annual Meeting, June 11, 1867* (Boston: Soldiers' Memorial Society, 1867), 3, 12–13; Faye Dudden, *Serving Women: Household Service in Nineteenth-Century America* (Middletown, Conn.: Wesleyan University Press, 1983).

30. Anna Lowell to Gen. C. H. Howard, Sept. 1, 1867, Letters Received, ACDC, BRFAL.

31. Anna Lowell to C. H. Howard, Dec. 4, 1866, Jan. 13, 1867, Feb. 6, Feb. 27. See also ibid., Oct. 25, 1866, and Nov. 1, 1866.

32. Anna Lowell to C. H. Howard, Jan. 13, 1867.

33. Anna Earle to Gen. C. H. Howard, Oct. 12, 1867; Jan. 24, 1868, Letters Received, ACDC, BRFAL.

34. Frederick Douglass to McKim, May 1865, Box 13, Samuel J. May Anti-Slavery Collection, Cornell University, Ithaca, New York; Jones, *Soldiers of Light and Love*, 148; Newman, *White Women's Rights*, 12.

35. Griffing to Eliphalet Whittlesey, Aug. 29, 1868, Letters Received, Office of the Commissioner, BRFAL. For more on Williams and Griffing, see Faulkner, *Women's Radical Reconstruction*, 129.

36. *Autobiography of Oliver Otis Howard* (New York: Baker & Taylor, 1907), 2:213–14. See also Farmer-Kaiser, *Freedwomen and the Freedmen's Bureau*.

37. S. N. Clark to Mr. E. Carpenter, Dec. 5, 1865, Letters Sent, ACDC, BRFAL.

38. Lucretia Mott to Martha Coffin Wright and Anna Temple Brown, Apr. 10, 1865, *The Selected Letters of Lucretia Coffin Mott*, ed. Beverly Wilson Palmer (Urbana: University of Illinois Press, 2002), 357.

39. Jacob R. Shipherd to Gen. O. O. Howard, Oct. 30, 1865, Letters Received, Office of the Commissioner, BRFAL.

40. Ibid. See also McKim to Shipherd, Jan. 10, 1866, McKim Letterbooks, Samuel J. May Anti-Slavery Collection, Cornell University, Ithaca, New York. For examples of Freedmen's Bureau agents attacking Griffing and other female reformers, see W. F. Spurgin to S. N. Clark, Nov. 1, 1865, and Jan. 1, 1866; Will Coulter to Gen. C. H. Howard, Nov. 5, 6, and 7, 1867; Maj. Vandenburgh to Coulter, Nov. 7, 1867; all in Letters Received, ACDC, BRFAL. See also Faulkner, *Women's Radical Reconstruction*, chapter 5 and passim.

41. *Fifteenth Annual Report*, 16.

42. *National Anti-Slavery Standard*, Feb. 20, 1869.

43. Griffing to Gen. O. O. Howard, Nov. 22, 1869, Letters Received by the Commissioner, BRFAL.

44. *Sixteenth Annual Report of the Rochester Ladies' Anti-Slavery Society* (Rochester, N.Y.: William S. Falls, 1867), 22; *National Anti-Slavery Standard*, May 1, 1869.

45. Stanton, Anthony, and Gage, eds., *History of Woman Suffrage*, 2:89; Newman, *White Women's Rights*.

46. Griffing to Elizabeth Cady Stanton, Dec. 27, 1870, in *The Selected Papers of Elizabeth Cady Stanton and Susan B. Anthony*, vol. 2: *Against an Aristocracy of Sex, 1866–1873*, ed. Ann Gordon (New Brunswick, N.J.: Rutgers University Press, 2000), 390–91.

Chapter 1: **Critical Thinking Questions**

Directions: Reflect on what you have read, and use information from the reading selections as a resource as you respond to the following critical thinking questions.

1. Do you think that the readings reflect the United States' development as a politically democratic republican or representative nation? Why or why not? Use examples to support your claims.

2. Do the readings illustrate some of the political struggles faced by the people populating the United States and how they worked to overcome those difficulties? Why or why not? Can you give an example?

Chapter 2

Culture and an Expanding Atlantic World

Readings in Western Atlantic World Culture and Social Changes from 1492 to 1877

Introduction

In this chapter we will explore the cultural and social developments and interchanges between indigenous Americans, Europeans, and Africans in the Western Atlantic world and the United States as the region took on a more diverse identity. Students should pay close attention to the dilemmas facing various groups and even subgroups. A major dilemma was maintaining a group's unique characteristics while living, working, and exchanging ideas with communities different from their own beginning with first contact in the fifteen century and continuing through the American Civil War. By examining these interactions students should find that communities influenced each other through various social means, at times resulting in levels of social synthesis, which resulted in pluralistic communities. This occurred despite attempts by indigenous people, Europeans, and Africans to maintain some level of cultural autonomy over themselves.

This chapter contains selected titles that center on the cultural dynamics of the emerging Western Atlantic world and the United States. From colonization through Reconstruction the cultural characteristics of indigenous, European, and African communities merged as people came to define and redefine themselves socially. The efforts of men and women seeking to shape the world around them are found in food ways, their medical practices, and their religious beliefs. Readings also reveal how communities saw their own identities and customs regardless of demographic and geographic changes in the United States, resulting in a multicultural population. This synthetic approach seeks to allow readers a glimpse into the fact that, although on the surface, marginalized groups, such as indigenous Americans, women, and Africans, sought to maintain a level of influence over their own lives, they would struggle to do so as white, male, and elite influence would work to suppress and minimize their impact.

The selections in this section also encourage readers to think about the following concepts.

1. How do the readings shape your understanding of the United States' development as a pluralistic or multicultural society?

2. Why do you think ideas of liberty seemed to elude many of the groups in the United States even though there appeared to be a belief in universal laws relating to liberty?

3. How did group's interpretations of other's cultural practices influence community beliefs surrounding medicine, religion, and identity?

Reading 2.1

The Columbian Exchange

Jeffery M. Pilcher

C OLUMBUS'S 1492 VOYAGE IN SEARCH OF a western passage to the Spice Islands began a fundamental transformation in the eating habits of all humans. The immediate biological and environmental consequences of contact between Europe and the Americas were dramatic, as exposure to Old World diseases killed more than 80 percent of the New World population within a hundred years. Aided by this unintentional germ warfare, Spanish conquistadors quickly subdued the vast Aztec, Maya, and Inca empires. European plants and animals flourished in the fields left open by demographic decline, transforming the ecology of the Americas, but the Spaniards succeeded only partially in their goal of establishing colonial replicas of their homeland. Surviving natives intermarried with European colonists and with African slaves, creating new ethnic blends. Highly productive food crops domesticated in the New World not only persisted as essential staples for both natives and newcomers alike, they were also carried back across the Atlantic and launched a demographic revolution in the Old World, helping set the stage for modern population growth.

Yet these changes were far from uniform. Peasants in China, Africa, and the Middle East began planting American staples as soon as they arrived in the sixteenth century, but in Europe and India these crops were largely ignored for hundreds of years. Fruits and vegetables likewise spread in an irregular fashion, and Europeans who had pioneered the new trade routes to America were the least likely to adopt the crops they had discovered. The circuitous routes by which new plants traveled also led to popular uncertainty about their origins.

Material and cultural factors combined to determine the acceptance of new foods. Ecology had a role, for plants grew best in environments similar to those in which they had been domesticated. Tropical crops could not resist freezing temperatures, but changes in altitude and microclimates allowed ecological flexibility. Productivity and compatibility with existing rotations also

Jeffery M. Pilcher, "The Columbian Exchange," *Food in World History*, pp. 19-26. Copyright © 2006 by Taylor & Francis Group. Reprinted with permission.

mattered to farmers considering new crops. Cooks likewise had their say, for an unfamiliar plant, however prolific, was unlikely to gain favor if it could not be prepared in a tasty and appealing fashion. Although a global process, the Columbian Exchange was nevertheless negotiated at the local level.

Mexico

The absence of domesticated animals, apart from turkeys and small dogs, distinguished the civilizations of Mesoamerica from other classical empires. Native Americans excelled at foraging for protein but still depended overwhelmingly on their staple grain, maize. Human labor provided the main source of energy, as women ground maize by hand while men carried heavy loads on their backs. The introduction of livestock by Spanish conquistadors therefore had the potential for improving livelihoods but also posed great environmental dangers for indigenous farmers unaccustomed to pastoral herds.

The Mesoamerican maize complex provided the foundation for a basically vegetarian diet. The grain supplied carbohydrates and up to 80 percent of total calories while beans added protein; complementary amino acids magnified the nutritional value of the pair by forming a complete protein when eaten together. Chiles, squash, tomatoes, and avocadoes offered vitamins, minerals, and interesting flavors. Native Americans supplemented this vegetarian cuisine by consuming virtually all available animal protein: deer, ducks, rabbits, seafood, and even rodents, insects, and lake algae.

Indigenous techniques for preparing maize tortillas were extremely labor-intensive. Mesoamerican women first simmered the kernels in a mineral solution, which loosened the indigestible husk and released niacin, a vitamin necessary to avoid the disease pellagra. The next step involved hand-grinding the wet dough, called *nixtamal*, while kneeling painfully over a grinding stone. Women then patted the smooth dough into thin, round tortillas and cooked them briefly on an earthenware griddle. Because tortillas quickly went stale and *nixtamal* fermented overnight, women had to rise hours before dawn to cook for men going to work in the fields. Midwives warned newborn girls: "Thou wilt become fatigued, thou wilt become tired; thou art to provide water, to grind maize, to drudge." The subjugation of the grinding stone inspired a particularly oppressive version of patriarchy in Mesoamerica.

With limited supplies, social hierarchies governed food distribution. Well-fed nobles stood some ten centimeters taller than commoners in the classical Maya city of Tikal (fourth–eighth centuries CE). A terrible famine in the year One Rabbit (1454), in the early stages of Aztec imperial expansion, focused attention on food supplies for the island capital of Tenochtitlan. At the time, Moctezuma the Elder used canoes to distribute maize to starving people, and in later years, the Great Feast of the Lords recalled this imperial beneficence through ceremonial handouts of tamales (maize dumplings) from canoes. The Aztec Empire demanded tribute of food and other goods from subject peoples, especially in the productive raised fields of Lake Chalco-Xochimilco. Among the warrior elite, civic and religious banquets assumed a competitive nature, with each host attempting to serve the finest chile pepper stews, tamales, and hot chocolate. Spanish conquistadors spoke with awe about the hundreds of lavish dishes served daily to Moctezuma the Younger (ruled 1502–1520).

Nevertheless, mutual disgust marked the culinary encounter between Spaniards and Native Americans. Moctezuma's emissaries reported that European bread tasted "like dried maize stalks," while Bernal Díaz del Castillo complained of the "misery of maize cakes" that served as rations during the conquest. Natives ranked pork fat among the tortures brought by the Spaniards, who were equally disgusted by the indigenous consumption of rodents and insects, dubbed "*animalitos*." Catholic missionaries attempted to propagate wheat in order to replace maize gods with the Holy Eucharist, but peasants found the Europe grain unproductive, expensive to grow, and prone to disease, although some entrepreneurial natives cultivated it for sale to urban Hispanic markets. As a result, wheat bread and maize tortillas became status markers within the racial hierarchy called the system of castes.

Even more devastating was the invasion of European livestock, as cattle and sheep reproduced at exponential rates and overran the countryside. The simultaneous growth of herds and collapse of human population due to disease made it appear as if the livestock were eating the natives. For a few decades in the mid-sixteenth century, meat sold for a pittance in Mexico City, but with uncontrolled grazing, herbivores soon exceeded the carrying capacity of the land, exposing the soil to erosion and rendering it unfit for farming or herding. In just a few decades, sheep turned the fertile Mezquital Valley into a barren desert, and by the end of the century, meat was again scarce in colonial markets.

Devastation and disgust notwithstanding, culinary fusion had already begun in sixteenth-century Mesoamerica. Although retaining their staple maize, native cooks learned to whip pork fat into tamales, giving the cakes a lighter texture and richer flavor. Spanish settlers meanwhile acquired a taste for beans and chile peppers, even while paying high prices for familiar wheat bread. This process of cultural blending was repeated in South America as well.

Peru

The Andes Mountains rise like some Brobdingnagian terraced field, with separate ecological niches providing a wealth of different foodstuffs. Abundant supplies of fish and shellfish supported complex societies as early as 2500 BCE in the otherwise desert climate on the

Pacific coast, where strong currents bring fog but no rain. Ascending the slopes into temperate highland valleys, the Mesoamerican maize complex coexisted with the Andean grain, quinoa. Farther up, in the cold, rainy zone above the treeline, human settlements depended on potatoes and other root crops such as *oca* and *ulloco*. At the highest elevations grazed llamas, domesticated camelids used to carry trade goods up and down the mountains, as well as smaller alpacas, which provided fine wool. Coca leaves, cultivated along the eastern slopes, were chewed as a stimulant by people living in the highlands. The exchange of food and other goods between such diverse climates became a central aspect of the diets and lives of Andean peoples.

To transport food such great distances without spoiling, Andean cooking relied heavily on methods for preservation. Highland farmers exposed potatoes to frost and sun to make freeze-dried *chuño*. Shepherds dried llama meat into *charqui* (hence the English word "jerky") and cooked blood into gruel similar to European black puddings. Meanwhile, salted and sun-dried fish arrived from the coastal lowlands. Guinea pigs, another important source of animal protein, reproduced so quickly as to obviate the need for preservation; they were simply boiled or roasted. Andean women likewise boiled and toasted maize. Without the need for laborious daily maize grinding, women worked as shepherds and farmers, planting and harvesting potatoes while men turned the soil with footplows, and as a result, they had greater social equality than in Mexico.

The Inca Empire (1438–1532) built a highly productive economy on Andean traditions of reciprocity, whereby leaders organized labor and redistributed wealth for the benefit of the entire community. Having conquered a vast realm, stretching 3,000 kilometers from present-day Ecuador to Chile, the Inca restructured these societies for maximum efficiency, for example, by resettling entire highland villages at lower elevations in order to increase the production of maize. The Inca not only uprooted communities but also dispersed them up and down the Andes Mountains, creating social "archipelagos" known as *ayllu*, in which kinfolk lived at different elevations and harvested seafood, maize, potatoes, and coca for exchange within these geographically extended families. *Ayllus* also had a responsibility for supplying labor tribute to herd llamas and to produce food, clothing, and other goods for the imperial government. The Inca maintained enormous granaries, both as military depots and as distribution centers, and kept careful records of food supplies using *quipus*, indigenous balance sheets that recorded numbers using a system of knots tied on strings. Local lords, called *kurakas*, served as intermediaries between the state and the people by allocating tribute duties and distributing food. The ideal of equality notwithstanding, nobles ate far more meat than commoners. According to early chronicles, Topa Inca (ruled 1471–1493) even ordered runners to carry "fresh fish from the sea, and as it was seventy or eighty leagues from the coast to Cuzco … they were brought alive and twitching."

Disease and brutality made the conquest of Peru as devastating as that of Mexico, but prior pastoral experience helped mitigate the environmental consequences of the Columbian Exchange. The rapacious Spaniards systematically looted Inca warehouses, seizing any treasure and selling off the foodstuffs. By the fall of 1539, less than a decade after their arrival, people were starving in Cuzco, despite the rapid population decline. Disease also decimated llamas, although from an indigenous source rather than a pathogen imported from Europe. Inca shepherds had carefully culled any animals infected with *caracha*, but after the breakdown of the native administration, this disease spread through the herds, killing two-thirds of the indigenous camelids. The conquistadors ordered Andean shepherds to tend cattle and sheep instead, a policy that at least helped protect indigenous farmers. Nevertheless, Spaniards often purposely turned livestock loose to damage indigenous fields and irrigation works in order to claim the land for their own uses, especially to grow wheat and sugar cane.

The development of food habits in post-conquest Mexico and Peru provides an interesting comparative study in cultural accommodation. Both colonies became productive centers for European agriculture, with diverse ecological niches supporting wheat, sugar cane, and livestock. Nevertheless, two other mainstays of the Mediterranean diet, olive oil and wine, flourished in Peru but not in Mexico. Favorable climates existed in both regions although unpredictable frosts frustrated early attempts at winemaking in Mexico. Nor does Spanish trade policy explain the differences because decrees establishing peninsular monopolies for these products came only after regional agriculture patterns had become fixed. Perhaps colonists in Mexico simply came to prefer the taste of substitutes—pork fat and hot chocolate—along with chiles and beans. Indigenous nobles in both colonies claimed status by adopting European foods, but commoners preferred their accustomed staples, maize and potatoes, and accepted imports at the margins of their diet; for example, *anticuchos* (grilled beef heart) became a street food of indigenous Peruvians in urban areas. Meanwhile, American crops had begun to transform the Old World.

Return Passages

In America, Columbus encountered foods that ultimately yielded far more benefits than the Asian spices he had originally sought, but Europeans proved curiously slow in exploiting those new culinary treasures. Instead of taking root in Iberian fields, these crops passed by way of Spanish and Portuguese merchants to the Middle East, Africa, and Asia. They gained European acceptance hundreds of years later. A number of factors helped determine the spread of new crops, including their productivity and fit within agricultural regimes, their ease of preparation and adaptability to culinary systems, and the cultural associations that they evoked.

Maize, the most versatile and productive plant domesticated in the Americas, illustrates the ambivalent reception of new crops. Columbus carried it back to Spain in 1493, but lacking the gluten to make leavened bread, it was prepared as porridge and considered to be a famine food at best. In 1597, John Gerard described it as "a more convenient food for swine than for men." By contrast, the American grain diffused rapidly in the Middle East, where porridges did not have such inferior status. Arriving in Lebanon and Syria by the 1520s, corn helped spur population growth under the Ottoman Emperor Süleyman the Magnificent (ruled 1520–1566). As a result, many Europeans referred to maize as the "Turkish" grain while in India it was known as "Mecca" corn. The Portuguese introduced it to West Africa, where it surpassed the productivity of millet and sorghum, although the latter was still more drought-resistant. From northern India, maize spread through inland Chinese provinces of Yunnan and Sichuan in the seventeenth century. The labor-intensive technique of making *nixtamal*, however, remained limited to Mesoamerica; Old World cooks prepared the new cultivar using familiar methods, either roasting it on the cob like a vegetable or else grinding it into flour for porridge or, in China, noodles.

Chile peppers likewise spread most rapidly in cuisines that already used spices liberally. Although colonists in New Spain quickly acquired a taste for chile sauces prepared by Native American cooks, western Europeans accustomed to powdered cinnamon, nutmeg, and pepper, hesitated to touch the hot plant, which burned the hands as well as the mouth. The principal staging point for the chile's invasion of the Old World was therefore India, where they were introduced by Portuguese traders and fit naturally into the complex spice blends, prepared as pastes and generically called "curry" by Europeans. Areas of Indian cultural influence such as Thailand quickly adopted the new condiments, and they were also carried overland on the Silk Road to Sichuan and Yunnan, Chinese regions now known for fiery dishes, as well as to Turkey and hence Hungary, where people became addicted to the chile powder, paprika. Chiles also spread widely through Africa as a complement to spices arriving from the Indian Ocean trade.

Social conditions influenced the diffusion of American crops, as can be seen by comparing the experience of China and India. Despite intensive agriculture, China's population had reached its ecological limits in the final years of the Ming dynasty (1368–1644). As famines struck, starving peasants eagerly adopted American foodstuffs, particularly the sweet potato, which provided multiple crops with a greater caloric yield even than rice, did not require laborious transplanting and paddy maintenance, and could be grown on otherwise marginal land. Whether baked, boiled, mashed, or ground into flour for noodles and porridge, sweet potatoes became a fixture of virtually every meal in South China. Maize and peanuts likewise complemented existing crop rotations, multiplying agricultural productivity. In India, by contrast, the Mughals ruled a more mobile society with considerable available land and relatively slow population growth. Farmers thus had little incentive to intensify production and largely ignored the American staples maize and potatoes until the nineteenth century.

European reluctance to adopt American crops begins to make sense when viewed from a broader perspective. Recurring bouts of plague left room for population growth until famines drove northern Europeans to adopt the potato, starting with Ireland in the seventeenth century and moving east through France, Germany, and Russia in the eighteenth and nineteenth centuries. Maize likewise became a staple in southern Europe but without losing its initial association as an animal fodder. Even the tomato, which had arrived in Naples by the 1550s, did not appear in Italian cookbooks until the end of the seventeenth century, although peasants had no doubt eaten it sooner. Thus, the lethargy with which medieval Europeans adopted Muslim crops continued to characterize the early modern spread of American foodstuffs.

Conclusion

Religious imperatives drove both Aztec and Inca imperial expansion, but the common belief in reciprocity took different forms in Middle and South America. The Inca, like the Chinese, emphasized the distribution of food as essential to good government, while the Aztec tribute system functioned primarily to supply food to the metropolis, as in imperial Rome, in addition to sacrificial victims for the maize gods. It is difficult to explain these differences considering material causes alone, but the labor-intensive production of maize tortillas does help account for the greater inequality of gender relations in Mesoamerica.

A broad view of material and cultural factors is likewise necessary to explain the uneven nature of the Columbian Exchange. Demographic pressure encouraged the adoption of new crops in Europe and Asia, while population declines helped spread livestock in the Americas. Landholding patterns and agricultural regimes also influenced the selection of new crops. Native Americans cultivated wheat only under Spanish compulsion because of the expense of heavy plows, grinding mills, and ovens. Disgust and fear also delayed the spread of both tomatoes and potatoes, which were considered potentially dangerous in Europe.

Although seeds often traveled independently of farmers, agricultural and culinary knowledge had an important role in the Columbian Exchange. Because Native American women, with their knowledge of *nixtamal*, did not travel to the Old World, populations that adopted maize as the staple grain were subject to the dietary deficiency disease pellagra. The limited inward migration to Europe during the early modern period may have slowed the diffusion of crops; indeed, American crops took hundreds of years to achieve their full demographic effect. By that time, Europeans had developed new systems of production and trade with profound historical consequences.

Further Reading

This chapter was inspired by Alfred W. Crosby, Jr., *The Columbian Exchange: Biological and Cultural Consequences of 1492* (Westport, CT: Greenwood Press, 1972). See also, Sophie Coe, *America's First Cuisines* (Austin, TX: University of Texas Press, 1994); John C. Super, *Food, Conquest, and Colonization in Sixteenth-Century Spanish America* (Albuquerque, NM: University of New Mexico Press, 1988); and Elinor G. K. Melville, *A Plague of Sheep: Environmental Consequences of the Conquest of Mexico* (Cambridge: Cambridge University Press, 1997). On the diffusion of American foods, William Langer, "American Foods and Europe's Population Growth, 1750–1850," *Journal of Social History* 8(2) (Winter 1975): 51–66; Nelson Foster and Linda Cordell (eds), *Chiles to Chocolate: Food the Americas Gave the World* (Tucson, AZ: University of Arizona Press, 1992); Sucheta Mazumdar, "The Impact of New World Food Crops on the Diet and Economy of China and India, 1600–1900," in Raymond Grew (ed.), *Food in Global History* (Boulder, CO: Westview Press, 1999); and Arturo Warman, *Corn and Capitalism: How a Botanical Bastard Grew to Global Dominance*, trans. Nancy L. Westrate (Chapel Hill, NC: University of North Carolina Press, 2003).

The Globalization of Disease After 1450

Sheldon Watts

Introduction

Thus far we have been examining medical systems developed in the context of a particular cultural grouping: ancient Greek, ancient Chinese and so on. From another perspective, it can be said that each of these medical systems was created by men who believed that the disease situations they themselves confronted were characteristic of their own particular society. Conversely, they believed that neighboring societies, living in a different type of setting, might have their own special diseases. These ideas about the cultural specificity of disease types (who was susceptible to which disease) unfortunately survived long after the breakdown of the physical barriers to permanent, sustained contact between peoples of widely different cultural backgrounds. This breakdown occurred soon after 1450 CE.

As we know, the conquest of the physical space, which before 1450 had separated Old World EurAsian and African civilizations from the New World, was achieved by Europeans using seaworthy ships of a sort they had only recently begun to build. However, we also now know that, by the early fifteenth century, the Chinese, the Indians and some Muslim North African peoples were also building seaworthy ships. Yet, in the event, none of the latter peoples chose to use their fine ships to cross the Atlantic or the Pacific (as the case may be) to the New World.

It would be of huge world historical significance that the discovery/rediscovery and exploitation of the New World (begun in 1492) was achieved by Europeans rather than by some other cultural grouping. As Chinese scholars such as R. Bin Wong have recently pointed out, in and after the mid-fifteenth century, the practice of combining trading/mercantile activities with state-supported conquest and armed violence seems to have become a distinguishing characteristic of the Europeans.

The American Continents: A Special Case

As late as the early months of 1492, the two American continents (North America and South America) contained perhaps a fifth or a sixth of all humankind. Then, in mid-October of that year, disaster struck. From that time onwards, within 20 or 30 years of a "first contact" experience with Europeans in any given setting, the Native Americans left remaining at that setting seldom numbered more than one-tenth of those who had been there before.

Given the vastness of the two continents, "first contact" was not a once-only affair. In the case of South America, "first contact" incidents began in the late 1490s when Spaniards began to trickle over to the mainland from their bases on the Caribbean Islands. Yet, in some parts of the rain forests of Brazil, "first contact" incidents were still taking place 500 years later. For indigenous peoples in the 1990s, these incidents had the same dire consequences as did all those dating from the years immediately after 12 October 1492. With respect to the earlier history of North America, as far as can be determined, the Norse settlers and explorers who were in Newfoundland and the Great Lakes region in the 1360s did not leave behind any long-term contagious diseases.

But in North America, *after* 1492, "first contact" incidents became part of an ongoing process which, on that huge continent, took nearly 300 years to work their way through. Thus, in remote areas such as present-day Oregon, Washington State and the Dakotas, first contact and accompanying population collapse did not happen until after the end of the American Revolutionary War against Britain (1783). This was 300 years after the initial first contact experience in Hispaniola.

That famous/infamous series of incidents began with the landing of Christopher Columbus on the island on 12 October 1492. Within a few decades, the ethnic group he and his crew had first encountered—the Taino—thought to have once been more than one million strong, had almost completely disappeared. Much of what happened during those terrible years remains shrouded in mystery, yet it seems quite certain that most Taino were victims of newly imported diseases and of a policy which purposefully destroyed an entire people and its cultural artifacts. Some aspects of this policy were graphically described by Bartholomé de Las Casas, a Dominican friar who came to Hispaniola in 1502. In his reports back to Spain, Las Casas created what was called the "Black Legend."

Similarly, in coastal North America, beginning in 1622 in the Virginia Colony (founded in 1607) and in 1637 in Massachusetts (founded in 1620), English settlers began to systematically destroy indigenous peoples. Though at times they regarded Native Americans as necessary allies against the French, as soon as the latter were defeated and expelled (with the fall of Quebec City in 1759 and then with the Peace of Paris in 1763), English and other European immigrant settlers had no qualms about killing off all Native Americans who stood in their way. Similarly, in Australia and the Island Pacific, a half century after first contact with whites (effectively beginning in the time of Captain James Cook in the 1780s), indigenous populations had been brought to the brink of extinction.

It is now understood that the massive reduction in the number of Native American and Island Pacific peoples—one-tenth what it had been before contact—was caused by a combination of three factors: (1) the actual diseases the invaders brought with them; (2) the settlers' genocidal practices—of the sort described by Las Casas—and, in the face of these horrible happenings; (3) the collapse of indigenous societies themselves. Their life-worlds shattered, and their triangles of curing wrecked, Native Americans and Pacific islanders failed to reproduce or to keep their newborn infants alive.

Explanations: Old World Disease Patterns and Mind-Sets

By 1450 almost the whole of the Old World (EurAsia and coastal North Africa) was well along in the process of becoming a unified disease zone. Long before that date, sophisticated Arab and Indian and Chinese businessmen and traders were crossing and re-crossing the Arabian Sea, the Indian Ocean and the South China Sea in large well-manned ships to visit focal points of progressive enterprise. In terms of global trade, western Europe was marginal. However, local peddlers, touring scholars, missionaries, mercenary soldiers and other agents did manage to maintain enough links with the Middle East to keep western Europe within the larger EurAsian disease zone.

Then, beginning around 1450, breaking out of the impoverished homeland that jutted out into the Atlantic, the Portuguese began to force their way into the Asians' and Arabs' trading networks. They first attacked coastal North Africa, then sailed around to the West African bulge, then round the Cape and northward along the coast to East Africa. From there, working their way further eastward on heavily armored ships with which they shelled and destroyed everybody else's shipping, the Portuguese proceeded to India (Goa) and finally on to China (Macao). Not to be outdone by their tiny neighbor, in 1492, the Catholic monarch of Castile (Isabella) with the support of her husband, Ferdinand, King of Aragon, invested in the expedition (headed by Columbus) which attempted to reach China and its fabled treasures by sailing west, rather than east as the Portuguese were doing.

Recent detailed studies have shown that most of the western European laymen who joined the fleets going out to the New World in and after 1492 were men-on-the-make. (In saying this I have purposefully excluded priests, monks and women: in early years, the latter were few in number). At home in Europe, none of these men-on-the-make had managed to achieve what Old World societies regarded as high status, either because of accidents of birth (aristocrats and gentlemen were "born" not made), or because they had failed to contract an advantageous marriage, or because they had failed in business dealing, or because of general bad luck. Leaving European ports with the expectation that their future lay in their own hands, these rugged men-on-the-make assumed that if they managed to survive the rigors of the unknown places beyond the seas and became wealthy, they would return to their natal lands and buy their way (or at least their children's way) into high status.

In short, these western Europeans were opportunists who—after escaping the moral bonds imposed by their home communities—were prepared to do *anything* to further their personal goals. Added to these characteristics, were the special traits of the Iberians (denizens of the Spanish kingdoms and of Portugal) who claimed to be descended from the Gothic peoples who had come into the land in the late Roman period. With the exiling of the Jews from the Spanish lands in 1492, and the fall of Granada and the murder of all remaining Muslims in the same year, employment opportunities at home for mercenary soldiers and for hireling thugs melted away. Accepting this reality, many of them made their way to the New World to seek their fortune.

Development and Disease

The literate few Iberians and Italians who sailed to America in the fifteenth, sixteenth and seventeenth centuries had a rough idea about what Hippocrates (in "Airs, Waters, Places") and later medico-philosophical synthesizers had said about disease causation. These approved writers held that someone might come down sick with a serious illness if he or she had recently undergone a "change" of climate or other dramatic alterations in life-style.

If the Hippocratic paradigm were correct, it should have been Columbus and later European adventurers who came down sick with fatal diseases after they left their home environment. Yet, in the event, it was the pagan New World peoples they met and mixed with who, in very large numbers, fell sick and died of diseases that seemed to leave the Europeans untouched.

As is well known, within a few years of their first arrival, Iberian Europeans began to realize that, in addition to mining silver, gold and other precious minerals for export back to the Catholic Kings in Spain, it was necessary to plant and harvest crops and to raise cattle and the like in order to supplement the foodstuffs brought in so irregularly from the Old World. They also finally realized that indigenous New World peoples tended to die off if made to work as slaves on European enterprises. Accordingly, in order to further their projects, the Europeans cast around for an alternative labor supply.

As it happened, by the early 1500s the Portuguese, the Iberian neighbors of the Spanish, were in the process of establishing large slave depots on the central west African coast (now Angola). Despite initial protests from their respective home governments, out in the colonies, Portuguese slave ship agents and Spanish slave purchasers very soon established a *modus vivendi*. With it, the infamous transatlantic slave trade came into existence. A few decades later, with the eclipse of Portuguese enterprise, first Dutch, and then English and Scottish slave ship owners provided the transport needed to bring more than 15,000,000 African slaves to the New World. Funding was provided by venture capitalists in Antwerp, London, Amsterdam, Augsburg and (between 1557 and 1627) Genoa.

With this, a working prototype of all later development projects came into being. At the center of the world-encompassing web of enterprise were venture capitalists, based in a handful of great European cities, who funded enterprises intended to bring in a huge return on investment. The enterprises were usually of the sort that collected or grew Non-western raw materials which would then be shipped to western Europe.

In the case of the Americas, by the early sixteenth century Europe's venture capitalists were funding the ships which brought fine manufactured cotton cloth from India to coastal Africa where it was handed over to local African leaders in exchange for slaves abducted from neighboring African societies. These slaves were then shipped across the Atlantic to provide the labor force needed on New World development projects.

One of the early types of development consisted of the sugar cane plantations of coastal Brazil and the Caribbean Islands. Grown and initially processed in the New World, when shipped across the Atlantic and further refined, cane sugar created an entirely new form of consumer demand. Because of its novelty and its popularity among ordinary people who had never before spent money on such trivialities, cane sugar did much to establish the pattern for our modern consumer society.

Setting the tone for later consumer societies, sixteenth-century European venture capitalists at the center of the worldwide web did not allow themselves to be swayed by moral concerns. They themselves were gentlemen. This meant that they could regard everyone else in the enterprise—ship crews, slaves, factors (merchants' traders) and plantation managers in the New World or in the far Pacific—as low status people who could be used for any purpose, whatever the consequences. In short, gentleman venture capitalists regarded the lives of their "factors" and servants as expendable.

Exemplifying this attitude, in the case of fellow white men in the far Pacific, were the practices of the Netherlands' East India Company (established in 1602). With its headquarters in Amsterdam and its "factories" (trading bases) in Indonesia, the Company could not fail to be aware of the short life-expectancies of its "factors" and servants out in the far Pacific. Indeed, in the 200 years after 1602, early death from fevers, dysentery and other water-related diseases found in the Archipelago drained away the lives of huge numbers of young men who otherwise would have remained at home and contributed to population growth in the Netherlands. As it was, between 1662 and 1795, Dutch population size remained static. Here then, by tending to "business" and not worrying about moral issues, the great merchant families of Amsterdam were able to build up and retain hegemonic control over Dutch society.

Disease Imports to the Non-West

In the first decades of exchange between the Old World and the Americas, the principal lethal diseases appear to have been influenza, smallpox, measles, typhus and malaria. With the establishment of the slave trade directly between west African ports and Brazil and the West Indies, and the return trade from the Americas to western Europe and thence south along the West African coast, the creation of a unified transatlantic disease zone was finally complete. Now, in addition to the diseases of western Europe and Asia, the New World was also subjected to a full range of African illnesses. Some of these, for example *falciparum* malaria, were far more lethal than the earlier malarial form (*vivax* malaria) which some scholars hold had been brought in to coastal North America from marshlands in western Europe.

Complicating matters, each killer disease actually consisted of two or more variant types. In the case of smallpox, there were three main variants, *Variola major*, *Variola minor*, *Variola intermedius*. When examined in sophisticated laboratories in the early 1970s, there were found to be a total of 450 sub-strains of smallpox, eight of them *Variola major*.

Each disease had its own specific causal agent (pathogen) and its own specific means of transmission. Some, as in the case of smallpox, needed no non-human intermediary. That virus was transmitted directly from one human to another, either through breathing air exhaled by a victim, or by coming into contact with the scabs or flesh which had dropped off the victim's body, or by coming into contact with a victim's clothing or blankets even weeks after the person had died. Measles, in its variant forms, was also transmitted directly from one infected individual to another.

Another early disease import to the New World was malaria (caused by a *plasmodia*) which was transmitted through an intermediary host, one or another type of mosquito. The malaria *plasmodia* (in one of its three forms) reached its full maturity within the human host, and infected this host's bloodstream, from whence it was transferred to another human, by way of a female mosquito of the appropriate sort (in which the *plasmodia* egg first hatched). Thus, even though the appropriate mosquito types might have been in the New World before the arrival of Columbus, they would only become bearers of malaria when females of their type bit and ingested some of the blood of a malaria-bearing migrant from the Old World. In a somewhat similar way, typhus (its causal agent is the *Rickettsia prowazeki*) was also transmitted to humans via an intermediary host, a human body louse, or to be more precise, the fecal matter deposited on human skin by a body louse.

As of the late fifteenth century, influenza (one of the five principal infectious disease killers newly introduced into the New World) was directly tied to the presence of domesticated animals of the sort not found in the Americas before. Indeed, within weeks of the landing on Hispaniola of Christopher Columbus and his henchmen, with their swine, cattle and other fresh meat on the hoof, local Taino people (until then a million in number) were struck down by swine fever, a form of influenza. Not until December 1518 were the Taino who had survived this epidemic attacked by virulent smallpox.

Thereafter, smallpox seems to have replaced influenza as the New World's principal killing disease. In a parallel development in the far Pacific, beginning in the 1750s, smallpox left by fishermen, indigenous to the island of Timor, who had dried their nets and gear on the north-eastern coast of Australia, became the principal killing disease of that continent's Aboriginal population.

Though only one of the five principal killer diseases brought to the western hemisphere around 1500 was directly linked with mammals (influenza, from swine), it would appear that in the distant past, three of the others (malaria, smallpox and measles) had also been linked in one way or another with EurAsian and African humankind's animal companions. [I]n the era between *c.* 13,000 BCE and early October 1492 CE there were no large mammals in the New World that could be domesticated and brought to live in close proximity to humans. Without close contact with friendly, cuddly animals of this sort, the processes of disease evolution which had occurred in the Old World in pre-historic times after sizeable cities had been established could not take place in the New.

In the case of smallpox (in the forms in which it was last known to ordinary scientists in 1977), the protective material originally used for vaccination against the illness, by Jenner in 1796, was derived from the udder of a cow suffering from cowpox. It would thus seem that through the mutative processes of natural selection, the causal agents of cowpox and smallpox had at some past time hived off from one another, to become two distinct diseases. As of 1977 (when it was abolished in the natural world), smallpox had no non-human host.

Turning again to malaria, African and Asian farmers have recently reminded visiting medical scientists that mosquitoes much prefer the blood of cattle to that of humans; if the two mammal types are in the same barn, the mosquitoes will light on the cattle every time. Thus it is likely that ancestral malaria, probably as found along the banks of the Indus River in India, began as a disease associated with cattle and only later became associated with humans.

Posited as happening at some time on the Indian subcontinent, a similar transference may also have taken place in West Africa where, after 1000 BCE, the cattle-keeping ancestors of today's Fulani mingled on a seasonal basis with agriculturalists. However, among adult Africans who in their lifetime did not travel far from their natal village, malaria would not be much of a problem, given that they had acquired immunity to the local variant while they were young children. Difficulties only began when large numbers of Africans were enslaved and taken far from their natal villages into new malaria zones where the immunity they had acquired to their local variant was not effective against the strange new types to which they were being exposed.

In Europe, by the early 1500s, when black African slavery had already become common in Portuguese ports and elsewhere in that mosquito-pestered little country, virulent malaria had become well established, brought in by the slaves and by their Portuguese captors. Virulent malaria was also well established in the mosquito-pestered flat lands south of Rome where absentee-owner estates held black Africans in bondage. In time, some of these estates became unfit for human habitation and fell derelict.

Acquired Immunity

In the half century after 1521 (when smallpox first struck the Aztec metropolis, Tenochtitlán), one reason why first generation white immigrants were convinced that they were chosen by God to inherit the western hemisphere was that they seemed to be immune to the sickness which was causing such havoc among indigenous populations. Medical historians now realize that early sixteenth-century white immunity existed not through the intervention of a supernatural force, but because very mild forms of smallpox were endemic in Europe at the time.

As I hinted earlier, endemic viral infectious diseases, such as smallpox (and yellow fever), tended to light on babies and young children, and rather than killing them all off (thus, in the long term, obliterating the virus's necessary hosts) caused only mild discomfort. In exchange for hosting it, the virus then provided recipients with life-long immunity to all further attacks. In the random logic of natural selection this meant that the infant human host (having served its purpose) would then reach maturity and produce infants, who in turn would host the smallpox virus (or the yellow fever virus) and thus enable it to perpetuate itself.

Like smallpox, a case of measles in one or another of its forms (also caused by a virus), similarly provided life-long immunity or near immunity. From the thirteenth century onwards measles was endemic in Europe, the Middle East and China, though in forms that were slightly different from those known today. Given what we know about its behavior in the 1530s, in EurAsia measles could sustain itself in mild form in interacting village communities numbering only a few thousand people.

Thus it happened that most of the Spanish and other Europeans who happened to be in the once heavily populated Valley of Mexico when measles struck in virulent epidemic form in 1531, found that they personally were immune (or suffered only light cases from which they easily recovered), even though indigenous people all around them were dying in great numbers. This confirmed the Europeans in their belief that Native Americans were cursed by God and that He intended that they should disappear.

In common with measles and smallpox, a mild attack of typhus also conferred life-time near-immunity to the disease. At a time when Spaniards abhorred bathing or changing their underclothes, it is likely that most of them were infested with body lice and that since infancy they had had experience with mild forms of typhus. By way of contrast, Native Americans abhorred body filth and bathed as frequently as circumstances permitted. Unfortunately, in prejudiced Spanish minds, this custom linked the peoples of the New World (none of whom had ever heard of the Prophet Muhammad or of Christ) with the ritually-well-washed Muslims who—until they had been killed off or sent into exile by Queen Isabella in 1492—had inhabited Andalusia in southern Spain.

Disease and the Destruction of New World Populations

Within 30 or 40 years of "first contact" (beginning in October 1492) in any particular "disease region" in the New World indigenous population numbers dropped precipitously, generally leaving only one person alive where there had been ten before. In defining a "disease region" one must take into account the special characteristics of the disease involved.

In the case of measles (which ravaged the Valley of Mexico in 1531–32) the "disease region" would be relatively small and self-contained, since the disease is highly contagious, usually acquired through direct contact with a sick person or with virus-laden droplets in the air which had been expelled from the lungs of the sick one. Here, the time between infection and the appearance of symptoms (the incubation period) was brief, limiting the geographic scope of disease transmission.

But the situation was quite different in the case of smallpox. Here, the virus causal agent was present in a bearer for a week or more before the person came down sick. During that time a Native American who happened to be in the business of carrying news and trade-goods between distant places might be able to travel 50 or 60 kilometers a day. This meant he might have traveled three or four hundred kilometers from the epicenter of a smallpox epidemic before falling sick and becoming an infective agent. For this reason, the "disease region" of smallpox might well include whole territories that had not yet been visited by whites.

The most famous example is that of the Incas of Peru, until the mid-1520s, rulers of a mighty empire that stretched for hundreds of kilometers along the Andes and the west coast of South America. Smallpox, probably brought in by Native American runners from the north, ravaged the heart of the empire in 1524–25. This was six years before the arrival of man-on-the-make Francisco Pizarro in 1531. In its early stages the epidemic killed the Inca king and many of the royal family, leading to a disputed succession and civil war. In the midst of this, Conquistador Pizarro (himself immune to smallpox) had no difficulty in coming in and taking charge.

We have already answered *part* of the rhetorical question, "Why did they die?". As we have pointed out, until 1492 no New World person had ever come into contact with smallpox or any other of Europe's cornucopia of infectious diseases. Not having acquired any immunity to these diseases, when they struck, New World peoples died in terrifyingly large numbers.

Yet, there may well be more to it than that. As every veterinarian (animal doctor) knows, no matter what disease hits a herd of cattle, some beasts survive, exemplifying the principle of "herd immunity." Of course, when dealing with domesticated animals it is assumed that a human owner is on hand to feed and water the sick animals until they recover. In the case of human beings, similar requirements have to be met.

Thus, wherever in the Old World smallpox broke out in lethal form, there would always be some responsible older people around (who had acquired immunity as children) to serve as carers during the ten to 12 days a smallpox patient was semi-delirious and unable to manage for her- or himself. But in the Americas, when an epidemic of smallpox first broke out as in the Valley of Mexico in 1520 or in the Pequot lands of New England in 1634, there would be no indigenous people around who had acquired immunity. Any family member brave enough to bring water and food to a sick person would soon fall sick herself. This sort of happening didn't have to repeat itself very often before all sane persons took to their heels and fled, spreading contagion into the countryside as they ran along. A famous example was the epidemic crisis that hit the Andean city of Arequipa and its densely populated hinterland in 1589, leaving more than a million dead.

Living as we do more than four hundred years after these terrible events, and in the absence of specimens of the disease casual agents that wrought such havoc (which could be analyzed using modern laboratory techniques), we can do no more than speculate about what happened and why.

This brings us to contentious topics. The first involves assessing the genetic make up of (long dead) individuals in particular population groups. The second is to assess the degree of disease-resistance *diversity* that might have been found in any given (long dead) population, say, "Population A" compared to some other (long dead) population, "Population B."

Let me begin with "Population A," the inhabitants of western Europe around 1200 CE. It is now known that the ancestors of the people who had come to settle in western Europe before 1200 CE had moved there from many far off regions. Some of these ancestors (or ancestral groupings) had come from central and western Asia, some from the Middle East and North Africa, some from eastern Europe and so on. Each of these ancestral groupings had their own distinctive genetic inheritance and, with it, their own distinctive clustering of chromosomes. At the level of the individual, each chromosome carried disease resistance units known as *alleles*.

After each of these various ancestors (ancestral groupings) settled down in western Europe, they and their progeny intermarried with women and men descended from other ancestral groupings. Happening over the course of several thousand years, emerging out of this mixing process were late-medieval Europeans. They were very much a mongrel people.

Because of this complex genetic situation in western Europe, there were a large number of possible combinations of alleles (disease resistance units) in the late medieval population. Indeed, given that alleles are attached to chromosomes, and that brothers and sisters do not share the same chromosomes, even siblings had slightly different immune systems. Next door neighbors also carried combinations that differed one from the other.

Thus, a disease pathogen attacking any member of the allele-rich population that was western Europe in the years after 1450 (the date after which most immigrants to the New World were born) would, in assaulting each individual person, confront a slightly different immune system. Sorting out these differences in defense systems and overcoming them one by one presumably had the potential to slow down the movement of the disease. It might even encourage it to remain in mild endemic form, rather than breaking out as a virulent epidemic. This then (in simplified form) was the situation in western Europe.

But in the New World, the accidents of settlement history were entirely different. Though much of this remains conjectural, it would seem that as of 11 October 1492 (the eve of Columbus' landing) the entire population of the Americas was descended from only four or five small Asian groupings (each perhaps under a dominant Patriarch). At various times 12 or 13 thousand years ago these small groups (two or three hundred strong) had made their way across dry land between present day Siberia and Alaska. Some of the descendants of these groups gradually made their way southwards, eventually to southern Chile.

Because the number of founding ancestors was very small (perhaps only a few dominant Patriarchs had initially been involved in the migration), the number of alleles possessed by their millions of descendants several thousand years later was also small when compared to mixed-breed European populations (with their far-flung and varied ancestral roots). It can be argued that as a result, in the whole of New World there was not much diversity in alleles. This meant that an epidemic disease, such as measles or smallpox, at work in that population, had far fewer immune system differences to overcome than would have been the case in western Europe. This would perhaps explain why, in the Valley of Mexico, measles went berserk every 20 or 30 years. Measles hit the Valley in epidemic form in 1531–32, in 1563–64, in 1592–93, and in 1595–97, leaving tens of thousands of people dead, many of them children.

Records kept in New Spain by Catholic priests suggest that later epidemics were marginally less severe. Perhaps this was because Spanish settler males (in the absence of Spanish females) tended to sleep around with Native American women and, in the process, gradually enriched the local gene bank and, with it, the diversity of alleles found in the population. Yet the lessening severity of epidemics in places that had been repeatedly ravished early on—such as the Valley of Mexico—may also be related to gradual mutations in the viral disease agents themselves.

Using the slippery technique, "argument by analogy" we can remind ourselves that a disease not before known in mainland Europe—venereal syphilis—had also been highly virulent when it first appeared in 1494 among military men and prostitutes in Italy and France. According to alarmists' reports at the time, heralding their early death, within a few weeks of contracting the disease the noses and penises of syphilis victims dropped off. However, 50 years later, medical authorities claimed that venereal syphilis had lost some of its most alarming symptoms and now took many years to complete its lethal work. If this were true, it would suggest that the disease had adjusted itself to a new environment, taking care not to kill off victims before they had time to breed children who could later serve as disease hosts.

A somewhat similar mutation in disease behavior (at first highly virulent, then much less so) *may* have happened to the viral agents of smallpox and measles in New Spain after 1650. However, without samples of actual disease causal agents from before and after 1650 that can be tested using modern laboratory techniques, suppositions about such changes remain only that.

Solid arguments, derived from biology, supplement, and may ultimately supersede, earlier "cultural" arguments. One "cultural" argument, most often applied to North America (based on two or three observations by bemused whites), held that according to native custom, whenever a community member fell sick, it was the duty of the whole community to visit, frequently. If the sick person had come down with an air-borne communicable disease—measles or smallpox—the visiting process would obviously put the entire community at risk.

A much less valid, but frequently repeated "cultural" argument, holds that Native Americans, when confronted with smallpox and its sores and pustules commonly resorted to steam baths in search of cleansing and cure. Modern historians who claim that this was the worst thing they could have done, are, unknown to themselves, simply reiterating sixteenth-century Spanish claims that bathing was "evil"—because it was a Muslim custom.

As we have seen throughout this book, "disease" is a reality (synonymous with disease agent/pathogen), but "illness" is—at least in part—a perceptual state. "Illness" (as perceived by "self") can be caused by *individual* misfortune and circumstances. But a state of mind conducive to serious illness would also be found among an entire ethnic group (or, as in the Aztec Empire, a collection of ethnic groups) whose lived-world had totally collapsed.

In the Spanish-ruled lands of America after 1492/1521, native people found themselves in a situation where their heads of government had been killed off by disease or murdered, where all their religious and cultural writings had been burnt, where their cities, temples and aqueducts had been dismantled and destroyed, where their lands had been stolen and their livelihoods destroyed, and where they had all been reduced to the dank equal status of serfs.

Here then, life-worlds of the sort known before the Conquest (not that these had been Gardens of Eden) were replaced by a new life-world in which control of "self" and overall control of the ethnic group were in the hands of an "Other." This "Other" consisted of Spanish landowners, Spanish entrepreneurs, Spanish priests (who insisted in collecting scattered rural communities into tight-packed, disease-ridden "congregations") and—at the center of the development web in Genoa and in northern European cities—gentleman venture capitalists.

In North America, the cast of characters in the "Other" was slightly different (in the English colonies there were no priests to speak of) but the end result was much the same. After the arrival of local whites as land-thieves, individual natives' sense of self-worth and personal identity was shattered.

Within the Americas—North and South—each ethnic group responded to this situation in their own way. In the Valley of Mexico, according to a survey taken in the 1580s, it would seem that survivors married at a younger age than had been the case before 1521, and had more live births. However, it would also seem that parents—demoralized by the Spanish regime—did little to keep their babies alive; the result was population stagnation, or continued decline. Further to the south, in the Andes, it would seem that a high proportion of married young people did not bother to have children at all. Given that very few Native American migrants were coming in, this too resulted in population decline.

A similar situation seems to have prevailed in much of North America. Here, demoralized Native American males often felt that since there would be no future worth living for, there was no point in marrying. Indeed many of them decided that there was no point in doing anything at all other than drink the whiskey and cheap rum which the white folks made available. In the late eighteenth and nineteenth centuries, drunken tribal chieftains readily agreed to treaties which handed over all tribal lands to white occupation, in perpetuity.

But in earlier centuries, some groups of Native Americans had clearly demonstrated that they would not easily accept being made into landless slaves. For example, in the spring of 1519 Aztec warriors had had no trouble in killing off most of the soldiers brought in by Cortés before they themselves were brought low by something other than western armaments. Two years later, when most Aztec warriors were in the process of dying from smallpox, Cortés had no difficulty in defeating them in battle; but then this was not exactly a fair fight.

Turning to the situation in North America, it is known that during the early years, Native Americans fought long and hard against land-grabbing settlers before they too were brought low by something else. In the absence of that "something else" (lethal European-borne diseases) it can be argued that had the full complement of New World people still been around in 1800 or 1850, they would have outnumbered European settlers by a factor of 50 to one. In the days before Gatling guns, man for man, Native American warriors were fully the equal of warriors of European stock.

The supposition that killing diseases (rather than just superior armaments and leadership) made possible the conquest of the Americas by Europe can, in part, be supported by evidence drawn from another part of the world, New Zealand. When, in the late eighteenth century, land-hungry British settlers came to North Island and South Island they found them occupied by the Maori. These people may well have been beneficiaries of a richer inheritance of alleles than were the indigenous people of Australia or the New World.

The Maori themselves had only come to New Zealand as conquerors around 1200 CE. As a peripatetic Polynesian people, it is possible that they had already had experience with some of the disease types found in East Asia. In any case, it would seem that they were not blitzed by European-borne diseases at first contact to the extent that most other Non-western people were. As a result, the Maori were able to retain their societal cohesion and their ability to defend themselves against European aggressors, sometimes using guns purchased from whites. Beneficiaries of a humanitarian governor, in 1840 the status of the Maori as a permanent element in the New Zealand population was recognized by the Waitangi treaty arrangement (this, at any rate is the reading in the Maori-language version of the treaty). Though they lost considerable ground in the next 90 years, by 1935 they were still very much present and were undergoing a major cultural revival. Their integrity and separate identity still intact, the Maori currently account for 15 percent of the population.

World Historical Consequences

In the New World, the processes of globalization (which were entirely dependent on development and development agents) could not have worked their way to fruition had not key regions in the two continents first been denuded of their Native American population. This denuding process, as we have seen, was achieved through the interaction of three factors: European-imported diseases, European sadistic behaviors and the collapse of Native Americans' lived-worlds.

In world historical terms, in the long run, the denuded region of most consequence was that lying inland from the Gulf of Mexico. Stretching from West Florida to beyond the Mississippi, in the years after 1815 this vast region became the home of *King Cotton*. Without this African slave-grown cotton (and England's own newly discovered reserves of coal), England's fledgling "industrial revolution" would probably have petered out and Britain would have joined Venice and Flanders/Netherlands as the home of yet another failed attempt at modernization.

But as Kenneth Pomeranz nicely demonstrates in his *The Great Divergence: China, Europe and the making of the modern world* (2000), Britain (rather than China—as late as 1750 China still had many things going for it) *did* achieve full modernization. Building on breakthrough achievements first in cotton, then in steam, after 1850 England's gentleman capitalists created the British world economic system. A century later, this world economic system was inherited by America.

Further Reading

For Spanish speakers: Sheldon Watts, *Epidemias y Poder: historia, enfermedad, imperialismo* (Barcelona: Editorial Andres Bello, 2000); in English as *Epidemics and History: disease, power and imperialism* (London: Yale University Press, 1997). The five hundredth anniversary of Columbus in America, 1492–1992, saw the production of many books which re-appraised Spanish achievements in the destruction of the New World. Particularly useful is Noble David Cook, *Born to Die: disease and New World conquest, 1492–1650* (Cambridge: Cambridge University Press, 1998) and David Stannard, *American Holocaust: Columbus and the conquest of the New World* (Oxford: Oxford University Press, 1992). An important article on alleles: Francis Black, "An explanation of high death rates among New World peoples when in contact with Old World diseases," *Perspectives in Biology and Medicine* 37 (2) Winter 1994, 292–307. A key book on the making of the modern world: Kenneth Pomeranz, *The Great Divergence: China, Europe and the making of the modern world economy* (Princeton, NJ: Princeton University Press, 2000): an update is the AHR Forum: "Asia and Europe in the World Economy": *American Historical Review* 107 (2) April 2002, 418–80.

References

Alchon, Suzanne Austin (1991) *Native Society and Disease in Colonial Ecuador*, Cambridge: Cambridge University Press.

Baker, Brenda J. and George J. Armelagos (1988) "The Origin and Antiquity of Syphilis: paleopathologic diagnosis and interpretation," *Current Anthropology* 29 (5): 732–7.

Bastien, Joseph W. (ed.) (1985) *Health in the Andes*, New York: American Anthropological Association.

Black, F. L. (1994) "An Explanation of High Death Rates among New World Peoples When in Contact with Old World Diseases," *Perspectives in Biology and Medicine* 37 (2), 292–307.

Blackburn, Robin (1997) *The Making of New World Slavery: from the Baroque to the modern 1492–1800*, London: Verso.

Braudel, Fernand (1985) *Civilization & Capitalism, 15th–18th Century*, Vol. 3, *The Perspective of the World*, London: Collins/Fontana Press.

Cook, Noble David and W. George Lovell (eds) (1991) *"Secret Judgments of God": Old World disease in colonial Spanish America*, Norman, OK: University of Oklahoma Press.

Cook, Noble David (1998) *Born to Die: disease and New World conquest, 1492–1650*, Cambridge: Cambridge University Press.

Crosby, Alfred W. (1972) *The Columbian Exchange: biological consequences of 1492*, Westport, CT: Greenwood Press. A pioneering work: some of its core concepts are now museum pieces.

Geary, Patrick (2002) *The Myth of Nations: the medieval origins of Europe*, Princeton, NJ: Princeton University Press. On the diverse origins of the settler/inhabitants of post-Roman Empire Europe.

Gruzinski, Serge (1993) *The Conquest of Mexico: the incorporation of Indian societies in the Western world, 16th–18th centuries*, Cambridge: Cambridge University Press.

Hall, Richard (1998) *Empires of the Monsoon: a history of the Indian Ocean and its invaders*, London: HarperCollins.

Henige, David (1986) "When did Smallpox reach the New World (and why does it matter)?" in Paul Lovejoy (ed.) *Africans in Bondage: studies in slavery and the slave trade*, Madison: University of Wisconsin Press: 11–26.

Inikori, Joseph and Stanley L. Engerman (eds) (1992) *The Atlantic Slave Trade: effects on economies, societies, and peoples in Africa, the Americas and Europe*, Durham, NC: University of North Carolina Press.

Joralemon, Donald (1982) "New World Depopulation and the Case of Disease," *Journal of Anthropological Research* 38: 109–27.

McCaa, Robert (1995) "Spanish and Nahuatl Views on Smallpox and Demographic Catastrophe in Mexico," *Journal of Interdisciplinary History* 25: 397–431.

MacLeod, D. Peter (1992) "Microbes and Muskets: smallpox and the participation of the Amerindian allies of New France in the Seven Years War," *Ethnohistory* 30 (1): 42–64.

MacLeod, Roy and Milton Lewis (eds) (1988) *Disease, Medicine, and Empire: perspectives on western medicine and the experience of European expansion*, London: Routledge.

Miller, Joseph (1988) *Way of Death: merchant capitalism and the Angolan slave trade, 1730–1830*, London: James Currey.

Pomeranz, Kenneth (2000) *The Great Divergence: China, Europe and the making of the modern world economy*, Princeton, NJ: Princeton University Press.

Porter, H. C. (1979) *The Inconstant Savage: England and the North American Indian 1500–1660*, London: Duckworth.

Stannard, David E. (1992) *American Holocaust: Columbus and the conquest of the New World*, Oxford: Oxford University Press.

Thomas, Hugh (1993) *Conquest: Montezuma, Cortés, and the fall of Old Mexico*, New York, Simon & Schuster.

Thomas, Hugh (1998) *The Slave Trade: the history of the Atlantic slave trade 1440–1870*, London: Papermac.

Thornton, John (1992) *Africa and Africans in the Making of the Atlantic World*, Cambridge: Cambridge University Press.

Ubelaker, Douglas H. (1992) "Patterns of Demographic Change in the Americas," *Human Biology* 64 (3): 361–79.

Verano, John W. and Douglas H. Ubelaker (eds) (1992) *Disease and Demography in the Americas*, Washington, DC: Smithsonian Institution Press.

Watts, Sheldon (1997) "Smallpox in the New World and in the Old: from holocaust to eradication, 1518–1977," in *Epidemics and History: disease, power and imperialism*, London: Yale University Press.

Wong, R. Bin (2002) "The Search for European Differences and Domination in the Early Modern World: a view from Asia," *The American Historical Review* 107 (2) April: 447–69.

Wright, Richard (1993) *Stolen Continents: the Indian story*, London: Pimlico.

Reading 2.3

Public Lands, Expansion, and the Native Americans

Ellen Holmes Person

I N A CHARGE TO THE GRAND Jury in 1783, South Carolina judge John F. Grimké celebrated the new nation's victory and congratulated his audience on their new position as the envy of Europe. He encouraged them to "behold the honor you are held in by them … see how they press to your hospitable shores." He charged his fellow citizens to "look forward to the immense Empire, the work of your hands, that you are creating." Expansion and attention from other nations were, according to Judge Grimké, "the rewards" of Americans' "Virtue and Bravery!"[1] Empire was certainly on the minds of the victorious Americans.

The new nation boasted endless potential for expansion on a continent that boundlessly stretched westward. Abundance of land and its ease of acquisition characterized and contributed mightily to the shaping of American identities from within and without. American and European alike recognized the potential for individual and national wealth that land brought.[2] Land and its accompanying natural resources were the new nation's most valuable assets, and after the Revolution, the job of granting land fell to state and federal government officials. What began as a matter for individual colonial charters and grants grew from local to federal in scale as expansion issues and their obstacles became more complicated. Lawmakers encountered challenges such as turf wars between local and federal governments, carelessly made or unrecorded surveys, and corruption of officials who administered land sales.

Many early national legal scholars watched the development of land law with great interest. For some, the concern was economic. For others, it was simply jurisprudential. For all, the distribution of territory—who lost the land and why, who got the land and how they used it—was central to their explanations of American identities. Although legists could use English law as the foundation of their property law, the English had never before dealt with the volume of land that North America boasted. Therefore, even more so than in inheritance law, Americans had to rely on legal innovations to shape their laws governing the transfer of land. In their lectures on land ownership, legists constructed histories of the growth of the American colonies, the abundance of land, and the ease with which settlers could gain title to it, and they pointed to these distinctive elements of their societies as important components of the American character. At some point in their lectures regarding the transfer and acquisition of real property, however, legists had to reconcile their desire for empire and wealth with the presence of the "original lords of the soil," Native Americans. No English precedent existed for such a situation. Indians' insistence on retaining their ancestral lands meant that white Americans had to employ new legal and moral tactics to obtain more territory so that they could satiate settlers' land hunger. Their justifications for displacing the first inhabitants of the land provide a glimpse into Anglo-Americans' sense of entitlement to territory and empire.

Americans of the late eighteenth and early nineteenth centuries looked upon their social, political, and cultural accomplishments as part of the natural course of human progress. They considered themselves more advanced than, hence superior to, Indians, who simply had not progressed as far culturally or socially. Some Americans compared Indians to their own primitive ancestors, believing that someday Native Americans would be as advanced as they. Therefore, it was fashionable in certain circles to exhibit optimism that Indians eventually could be "civilized" and thus assimilated into white society. In yet another example of the innovations possible in America's experimental republican polities, leaders of these new, expansive societies could transform the Indians from primitive, simple savages into "civilized" human beings. The eyes of the world would be upon them as they effected this transformation and proved the virtues of their republics. Men like George Washington's secretary of war Henry Knox, Thomas Jefferson, and other leaders were convinced that such a civilization program would work.[3]

But increasingly in the early nineteenth century, some legal scholars, like many Americans, began to voice the conviction that Indians were not capable of civilization and eventual assimilation into the Western world. Moreover, they became convinced that Native Americans' rejection of whites' philanthropic efforts to "improve" and civilize them would lead to their eventual destruction. They had to face the fact that many whites not only opposed the assimilation of Indians, but also wanted to destroy Native Americans and snatch their lands by any means, legal or illegal. As they crafted their historical and legal lessons about whites' attempts to civilize Indians and appropriate Indian lands, legists struggled with the challenge of making this part of the American character a positive attribute.

I

In the early national period, private citizens and public concerns alike took advantage of land's profit potential. Land was a valuable resource, and states sold off millions of acres of their western holdings to wealthy men who could afford to purchase large tracts of land. New York, Virginia, and Pennsylvania, among others, rewarded their Revolutionary War veterans with acreages that land speculators then bought and gathered into large parcels. With the consolidation of western lands under the federal government and the Northwest Ordinances of the 1780s, the U.S. government implemented plans designed to bring in much-needed revenue from the sale of lands. Speculators took advantage of this opportunity as well. They already possessed the social prestige and authority that land brought, and they did not intend to draw wealth from the land as long-term investments. Their goal was to turn quick profits by capitalizing on the added value that rapid post-Revolution population growth and increase in material wealth brought.[4] Many of the nation's legal scholars invested in western lands, with mixed results.

Whether or not they invested in western lands, the states' leading jurists and legal scholars observed the sale and settlement of the new territories with concern.[5] Poorly trained surveyors and careless land officers left many deeds erroneously measured or recorded. Some officials took bribes to record deeds inaccurately or not to record them at all. Overlapping claims due to careless surveying and recording were especially common in the Southern states.[6] Officers conspired with government officials to acquire land in shady deals that benefited both parties. Perhaps the most famous land speculation scandal of the early republic occurred in Georgia, where the legislators voted to sell four speculation companies forty million acres for $500,000. An investigation led to the discovery that all but one of Georgia's legislators had invested in one of the land companies or had taken a bribe to vote in favor of the transactions.[7] America's legal scholars watched these scandals unfold and worried about the integrity of their own states' land practices.

Virginia's inefficient land policy provoked St. George Tucker to call for reform similar to the innovations contained in the federal government's management of expansion. In his edition of Blackstone's *Commentaries,* Tucker criticized Virginia's system of land grants, calling the state's laws an open season for speculators and con artists. In the early 1800s, Virginia land patents—both legitimate and fraudulent—served as currency in the state and beyond it. Unscrupulous speculators took the patents to Europe to sell to unsuspecting investors, and the loopholes allowing this practice had not been closed in subsequent legislation. Virginia's General Assembly required that the governor issue grants after reviewing the claims and comparing them to land surveys. This process, Tucker complained, was flawed, because claims were often not adjacent to each other. Considerable tracts of lands were sometimes interspersed with small parcels that had been claimed and patented separately. Those who claimed the leftover lands sometimes had to cobble together a patchwork of unconnected parcels. Tucker asserted that the law should have required that claim locations be made adjacent to one another, or it should have limited the amount of land to be granted in a single patent "to any reasonable number of acres." He accused "rapacious land-mongers" of preventing productive amendments to the regulation because they did not want to pay for a full survey. Instead, they referred to "some well known natural boundary ... with a reservation of prior claims, of which there might be an hundred or five hundred, founded upon prior patents." Because Virginia law did not require precise surveys of patents, unsuspecting patentees received "an emmense extent of territory to appearance, whilst perhaps in reality there was not a single acre of arable land within their bounds, which was not comprehended in the reservation of prior claims." Moreover, Virginia law did not require that speculators survey the entire claim, but rather they merely had to survey a few lines, because surveys for prior claims had already been done. Tucker saw in this practice unlimited potential for lawsuits and messy settlements, "endless contention, and controversies between those who may be unfortunate enough to derive their titles from such an impure source." The General Assembly tried to plug this loophole in 1795 by prohibiting the land office from accepting any plat and certificate of survey that conflicted with prior claims. However, according to Tucker, the solution was too late to prevent many people from being swindled.[8] The Old Dominion's land records remained a disorganized mess for years after the law went into effect.

Tucker looked to the Northwest Ordinance of 1787 as an ideal format for parceling out territory. It provided for the orderly division of the territory northwest of the Ohio River in north and south lines, apportioning the land into townships of six square miles, except in those places where natural boundaries or treaty boundaries with Indians prevented straight lines. He admonished his fellow Virginians: "The United States will obtain as much for *one* acre of their land, as Virginia gets for an *hundred*." Moreover, Virginia would lose industrious men to the more efficient system in the Northwest. A settler who wanted "to set down in peaceable possession of his lands; to improve them, and to transmit them to his posterity" would, Tucker concluded, "turn his eyes to the northwest of the Ohio for an establishment." Those who wished "only to deceive and defraud others, who buy, merely to sell; who regard not in what miseries or perplexities they may involve ignorant persons, and foreigners, will, until the *bubble bursts*, continue to traffic in parchment" to the injury of the innocent.[9] Other areas would win the competition of land management, while Virginia lagged behind because of her lawmakers' lack of foresight. The "bubble" continued to move westward for decades, causing Tucker's descendants and others of future generations much consternation and enriching many along the way. Corruption and inefficiency continued to plague expansion, not just in Virginia, but throughout new territories of the United States. But the obstacle that preoccupied legal scholars even more involved conflicting claims to territory from Native Americans.

II

In his *Commentaries on American Law,* James Kent wrote that "the subject of the treatment of the Indians is one which appears to be, in every view, replete with difficulty and danger." Their interaction with whites, Kent observed, seemed to "have had an immoral influence upon Indian manners and habits, and to have destroyed all that was noble and elevated in the Indian character." Because they simply seemed unable—or unwilling—to accept the Anglo-American version of "civilization," Kent predicted that "the Indians of this continent appear to be destined, at no very distant period of time, to disappear with those vast forests which once covered the country."[10] He did not address the Native Americans' condition in his treatise simply because he was concerned about their plight. Because early national legal scholars like Kent considered themselves teachers of much more than the law, they expended considerable energy defending their nation's right to territory, justifying the taking of land and alternately condemning or apologizing for European Americans' treatment of America's First Peoples. Their visions of Indians' place in America's history and in contemporary society provide insight into their self-conceptions, as well as into the meanings that they invested in the images of "America" and "Americans."

Early national legal scholars had to negotiate the "narrow confines" of safe Indian policy and judicial politics.[11] It was difficult for them to find a comfortable spot in their histories for those peoples who held original title to North America. Their explanations of Native American property rights incorporated a variety of ideas about race, civilization, and rights to occupy or possess land.[12] Early national legists espoused Enlightenment-era scientific theories about race and progress. They were, with a few notable exceptions, detached from the frontier struggles between Indians and white settlers, but they expressed dismay over the violent tactics that white migrants adopted to drive Indians from their ancestral lands.

Early Americans were quick to point out the differences between their own modes of land acquisition and possession and Native American practices, but they were less willing to admit to similarities. With regard to differences, European observers consistently noted that Native Americans did not recognize individual ownership and individual right to convey land away from the nation. Similarities were harder for Europeans to see. For example, both Europeans and Indians shared customs of marking boundaries with piles of stones, colored posts placed in the ground, or marks in trees. However, whites refused to recognize the legitimacy of Indians' marks as signs of possession. Additionally, claims to sovereign territory rested on military success for both cultures. Victory in war meant territorial gains. Although English customs of common land use lasted through the sixteenth century, by the seventeenth century the enclosure system had erased English ideas about use of certain lands in common.[13] The transition to enclosure and individual use and possession of land drove a cultural wedge between white and Native American ideas about possession.

Because they had to keep the "big picture" of America's Revolutionary mission intact, legists had to be careful about how they constructed their histories of European-American seizure of Indian lands. Because Blackstone had laid out the argument so neatly in his discussion of *Calvin's Case,* the easiest justification for this appropriation would have been conquest.[14] But Americans could not comfortably characterize their possession of all lands in North America as a result of conquest. Pre-Revolutionary political debates over America's designation as conquered territory threatened the legitimacy of Americans' claims to common-law protections.[15] Legal scholars believed that they had put to rest the argument that British American colonies had originated in conquest. They asserted their claims to the common law under the argument that American colonies were not born of conquest and, therefore, were not inferior to Britain. In his version of colonial history, Wilson depicted a confident and independent group of English citizens who, "permitted and commissioned by the crown, ... undertook, at their own expense, expeditions to this distant country, took possession of it, planted it, and cultivated it."[16] Of course, Wilson's story of peacefully settled lands omitted the constant struggles between European settlers and Native Americans.

The conquest theory rested on the assumption that a conquered *people* accompanied a conquered land, therefore it was in Americans' interest to portray their land as unpopulated or containing an easily removed people. Indeed, most history lessons about the settlement of colonial America bore a resemblance to St. George Tucker's description of it as settled by "the conquerors themselves, or colonists, settling a vacant territory." Echoing Thomas Jefferson's sentiments, Tucker asserted that status of conquered territory simply did not apply "to any colony, which was settled by English emigrants, after the Indian natives had ceded, or withdrawn themselves from, the territory."[17] Instead, Tucker found "repeated proofs of purchase" of land throughout the South, and he asserted that the northern part of the United States was "acquired altogether by purchases made in the most unexceptionable form."[18] In his version of colonial-era Indian/white relations, the Indians voluntarily disappeared from the picture by ceding their lands to whites. By the time English settlers came in any number, the Indians had already melted into the wilderness, and by the end of the eighteenth century, according to Tucker, Virginia's Indian population was "too small to require particular notice."[19] A history lesson that peacefully erased Native Americans from the landscape supported the notion that Englishmen had no competitors for the land. Thus, Tucker's "disappearing Indian" cleared the way for discussions of conveyance and possession among whites without the complications of conflicting claims.

In Peter DuPonceau's case, the Indian was barely there from the beginning. DuPonceau was fascinated with Native American languages and enamored of their sense of order and logic, but he did not accord Indians a significant role in Pennsylvania's history. In a speech to the American Philosophical Society, DuPonceau gave the Native Americans little notice.

When he did mention them, they seemed to be a part of the landscape rather than actors in the drama of discovery or possession. In his narrative of the arrival of the first ship in William Penn's contingent, DuPonceau set the scene of a "gallant ship" sailing up the Delaware River, decks covered with passengers "enjoying the mild temperature of our climate, and the serenity of our autumnal sky." He described the vast forests as nearly vacant wilderness: "No noise is heard around them, save that of the deer rustling through the trees, as she flies from the Indian who pursues her with his bow and arrow. Now and then a strange yell strikes the ear from a distance, which the echoes of the woods reverberate, and forms a strong contrast to the awful stillness of the scene."[20] DuPonceau's history lesson included the Indian only as part of the wildlife. He depicted Native Americans as invisible, but not unheard, predators.

DuPonceau acknowledged one distinctive Indian personality in his history of the Penn settlement, the Lenni Lenape chief Tamanend, whom he described as unequaled in virtue and goodness. His account of Penn's meeting with Tamanend was designed to tell his audience as much about Penn's character, and Tamanend's trust of the English proprietor, as it did about Tamanend himself: "His [Tamanend's] eye is steadily fixed on William Penn! His great mind has already discovered in him a congenial soul; alone among his tribe, he shews by his looks that noble confidence which will not be deceived." DuPonceau contrasts Tamanend's reception of Penn with the other Native Americans who greeted the Englishmen, "a motley group ... whose anxiety manifests itself on their countenances, and who view the new comers with looks in which suspicion seems as yet to predominate."[21] He characterized the group of Indians as nervous and suspicious of whites, but not threatening. Collectively, DuPonceau's indigenous peoples were barely there, simply a part of nature. However, DuPonceau bestowed redeeming human qualities on Tamanend, whom he depicted as honorable.

Legal scholars, American and European alike, often used William Penn as the ideal man of honor who treated Native Americans well, and DuPonceau echoed other authors' accolades of Pennsylvania's founder by assuring his audience that, in Penn's lifetime, the treaty he signed with Tamanend was not broken. However, DuPonceau admitted, the treaty did not last long after Penn's descendents were out of power. Moreover, he candidly placed the blame for deterioration of Indian relations on the white leaders who succeeded Penn's descendents.[22] DuPonceau carefully protected Penn's heirs from the taint of corruption, but he found subsequent generations of colonial leaders guilty of succumbing to land hunger and, thus, breaking promises to Pennsylvania's first peoples.

III

Whether they lived in places where American Indians were disappearing, like Tucker's Virginia, or were barely visible, like DuPonceau's Pennsylvania, or whether they lived in states where Native Americans made their presence known by pressing their land claims in the courts, early national legists used natural law concepts of discovery and occupancy and the notion of consent to justify appropriation of Indian lands. They acknowledged that the law of nature vested rights to land in the first occupant. But in 1814, frontier jurist and Indian-hater Hugh Henry Brackenridge disagreed with the idea that Indians possessed natural rights of occupancy in his *Law Miscellanies*. Brackenridge could look to Vattel's *Law of Nations*, the most popular reference for natural-law concepts of territory possession, to justify his objection. According to Vattel, every nation was bound by natural law to cultivate the land. Those who adopted the lifestyle of hunting occupied more land than they should; therefore other nations that intended to use the land for agriculture had a right to occupy the unused land.[23] He acknowledged that the Indians had, "from earliest times ... possessed their country." But, Brackenridge complained, "shall a few tribes thinly scattered over an immense continent retain possession of it, while other parts of the globe are overcharged with inhabitants?"[24] Brackenridge took Vattel's ideas about territorial rights and turned the question of rights to property into a question of what was best for the largest number of people—at least for the largest number of white people.

James Kent crafted a more sophisticated answer to the Indian question with his 1823 *Goodell v. Jackson* decision and his masterful explanation of Native Americans' right to territory and whites' right to usurp Indian claims in his *Commentaries*.[25] His interpretation of Native American property rights blended older notions of property ownership as a conservator of traditional social order and more progressive views of property as a commodity. From Kent's point of view, Native Americans' refusal to accept whites' version of civilization disrupted the social order *and* stood in the way of economic progress.[26] Kent claimed that Indians' title to the land "was imperfect" because it was limited to title by occupancy. He offered a more elegantly worded version of Brackenridge's complaint when he argued that the foundation of European claims to North American territory was based on "the sounder claim of agricultural settlers over tribes of hunters; and from the loose and frail, if not absurd title of wandering savages to an immense continent." Thus, Kent concluded, Americans' moral obligation to possess, "subdue, and cultivate" the land created a superior title to the land.[27]

Though Kent flirted with the idea of conquest as historical justification for American land claims, he seemed more comfortable resting claims to American territory on rights of discovery, "immemorial usage of the land," and the Indians' consent to transfer land to whites.[28] Kent borrowed liberally from *Johnson v. M'Intosh*, a Supreme Court case also decided in 1823, which, in his words, confirmed as "historical fact" that discovery of the continent was considered to have given the government of the discoverers "the sole right of acquiring the soil from the natives as against all other European powers."[29] Each nation subsequently regulated the relationship between Indians and its citizens, and the new relationship "necessarily impaired ... the rights of the original inhabitants" as Europeans asserted a superior title to the land. Europeans' "superior genius ... founded on civilization and Christianity, and on their superiority in the means, and in the art of war" entitled them to the land, according to Kent.[30] Kent's version of discovery implied that the threat of conquest, because of Europeans' superior military technology, was often enough to bring indigenous peoples and their territory under European control.

After establishing "title to the soil" through discovery, European nations allowed Indians the right of occupancy. St. George Tucker explained that colonial governments became the sole grantors of territory in a colony, and all grants had to be approved by the colonial assembly and governor. The state and federal governments continued that practice after Independence.[31] Kent elaborated on the history of American land claims by explaining that these local governments possessed the "exclusive right to extinguish the Indian title by purchase or conquest, and to grant the soil, and exercise such a degree of sovereignty as circumstances required." In other words, this superior claim to American lands meant that Indians had no permanent right, not even of occupancy, to these lands. Indians' claims to title were "obliged to yield to the combined influence with military, intellectual, and moral power," in the form of European immigrants.[32] But despite local governments' superior claims to Indian lands, officials still tried to negotiate the sale or trade of lands rather than forcing Native American tribes to cede territory. For Kent, as for many of his contemporaries, the peaceful method of consent was preferable to coercion. However, Kent was willing to sanction the use of force to acquire land, if that force was in the form of a "just and necessary war."[33]

Kent claimed that whites had a moral obligation to assert their rights to the soil, because "to leave the Indians in possession of the country was to leave the country a wilderness."[34] To allow land to go to waste without improvement was a grave offense in Anglo-American culture. Until Native Americans adopted American modes of civilization, Kent found it impossible to consider allowing indigenous peoples the same rights and privileges to property that whites enjoyed. He believed that Indians did not have the moral or intellectual capacity to own or convey real property, and he seemed to hold out little hope that they would ever progress beyond a state of "dependence and pupilage." Therefore, according to Kent, not only did governments have to carefully assert their rights to territory, but they also had to offer a certain measure of protection to the Indians. As long as they held fast to their traditional lifestyles, Indians had to be kept "separate, subordinate, and dependent, with a guardian care thrown around them for their protection."[35] To illustrate his points about the benefits of offering protection and peaceful land exchanges to Native Americans, Kent offered the example of New York's relationship with the Six Nations, who "placed their lands under the protection of [the New York] government from the earliest periods of the colony administration." Glossing over a rather bumpy history of Iroquois distrust of the colonists, their preference for neutrality, and their divided sympathies during the Revolution, Kent praised their loyalty to America, even in the face of war "and the artful means which were used from time to time to detach them" from American alliances. He expressed admiration for "the intrepid spirit" of those "generous barbarians."[36]

In a lengthy footnote to his ode to the Iroquois, Kent mourned the Six Nations' disintegration. He explained that, at the close of the seventeenth century, the confederacy contained as many as ten thousand warriors. But by 1747 the number was less than fifteen hundred.[37] Kent added to his description of the Iroquois population decline in his third edition, published in 1836. Because of "their paucity in numbers and insignificance (with the exception perhaps of the Senecas)," Kent claimed that the Six Nations had "ceased to exist in a distinct national capacity as tribes, exercising self-government, with a sufficient competency to protect themselves." He noted that in 1822, the state of New York asserted criminal jurisdiction over the Indians, inside and outside of the reservations.[38] In his fourth edition, published in 1840, Kent explained that in September of 1836, the United States and the "New York Indians," which Kent defined as the remains of the Six Nations, negotiated a treaty by which the Iroquois voluntarily removed to Indian Territory west of Missouri. He assured his audience that the treaty included "liberal provisions for their removal and support."[39] Even in the fourth edition, the last edition that Kent edited, he still praised the Iroquois confederacy as a great empire that had driven out or exterminated many of its rivals. But Kent's version of the confederacy's history only served as a foil for his image of the Six Nations' degraded state by the Revolution, and its continued deterioration in the early nineteenth century. With his story of the rise and fall of the Iroquois Confederation, Kent made his point that even the strongest of Native American nations eventually required the protection of the culturally superior white Americans.

IV

Even among those who looked upon them as uncivilized, First Peoples had their advocates. These champions, however, often were the same men who condemned Native Americans for their resistance to white civilization and for stubbornly refusing to abandon their wandering ways. Kent's description of Native American/white conflicts over land combined elements of the two most popular nineteenth-century images of Native Americans: Indian as cruel and inhuman beast and Indian as noble savage.[40] He created his own historical version of conflicts between American Indians and whites in which, conveniently omitting the numerous instances of Indian military victories, he asserted that Native Americans' powers and means of war had never been equal to those of whites. He characterized Native tactics in war as "ferocious and cruel," yet he pointed out that "there was still much in the Indian character, in their earlier and better state, to excite admiration, and in their sufferings, at all times, to excite sympathy."[41] Despite Kent's depiction of Native Americans as shadows of their former selves, indigenous peoples still invoked fear in many Americans, and the New York jurist tried to downplay the image of the savage Indian.

Kent defended American Indians' actions against whites, insisting that although conflicts were "never unjustly provoked by the colonial governments or people, ... they were, no doubt, stimulated on the part of the Indians, by a deep sense of injury, by a view of impending danger, by the suggestions of patriotism, and by a fierce and lofty spirit of national independence."[42] This notion that Native Americans could harbor nationalistic sentiments may have surprised many of Kent's contemporaries. Kent illustrated Indians' sense of nationhood through their ties to a larger, pan-Indian community, using examples from the distant past: the alliances among New England Natives in the Pequot War of 1637 and the pan-Indian movement attempted by Metacom in 1675. He ignored more recent examples, such as Pontiac's pan-Indian movement of 1763 or, even closer to home, the early nineteenth-century conflicts between whites and Tecumseh's alliance. There was safety in temporal distance, and perhaps more recent examples of patriotism and "fierce and lofty national independence" would have worked against his theory that in recent years the noble spirit of the Indians had degenerated into weakness and dependence. His description of their weakened state offered additional justification for taking their lands and placing Native Americans more firmly under the "pupilage" of the U.S. government.

Kent was not the only early national legal scholar to tell his audience that these noble—and very American—patriotic impulses existed among the savages of North America. In his *Sketches of the Principles of Government*, published in 1793, Nathaniel Chipman used similar language to describe Native American character, though his ideas about how Native Americans demonstrated their patriotism differed from Kent's. For Chipman, ties to place and cultural tradition demonstrated patriotism. He used plenty of fashionable rhetoric about Native Americans in his treatise, describing them as vengeful hunters who treated their women "little better than slaves."[43] But he rejected observations that First People's nomadic ways left them without territorial attachments, and he insisted that their patriotism, which he simply defined as "love of country," was apparent through their ties to the soil. He pointed out that although they occupied "but a small part" of "their country," Native Americans claimed these larger pieces of land as their own. Only extreme circumstances, such as war, famine, "or some more powerful cause," could compel them to relinquish their territory.[44] He illustrated his point with a story in which the French proposed to remove some Canadian Indians from their native soil. He quoted a chief who allegedly responded to the French, "We were born ... on this ground. Our fathers lie buried in it. Shall we say to the bones of our fathers, Arise, and come with us into a foreign land?" Was this, Chipman asked, "the language of a people ... [w]ho have no national attachments? No republic? No social state?" He related another story of Logan, a Mingo chief who, for the good of his nation, refused to wage war to avenge the murder of his entire family, a sacrifice that Chipman lauded as the ultimate act of patriotism. The Vermont legist reminded his readers that Americans "who have had frequent occasion to transact business with the American natives, both as individuals, and in their national councils, know the strength of their national attachments."[45] With his version of Native American histories, Chipman tried to find common ground between First Peoples and white Americans.

Chipman did not mean to imply, however, that American Indians possessed "civilized" traits like patriotism. Instead, he pointed out that the "love of country" was a trait that even "uncivilized" people could own. He quoted Abbe Raynal, in his history of the East and West Indies, as saying that patriotism was not a natural passion of man. Raynal used the indigenous peoples of Brazil as examples, asserting that they had "no particular attachment to their native place. The love of country, which is a ruling passion in civilized states; which, in good governments, rises to enthusiasm, and in bad ones grows habitual; *this love of our country* is but a fictitious sentiment arising from society; but unknown in a state of nature."[46] Chipman was not convinced. He stated that though Raynal wrote of indigenous Brazilians' "want of attachment to their native soil," Raynal's evidence refuted this assertion. Chipman pointed out that in the case of the Brazilians, "love of country" was equal to "love of community." According to Chipman, "an attachment to the soil collects, limits, and fixes the passion, and gives a locality to its object; but is not necessary to its existence. Take from the country the community, all its inhabitants, the object ceases." He asserted that in all peoples, an attachment to community was present. He used the "ancient barbarians of the north," ancestors of Europeans, as examples of peoples who possessed this national attachment, but he acknowledged that "their attachment to the soil was not so strong." This attachment, he explained, was "fixed, principally, by the cultivation of the earth for subsistence, which collects the interest and attention to one pot, and gives a locality to conveniences."[47] Therefore, at least in the case of the First Peoples of Brazil, patriotism did not require ties to the soil. Chipman implied that removal from the land would not eliminate a people's ties to community, because their ties were not to a particular place, but rather to one another. However, this assertion did not seem to match the argument he made for North American Indians.

Chipman's self-contradictions tell the reader much about his place and time. Around the time that he wrote his *Sketches*, Chipman's home territory, Vermont, was applying for admission to the union as a state. Their bid was not warmly received, however. Some of the same questions about Native Americans' abilities to become civilized were being raised about Vermonters, who had a reputation for being a rough and wild bunch. This personal experience could have given Chipman some measure of empathy for the Indians' situation at the hands of the U.S. government. However, shared experience did not offer him enough reason to believe that Indians were cultural equals. Even as he complimented them, Chipman designated American Indians a less-civilized people.

Chipman used the "savages of America" as examples of beings who lived in the state of nature. These peoples, he asserted, "esteem war and hunting almost the only pursuits worthy of a man," while leaving most other labor to their women, "who are little better than slaves." Because men's attention was devoted to hunting and war, Chipman characterized them as exhibiting "an excessive ferocity of manners." He explained that "their resentment is keen, and revenge their most darling gratification." Part of Indians' lack of civility, according to Chipman, stemmed from their lack of a legal or justice system. In Indian society, Chipman stated, "every man is left to judge in his own cause, and to avenge his own wrongs." However, in the next paragraph, he noted that "the injuries of an individual are resented as national," a comment that bestowed a strong sense of community on the Indians. An Anglo-American would have considered property ownership individual, and therefore trespass onto property should have been a matter between individuals, rather than a community problem. However, because Indians' lives were tied to hunting rather than agriculture, their communal property meant more to them than would individual agricultural plots. Chipman projected Anglo-American imperial ambitions onto Native Americans when he claimed that "the possession of a hunting ground is, to them, the possession of an empire." Disputes over hunting grounds were "sources of frequent wars," causing "butchering and scalping of old men, women, and children, of torturing and burning of prisoners, in cold blood, with the most shocking circumstances of cruelty." These acts of violence were public and "under what is to them, the law of nations."[48] With this example, Chipman's own evidence refuted his assertion that Indians had no law or justice system. He attributed to them the potential for great violence and cruelty, yet on the next line, he bestowed upon them a primitive sense of order brought by law.

Chipman's account of the Native American character is full of such contradictions. Even when he laid lavish compliments on them, Chipman somehow found a way to take away the virtues that he briefly bestowed. For example, the Vermonter carried on a rather curious discussion of the American Indians' talent for "hospitality," a characteristic that he believed whites had all but lost in the civilization process and that he considered "the finest trait" in Native Americans' character. But while American Indians' practice of the art of hospitality indicated "some advance in civilization," the absence of further progress in the forms of an increase in population and the establishment of inns and other places of lodging made this trait obsolete. Therefore, Indians' generous hospitality attested to their backward society. Besides, in Chipman's estimation, the "North American natives have never been equally noted for the practice of this virtue, with the ancient Germans, or the more ancient inhabitants of Greece."[49] They did not measure up to the great ancient societies in their practices of primitive forms of hospitality.

In fact, Chipman complained that the simple state of the savage was overrated. He criticized those who saw virtue in natives' simplicity, stating that those writers who looked at Indians with a "romantic eye" saw too much virtue in the uncivilized. He noted Indians' lack of concern about the future, stating that they were "too indolent to think of making an adequate provision against the inclemency of the season, or, indeed, against any future want." Chipman considered this sort of simple life a double-edged sword. While Indians did not have as many vices as "civilized" men, they also possessed "fewer virtues than more civilized nations." He described the Indians as possessing "little curiousity, and no conception of any knowledge which can be of use, beyond that of forming the bow, or some instrument of the chace."[50] Fellow New Englander James Sullivan agreed with Chipman. He laid the blame for Native Americans' decline on their refusal to pursue Western modes of learning and culture. He accused Indians of leading a lifestyle that "excluded all ideas of civilization, and shut up the human mind from cultivation; rejected the arts and sciences, and quite subverted the embellishment and prevented the extension of the rational faculties of man." In a surprising departure from prevailing theories of race, Sullivan elevated Africans' propensity to cultivation over that of Native Americans. He asserted that Africans had "frequently been induced to attend to letters, painting, and some of the finer arts." He also noted their "natural turn to music," but Native Americans, on the other hand, had "no organs suited to a taste for literature, poetry, or music."[51] Ironically, Europeans had leveled similar criticisms about a lack of indigenous culture on the new American nation. Yet, Sullivan suggested that if Native Americans were willing to improve themselves, white Americans would be willing to help.

Sullivan emphasized whites' paternal efforts to help Indians to progress toward civilization, but he also warned that the Native Americans' disappearance might be inevitable. It was possible that Indians were destined not to listen to whites' advice. "Divine Providence" dictated that the New World should be inhabited and used by God's "rational offspring." After "expensive attempts" to teach Indians agriculture, Christianity, and other white ways failed, Sullivan argued that they might not be destined to be a part of the civilized world.[52] The idea that Native Americans' disappearance was an inevitable result of their own intransigence relieved white Americans of any responsibility for the First Peoples' fate.

V

Hugh Henry Brackenridge was not willing to wait on divine providence to rid the United States of Native Americans. His opinions about Indians and their rights to territory were, perhaps, products of his experiences in the backcountry, although he seemed to have been inclined toward a hatred of Native Americans even before he relocated to the frontier hamlet of Pittsburgh. Brackenridge was among the more colorful figures in early American legal history. He was a frontier lawyer and judge, a poet and a literary figure. Some legists questioned Brackenridge's credibility as an expert on the law, but he made a valuable contribution to early American legal literature with his *Law Miscellanies*. Brackenridge's encounters with Indians in western Pennsylvania shaped his attitudes toward Native American wars, treaty negotiations, and removal. While many of his contemporaries lived far from Native American strongholds, Brackenridge settled at the epicenter of contentions between whites and American Indians. Therefore, the frontier legist brought a very different perspective to the table in his discussions about the foundation of title to land. Though his fundamental ideas about treaty negotiations and Native American rights to land were the same regardless of his audience, his rhetoric underwent transformations depending on whether he was building an argument for one of his legal or political treatises, or whether he was writing for a more general audience. Always, his mission was to persuade his audience that Indians had no natural right to the land, and that they could be—and ought to be—relocated or exterminated to make way for the more "civilized" whites.

Brackenridge was practiced in appealing to a myriad of audiences. While a student at Princeton, he composed and read an epic poem, "The Rising Glory of America," at commencement in 1771. From the Revolution onward, he authored patriotic tragedies and political pamphlets. During the Revolution, he founded and edited the *United States Magazine* in Philadelphia. After moving to Pennsylvania's frontier, he founded the *Pittsburgh Gazette*. In 1783, Brackenridge edited and published an Indian captivity narrative entitled *Narratives of a Late Expedition against the Indians with an Account of the Barbarous Execution of Col. Crawford; and the Wonderful Escape of Dr. Knight and John Slover from Captivity, in 1782.*[53] This narrative, Brackenridge hoped, would convince lawmakers to provide more protection for frontier dwellers against the "savage" Indian. He embellished the description of Colonel Crawford's ordeal and execution, providing grisly details of the hours-long torture in order to illustrate even more graphically the Indians' propensity toward cruelty. The story appealed to popular interest in captivity narratives and certainly gained popular support for the eviction or elimination of Native Americans on the Pennsylvania frontier. In the 1790s and early 1800s, Brackenridge published a four-volume comic narrative in the style of Don Quixote, entitled *Modern Chivalry*. And in an effort to provide American lawyers with an "American Blackstone," Brackenridge published *Law Miscellanies* in 1814. Always mindful of his genre and audience, Brackenridge modified his rhetoric for maximum effectiveness.

The rhetoric and tone that Brackenridge used in his *Law Miscellanies* differed from those in "Thoughts on the Present Indian War," and these variations reveal his self-consciousness when it came to audience. His legal treatise called for a more reasoned approach, therefore Brackenridge toned down his descriptions of Indians and concentrated on explaining the theories of discovery and occupancy that justified removal. But, instead of relying on legal precedent to support his points, he resorted to biblical stories and Lockean ideas about labor and property. He first addressed the law of nature and what he considered man's natural right to dominate the earth. Because man cultivated the earth, Brackenridge explained, man's labor gave him the right to possess land and to dominate the earth and "brute animals." He considered "savages who do not cultivate the soil, or sustain themselves to much extent" through agricultural means the same as "the beasts." Like other contemporary legal scholars, he described rights to the soil as founded on discovery, although that right was "limited in its extent, by the right of the natives," as well as the rights of other nations that may have discovered certain lands first. To counter the argument that the rights of Natives excluded others because the right to soil should be vested in its first occupant, he employed an argument around agricultural labor that limited Native American claims. Brackenridge invoked the biblical charge to "be fruitful and multiply and replenish the earth, and subdue it." He noted the crucial differences between natural law, or God's law, and civil policy by pointing out that God's charge did not convey the right of primogeniture, nor any other right by which one man could hold a larger portion of the soil than his neighbor. Those rights, he explained, were not part of God's law, but rather they were civil law, not arising from a state of nature, but rather from a state of society.[54] In other words, he turned Blackstone's arguments about the positive laws of inheritance to his advantage as he asserted whites' right to territory.

Brackenridge applied his definition of the law of nature and equal distribution of property to Indians, asking whether the Indians, who were "inferior in number to perhaps one twentieth of the inhabitants of Europe," should "possess ten times the territory." Their defenders would argue that their "manner of life" made more territory necessary because they lived by hunting, but he asked whether the laws of nature ought to allow every man to live as he pleased, rather than living in a way that would help the largest number of people. He resurrected the biblical story of Adam's "lapse" and banishment from Eden, asserting that "the Lord God sent him forth from the garden of Eden, to till the ground." Therefore, if God's order was to till the ground, then the Indians were not obeying God. Brackenridge asserted that the law of nature, even where God's law was not yet known, dictated that all men should have equal access to land so that all could "pursue that manner of life which is most consistent with the general population of the earth, and the increase of happiness to mankind." Moreover, Brackenridge argued, a life of hunting retarded the progress of the race. When men lived by hunting rather than agriculture and thus were "necessarily scattered" over thinly settled territory, "the powers of genius are inactive, the arts and sciences remain unknown, and man continues to be an animal differing in nothing but in shape from the beasts of prey that roam upon the mountain."[55] They were, in other words, not leading a "human" life if they were not encouraging progress through their chosen lifestyle. Indians, he insisted, did not have a solid claim to a place they had never cultivated. The most they could claim was the place "where their wigwams have been planted, and to so much of the soil around them as may be necessary to produce grain to support them" and their families. If they wanted to move away, however, Brackenridge was perfectly willing to allow them "a right to occupy a different country," where they might be able to continue living as hunters.[56] In this way, two incompatible peoples could continue to live peacefully—and separately.

His comments in the *Gazette* emphasized racial characteristics, but in *Law Miscellanies* Brackenridge was careful to present an argument that was based on what was best for the community. Brackenridge stated that all nations should be judged by the same standards for territorial claims as he set out for the Indians. No nation or nations, he insisted, should "possess a more extensive tract of country, than is necessary for their particular subsistence." Therefore, a nation with more people, "whose numbers overcharge the soil, have a right to demand territory from a nation in possession of a soil equally fertile, and less abounding with inhabitants." Even the right of discovery, according to Brackenridge, did not give any nation a right to take any more territory "than is necessary for subsistence; and not indeed any portion of it, unless the visitant remains to occupy and dwell upon it."[57] This comment applied to other territorial rivals in addition to Indians. He had in mind specific European targets as well, namely the French and Spanish, who had laid claim to parts of North America, yet settled very few of their citizens on the territory that they claimed. European rivals for empire in North America still existed, and Brackenridge was well aware that his arguments worked equally as well against the French, Spanish, and even the English, as they did against the Indians.

Brackenridge used the history of overlapping, conflicting and usurping claims among the European nations as evidence that the mere right of discovery did not give any nation exclusive control over the vast tracts of land in the New World. He accused the Swedes and Dutch of ignoring Britain's claim in North America through explorer Sebastian Cabot's discovery. But Brackenridge actually sanctioned this kind of disregard, because "no expence, enterprize, or labour of a nation, or of any individual, can give a right which in its operation would defeat the end in view by the Creator, which was, that the earth be fully stocked with inhabitants." Therefore, the claims of the first discoverers should have been only to as much of the soil as their settlers were able to inhabit and cultivate. But he admitted that because the nations and their explorers bore the expense and effort of exploration and discovery, they were entitled to reap the profits of that discovery, and they should be given time and opportunity to encourage their countrymen to emigrate. In this way, the earth would "become peopled," according to "the will of the Creator."[58] Even the natural law, according to Brackenridge, did not favor Native Americans having more land than they could cultivate.

Brackenridge did not explicitly advocate the extermination or wholesale removal of the Indians in his *Law Miscellanies*. Instead, he took a milder stance that called for containment of Native Americans on only as much land as they could cultivate, while redistributing their vast hunting grounds so that whites could "subdue and cultivate the earth." Even as he deemed North America to be "a vacant country and liable to become the property of those who should take the trouble to possess it," he was careful to point out that he was not advocating war against the Indians, nor was he pushing for their extermination. However, he encouraged a calculated "encroachment on the territory claimed by them, until they are reduced to smaller bounds, and under the necessity of changing their unpolished and ferocious state of life, for fixed habitations and the arts of agriculture." Brackenridge encouraged purchase of Native American lands, "if it may be done conveniently." He reasoned that it was more humane not to take property by force, because that tactic could involve "the shedding of the blood of those, who though sunk beneath the dignity of human nature, yet bear the name and are seen in the shape of men."[59] When writing for an audience of lawyers, Brackenridge carefully asserted that even those who barely qualified as human beings should only be treated with violence as a last resort.

When writing for a broader audience, Brackenridge cast the same argument in more emotional language. He used the legal lingo of "occupancy" and "discovery" in his popular publications, but with more dramatic illustrations and examples. In an afterword to his edition of the *Narratives of a Late Expedition against the Indians,* Brackenridge elaborated on an essay that he wrote for the *United States Magazine* in 1779, in which he argued that Indians had no right to the soil. Using vivid imagery to illustrate the defense of Indian rights to the soil on occupancy, he wrote: "A wild Indian with his skin painted red, and a feather through his nose, has set his foot on the broad continent of North and South America" and claimed it as his own, bidding all other comers "take his foot off the continent, for he being first upon it, had occupied the whole, to kill buffaloes, and tall elks with long horns." Brackenridge admitted that some believed the claim to be just.[60] In his *Gazette Publications*, Brackenridge spared the reader his savage image of the claimant, but he used the same image of the Indian "having his foot first on the continent." He considered the claim unreasonable because of the uncertainty over the number of claimants there must be to uphold such a right. Equally uncertain was how much territory they could claim. He insisted on a fixed principle on which the right to soil depended. Under the law of nature, he argued, a person only had right to enough land as would provide subsistence. Moreover, the amount of land should be measured by agriculture, rather than by "pasturage and hunting." If a society used that criteria, then more people could subsist off the land.[61] Because Native Americans had not followed

God's charge to till the ground, they had not made proper use of the soil, and therefore, "not having made a better use of it for many hundred years," he concluded that "they have forfeited all pretence to claim, and ought to be driven from it."[62]

The frontier legist reminded his readers that, according to the Bible, all of the earth was given to man, and all descendants of Adam should have an equal share. To those who argued that, in a state of society, some men could hold more land than others and, therefore, Indians had a right to own large tracts of land, Brackenridge responded that these unequal holdings were because of civil law, the laws to which citizens of a society had consented. Men living under a state of society were protected by laws that secured property in that unequal manner. However, while wealthy men or large families might lay a civil claim to more space on which to live or garden, "an agile, nimble runner, like an Indian," should not expect more land than his neighbors "because he has traversed a greater space."[63] In other words, exceptional physical strength should not trump intellectual and moral superiority.

Brackenridge was not among those white Americans who believed that Indians could eventually be civilized and assimilated into white society. He related examples of instances when "several of these creatures" were taken from their homes and placed in American schools to learn trades and "civilization." He claimed that he did not know of "one who has even by these means been rendered a useful member of society: they retain the temper of their race." He held up John Montour, son of mixed-blood cultural intermediary Andrew Montour, as an example of the uncivilizable Indian who was educated "at one of the northern seminaries, [was] taught Greek and Latin, and in [the Revolution] dignified with a commission of captain. No greater savage ever existed." Brackenridge accused Montour of killing many of his own people and being forced to flee his people's vengeance because of his actions. This breach of honor, according to Brackenridge, was unforgivable. To punctuate his description of Montour, he told his audience that he saw "this man with the bloody scalp of an Indian in his hand, which he had just taken off, having first tomahawked the creature, though submitting and praying for his life." Brackenridge was convinced "that for a keg of whiskey you might induce any Indian to murder his wife, child, or best friend."[64] Persons of this character, Brackenridge insisted, were not to be defended, nor should their rights be protected.

Brackenridge leveled harsh criticism at those whites who defended Native American rights to territory. In his "Thoughts on the Present Indian War," published in the *Pittsburgh Gazette*, Brackenridge responded to congressional debates over Native American rights to territory. He characterized defenders of Native American territorial rights as "philosophers," an occupation that did not garner much respect on the frontier, where men valued action more than reflection. He accused those who were "soft" on the Indian territorial question of being ignorant of the situation. He compared defenders of Native American character and rights to "young women who have read romances, and have as improper an idea of the Indian character in the one case, as the female mind has of real life in the other." In other words, Brackenridge characterized his opponents in this debate as soft, effeminate, of little resolution, misinformed, and romantic. These traits simply did not sit well with the frontier-dwelling readers of the *Gazette*. Using a popularized version of the anti-natural rights argument, Brackenridge accused defenders of Indian territorial rights of trying to "affect the public mind by holding up *the original right* of these aborigines to the soil." He described their defense as "the claim of the children: it is mine, for I first saw it." He then paraphrased Vattel's ideas about natural right to the soil by asserting that the earth was given to man in common, and each man should only use as much as he needed, so that all may have their share. He wrote that the land should be used in a way that would sustain the greatest number of people and provide "the greatest sum of happiness; that is, the cultivation of the soil." Any right not housed in "agricultural occupancy," according to Brackenridge, was not valid.[65] Improvement of land brought progress, which, for Brackenridge, represented a greater good.

Brackenridge derided the ideas of those who believed in the virtues of "the unimproved state." The misguided "philosopher," according to the frontier jurist, saw "green fields and meadows in the customs and virtues of the savages." He assured his audience that only experience could correct this image. Brackenridge was a firm believer that "all that is good and great in a man, results from education; an uncivilized Indian is but a little way removed from a beast who, when incensed, can only tear and devour, but the savage applies the ingenuity of man to torture and inflict anguish." He used as an example the story of a French botanist and "philosopher" who claimed "the man of nature" as his "darling favourite." Unarmed and with only two other men, the botanist undertook an expedition on the Ohio River, confident that any Indians he encountered "could wish him no harm." But while on his expedition, he met a party of Indians who, he thought, approached to "pay their respects to him; but the first circumstance of ceremony when they came on board, was to impress the tomahack [*sic*] and take off the scalp of the philosopher."[66] According to Brackenridge, whites held no moral obligation to protect those who did not feel a reciprocal obligation of protection.

Brackenridge saw no reason to treat with Native Americans, because, from his perspective, they would only break the treaty when it was in their interest. He laid the blame for tensions between Anglo-Americans and Native Americans squarely on Indians' failure to honor treaties. In his "Thoughts on the Present Indian War," Brackenridge provided colonial-era examples of treaties that Indians broke with the British in order to ally with the French in Canada. Because it was not in the Indians' interest to have Britain and France at peace, they instigated war at the expense of treaties. The United States was, Brackenridge asserted, still in the same situation, now that Canada was a British possession. Native Americans in Canada had already shown that they would not honor treaty terms; therefore, he argued, the U.S. government should not negotiate with them at all.[67] He even blamed the Indians for the U.S. government's need to sell, rather than give away, land in the Old Northwest to white settlers, because "they have been at expence in combating the false claim of the savages, and ought to be paid for it."[68] Their claims to territory not only cost lives, Brackenridge complained, but such claims also cost the money of settlers who were willing to populate the western lands. The roadblocks that Indians threw in the way of America's progress toward empire enraged the Pennsylvania jurist.

Brackenridge refused to acknowledge that whites may have instigated some conflicts with Indians. He claimed that he knew of only three instances in which an Indian had been hurt by a white since the Revolution, yet Native Americans became more dangerous and less trustworthy by the day. His stories about Indian chiefs "driven out of a kitchen by a maid with a broomstick, lest [they] should steal a tin cup or a table spoon" supported his claim that Indians' dishonesty extended to their word. They respected no treaty.[69] The only recourses, Brackenridge insisted, were "war and reduction," doing away with the government's system of agents and interpreters and making the Native Americans "stay in their woods and negotiate an equal trade" for their land. Better relations could be achieved only when "the line of savages that are at present hostile, is removed," because he believed that other Indian nations further west were more open to negotiation with the United States for trade and territory.[70] In a poem published in the *Pittsburgh Gazette*, Brackenridge pleaded with government officials, especially secretary of war "General [Henry] Knox" to

> stick to war; at least,
> until they're properly repress'd
> And if they will treat, why then treat
> But give them neither strouds nor meat
> But leave to live as they do us,
> Nor dare again to be our foes.[71]

The captivity narratives that Brackenridge edited provided even more graphic evidence for his assertions that Native Americans could not be trusted. Indians may have "the shapes of men and may be of the human species," he wrote, "but certainly in their present state they approach nearer the character of devils: take an Indian; is there any faith in him? ... Can you trust his word or confide in his promise?" Brackenridge further exploited the emotion of the narratives by asking his reader, fresh from the gory tale of Colonel Crawford's agony and death, that when an Indian "makes war upon you, when he takes you prisoner and has you in his power[,] will he spare you?" According to Brackenridge, the merciless Indian "departs from the law of nature, by which ... it is unjustifiable to take away the life of him who submits; the conqueror in doing otherwise becomes a murderer, who ought to be put to death." In Brackenridge's eyes, the Indians violated the law of nature; therefore, there should be no debate over their right to land. According to Brackenridge, "The tortures which they exercise on the bodies of their prisoners" justified their extermination.[72] Because of the duplicitous character of the Indians, he concluded that the United States' "best defense is *offence*. Instead of warding off blows, give one." Instead of "watching beasts of prey," he suggested that American troops should "penetrate the forests where they haunt, and extirpat[e] the race."[73] The frontier judge proposed to

> dispossess them of the goodly lands, springs and rivers to the westward, which they have so long made a scene of horror by their practices. ... Instead of forming treaties, and sending any other talk to them, and prophaning ourselves by calling them brothers, I would simply let them know that they are no longer to show themselves below the heads of the great rivers that fall from the westward into the Ohio and Mississippi waters.

Brackenridge wished for them to be driven further north and west into the cold, "where darkness reigns six months in the year," where "their practices shall be obscured, and the tribes gradually abolished."[74]

The language of violence against American Indians did not appear in Brackenridge's *Law Miscellanies.* He reserved such unabashedly hateful prose for popular audiences. However, even in his legal treatise, Brackenridge's argument departed from those of many of his colleagues. His reliance on biblical history and active advocacy of dispossession contrasted with Kent's explorations of legal precedent and Tucker's dismissal of the Indians as already gone. While Brackenridge advocated dispossession and extermination in his popular publications, his contemporaries took a more passive approach, generally answering the fate of the Indians with embarrassed efforts to erase them from American histories—or, at least, from the present and future of early national America.

VI

As legal scholars built their opposing images of Native Americans, James Kent simultaneously crafted a dual image of whites. Kent developed his thinking on this subject more fully, and over a longer span of years, than any other legal scholar. In his first edition, Kent depicted the government's treatment of Native Americans as benign and paternal while acknowledging a few individuals' cruelty toward the Indians. He insisted that whites had acquired Indian lands with "as little violence and aggression ... as were compatible with the fact of the entry of a race of civilized men into the territory of savages." He echoed Vattel's and DuPonceau's words of praise for men like William Penn, who purchased land from the "Indian proprietors." He acknowledged, however, that not all lands had been acquired peacefully, and he blamed the wars on "the fact of the presence and location of white people" and the Indians' realization "that the destruction of their race must be the consequence of the settlements of the English colonists, and their extension over the country."[75] The New York jurist chose language that characterized as passively as possible whites' contributions to Native Americans' eviction. For Kent, it was whites' "presence and location," not their aggressive migrations into Indian territories, that provoked Native Americans to violence.

Again, Kent emphasized U.S. government officials' good intentions when he described their efforts to protect Indians "from wars with each other, from their own propensity to intemperance, from the frauds and injustice of the whites." These philanthropic and paternal efforts, Kent claimed, reflected "the luster" of America's "national character."[76] Kent did, however, differentiate between the American government's "uniformly just and benevolent" intent with regard to First Peoples and the practice of certain individuals whose negotiations with the American Indians were "attended with much abuse … and with very injurious effects upon the moral and civil condition of the Indian tribes."[77]

Kent's ideas about the place of indigenous peoples in America followed the same lines of logic as one of his more prominent contemporaries. In the first edition of his American *Commentaries*, he echoed Chief Justice John Marshall's opinion that the discovery doctrine had "necessarily impaired" Native Americans' rights to territory, and it privileged European claims to land over those of the Indians.[78] However, when Marshall retreated from his position on the discovery doctrine, Kent followed suit. The case *The Cherokee Nation v. The State of Georgia* (1831) appeared in Kent's second edition, with the majority opinion that the Cherokee nation was not a foreign state as defined by use of the term in the Constitution. Instead, the Cherokees "were *a state*, or distinct political society, capable of managing its own affairs, and governing itself." The difference, then, was in their "peculiar" relation to the United States, in that they were "domestic dependent nations, and their relation to us resembled that of a ward and guardian; and they had an unquestionable right to the lands they occupied, until that right should be extinguished by a voluntary cession to our government."[79] He went on to discuss *Worcester v. The State of Georgia* (1832), in which Georgia claimed sovereignty over the Cherokee nation and proclaimed that the Cherokee government could not be sovereign within the boundaries of an established state. Writing for the majority, Chief Justice Marshall declared that the right of discovery gave the discovering nation exclusive right to purchase, but that nation had to procure the consent of the Indian possessor to sell. The Court upheld the Cherokee nation's status as a "distinct community, occupying its own territory … in which the laws of Georgia cannot rightfully have any force."[80] Kent's reaction to *Worcester* was fresh in the second edition of the *Commentaries,* which also came off the press in 1832. He pointed out that the Supreme Court's decision did not represent "the promulgation of any new doctrine." The principles of discovery and sovereignty outlined in the decision had been the custom for generations. Without explicitly pointing out the reversal, Kent implied that Marshall had departed from custom in his *Johnson* opinion, and that *Worcester* had restored the common-law understanding of Native Americans' legal relationship to their ancestral lands.[81] Unfortunately, subsequent court decisions ignored Marshall's revision of the discovery doctrine's meaning and continued to use Marshall's *Johnson v. M'Intosh* definition.

Kent expanded his own definition of the nature of Native Americans' dependence on the U.S. government by adding some local descriptions of how American Indians' dependent status affected their relationships with the states and the federal government. Kent referred to his own opinion in *Goodell v. Jackson* and an 1810 case in Tennessee, *Jackson v. Wood,* which "explicitly recognized the historical fact" that Indians were governed by their own laws, "under their own chiefs, and competent to act in a national character, and exercise self-government ... owing no allegiance to the municipal laws of the whites." Indian nations had, as Kent pointed out with his example of the Iroquois, "placed themselves under the protection of the whites, and they were cherished as dependent allies, but subject to such restraints and qualified control in their national capacity, as were considered by the whites to be indispensable to their own safety."[82] Kent's descriptions of Indians' dependent status emphasized the U.S. government's moral obligation to protect Native Americans from predatory whites as well as from one another. Moreover, Kent implied that the federal government had fulfilled its obligation, at least up until President Andrew Jackson took office.

Kent still emphasized Indians' dependent status in editions of his *Commentaries* published during and after efforts to remove Indian nations from their ancestral lands in Georgia, Tennessee, and Alabama. In the third edition published in 1836, the *Worcester v. Georgia* decision and state legislation hedging the legal rights of Native Americans, particularly the Cherokee, became the centerpiece of his chapter on the foundation of title to land. Emboldened by the Georgia court's successful refusal to abide by the Supreme Court's *Worcester* decision, the Alabama and Tennessee legislatures quickly extended civil and criminal jurisdiction over all of the Indian territories within their limits. However, Kent defended these actions by insisting that the extension of their laws over Indian territory "was made with mild and reasonable qualifications, in respect to the Cherokees, compared with similar acts in some other states." The laws prohibited confiscation of Native American property and encroachment on Indian lands by whites. Kent compared Alabama and Tennessee's laws to a New York law of 1822, which asserted jurisdiction over any crimes committed in the Indian territories within the boundaries of that state. He also claimed that the Tennessee act was necessary, given the reduced numbers of Cherokee in that state "and the too great imbecility of their organization and authority to preserve order, and protect themselves from atrocious crimes."[83] Again, Kent justified laws that hedged Native Americans' rights by invoking whites' moral obligation to protect inferior beings. Unfortunately, white authorities rarely enforced the provisions prohibiting white encroachment on Indian lands.

Beginning with his second edition, Kent paid more attention to colonial and state legislation regarding diplomatic exchanges between Europeans and Native Americans. He seemed to have two objectives for these history lessons. First, he supported the popular argument that most Europeans tried to maintain peaceful relations with the Indians and tried to use peaceful means to conduct land transactions with them. With these examples he also implied Native American sovereignty. European negotiations of land sales with Native Americans helped to prove sovereignty of Indian nations. He argued that from the beginning of English, French, and Spanish settlement, most European nations tried to maintain peaceful relations and to use peaceful means to conduct land transactions with the Native Americans. They established regulations that restricted dealings with First Peoples to transactions between authorized members of tribes and the colonial governments. Individuals could not contract with Indians for land.[84] He also added a footnote with examples of a North Carolina law of 1783 and an 1830 ruling of the Tennessee Supreme Court that upheld Native American national sovereignty and affirmed that indigenous people's lands were held under the "right of exclusive occupancy and enjoyment." He noted an 1813 New York law authorizing the governor to pay the Oneida Nation for lands ceded to the state under a treaty.[85] With these examples, Kent tried to help Marshall to set the record straight on America's obligation to uphold Indian sovereignty and to protect Indians' rights to their territory.

Kent edited four editions of his *Commentaries,* and with each iteration the footnote explaining the fate of America's remaining Indian nations lengthened. As treaties and coercion pushed the Native Americans further westward, Kent added to his commentary on the fate of the Indians who remained under the "pupilage" of the United States. He alternated between defending and condemning the government's actions, although he continued to assert that, while government officials in general tried to treat Indians fairly and equitably, certain individuals were not so inclined. Unfortunately, starting in 1828, one of the individuals was the nation's president, Andrew Jackson.

As part of his defense of the U.S. government, Kent pointed out the money and effort that the government put forth to help the nations with removal and rebuilding. He listed over forty Indian nations that benefited from a congressional act of March 3, 1835, that granted $1,830,000 in appropriations to those tribes. He continued to defend "the intentions of the government of the United States" as "uniformly just and benevolent"—until 1829, when President Jackson's administration "essentially changed" the policy and course of conduct toward the Indians. Kent claimed that Jackson's administration withdrew protections afforded Indians under treaties and legislation negotiated in previous administrations. The Cherokees in particular, Kent stated, were "left in a defenceless state, to the penal laws of the state of Georgia." Kent quoted from Jackson's 1832 messages to Congress regarding his continued insistence that the "entire and speedy migration" of Indians westward must continue, and his threat that any Indians that did not remove from the settled portions of the nation would be left with "such privileges and disabilities as the respective states within whose jurisdiction they be may prescribe."[86]

The 1840 edition gave his audience the end of the Cherokees' struggle to maintain their territory in the east. Kent wrote that since his previous edition in 1838, "those Indians have been expelled, by military force, from the southern states, and transported across the Mississippi." He described President Martin Van Buren's "elaborate vindication" of the government's actions, in which Van Buren held that "a mixed occupancy of the same territory by the white and red man, was incompatible with the safety and happiness of either, and that their removal was dictated by necessity." Kent also related Van Buren's assurance that the "upwards of one hundred and sixteen millions of acres of land," the removal to which the federal government had paid "upwards of seventy-two millions of dollars to and on behalf of the Indians, in permanent annuities, lands, reservations, and the necessary expense of removal and settlement of them," was now "guarantied" to the Indians as their own, for their "exclusive and peaceful possession."[87] Kent used the language of law, not the language of emotion, to describe the Indians' fate at the hands of American settlers and their polities. But he appeared to be deeply saddened by the First Peoples' situation.

In his lecture "Of the Foundation of Title to Land," Kent admitted that, all too frequently, whites only dwelled on "the darkest traits in [Indians'] character." Because Native Americans were, according to Kent, "ignorant of letters" and had no historians of their own, they had no one to "transmit to posterity the specimens of their genius, to portray their feelings, to record their grievances, to vindicate their character, or to perpetuate the memory of their daring achievements."[88] Kent's sympathetic, ethnocentric remarks about the shortcomings of Native American culture illustrated the kind of "help" that Indians could expect from whites who were sympathetic to their cause. Kent and a few other policy makers and legal scholars felt obligated to defend Native American character with descriptions and histories that were ambivalent mixes of compliments and affronts. They were motivated by the obligation to justify their states' and nation's policies toward expansion, land possession, and dispossession, issues in which Indians figured prominently.

With his histories of a once-noble culture of "generous barbarians," Kent managed to balance his own patriotic impulse to justify the U.S. appropriation of Native American territory with his perceived obligation to protect the only thing that he believed many Indians had left—their noble and honorable pasts. Kent did not, however, harbor any optimism for the Indians' fate. He carefully situated his admiration of the Native American character in his colonial history lessons and reserved his sympathetic rendering of their "poverty and misery" for more recent times. Their interaction with whites, Kent observed, seemed to "have had an immoral influence upon Indian manners and habits, and to have destroyed all that was noble and elevated in the Indian character." While Kent condemned the frontiersmen for their "fierce and lawless manners," he could not lose sight of America's expansionist vision. The new waves of white settlers, Kent insisted, "must have" these Indian territories.[89] Kent predicted that America's Indians were "destined, at no very distant period of time, to disappear with those vast forests which once covered the country," because they simply seemed unable—or unwilling—to accept the Anglo-American version of "civilization."[90] This tone of inevitability, combined with enthusiasm for territorial expansion, helped give the next generation of legal practitioners the intellectual tools to participate in, and justify, imperial expansion.

Notes

1. Grimké, *State of South Carolina. At the Courts of General Sessions ... November, 1783*, 2.
2. For more on land and the new nation, see Abernethy, *Western Lands and the American Revolution*; Berkhofer, *The White Man's Indian*; and Sakolski, *The Great American Land Bubble*.
3. Berkhofer, *The White Man's Indian*, 44–49; Horsman, *Race and Manifest Destiny*, 104–8; Sheehan, *Seeds of Extinction*, 89–116.
4. Sakolski, *The Great American Land Bubble*, 32–46. For interpretations of changing ideas about property in the early national period, see Alexander, *Commodity and Property*; and Horwitz, *The Transformation of American Law*, 31–62.
5. For more on early national political and legal leaders' investments in land, see Grimké, *The Petition and Memorial of the Subscriber*; Royster, *The Fabulous History of the Great Dismal Swamp Company*; and Sakolski, *The Great American Land Bubble*, 2–12, 20.
6. For more on early speculation, see Abernethy, *Western Lands and the American Revolution*; and Sakolski, *The Great American Land Bubble*.
7. Sakolski, *The Great American Land Bubble*, 124–41.
8. St. George Tucker, *Blackstone's Commentaries*, 3:A69–70.
9. Ibid., 3:A70–71 (Blackstone's italics).
10. Kent, *Commentaries on American Law*, 3:319n.
11. Lerner, *The Thinking Revolutionary*, 142.
12. Some of the more prominent works on the connections between early modern theories of race and progress and American attitudes toward Native Americans are Horsman, *Race and Manifest Destiny*; Pearce, *The Savages of America*; and Sheehan, *Seeds of Extinction*.

13. Blackstone, *Commentaries on the Laws of England*, 2:32–34. For an innovative look at cultural similarities between whites and Native Americans, see Shoemaker, *A Strange Likeness*, especially 2–31.

14. Blackstone, *Commentaries on the Laws of England*, 1:106; Berkhofer, *The White Man's Indian*, 122.

15. For colonial and Revolutionary-era debates over the question of whether America was a conquered territory, see Black, "The Constitution of Empire," 1199–1200; Greene, *Peripheries and Center*, 24–28; and Reid, *In Defiance of the Law*, 79–80.

16. "Of Legislative Authority," in *The Works of James Wilson*, 2:739–40.

17. St. George Tucker, *Blackstone's Commentaries*, 1:A382. For Adams's arguments, see Adams and Leonard, *The American Colonial Crisis*; and Adams, *Works*, 4:126.

18. St. George Tucker, *Blackstone's Commentaries*, 2:A4.

19. Ibid., 2:66.

20. DuPonceau, *A Discourse on the Early History of Pennsylvania*, 21, 24.

21. Ibid., 24–25.

22. Ibid., 26.

23. Vattel, *Droit des gens*, bk. 3, chap. 2, pp. 37–38. For information on Americans' use of these rights with regard to possession of territory, see Green and Dickason, *The Law of Nations*; Horsman, *Race and Manifest Destiny*; Jones, *License for Empire*; Pearce, *The Savages of America*; and Sheehan, *Seeds of Extinction*.

24. Brackenridge, *Law Miscellanies*, 122.

25. *Goodell v. Jackson*, 20 Johnson's Reports [N.Y.] 693 (1823).

26. For a detailed discussion of Kent's blending of proprietarian and commercial purposes of property, see Alexander, *Commodity and Property*, 127–57.

27. Kent, *Commentaries on American Law*, 3:310.

28. Ibid., 3:309; see also White, "Symposium."

29. *Johnson v. M'Intosh*, 21 U.S. 543, 550–51 (1823); Kent, *Commentaries on American Law*, 3:309. The most detailed interpretations of *Johnson v. M'Intosh* are Robertson, *Conquest by Law*; and Williams, *The American Indian in Western Legal Thought*.

30. Kent, *Commentaries on American Law*, 3:309.

31. St. George Tucker, *Blackstone's Commentaries*, 2:A5.

32. Kent, *Commentaries on American Law*, 3:309.

33. Ibid., 3:310.

34. Kent lifted this passage verbatim from Chief Justice John Marshall's opinion in *Johnson v. M'Intosh*, 21 U.S. 590 (1823).

35. Kent, *Commentaries on American Law*, 3:309.

36. Ibid., 3:317.

37. Ibid., 3:317n. Kent does not cite his source for numbers of warriors.

38. Ibid., 3d ed., 3:394n.

39. Ibid., 4th ed., 3:395n.

40. Horsman, *Race and Manifest Destiny*, 103; Sheehan, *Seeds of Extinction*, 89–116.

41. Kent, *Commentaries on American Law*, 3:315.

42. Ibid., 3:315.

43. Chipman, *Sketches of the Principles of Government*, 23.

44. Ibid., 59.

45. Ibid., 62.

46. Raynal, *A Philosophical and Political History of the Settlements and Trade of the Europeans in the East and West Indies* (1776), as quoted in Chipman, *Sketches of the Principles of Government*, 56 (italics in Chipman).

47. Chipman, *Sketches of the Principles of Government*, 56, 58–59.

48. Ibid., 24.

49. Ibid., 25–26.

50. Ibid., 26.

51. Sullivan, *History of Land Titles in Massachusetts*, 29–30.

52. Ibid., 29–30.

53. Brackenridge, *Narratives of a Late Expedition against the Indians*.

54. Brackenridge, *Law Miscellanies*, 122–23.

55. Ibid., 123.

56. Ibid., 124.

57. Ibid., 125–26.

58. Ibid., 126.

59. Ibid., 125.

60. Brackenridge, *Narratives of a Late Expedition against the Indians*, 32.

61. Brackenridge, *Gazette Publications*, 102–3.

62. Brackenridge, *Narratives of a Late Expedition against the Indians*, 35.

63. Ibid., 33–34.

64. Ibid., 37–38.

65. Brackenridge, "Thoughts on the Present Indian War," 94.

66. Brackenridge, *Gazette Publications*, 99–100.

67. Ibid., 95.

68. Ibid., 103.

69. Ibid., 99–100.

70. Ibid., 101.

71.   Ibid., 106. Knox opposed removal of Native Americans; instead, he advocated a strategy that combined "civilization" with assimilation.

72.   Brackenridge, *Narratives of a Late Expedition against the Indians*, 26.

73.   Brackenridge, *Gazette Publications*, 98.

74.   Brackenridge, *Narratives of a Late Expedition against the Indians*, 38.

75.   Kent, *Commentaries on American Law*, 3:318.

76.   Ibid., 3:318.

77.   Ibid., 3:318n.

78.   *Johnson v. M'Intosh*, 21 U.S. 543, 550–51 (1823); Kent, *Commentaries on American Law*, 3:309.

79.   Kent, *Commentaries on American Law*, 2nd ed., 3:382; *The Cherokee Nation v. The State of Georgia*, 30 U.S. 1 (1831). For a discussion of Chief Justice John Marshall's reconsideration of the discovery doctrine, see Robertson, *Conquest by Law*, 117–44.

80.   *Worcester v. The State of Georgia*, 31 U.S. 515 (1832).

81.   Kent, *Commentaries on American Law*, 2nd ed., 3:383; Robertson, *Conquest by Law*, 133–35.

82.   Kent, *Commentaries on American Law*, 2nd ed., 3:385–86; *Goodell v. Jackson*, 20 Johnsons Reports [N.Y.] 693 (1823); *Jackson v. Wood*, 5 Tenn. Reports 348 (1824).

83.   Kent, *Commentaries on American Law*, 3rd ed., 3:381–82.

84.   Ibid. See also Kent's footnotes, in the 2nd edition of this work, on pp. 390, 392, and 393; in the 3rd edition, on pp. 377, 379, 388–89, and 392; and in the 4th edition, on pp. 376, 378, 379, 385, 387–89, 390, and 392.

85.   Kent, *Commentaries on American Law*, 3rd ed., 3:385.

86.   Ibid., 3:399n.

87.   Kent, *Commentaries on American Law*, 4th ed., 3:399.

88.   Ibid., 3:318.

89.   Ibid., 3:318n.

90.   Ibid., 3:319n.

Bibliography

Case Law

Goodell v. Jackson, 20 Johnson's Reports [N.Y.] 693 (1823)

Johnson v. M'Intosh, 21 U.S. 543, 550–51 (1823)

Worcester v. Georgia, 31 U.S. 515 (1832)

Published Sources

Abernethy, Thomas Perkins. *Western Lands and the American Revolution*. New York, 1959.

———. *The Works of John Adams*. Vol. 4. Boston, 1851.

Adams, John, and Daniel Leonard. *The American Colonial Crisis: The Daniel Leonard–John Adams Letters to the Press, 1774–1775.* Edited by B. Mason. New York, 1972.

Alexander, Gregory. *Commodity and Property: Competing Visions of Property in American Legal Thought, 1776–1970.* Chicago, 1997.

Berkhofer, Robert F., Jr. *The White Man's Indian: Images of the American Indian from Columbus to the Present.* New York, 1979.

Black, Barbara. "The Constitution of Empire: The Case for the Colonists." *University of Pennsylvania Law Review* 124 (1976): 1157–1211.

Blackstone, Sir William. *Commentaries on the Laws of England.* Facsimile of the 1st ed. of 1765–69. Edited by Stanley N. Katz. Chicago, 1979.

———. *Gazette Publications.* Carlisle, Pa., 1806.

———. *Law Miscellanies: Containing an Introduction to the Study of the Law, Notes on Blackstone's Commentaries, shewing the Variations of the Law of Pennsylvania from the Law of England, and what Acts of Assembly might require to be Repealed or Modified; Observations on Smith's Edition of the Laws of Pennsylvania; Strictures on Decisions of the Supreme Court of the United States, and On Certain Acts of Congress, with Some Law Cases, and a Variety of Other Matters, Chiefly Original.* Philadelphia, 1814.

———, ed. *Narratives of a Late Expedition against the Indians with an Account of the Barbarous Execution of Col. Crawford; and the Wonderful Escape of Dr. Knight and John Slover from Captivity, in 1782.* Philadelphia, 1783.

———. "Thoughts on the Present Indian War." In *Gazette Publications.* Carlisle, Pa., 1806.

Brewer, Holly. *By Birth or Consent: Children, Law, and the Anglo-American Revolution in Authority.* Chapel Hill, N.C., 2005.

———. *Sketches of the Principles of Government.* Rutland, Vt., 1793.

DuPonceau, Peter S. *A Discourse on the Early History of Pennsylvania: Being an Annual Oration Delivered before the American Philosophical Society, held at Philadelphia, for Promoting Useful Knowledge; Pursuant to their Appointment, in the Hall of the University of Pennsylvania, on Wednesday, the 6th of June, 1821.* Philadelphia, 1821.

Green, L. C., and Olive P. Dickason. *The Law of Nations and the New World.* Edmonton, Alberta, Canada, 1989.

———. *Peripheries and Center: Constitutional Development in the Extended Polities of the British Empire and the United States, 1607–1788.* New York, 1990.

———. *The Petition and Memorial of the Subscriber, in behalf of the Company incorporated by law, for opening the Navigation of the Catawba and Wateree Rivers.* Charleston, S.C., 1808.

———. *State of South Carolina. At the Courts of General Sessions of the Peace held for the districts of Cheraws and Camden, the 15th and 26th of November, 1783, before the Hon. Judge Grimke, the Grand Juries of the above districts having requested that the Charge delivered by the Court be published, together with their Presentments.* Charleston, S.C., 1783.

Horsman, Reginald. *Race and Manifest Destiny: The Origins of American Racial Anglo-Saxonism.* Cambridge, Mass., 1981.

———. *The Transformation of American Law, 1780–1860.* Cambridge, Mass, 1977.

Jones, Dorothy V. *License for Empire: Colonialism by Treaty in Early America.* Chicago, 1982.

———. *Commentaries on American Law.* 2nd ed. 4 vols. New York, 1832.

———. *Commentaries on American Law.* 3rd ed. 4 vols. New York, 1835.

———. *Commentaries on American Law.* 4th ed. 4 vols. New York, 1841.

Lerner, Ralph. *The Thinking Revolutionary: Principle and Practice in the New Republic.* Ithaca, N.Y., 1997.

Pearce, Roy Harvey. *The Savages of America: A Study of the Indian and the Idea of Civilization.* Baltimore, 1965.

———. *In Defiance of the Law: The Standing Army Controversy, the Two Constitutions, and the Coming of the American Revolution.* Chapel Hill, N.C., 1981.

Robertson, Lindsay G. *Conquest by Law: How the Discovery of America Dispossessed Indigenous Peoples of Their Lands.* New York, 2005.

Royster, Charles. *The Fabulous History of the Great Dismal Swamp Company.* New York, 1999.

Sakolski, A. M. *The Great American Land Bubble: The Amazing Story of Land-Grabbing, Speculations, and Booms from Colonial Days to the Present Time.* 1932. Reprint, New York, 1966.

Sheehan, Bernard W. *Seeds of Extinction: Jeffersonian Philanthropy and the American Indian.* New York, 1974.

Shoemaker, Nancy. *A Strange Likeness: Becoming Red and White in Eighteenth-Century North America.* New York, 2004.

Sullivan, James. *History of Land Titles in Massachusetts.* Boston, 1801.

Tucker, St. George. *Blackstone's Commentaries: With Notes of Reference to the Constitution and Laws of the United States and of the Commonwealth of Virginia: With an Appendix to Each Volume, Containing Short Tracts upon Such Subjects as Appeared Necessary to Form a Connected View of the Laws of Virginia as a Member of the Federal Union.* 5 vols. Philadelphia, 1803. Reprint, Chicago, 1986.

Vattel, Emmerich de. *Droits des gens.* Translated by Charles G. Fenwick. Washington, D.C., 1916.

White, G. Edward. "Symposium: The Chancellor's Ghost." *Chicago-Kent Law Review* 74(1988): 254–62.

Williams, Robert A., Jr. *The American Indian in Western Legal Thought: The Discourses of Conquest.* New York, 1990.

Wilson, James. *The Works of James Wilson.* Edited by Robert Green McCloskey. 2 vols. Cambridge, Mass., 1967.

Reading 2.4

"Being Affected Together"
Revivalism, Slavery, and Empire

Paul Harvey

W HEN FRANCIS ASBURY, ONE OF THE founding itinerant Methodist ministers and bishops in America, came to Leesburg, Virginia, in the 1770s, he found a chapel full of white and black worshipers, with crowds outside the door unable to get in. Preaching from Ezekiel's vision of dry bones, he attempted to compose an audience convulsed with emotion. But the cries to God only grew. At another revival near Petersburg, Virginia, in 1776, as early Methodist Jesse Lee described it, whites and blacks sang together "and being affected together would begin to pray ... and they would continue their cries until some of them would find peace to their souls." Three decades later, thousands (and sometimes tens of thousands) gathered in the great camp meeting revivals that swept portions of the South, especially Kentucky and surrounding regions where migrants sought fresh land and a new start. The religious "enthusiasm" of the eighteenth-century Awakenings metamorphosed into the great revivals of the first third of the nineteenth century, now collectively grouped under the heading the "Second Great Awakening." Such labels certainly oversimplify, but they also suggest something of the impact of these movements. The revivalists revolutionized the South in ways that the American revolutionaries scarcely could have countenanced.[1]

Asbury and the succeeding generation implanted evangelicalism as the most powerfully expansive religious presence of the nineteenth-century South. When that religious movement encountered the even more powerful movement of peoples (both voluntary and forced), financial instruments, and agricultural technologies into newly opening states, "the South" as it is popularly conceived began to emerge. This was the land of cotton, slavery, and Christianity; of King Cotton and King Jesus.[2]

The southern evangelical Awakening took off just as fears of decline seized postrevolutionary evangelicals. The Awakening leader Devereux Jarratt declared the prospect of religion in

Virginia in 1796 to be "gloomy and truly suspicious and discouraging." Other travelers and observers just after the American Revolution found abandoned church buildings and spiritual indifference among the populace. Evangelical leaders determined to light the revival fires anew, in part because of their deep fears about the irreligiosity and infidelism they saw all around them in the early Republic. Defeating deism and skepticism became the millennial mission of the revivalists.[3]

In the early nineteenth century, religious seekers flocked to hear the Word and share in the excitement of the epic revivals of that era. The gatherings at Cane Ridge, Kentucky, for example, reportedly numbered from 12,000 to 25,000, as New Light Presbyterians from North Carolina ignited the Great Revival of 1801 in Kentucky. Around Lexington, Kentucky, exclaimed one correspondent, religious fire once confined was now "spreading with a rapidity that is indescribable." Correspondents reported in wonder at the number of people spiritually gathered at the camp meetings, including both whites and blacks. One estimated about 10,000 people and 500 wagons at his camp meeting in Bourbon County, Kentucky, in August 1801. Among the saved were former skeptics, deists, and infidels who had been made to "bow the knee, and throw down their weapons of rebellion." In a typical passage from memoirs of the revivals, one observer wrote that he had seen the "stoutest of men instantly fall as dead men to the ground and lay motionless, and seemingly breathless for hours"; others would "Roll and tumble and scream for mercy; the awful agony into which they would get before their deliverance."[4]

These camp meetings and other revivals became the staging ground for the evangelical assault on southern deists, freethinkers, and skeptics. The revivals underscored that the visions of the revolutionaries were giving way to the millennial dreams of the revivalists. This transformation coincided with the early years of the "internal Middle Passage" of African Americans from the Eastern Seaboard south to the newly opening Bluegrass and Deep South, as well as with the conflicts raging in the Southeast over Indian lands. It went along as well with rapid economic growth in the lands that became the Deep South states, with exploding markets for their products (especially cotton) that drew in speculators, financiers, settlers, and forced laborers. The confluence of these forces—internal mass migrations, land expropriation and settlement, and evangelical revivalism—fundamentally shaped the nature of the slave society of the nineteenth-century South.

Religion and Slavery in the Postrevolutionary South

Controversies over slavery inevitably drew evangelical churches into difficult discussions of fundamental issues. The black converts who attended churches with their masters or, in some cases, independently kept the issue visible to evangelicals. Trouble also arose when a number of early evangelicals expressed opposition to, or at least ambivalence about, slavery. Yet evangelical leaders also knew that forming strong religious institutions required the intellectual and financial resources of wealthy and educated whites.

Dissension within evangelical churches about slavery raged in the 1780s and 1790s. Antislavery Baptist associations took their quarrel against the peculiar institution to new homes in Kentucky. When confronting the issue of slavery directly, though, Baptist antislavery advocates quickly hit the limits of what congregants could tolerate. John Leland, a native of New Hampshire who became an important early Baptist spokesman, persuaded the Baptist General Committee in Virginia in 1790 to pass this resolution: "That slavery, is a violent deprivation of the rights of nature, and inconsistent with a republican government; and therefore recommend it to our Brethren to make use of every legal measure, to extirpate the horrid evil from the land." This resolution arose after representatives at the General Committee reported back that "they could not agree in their opinions upon the subject" but instead simply allowed Leland to raise the resolution for a vote. One could make much of the appearance of the resolution in the minutes. Yet its brief presence at the end of a document primarily concerned with other church and social matters suggests that it was more a sign of respect for Leland than a widely held sentiment. In a few other cases, Baptist associations and state committees passed similar resolutions. In 1796 the Portsmouth (Virginia) Baptist Association, for example, decried the "covetousness" that led to keeping people in slavery *contrary to the laws of God and nature.*"[5]

From the 1780s to the early nineteenth century, local Baptist associations fired back passionately against such condemnations of slavery. Some advised the General Committee "not to interfere" in questions about slavery; others indicated that they were "not unanimously clear" on the subject. On November 10, 1785, for example, 266 church members in Brunswick County affixed their signatures to protest the tide of antislavery sentiment. In scripture, they insisted, God clearly commanded his followers "to buy of other nations and to keep them for Slaves." Nothing in the New Testament contradicted or forbade the practice; instead, the apostle Paul had simply given "exhortations to Masters and Servants how to conduct themselves to each other." Many other petitions cited biblical support for slaveholding. Most seem to have come from the same original source, the equivalent of mass mailings to congressmen organized by political pressure groups. One petition submitted from churches in two Virginia counties recounted how congregants had "risked our Lives and Fortunes, and waded through Seas of Blood" during the trying years of the American Revolution. Yet the congregants now faced an effort to strip them of their slave property. Such false teachings ignored the fact that God expressly permitted slavery in the Bible and nowhere forbade it. Christ came to bring freedom from the "the dominion of Mens Lusts and Passions," the petition concluded, but as for their "Outward Condition, whatever that was before they embraced the Religion of Jesus, whether Bond or Free, it remained the same afterwards." The churches also feared "all the Rapes, murders, and Outrages, which a vast Multitude of unprincipled, unpropertied, revengeful and remorseless Banditti are capable of perpetrating."[6]

Through such reasonings about God's evident will, the people's voice grew clearer. By 1793 church bodies increasingly dismissed the subject as properly belonging to a civil legislative institution, not a church organization. The church might regulate marriages, prices in the marketplace, or various forms of participation in civic life, but not slavery.

In the age of the international revolutions from France to Haiti, mythic nightmares would quickly outrun formal theology. One planter in 1807 complained to the governor of South Carolina that the state housed numerous religious "Enthusiasts" who preached "very dangerous Doctrines" that inevitably would "lead to fatal results."[7] He might have been thinking about people such as a slave named Winney. Owned by a woman who had been admitted to Forks of Elkhorn Baptist Church in Kentucky, the Baptist slave had become convinced that Christians could not be slave owners. She had tried to be a faithful servant, but after her salvation, she stopped believing that Christians should keep Negro slaves. White slave owners, she announced, were "Wallowing in Hell for their treatment to Negroes."[8]

That was too much for her fellow church members, who quickly expelled Winney. In 1805 the Elkhorn Baptist Association in Kentucky concluded that ministers and churches should not "meddle" with questions such as slavery "or any other political subject." Considering a query about whether slavery could be "supported by scripture and the free principles of a republican government," the Ketocton Baptist Association of Virginia answered that its only business was to "give advice to the Churches respecting religious matters." These replies extended to controverted questions about slave marriages and the ability of owners to "discipline" disobedient slaves who might happen to be members of the same congregation. As a Baptist association in South Carolina decided in the 1790s, masters and parents alike still possessed the "right to govern their household, and to use the rod, if need be, yet are subject to the discipline of the church, for cruelty or oppression."[9] That fraught balance between recognizing the rights of masters and husbands while monitoring sinful conduct governed relations between evangelical churches and individual households for much of the century.

A remnant of antislavery southern Baptists carried on the fight. Born in 1753 in Brunswick County and converted at age seventeen, the antislavery Baptist minister David Barrow went to serve the General Baptist congregation in Isle of Wright County (Virginia), in 1772. He freed his own slaves in 1784. In doing so, he found it impossible to compete economically with other farmers in Virginia and headed out to Kentucky. There, in 1798, he published a pamphlet denouncing slavery. The "business of speculation" was incompatible with the ministry, he had found, and "that of holding, tyrannizing over, and driving slaves, I view as contrary to the laws of God and nature." After his move to Kentucky he created the "Baptized Licking-Locust Association Friends of Humanity." Combining a conventional Baptist creed and a Jeffersonian political philosophy, Barrow looked forward to the time when slaves would be free of the "iron talons of their *task-masters*, and joyfully put off the galling yoke of slavery." He vilified Baptist associations that had been "Blinded by covetousness and intoxication with the cup of Babylon," making them "call evil good and good evil."[10]

Barrow and other emancipationist Baptists connected their case with the broader themes of republicanism. Slaves, they said, had "never forfeited their natural right to liberty." The bulk of southern Baptists, however, moved to the position that, regardless of the morality of the existence of slavery, ultimately it was a civil and legislative concern, best dealt with by the state. Some antiemancipation Baptists even sought to discipline abolitionist Baptists for fomenting internal dissension. The North District Baptist Association of Virginia, for example, condemned Barrow for preaching about emancipation to the "hurt and injury of the feelings of the brotherhood." The association warned against those who were deluded enough to "encourage disobedience in servants, and a revolution in our Civil Government." The association eventually expelled Barrow from the body.[11]

Even the emancipationist Baptists eventually came around to that position; some formed emancipation societies requiring no religious profession, allowing them to pursue their political aims outside the boundaries of the church. Some emancipationist advocates who had been expelled from church were readmitted. Associations formerly divided over the issue came to a reconciliation. One concluded that slavery might be an evil but "how to Remedy it none can devise."[12]

Methodist views on slavery followed a similar trajectory. Often suspected of being Tories or pacifists, American Methodists endured difficult years during the American Revolution. After his conversion in 1775, Freeborn Garrettson, a Maryland-born Methodist who later would have a long career as a minister in New York and among free blacks in Canada, heard God's voice telling him to "let the oppressed go free." After he emancipated his own slaves, Maryland charged him with being a "Fugitive Disaffected Person."[13] Early Methodist leaders such as Francis Asbury found slavery repugnant to the spiritually egalitarian principles of Methodism. At the Baltimore Methodist conference in 1780, American Methodist leaders declared slavery contrary to the Golden Rule. Four years later, they tried to give Methodist slave owners time to free slaves and to disallow admitting more slave owners to the church—except in states that did not allow manumission. Methodist leaders instructed that whites should lead blacks in class meetings and not allow meetings to run late or to be conducted without white supervision. The General Conference of 1800 allowed for the ordination of black deacons, over the objections of southern delegates. Critics of the national Methodist leadership feared the abolitionism and social disorder they saw emanating from Methodism.

Many Methodists, as well, expressed concern that the General Conference had been too censorious about slavery, with inflammatory language calculated to "irritate the minds of the people."[14]

The early and somewhat-halting antislavery efforts in Methodist conferences met a quick response. Critics accused antislavery Methodists of being "the Enemies of our Country, Tools of the British administration." Slave-owning Methodists in Virginia put up a vigorous defense of slavery as a social institution. Petitions to legislatures from evangelical congregations enunciated proslavery arguments. These petitions frequently mentioned scriptural passages on the duties of servants and freemen. Emancipation threatened the entire moral economy of the region, they said; it would be "ruinous to individuals and to the public," productive only of "want, poverty, distress, and ruin for the free citizen, neglect, famine and death to the helpless black infant and superannuated parent." It would lead to "inevitable bankruptcy to the revenue and consequently breach of public faith and loss of credit with foreign nations; and lastly, ruin to this now free and flourishing country."[15]

Antagonism toward enslaved and antislavery Methodists grew rapidly during the last part of the eighteenth century. Local ordinances restricted or prohibited night meetings by slaves. In 1789 a sheriff in Virginia attacked groups of Methodists who were praying with a "sett of the greatest Roges of Negroes in this County." He felt obliged to break up such meetings, for blacks imbued with improper notions of freedom might free themselves of white command and drive away slave patrols (local militias of white men who patrolled the countryside for runaway slaves). Attacks also grew against black Methodists in James Meacham's circuit in southern Virginia. A dedicated Methodist itinerant and opponent of slavery, at one meeting in 1789 he had just finished a sermon when he reported that "the dear black people was filled with the power & spirit of God and began with a great Shout to give Glory to God," which only "vexed the Devil." Soon thereafter, white men organized by the local magistrate stormed the church, beating the slaves with clubs. The persecution only strengthened Meacham's resolve. "The proud whites can live in luxury and abomination making a [mockery] of God and his word, the African upholds him by his Swet and labour of his willing hands," he lamented. "O America how she groans under the burden of slavery."[16]

Several major Methodist leaders, including Francis Asbury, William McKendree, and Jesse Lee, urged the Methodist General Conference in 1800 to petition state legislatures to enact gradual emancipation laws. They wanted deacons and preachers to press the issue until emancipation was accomplished. Four years later, however, newly rewritten Methodist denominational rules exempted churchgoers in several southern states from ecclesiastical rules that discouraged slaveholding. Methodist leaders such as Asbury determined that converting slaves, not freeing them, best ensured the spread of Methodism into areas of the country experiencing explosive population growth.[17]

The prominent role women played in early southern Methodism only increased fears of a religious world turned upside down. One of the best known of these early Methodist women, Sarah Jones, converted to Methodism despite the violent objections of her husband, who threatened to shoot her if she went to church. Methodist women frequently testified during services, often elaborating on their visionary experiences. During the Revolutionary War, women came to the rescue of embattled itinerants, including those attacked by mobs. At an annual conference in 1791, one woman delivered a spontaneous antislavery testimony criticizing the increasingly close relationship of the church to the world. In Charleston, after the circulation of an 1800 Methodist broadside urging church members to petition state legislatures on behalf of abolition, angry residents went looking for John Harper, who had shown the incendiary Methodist publication to another minister. They missed him but abducted his colleague George Dougherty, who already was under suspicion for instructing black children in a Methodist school. They tried to drown him by holding his head under a water pump. A local female Methodist blocked the water spout with her shawl, saving the threatened cleric. Subsequently, mobs threatened other clerics who ministered to blacks. John Harper subsequently assured Charlestonians that he would not circulate the 1800 address to any slave. The governor of South Carolina condemned the address, while the state legislature authorized lawmen to "disperse or whip" preachers or congregants at gatherings where whites taught blacks without proper supervision. The vitriolic response to the last-ditch Methodist antislavery effort ensured that antislavery Methodism in the South ultimately would be drowned by the flood of antiemancipationist (and eventually proslavery) sentiment.[18]

This evolving evangelical stance on slavery was shared by a devoutly evangelical sect of Central European immigrants, the Renewed Unity of Brethren (referred to in shorthand as the Moravians), who settled in the western Piedmont region of North Carolina beginning in 1753. Their theology and history of avid proselytization among blacks in parts of the Caribbean promised an egalitarian idealism that might shape a different social order on the North American continent. Ultimately, however, a similar story of spiritual equality and increasing temporal inequality unfolded among them as it did elsewhere in the South. Moravian settlements in the colonial era typically modeled very different relations between Europeans and others. Their theology, stemming from an intensely felt connection to Christ's human blood shed on the cross, afforded Moravians a strikingly egalitarian view of Christian brotherhood. The Moravians practiced close physical fellowship with other believers, including "love feasts," holy kissing, and washing feet. When faced with difficult decisions, Moravians resorted to sortilege, drawing a piece of paper from a container to reveal the divine answer ("yes," "no," or "maybe"). Attempting to decide whether to purchase a slave named Sam in 1769, they drew the lot. At that fateful moment, with the sign of divine approval, American Moravians became slaveholders.

Over the next two generations, the Moravian Church, now based in Salem, North Carolina, purchased slaves to help with the community's labor requirements. By the early nineteenth century, they owned seventy-three slaves. They also rented out those slaves to local businessmen and farmers. Slavery shaped how the Brethren understood God's will and how they formed their economic order. Church members, for example, recognized that renting slaves provided the cheapest method to erect new buildings for congregations.

Ceding to pressure to separate out blacks from white congregations, Moravian leaders gradually created separate "mission" churches for black Moravian believers. They withdrew from the kinds of physical contact that maintained social harmony among believers. They encouraged black conversion, thinking that this was the best way to discourage revolts, but they physically separated themselves from black believers. White Moravians offered a handshake rather than a holy kiss to new black members of the church. Black Moravians took their final rest in separate cemeteries, segregated in death as in life. The inherently inegalitarian social order of slavery had overcome the original vision of the most radically egalitarian of eighteenth-century evangelicals.[19]

Ultimately, white southern Christians determined that their social order reflected the will of God and that God expected men and women to perform their duties within the social stations given them in that order. In doing so, they thus reinforced and policed racial boundaries in American society.

The spread of Christianity into the newly opening states of the Southeast also brought southerners into direct conflict and competition with those who possessed those lands already. A myth of innocence wrapped together "benevolent" and violent expansion into a single ideological and material force that subsumed other peoples, propelled the massive slave trade from the older Eastern Seaboard states to the new states of the Deep South, and created the conditions for the rise of the evangelical South of the antebellum era.

Missions, Colonialism, and Native American Awakenings

From the 1790s to the 1820s, Indians carried on an increasingly desperate struggle for protection of their lands and survival of their people. Territorial expansion and the evangelical revolution worked in tandem, each a justification and impetus for the other. The result, for southern Native peoples, was sometimes Christianization but always conquest. The growth of slaveholding and of plantation agriculture among certain tribesmen of the Southeast, as well, demonstrates the deep-rooted effect of the economic ways of the American nation-state on Natives who increasingly were hemmed in on all sides by settlers of the newly growing states of the Southeast.[20]

Prophets from various parts of Native America came to the Southeast and delivered visions of the struggle to come. In 1807 an Ottawa Indian recounted visions of the "first man whom God created," said to be living among the Shawnees. The visionary was probably Tenskwatawa, a Shawnee prophet and brother of Tecumseh who had lived among the Delawares. Tenskwatawa had been sleeping when he was awakened by the Great Spirit, who was set to "destroy the Earth" before the first man managed to obtain a reprieve in order to reclaim his "*Red Children*." The Great Spirit told the Red Children not to associate with whites, whether they be French or English. But the Spirit singled out the special villainy of the white people of the United States, who had come from the "scum of the Great Water, when it was troubled by the Evil Spirit." As was typical for Native prophets, Indians were commanded to rid themselves of European goods (especially hats, the historic Indian symbol for whites) and to return to Indian customs. Indian prophets instructed their people to avoid internal wars and instead unite in alliances to drive away whites.[21]

The Anglo-American presence increasingly spurred tribal groups who might have been enemies in the past to form alliances to respond to white encroachment. Tribal ceremonies bonded these new allies and provided traditionalists with a venue to practice what they preached: ritual cleansing and the recapturing of sacred power through proper ceremony. Religiously inspired prophetic resistance ran through Indian communities from the Great Awakening forward—from the visions of the Delaware Neolin in the mid-eighteenth century to those of the Shawnee prophet Tenskwatawa and militant nativists among the Creeks and Seminoles in the Southeast in the early 1810s. It continued from the imperial and revolutionary wars of the later eighteenth century into the era of Anglo-American expansionism of the first part of the nineteenth century.

Although widely separated in time and geography, common visions and dreams unite the stories recounted by the Indian nativist prophets. Each of them took dream journeys and reached forks in the road along the way, with narrow roads leading to paradise and wide and more easily traversed paths taking the journeyer to some form of hell. Indeed, the concept of hell itself was probably the closest connection of these dreams to Christian theology; few Native American groups had any such definite idea of eternal torment prior to the introduction of Christianity. Those who took up the European vices, especially alcohol, found punishment. One of Tenskwatawa's visions was of a feast in which Indians "danced and rejoiced before the Great Spirit and proposed to revive the religion of their ancestors." Nativists and prophets insisted on the separate creation of peoples and the notion that the "Great Spirit did not mean that the white and red people should live near each other." After all, whites had "poison'd the land."[22]

Like the prophets of a generation earlier, Cherokee traditionalists opposed American influence, informing visiting missionaries and agents of the federal government, for example, that the "great spirit is angry with [Native peoples] for adopting the manners, customs, and habits of the white people who they think are very wicked." These Cherokees kept alive the notion of a separate and distinct creation as well: "You yourselves can see that the white people are entirely different beings from us; we are made from red clay; they, out of white sand."[23]

In other cases, especially among the Cherokee, active missionary work carried out by the American Board of Commissioners for Foreign Missions, the American Baptist Home Mission Society, and the Moravians found some success in implanting Christianity into Indian life in the Southeast. Often this came at the expense of tribal splits between traditionalists and those who saw in Christianity a way to access new forms of power. Southeastern Indians, Christian and non-Christian alike, debated their place in a world defined by Christian power. They incorporated elements of Christian thought and myth into their understanding of the world, thereby finding ways to explain the origins of white and black men, for example, and they explored the uses and possibilities posed by a new religious tradition such as Christianity.[24]

After a slow start by the Moravians in the early nineteenth century, American Protestant missionaries had made inroads among the Cherokees in the 1820s and 1830s, especially through educating children in institutions such as the Brainerd Mission school in Chattanooga, Tennessee. John Ridge, son of a Cherokee warrior who was educated in Moravian mission schools and later served as an assistant to Albert Gallatin in the federal government's dealings with the Creek Indians, noted the spread of Christianity among his people: "Portions of Scripture & sacred hymns are translated and I have frequently heard with astonishment a Cherokee, unacquainted with the English take his text & preach, read his hymn & sing it, Joined by his audience, and pray to his heavenly father with great propriety & devotion."[25]

Some Indian female Christian converts blended Christian and Native traditions. A young Cherokee woman named Catharine Brown, for example, attended Brainerd Mission school and became a nationally known figure when her letters were posthumously reproduced in northern missionary magazines. She came to Christianity through a dream in which she struggled to reach the top of a steep hill, helped by "a little boy standing at the top, who reached out his hand; She grasped his thumb, & at this moment she was on the top and some one told her it was the Saviour."[26] Brown's melding of Cherokee stories and cultural systems with a Christian belief in salvation and heaven was a common synthesis for Natives making sense of the two powerful cultural forces shaping their lives.

Despite the influence of Christianity, plantation agriculture, and the printed word, the number of people favoring Indian removal continued to grow. Some Cherokees, including the editor of the *Cherokee Phoenix*, Elias Boudinot, noted the irony that Indian removal was occurring at precisely the same time that the Cherokees evidenced a form of "civilization" that Anglo-Americans could recognize: farming, creating an alphabet and spreading literacy among their people, attending Christian churches, and adopting black slavery into their economy. Cherokees themselves split over the wisdom of removal. "The land was given to us by the Great Spirit above as our common right, to raise our children upon, & to make support for our rising generations," a group of Cherokee women said. In 1818 they petitioned Cherokee headmen to urge them to resist the sale of lands. Also, as they pointed out, many had been Christianized, "civilized & enlightened, & are in hopes that in a few years our nation will be prepared for instruction in other branches of sciences & arts."[27] Northern Baptist missionaries such as Evan Jones allied themselves with the southeastern Indians, believing that the civilizing influence of education and Christianity would bring a peaceful solution to conflicts between whites and Natives in the Southeast.

Moravian missionaries in northern Georgia assumed much the same. The earliest Moravian missions in the colony of Georgia dated from the late 1730s. In the early nineteenth century, the Moravians established a mission at Spring Place (in northwestern Georgia, near present-day Chatsworth), right on a main thoroughfare connecting the roads leading out of Augusta and through north Georgia toward Nashville and other important market destinations in the region. Spring Place played host to a constant stream of visitors, whites and Indians alike, becoming a central meeting place in the heart of Cherokee country. Unlike Wachovia in North Carolina, which began as an economic concern and then over time took in slaves and opened schools, Spring Place operated as a mission from the beginning. At the Cherokees' demand, the Moravians took in Indian students as pupils. For the Cherokees, the main point was practical education; few evidenced much interest in Moravian religious doctrines, perhaps in part because the Moravian emphasis on consuming the body and blood of Christ conflicted with Cherokee notions of the meaning of flesh and bodily fluids.

From 1805 to 1821, the Moravian couple John and Anna Rosina Gambold took charge of the Spring Place mission and the school. The records they kept provide one of the most complete accounts of this portion of Indian country during the time of white expansion and settlement, the Christianization of particular Indian tribes, and the wars of resistance waged by others. One Cherokee leader told the Gambolds, "We do not view you as *White people* at all, but rather as *Indians*." These Moravians did not seem to possess the same rapacious desire for land that the Indians had encountered among other whites.[28]

Evolving traditions, stories, and religious practice suggested the struggles waged by Indians to comprehend the new world coming into being in the Southeast. The Moravians recorded the stories of one visiting group of Cherokees. While they were traveling, they went to an unoccupied house near a mountain. They heard a noise and looked out to see "a whole host of Indians arrive on the mountain from the sky. They rode on small black horses and their leader beat a drum and came very close to them." The leader urged them not to be afraid, for God had come to him and commanded him to let the Indians know that

God is dissatisfied that you so indiscriminately lead the white people onto my land. You yourselves see that your game has gone. You plant the white people's corn. Go and buy it back from them and plant Indian corn and pound it according to your ancestors' ways. Make the people go away. The mother of the nation has left you, because all her bones are being broken through the milling. She will return, however, if you get the white people out of the country and return to your former way of life. You yourselves can see that the white people are completely different from us. We are made from red earth, but they are made from white sand.

The leader told them to look at the sky, after which it opened up and out of it came an "indescribably beautiful light in which were four white houses. From such houses, the leader said, you should build your old 'beloved Towns.'"[29]

In 1815 a Cherokee related another origin story that explained the relative economic power of whites and Natives. The narrative told of a mother who had two sons, who disliked her and plotted against her. She determined to ascend to heaven and remove herself from their schemes. When their mother ascended, their father handed them a book with instructions for trade and commerce. The first son snatched the book, and a line (the sea) was drawn between the two brothers. Both brothers were white, but the second did not take care to protect himself against the sun and so became darker. The people from one side of the line, led by King George, made great boats and followed the course of the sun until they finally came to the land on the other side. The king sent gifts to both brothers, but the first "grabbed all these gifts." The first brother kept the gifts for himself, leaving the second brother poor. The Moravians recording these stories grieved at the "lies" contained within them and prayed for the Indians to comprehend the gospel truth. But the historical accounts they record provide an invaluable documentary record of Indian religious interpretations of the rapid expansion of the Anglo-American empire into the Southeast.[30]

One of the climactic episodes of the encounter of the expansionist American state with the land's aboriginal peoples occurred in the early nineteenth century. The result was an expansion of Georgia, the creation of the state of Alabama in 1819, the rapid spread of cotton and slavery into the Southeast, and the bloody crushing of a prophetic revolt. Hemmed in by land sales and outright fraud, internally riven by an incipient civil war between a faction aligned economically and politically with Anglo-Americans and a faction that resisted all white influence, tormented by problems with alcohol, and economically devastated by a rapid decline of the deerskin trade, which had been at the heart of their economy, Muskogees cried out for a prophetic interpretation of contemporary catastrophes. Muskogees who sought renewal listened intently to natural signs—in this case a series of earthquakes in 1811–12 that seemed to signify the displeasure of the Maker of Breath—as well as to those who related visions. Drawing from their own traditions of purging rituals and renewals, replayed yearly in the Busk, or Green Corn, ceremony, Muskogees sought to imbue their struggle for survival with sacred power.[31]

By this time, however, the alliance between nativists and accommodationists that had formed in the revolutionary era struggles had disintegrated, largely due to the growing power of the American presence. In the case of Alabama, Lower Muskogee chiefs, many of whom had economic ties with American agents such as Benjamin Hawkins, mostly refused to join the Redstick Revolt of the early 1810s. Their residence directly next to the state of Georgia instilled in them an awareness of their imminent peril. Hawkins's hopes for a subsiding of the "Fanatical fright" among the Redsticks were too optimistic, however. Muskogees had been listening to the Shawnee leader Tecumseh and his brother and prophet Tenskwatawa. They viewed themselves not as members of individual tribes but as red men militantly opposed to white men. They purged themselves of white influence as a necessary first step to the renewal necessary for a recapturing of sacred power sufficient to resist the growing secular power of the Anglo-Americans. The targets of the Muskogee prophets were at first the chiefs friendly to the United States. The Redsticks' attacks set them against well-armed and aggressively counterattacking US forces, who squashed them in battle. US commander Thomas Pinckney declared that Almighty God had "blessed the arms of the United States" against the "insolent" and "perfidious" Muskogees. By the end of 1814, the "sacred revolt" was over. Over the next quarter century, forcible removal of Indians from their ancestral lands would proceed inexorably, regardless of any previous resistance to or accommodation of American demands.[32]

Except in Florida, where the Seminole Wars continued for several more decades, Native Americans of the Southeast could do little in the face of Anglo-American expansion. Whether they chose to Christianize and Anglicize (as did a sizable minority of many southeastern tribes, especially the Cherokees), whether they engaged in limited economic commerce with Europeans but otherwise maintained their own cultural practices, or whether they resisted violently under the leadership of messianic individuals, the outcome was more or less the same: forcible removal from their lands, repression of Native religious practices, and exile far westward out of the way of white settlers. At the same time, however, Creeks, Cherokees, and others in Georgia and elsewhere picked up white allies, namely missionaries intent on using the Americans' own legal codes to provide some degree of protection for besieged natives.

In Georgia, the state legislature employed every means necessary to clear out areas for land-hungry settlers and for the coffles of slaves being transported overland to the newly opening regions. Missionaries from the American Board of Commissioners for Foreign Missions, including Samuel Austin Worcester, refused to sign an oath of allegiance to the state of Georgia, insisting that the state had no authority over them in the lands of the

Cherokee nation. In *Worcester v. Georgia* (1832), Chief Justice John Marshall ruled in the Cherokees' favor, suggesting in effect that since the Cherokees were semi-sovereign and semi-wards of the federal government, the state of Georgia did not have legal authority to disperse them and enforce laws within the bounds of the Cherokee lands. President Andrew Jackson famously disregarded the Court's edicts. He knew military force trumped Supreme Court doctrine. Jackson supported Georgia's position of maintaining sovereignty within its own borders and further suggested that segregating Indians from contact with whites would lessen chances for their degradation. Previously, Jackson had signed the Indian Removal Act in 1830, which eventually displaced approximately one hundred thousand Indians. Whites soon flooded into Cherokee lands, despite the Supreme Court's defense of Cherokee sovereignty. Meanwhile, the missionary after whom the case was named, Samuel Worcester, later asked for a pardon from the governor of Georgia and advised Cherokee leader John Ross to accept the inevitable—removal from the Southeast to new lands to the west.[33]

By 1830 a South of evangelicalism and slavery had emerged from the competing streams of religious traditions that had come into the region starting in the sixteenth century. That outcome was far from inevitable. Evangelicals fought their way into the social hierarchy, met considerable resistance, but ultimately helped to define how a society with slaves became a slave society. The real revolutionaries, as it turned out, were the revivalists. They revolutionized the region in ways that the American revolutionaries scarcely countenanced or understood. Their world underlay a political and economic juggernaut whose ruling principles rested on violence, acquisition, expansion, and coercion. In that way, the evangelical explosion and the rise of the kingdom of slavery worked in tandem. But the violence necessary for the southern synthesis would ultimately extract a heavy price from its defenders.

Notes

1. Francis Asbury, *An Extract from the Journal of Francis Asbury, Bishop of the Methodist Episcopal Church in America, From August 7, 1771 to December 29, 1778*, vol. 1 (Philadelphia, 1792), 269–71; and Jesse Lee, *A Short History of the Methodists, in the United States of America* ... (Baltimore: Magill and Clime Booksellers, 1810), 134.

2. The classic study of this era is Christine Leigh Heyrman, *Southern Cross: The Beginnings of the Bible Belt* (Chapel Hill: University of North Carolina Press, 1998).

3. Amanda Porterfield, *Conceived in Doubt: Religion and Politics in the New American Nation* (Chicago: University of Chicago Press, 2012), 5.

4. Ibid., 97–98; *Gospel News, or a Brief Account of the Revival of Religion in Kentucky, and Several Other Parts of the United States* ... (Baltimore, 1801), 3–8; and John Brooks, *The Life and Times of the*

Reverend John Brooks, in which are Contained a History of the Great Revival in Tennessee (Nashville: Nashville Christian Advocate Office, 1848), 22–25.

5. Baptist General Committee (Virginia), *Minutes of the Baptist General Committee: at their yearly meeting, held in the city of Richmond, May 8th, 1790* (Richmond, VA, 1790), 6–7, original copy at Virginia Baptist Historical Society, digital copy available through Early American Imprints. See also the extensive discussions of the resolution in Monica Najar, *Evangelizing the South: A Social History of Church and State in Early America* (New York: Oxford University Press, 2008), 145–48; and Randolph Ferguson Scully, *Religion and the Making of Nat Turner's Virginia: Baptist Community and Conflict, 1740–1840* (Charlottesville: University Press of Virginia, 2008), 110.

6. Najar, *Evangelizing the South*, 147; and Fredrika Teute Schmidt and Barbara Ripel Wilhelm, "Early Proslavery Petitions in Virginia," *William and Mary Quarterly*, 3rd ser., 30 (January 1973): 133–46 (quotation on 140).

7. Jeffrey Robert Young, *Domesticating Slavery: The Master Class in South Carolina and Georgia, 1670–1837* (Chapel Hill: University of North Carolina Press, 1999), 143.

8. The story of Winney comes from the minutes of the Forks of Elkhorn Baptist Church, January and February 1807, quoted in Najar, *Evangelizing the South*, 157. The original minutes from those months are also transcribed at http://nationalhumanitiescenter.org/pds/livingrev/religion/text5/elkhorn.pdf.

9. Porterfield, *Conceived in Doubt*, 138; and minutes from Ketocton Baptist Association (Virginia) and minutes from Bethel Baptist Association (South Carolina), 1794, Early American Imprints.

10. Carlos R. Allen Jr., "David Barrow's Circular Letter of 1798," *William and Mary Quarterly*, 3rd ser., 20 (July 1963): 440–51 (quotations on 445, 450–51); and Najar, *Evangelizing the South*, 157–60.

11. Najar, *Evangelizing the South*, 155.

12. Ibid., 161.

13. Cynthia Lynn Lyerly, *Methodism and the Southern Mind, 1770–1810* (New York: Oxford University Press, 1998), 22, 24.

14. Jesse Lee, *A Short History of the Methodists, in the United States of America: Beginning in 1766, and Continued Till 1809 ...* (Baltimore, 1810), 72, 134, 270 (quotation).

15. Fredrika Teute Schmidt and Ripel Wilhelm, "Early Proslavery Petitions in Virginia," *William and Mary Quarterly*, 3rd ser., 30 (January 1973): 139, 141–45; Lyerly, *Methodism and the Southern Mind*, 125; and Robert Calhoon, *Evangelicals and Conservatives in the Early South, 1740–1861* (Columbia: University of South Carolina Press, 1989), 126–27.

16. "A Journal and Travels of James Meacham," original from Methodist General Commission of Archives and History, Drew University, Madison, NJ, digitized copy available at https://archive.org/details/journaltravelofjoojame, 88, 94–95.

17. *Methodist Episcopal Church, Conference, 1800, An Address of the General Conference ...* (Baltimore, 1800), Broadside Collection 29, Library of Congress, consulted at Early American Imprints; and

Sylvia Frey, *Water from the Rock: Black Resistance in a Revolutionary Age* (Princeton, NJ: Princeton University Press, 1991), 256.

18. Lyerly, *Methodism and the Southern Mind*, 103, 105, 117, 127; and Frey, *Water from the Rock*, 256. The Dougherty story comes from Nathan Bangs, *A History of the Methodist Episcopal Church* (New York: T. Mason and G. Lane for the Methodist Episcopal Church, 1839), 2:125.

19. The full story briefly summarized here is told in the classic work of Jon Sensbach, *A Separate Canaan: The Making of an Afro-Moravian World in North Carolina, 1763–1840* (Chapel Hill: University of North Carolina Press, 1998).

20. Robbie Ethridge, *Creek Country: The Creek Indians and Their* World (Chapel Hill: University of North Carolina Press, 2003); and Claudio Saunt, *A New Order of Things: Property, Power, and the Transformation of the Creek Indians, 1733–1816* (Cambridge: Cambridge University Press, 1999).

21. Gregory Dowd, *War under Heaven: Pontiac, the Indian Nations, and the British Empire* (Baltimore: Johns Hopkins University Press, 2004), 272–73.

22. Gregory Dowd, *A Spirited Resistance: The North American Indian Struggle for Unity, 1745–1815* (Baltimore: Johns Hopkins University Press, 1993), 128, 142.

23. Ibid., 173–75.

24. See the essays collected in William McLoughlin, *The Cherokees and Christianity, 1794–1870: Essays in Acculturation and Cultural Persistence* (Athens: University of Georgia Press, 1994).

25. Theda Perdue and Michael D. Green, eds., *The Cherokee Removal: A Brief History with Documents* (Boston: Bedford Books, 1995), 39–40 (quotation), 48.

26. Catharine Brown, *Cherokee Sister: The Collected Writings of Catharine Brown, 1818–1823*, ed. Theresa Strouth Gaul (Lincoln: University of Nebraska Press, 2014), 17.

27. Perdue and Green, *Cherokee Removal*, 125, 137.

28. Material about the mission comes from introduction to *The Moravian Springplace Mission to the Cherokees*, ed. Rowena McClinton, vol. 1 (Lincoln: University of Nebraska Press, 2007), esp. 18–40. Volume 1 of these records covers 1805–13; volume 2 covers 1814–21. Quotations are from the introduction and various diary entries (see, e.g., May 10, 1811) in 1:431–32. For more basic background information about various denominational missions to southeastern Indians, see Rowena McClinton, "Indian Missions," in *New Georgia Encyclopedia*, http://www.georgiaency-clopedia.org/articles/history–archaeology/indian–missions.

29. *Moravian Springplace Mission*, 1:411–12 (February 1811).

30. Ibid., 2:87 (October 13, 1815).

31. Joel Martin, *Sacred Revolt: The Muskogees' Struggle for a New World* (Boston: Beacon Press, 1992), 115.

32. Ibid., 143, 164.

33. Perdue and Green, *Cherokee Removal*, 73, 69, 88–89; and William McLoughlin, "Two Bostonian Missionaries," in McLoughlin, *Cherokees and Christianity*, 72.

Reading 2.5

Temperance Counter-Cultures and the Coming of the Civil War

Holly B. Fletcher

"Millions of slaves sighing for freedom; the greatest soul of Womanhood crushed and degraded; outcast children and drunken parents, should not be left to suffer. ... I have a bright ideal for the Future ... that each man and each woman may give to his own intellectual, moral and physical nature the fullest development."

—Lucy Stone to Henry Blackwell, 1853[1]

Lucy Stone's words to her husband clearly demonstrate that the culture of the self-made man existed alongside other temperance cultures and visions in the antebellum movement. Stone viewed temperance not in terms of white, middle-class male achievement, identity, or authority but in terms of the exclusivity of that world in its denial of independence, individuality, and opportunity to those outside its boundaries. For Stone, temperance underscored the dignity and rights of all human beings, not that of a single group.

Stone's words also highlight the intersections between the antebellum reform cultures of temperance, abolition, and women's rights. Within the temperance movement, the influence of the latter two reforms proved to be incredibly divisive. This was the case on both an ideological level, as racial and gender equality countered patriarchal assumptions, and on a practical level, as the American Temperance Union tried to maintain national unity as the Civil War drew near. An examination of the feminist and abolitionist employment of temperance illuminates how temperance became an arena for debating the gendered and racial structures of society and how the movement was embroiled in the emerging divide between North and South. In this political climate, the icon of the self-made man became a lightning rod for conflict instead of a unifying symbol.

The ways in which temperance fit within this larger dialogue also demonstrates the diversity and elasticity of temperance ideology. In other words, different groups and individuals conceived of temperance in different ways and to different ends. Even taken as an insular reform, temperance was no singular movement of white, middle-class men. The working-class Washingtonian movement comprised a notable departure from the mainstream. In particular, the Washingtonians demonstrated new ways of thinking about gender roles and definitions within the context of temperance. Although there is no evidence that the Washingtonians directly influenced or contributed to the brewing conflict over gender and racial equality, within temperance and without, they subtly subverted the culture of the self-made man and illuminated the complexities of temperance discourse.

Historians have documented well the roots of the Washingtonian movement in the late 1830's, when the temperance movement, as well as the American economy, entered a period of decline. Disputes over the extent of teetotalism and the use of legislative action were partly to blame. In addition, the dire economic situation resulting from the Panic of 1837 depleted the American Temperance Union's coffers.[2] It was at this point, in 1840, that six working-class Baltimore alcoholics pledged to each other they would quit drinking. With unemployment on the rise, they viewed it as a practical step toward greater personal security and never intended to begin a mass movement of abstinence among working-class men and women. Within six months, however, twenty thousand people formed fifty new "Washingtonian" temperance societies, injecting the temperance movement as a whole with new life—and infusing it with new ideas and directions that challenged the iconography of the self-made man.[3]

The Washingtonians were primarily artisans on the upper end of the working class; the culture of their movement differed considerably from that of their middle-class counterparts.[4] Like the ATS/ATU, Washingtonian societies appointed agents who went on nation-wide speaking tours, exhorting people to sign total abstinence pledges. But all Washingtonian agents were reformed alcoholics, and their stump speeches were tales of their own dramatic "conversions." As a result, Washingtonian meetings took on the appearance of religious revivals of the most emotional sort. At one meeting in St. Louis, "the whole audience was overcome. ... The house resounded with shouting and clapping" when a "confirmed drunkard" came forward to sign the pledge.[5] Whereas clergymen led the mainstream movement and acted as its agents, Washingtonian agents were untrained and uneducated laymen who gave their movement a decidedly democratic feel. Though their meetings manifested a kind of religiosity, the Washingtonians adhered to "neutrality" in spiritual matters and steered clear of doctrinal or theological statements. This was much to the dismay of mainstream, middle-class reformers, especially the clergy among them, who explicitly linked temperance with Protestant Christianity. Middle-class reformers also resented the Washingtonians' opposition to the legislative work that had come to dominate the mainstream movement.[6]

On a deeper level, the Washingtonians created a culture of temperance—and of masculinity—that was at odds with the middle-class version. Whereas mainstream reformers flocked to the temperance movement to ensure their continued success, the Washingtonians arrived out of an already-realized failure. Whereas middle-class men pledged temperance as an individual endeavor of self-mastery and achievement, the Washingtonians did so as a communal exercise of mutual encouragement and support. And whereas self-made men exalted their own independence, reformed drunkards admitted their continued dependence, now on their community instead of on alcohol.

The Washingtonian view of the drunkard highlighted the working-class movement's unique culture. The biggest change the Washingtonians wrought on temperance activity was to shift its focus to the alcoholic, to recast him as a victim rather than a villain, and to act on a belief that he could be reformed with the help of friends. At Washingtonian meetings, "the drunkard unexpectedly found himself an object of interest. He was no longer an outcast."[7] The Augusta, Maine *Washingtonian* noted the differing approaches of the new movement and the mainstream movement, with regard to drunkards. Of the mainstream movement's tendency to bind "the seller and the drinker together, and [exclude] them both from the society and patronage of the community," the *Washingtonian* declared, "a greater system for making hypocrites and drunkards could never have been invented."[8] The Washingtonian motto, "Never forsake a brother," manifested itself through kind pleading, consistent encouragement, and material aid.[9] "Tell them what useful men they might be, what good citizens they might make, and how happy they can make themselves as well as relatives," one paper exhorted, "Treat a drunkard well and you can reform him."[10] In order to start anew, the reformed drunkard required food, medicine, and especially clothing; "he had need to lay off his 'filthy rags' for a 'teetotal dress' before he could seek employment with any hope of success."[11] These working-class reformers "actually *washed* the filthy, clothed the naked, fed the hungry and provided lodging for the houseless inebriate," if he would sign the pledge.[12] A pledge of sobriety, instead of marking a man as "self-made," integrated him into a community of aid and comfort. The source of self-possession was the mutual support of the group.

Conversely, the group culture formed around the individual experiences of its members and, more specifically, around the collective and sentimental enterprise of telling and hearing those experiences.[13] Attendees at Washingtonian meetings heard personal, seemingly spontaneous tales of drunkards' doleful lives and their glorious redemptions. Speakers formed an emotional bond with the audience; tears flowed freely. John Hawkins, one of the movement's founders, reported that at one "experience" meeting, "more tears were never shed by an audience in one evening. ... Old gray haired men sobbed like children, and the noble and honorable bowed their heads and wept."[14] Whereas middle-class reformers spoke "from the head rather than the heart," Washingtonians spoke a language to which the lowly alcoholic could relate and respond, one of personal experience and empathy.[15]

Given that much of the audience and all of the speakers at such meetings were men, Washingtonians presented not just their own version of temperance but unique ways of linking it to male identity. The Washingtonian's manhood was decidedly sentimental, emotional, and affectionate. It was communal more than competitive. These men related to each other outside the realms of the political, the commercial, or even the intellectual, as they were more interested in the telling of personal narratives than the construction of convincing arguments. As the mainstream movement shifted its focus away from moral suasion to legislative action, the Washingtonians continued to shun all tactics except love, care, exhortation, and "brotherly kindness."[16]

Washingtonians appreciated the unique culture they created. Despite gestures from middle-class reformers to unify the two groups, Washingtonians insisted upon maintaining their own identity simply because it was one other temperance men did not share. "We are a class of men who have associated together heretofore; we have taken the social glass together. ... We have now ... reformed together," while mainstream reformers "have never used intoxicating drinks. ... They take pride in saying they have never had an inclination to drink. Then what possible service can they be to us?" Though Washingtonians bore no ill-will toward the "old temperance men," many thought it best to "let each of us move in our own particular spheres."[17] The use of the gendered word "sphere" is interesting; it suggests that the differences between the Washingtonians and other temperance men did not arise simply from class, tactics, or prior experience but from gender identity. Washingtonians were not the "self-made men" of the ATS/ATU, individuals striving for greater mastery and personal success; they were a community of men, leaning on each other, encouraging each other, bearing each other's burdens.

The Washingtonian movement, though predominantly a male movement, incorporated women in significant ways into its larger community of support. In many respects, however, the gender ideology of the Washingtonian movement differed little from its middle-class counterpart. Women retained immense moral authority in both. In fact, an article appearing in the *Worcester County Cataract*, a Washingtonian paper, in 1843 on women's obligation to the temperance movement was a verbatim reprint of a speech given by reformer W.K. Scott nine years earlier. Both listed reasons why women should be involved: "They control the fashions of the day. ... The sphere of life in which they move, and the peculiar duties they are called upon to perform, render them more susceptible to feelings of humanity. ... They can do more than men to prevent the formation of intemperate habits in the young. ... The heaviest calamities occasioned by intemperance fall on them."[18]

In other ways, however, Washingtonian temperance was far more open to the presence, influence, and activism of women than was the middle-class version. A middle-class gender ideology that enshrined women as moral authorities combined with an emphasis on material aid gave Washingtonian women, or Martha Washingtonians, greater importance within the working-class movement and more opportunities for active participation.[19] The first Martha Washingtonian society began in New York in May 1841. Soon dozens dotted the nation. Women joined by signing a total abstinence pledge and paying small monthly dues. These dues went toward buying second-hand clothing, medicine, and lodging for reformed drunkards and their families or for the families of alcoholics who had yet to reform.[20]

Performing charity work comprised the bulk of the women's activities. This work became their exclusive domain, while Washingtonian men focused their energies on speaking and soliciting new members. Men and women went together into the poorest neighborhoods, "visiting," inviting people to their meetings, checking on those who had signed the pledge already, and assessing physical needs. Then, the women assumed responsibility for meeting those needs. This might mean taking in a homeless woman and her children, as one Martha Washingtonian directress did,[21] or mending items of clothing for dispersal among the "half-clad reformed inebriates" so they might have something to wear on job searches.[22] The Washingtonians, male and female, had limited means themselves but made up "the deficiency of funds in the labor of their hands."[23] The object of material assistance was not only "to aid the poor, simply because they are poor," but to make the work "a powerful lever in their hands for raising the individual with whom they communicate to better *habits* and to an improved state of mind and feelings."[24] Moreover, unlike "many persons of wealth [who] impart pecuniary aid as a *condescension*," Martha Washingtonians approached their work with great empathy.[25] They were not much higher on the socio-economic ladder than the recipients of their charity, just more "respectable" in terms of their behavior.[26]

In addition to affording material help, women in the Washingtonian ranks were the missionaries of the temperance gospel to their own sex. Much more so than the mainstream movement, the Washingtonians realistically acknowledged that, despite women's overall moral superiority, not all of them fulfilled the potential of their gender. Reports of drunken women made frequent appearances on the pages of the movement's newspapers. The *Samaritan and Total Abstinence Advocate* out of Providence, Rhode Island estimated that there were "hundreds of vicious females ... in our community who need to be reclaimed."[27] The *Michigan Temperance Journal and Washingtonian* included a report from New York "that the drunken females who have come under the official cognizance of the police during the week—God only knows how many there are whose cases have not been reported—number *only* one hundred sixty-six!" The paper concluded, "If women will get drunk, it's all their own fault," indicating that Washingtonians no less than other temperance workers held women to higher standards.[28]

It was up to the Martha Washingtonians to help them live up to these standards. This was work only women could do successfully because of their "tender, sympathetic bearing toward the sorrowing, suffering and disconsolate."[29] Many female reformers had been rescued from drunkenness themselves, and they offered their alcoholic sisters their "friendship and confidence."[30] Their methods produced successful results, even with the most "filthy and degraded" women. One Martha Washingtonian took in a woman found in a debilitated condition on the streets of New Haven; three months later the reformer had made her over into "the image of respectability."[31]

Washingtonian men were similarly "domesticated" by women, just as middle-class men were. But in the Washingtonian movement, the *process* of female influence gave women more opportunities for publicity and power. As the culture of the working-class movement embraced a mutual dependence between members, it also affirmed male dependence on women. Women played a major role in the conversion of male drunkards, particularly their husbands. Sometimes wives publicly pleaded with their husbands at experience meetings; one woman did so "with an earnestness that seemed all unconscious of the crowd," an act that moved other men to follow her spouse to the front.[32] Once these men entered the temperance fold, women kept them accountable. They did so primarily by providing entertainments that served as alternatives to and distractions from the temptations of the saloon. The Fourth of July was the big Washingtonian event of the year, marking not only the nation's independence but that of members from alcohol. But the celebration also displayed reformed men's *dependence* on women for their sobriety. Women largely organized the event, making banners, cooking, and decorating for the picnic. During the rest of the year, they organized other entertainments—concerts, parties, teas, and picnics. Attendees "could not fail of noticing the striking difference [from] ... those they attended before the temperance reform began. ... Then intoxicating drinks met at every turn ... consequently the female portion of the community were excluded from all part in those celebrations, while the other sex brutalized themselves."[33] Martha Washingtonians were thus significant in the construction of a sober, working-class masculinity. They also helped put a respectable face on a movement that middle- and upper-class Americans might otherwise have viewed with suspicion. As Sean Wilentz noted, Washingtonian experience meetings could be rowdy affairs, including "barroom boasting stood on its head, a recitation of past exploits transformed into a confession."[34] The sizable presence of women helped to protect the movement from the criticism of the members' social superiors.

Washingtonians' urgent need of female aid is clear in the sometimes harsh denunciations of women who did not give their full energies to the cause or those who actively harmed the cause, even if unintentionally. Although mainstream temperance literature at times admonished women for dereliction, it primarily portrayed women as victims or angelic moral guardians, both largely passive roles. Washingtonian literature more often included tales of women who endangered the sobriety of reformed drunkards. In fact, so harshly did Washingtonian papers deal with women, one female reader wrote into the *Michigan Washingtonian* to complain, saying that in all the stories published, "the lady is made to drive the gentleman into deeper drunkenness."[35] In one such story, a Washingtonian's wife reportedly told him he would never be anything but a drunk and taunted him with "what he had been, instead of hiding the past from his mind." Indeed, "he was almost driven to his cups by the unkindness of his wife," and it was only the sympathy of others that kept him sober. He did not stay that way, however. Another woman, a lady saloonkeeper, lured him to his demise with her hospitality, which stood in stark contrast to his wife's coldness.[36] A reformed man needed the personal support of his female relatives to stay sober, but more importantly, he needed the collective aid of the female community to redefine and resituate the arenas of leisure. A renewed life of alcoholism was as close as the nearest saloon, which stood at the center of working-class male sociability.[37]

The story of the lady saloonkeeper reveals the extent to which Washingtonians articulated a male culture of dependence that stood in contrast to the insistence on independence at the center of middle-class masculinity. The drunkard's fate in the above story was completely at the mercy of others, and more significantly, at the mercy of *female* others, a fact that underscored his dependence. The Washingtonians, having once been slaves to alcohol, exhibited far greater comfort with personal need than did middle-class reformers. Not surprisingly, then, Washingtonians also displayed much less ambivalence towards female activism. The temperance organization functioned in almost opposite ways for middle- and working-class men; for the former, it distanced them from female influence, while for the latter, it removed distance. Washingtonian papers urged readers to "shun the bar-room," the more familiar domain of a working-class man, and to "reverence the fireside. Admit no rival here."[38]

Although Washingtonian gender ideology subverted the idea of male independence and offered women a more prominent and active role in reform, it was still generally patriarchal, and Washingtonians would be dismayed when their efforts helped spawn temperance participation by women who championed the full individuality and equality of their sex. The Augusta, Maine *Washingtonian* expressed horror that "there are ... schemes in contemplation to make the Washingtonian cause tributary to the advancement of matters having no connection with the reformation of the drunkard." Specifically mentioned were the "movements of female preachers of 'moral reform,' and other theories no less odious to well wishers of society," and "doctrines notoriously demoralizing and polluting to the mind of youth."[39] Although the Washingtonian movement's cultural challenge to the mainstream movement still affirmed patriarchy, its feminized masculinity and the access it afforded women suggested that alignments between temperance and gendered roles and identities were by no means at fixed points.

One woman with whom the Washingtonians would undoubtedly find fault, Amelia Bloomer, began her temperance career subsequent to her initial contact with the working-class reformers. When the movement arrived in Seneca Falls, New York in 1840, Bloomer reported that it "produced a great sensation, almost revolutionizing public sentiment on the subject," and not simply among those of lower station.[40] She found herself inspired, as she heard Washingtonian speakers depict "in burning words the sad lot of the drunkard and his family."[41] Bloomer's curiosity led her into a variety of activities—attending gatherings, serving on committees, and writing articles for the local temperance paper, *The Water Bucket*.

Her interest had been aroused, and she was not alone. By 1841, there were enough active women in her town to organize a Female Temperance Society with a membership of hundreds. In 1848, the society, reconstituted with new zeal, founded a newspaper edited by Bloomer that represented the unique perspective of women on temperance. After an inauspicious start (including a swindling by a male temperance lecturer who offered his aid), the *Lily* published its inaugural issue on January 1, 1849 as the nation's first and only newspaper owned and operated by a woman.[42] "It is *Woman* that speaks through the *Lily*," Bloomer wrote in her first editorial, "It is an important subject, too, that she comes before the public to be heard. Intemperance is the great foe to her peace and happiness. ... Surely she has the right to wield the pen for its suppression."[43]

Other prominent women duplicated Bloomer's path into temperance activism through the Washingtonian movement. Mary Livermore, who would become a leading temperance and women's rights advocate after the Civil War, began her temperance work in the wake of the Washingtonians' arrival in her town of Duxbury, Massachusetts.[44] She joined the editorial staff of a local temperance newspaper and began work with the children's Cold Water Army. Susan B. Anthony likewise began her illustrious career as an activist within the Daughters of Temperance, an offspring of the Washingtonian movement.[45] That organization blossomed in the early 1850's with a membership of twenty thousand. Bloomer, herself a member, called the organization "a salve to the wounded feelings of the women," who had felt excluded for much of the antebellum movement's run. It was "the first organized movement ever made by women to make themselves felt and heard on the great temperance question."[46] It seems the Washingtonians did not simply revolutionize female participation for working-class women; they also influenced the position of women within the larger temperance ranks. The example of working-class women seemingly ignited enthusiasm in women of higher stations by offering them alternative activities to the middle-class movement's increasingly political ones.

Bloomer's early temperance work makes clear that her initial concerns were of a decidedly domestic nature. She reserved most of her criticism for women themselves, those who continued to cook with alcohol or those who had yet to involve themselves against it. Of the former category, Bloomer wrote, "What examples these ladies are setting! Have they a husband, a brother, or a son, and have they no fear that the example they are not setting them may be the means of their filling a drunkard's grave? Have they a daughter? Their example teaches her to respect moderate-drinking young men."[47] Indeed, "a word, or a look from women, may and has had an influence to save many from drunkards' graves."[48] She confronted apathetic women with "the experience of thousands of their own sex," whose lives had degenerated from "every happiness that wealth and station can impart" to the "lowest depth of misery and degradation" as a result of alcohol's destructive power.[49] Woman's calling came from her "peculiar goodness," that "her gentle voice" could "persuade men's sterner souls to leave the path of sinful strife."[50] As a powerful moral figure, woman might lead the drunkard "back to the paths of sobriety and virtue, and to bind up the wounds of the afflicted and broken hearted." Bloomer expressed her belief that women's particular calling to temperance work grew out of alcohol's invasion of the home—woman's "empire"—and that they could fulfill that calling "in a manner becoming the retiring modesty of our sex."[51]

Over the next several years, however, Bloomer's newspaper and the work of other female temperance reformers gradually fed into a more direct and gendered critique of the larger movement. The apparent lethargy of the cause, the lack of real results in reducing alcoholism, and the continued suffering of women as the chief victims of drunkenness drew the ire of female reformers. "Men have too long dallied with the subject," Bloomer wrote in 1850, "while thirty thousand of their fellow beings are annually swept into the drunkard's grave. ... We want something more than talk to convince us that men are sincere in their professions."[52] She declared she was "disgusted" with male reformers and the meager results of their efforts and called for women to take a greater role.[53] But women found that when they tried to expand their activities, they faced resistance and poor treatment from male reformers, who preferred to assign women merely trivial work. Susan B. Anthony railed against the "senseless, hopeless work that man points out for woman to do," while men heaped upon "angel woman" empty rhetorical praise for their moral superiority.[54]

Increasingly, temperance-minded women chastised men for what they perceived to be lackluster attempts to destroy drunkenness through political and legal channels. Anthony pleaded with the women in attendance at an 1853 temperance meeting in Walworth, New York to "agitate on this Temperance question, do all in your power to awaken the true temperance men of your town." The "secret of the defeat of temperance tickets," she claimed, was that temperance men put too much trust in "the old parties to nominate true men." If women could not participate in the legal and political fight against temperance, they could not ensure that "he who votes for you by proxy, be duly instructed, that he may not long misrepresent you at the Ballot Box."[55] She told another audience in Albion, New York that "to merely relieve the suffering of wives and children of drunkards, and vainly labor to reform the drunkard was no longer to be called temperance work," and argued that "woman's temperance sentiments were not truthfully represented by man at the Ballot Box."[56] Anthony's statements make clear that by the 1850's some women reformers rejected moral suasion, the traditional and acceptable tool of female reform, as an effective tactic. Bloomer, too, wrote in 1854, "People have gradually lost confidence in individual moral action, as a *measure* ... to destroy drunkenness." Prohibitory legislation like the Maine Law was "the only cure—the last resort."[57]

As previously noted, the movement's shift to legal measures was motivated at least in part by the desire to strengthen male authority in the home. But this change in tactics ironically gave women in the movement an argument for suffrage.[58] Though women, "having no political rights available ... *seem*[ed] to be excluded," they continued to believe they had an apposite claim to temperance work as moral authorities and victims of drunkenness.[59] In this, they simply reflected the sentiments long advanced by the larger movement. The conclusion drawn by many female activists was that legislative action was part of woman's domain as well. "In the name of all that is sacred *what is woman's business* if the law and customs which bring misery, crime, degradation and death to her home and hearthstone be no concern of hers?," Bloomer asked a New York audience in 1853.[60] By continuing to insist temperance was an issue that affected the domestic circle yet adopting prohibitory means, temperance reformers created a link between the imagined gendered spheres of society, a fact not lost on female reformers like Bloomer, and certainly not on their more radically feminist sisters.[61]

It was this latter group of women, most notably Elizabeth Cady Stanton, who channeled the frustrations felt by women within the temperance movement into outright feminist reform. Stanton's influence on Susan B. Anthony is well-documented, but Amelia Bloomer also credited Stanton with awakening her to the fact that "there was something wrong in the laws under which [women] lived" and ushering her into more radical reform work.[62] The three women joined forces in 1852 to begin the New York Women's State Temperance Society, which promoted a decidedly radical agenda while under Stanton's leadership.

The immediate impetuses for the society's formation were the repeal of an 1846 prohibitory statute and female reformers' continued frustration with the limitations male-led temperance groups placed on their activity. Stanton noted that when women acted as victims, as did some New York women who violently protested the repeal of the License Law, they were "applauded for these acts of heroism by the press and temperance leagues." But when women sought to engage the cause as men's equals, through associations and conventions, "then began the battle in the temperance ranks, vindictive and protracted for years."[63] The new women's temperance society angered many male reformers immediately. This was particularly the case when Stanton issued a circular to the women of New York that urged the wives of alcoholics to divorce their husbands. When delegates from the society attended the state's temperance convention in June 1852, the men present treated them cordially at first. But when Anthony tried to mount the platform, the proceedings erupted in angry debate over the right of women to participate fully.[64]

Other prominent women's rights advocates became heavily involved in the cause all around the country in the early 1850's. Francis Dana Gage assisted the Woman's State Temperance Society of Ohio, which had formed in the wake of the Maine Law debate at the state's constitutional convention. She attended two of the society's conventions in Cincinnati and Dayton in 1851 and 1853, respectively. Gage recollected that the Dayton community nearly shut out the convention; it finally secured a meeting hall from the local Sons of Temperance. Another women's rights reformer and the editor of the *Windham County Democrat* in Vermont, Clarina Howard Nichols, traveled around Wisconsin as an agent of the state's women's society. She argued that women's claim to being the "'greatest sufferers,' the helpless victims of the liquor traffic" was made possible only by man's "disabling laws" and the "legal and political disabilities" with which they left women vulnerable. Male community leaders and the state's male Temperance League vigorously protested her work wherever she traveled.[65]

Sometimes other women opposed the melding of temperance with women's rights. A group of Dayton, Ohio women interrupted the 1853 convention attended by Gage to express their disapproval of women calling temperance conventions. They also termed the conduct of Antoinette Brown, an ordained minister who attempted to mount the platform at the 1853 World's Temperance Convention in New York, "unseemly and unchristian."[66] Even within the New York State Women's Temperance Society, feminist agendas met with mixed reviews; the society garnered a diverse membership, and Stanton's views on divorce and suffrage did not match those of all her constituents. At the first annual meeting of the society, in June 1853, Stanton forcefully argued that temperance "carries us legitimately" into a call for women's full equality and characterized those who worked exclusively for temperance, "superficial reformers, mere surface workers." Many of those present disagreed, including one woman who said she hoped that the society "would not take in all the 'ites' and 'isms' and 'ologies' and then baptize the whole with the name of temperance." Stanton was not returned to the presidency.[67]

Unlike Bloomer and Anthony, Stanton never saw temperance agitation as an end in itself but as work that informed and enlightened women on their overall degradation and domination by a patriarchal society. She wrote to Anthony in 1853, "The right idea of marriage is at the foundation of all reforms. ... I ask for no laws on marriage. ... Remove law and false public sentiment and woman will no more live as wife with a cruel, beastly drunkard, than a servant in this free country will stay with a pettish, unjust mistress."[68] After Stanton's ouster from the presidency of their temperance organization, she instructed Anthony "to waste no powder" on the matter: "We have other and bigger fish to fry."[69]

In the 1850's, such female reformers did indeed make temperance a major weapon against the larger enemy of gender inequity. Temperance arguments gradually blended with agitation for divorce reform and women's suffrage and against the patriarchal notion of coverture. Nowhere was this more apparent than in the verbal attacks women reformers leveled at drunkards and even drunkards' wives, those sorrowful creatures who sacrificially stood by their husbands even unto death. The mainstream temperance movement portrayed the drunkard's wife as the embodiment of feminine virtue, a caricature that enraged feminist reformers. The *Lily* blasted an article in the *New York Organ* that instructed women to "cling to the besotted and rotten carcasses of their husbands, even if by doing so they suffered ten thousand deaths," and "spoke glowingly of the opportunity thus afforded the drunkard's wife for exhibiting the noblest and most heroic traits in her character." The *Lily* mused that "it almost made drunkenness itself a virtue" and suggested that the "rum suckers and beer swillers" deserved kicks, not kisses, from their wives.[70] Jane Grey Swisshelm, editor of the reform paper the *Pittsburgh Visitor*, saw a gendered motive in "the diagnosis of drunkenness ... [as] a disease for which the patient was in no way responsible;" it made long-suffering women out to be "angels" called to re-make men through their own submissive endurance. "It may be very angelic for a pure-minded, virtuous woman to love and caress a great drunken beast," she wrote, "But for our share we have not the slightest pretensions to being an angel."[71] In expecting higher sacrifice and morality from women, men denied their equality and individuality. The drunkard's wife's own happiness, and even her life, was incidental compared to its sacrifice for the sake of her husband. For feminists, the families of alcoholics exhibited not the elevation of female virtue but the loss of female personhood. Just as bad, misguided conservative temperance reformers exalted this erasure as inspirational sacrifice.

Feminist temperance advocates went further to argue that such sacrificial living only enabled the drunkard's lifestyle and that a wife might do her husband (and herself) better service to simply "leave him, and take with her the property and the children."[72] The alcoholic's knowledge that "the gentle being whom the law and public sentiment declares to be his wife is his slave" gave him little real incentive to reform.[73] Jane Swisshelm put it more baldly; to require a wife to stay and minister to her drunken husband "is a violation of the laws of God, and the dictates of common sense and common decency. A woman who will persist in so living should be shut up in a lunatic asylum."[74]

Such talk raised red flags for many male reformers, who viewed the use of temperance by these women as subversive of not only one of the favorite devices of the movement—the drunkard's pathetic family—but of the institution of the family itself, as it rested on male authority and female dependence. The ATU commented that although the idea of a woman's temperance society was "very imposing," it could not approve of the activities of Stanton, Stone, Anthony, and their cohorts, as they instructed women "that the marriage covenant is only a matter of convenience." The argument that drunkenness was an acceptable cause for divorce was "at variance with the Bible and cutting off also the last hope of reform for the unfortunate inebriate."[75] Anthony called these suspicions "all wrong and calculated to produce much evil in society."[76] She insisted that she and her colleagues advocated legal separation, not divorce, in the case of intemperance. A woman should remove herself, her children, and the family's property out of the reach of the offending husband until he reformed.[77] But more radical feminists, including Elizabeth Cady Stanton and Lucy Stone, did employ temperance to argue for the relaxation of the nation's divorce laws. They believed that the "marriage question ... underlies the whole movement" and divorce was "a doctrine which is to strike the most effective blow at the sin of drunkenness."[78] At the June 1853 meeting of the New York Women's State Temperance Society, Stanton went so far as to argue that a marriage should be dissolved any time "the unity of soul" disintegrated, whether it be from intemperance or any other cause. In a bold assertion of individual rights, she declared, "Any law or public sentiment that forces two high born souls to live together as man and wife, unless held there by love, is false to God and to humanity."[79] Few other members of the society fully agreed with such a radical statement on marriage, most preferring Anthony's more moderate stance.

Less controversial among women's rights supporters was female suffrage. As with the issue of divorce, complaints about men's impotence or indolence in passing prohibitory legislation fed into a call for women's political participation. "The sad truth [is] that hitherto those who have claimed to be woman's rightful representatives and protectors have legislated against her interests and happiness and turned loose upon her a fearful foe to desolate her home and subject her to a life of poverty, shame and sorrow," Bloomer told a Council Bluffs, Iowa audience.[80] "It is quite time that their rights should be discussed, and that woman herself should enter the contest."[81] Consequently, instead of being woman's protector, the law became her enemy. Swisshelm wrote that "self-preservation" was a law higher than the Constitution, and women would obey it first. Woman "cannot preserve her home, her happiness, her life without setting your wily, wicked laws in defiance."[82] Feminists therefore supported women who took the law into their own hands and vandalized saloons in the 1850's. Although conservative temperance men praised such action by female "victims" of intemperance, feminists offered a different interpretation. "'Moral suasion'" deemed "useless," "the ballot-box ... closed against her ... the law-making power ... denied her," and "men lack[ing] courage and efficiency to do what they have the power to do," women must "rely on the strength of her own right arm ... meet the foe face to face."[83] By physically and often violently coming to their own defense, even "horse-whipping" rumsellers, as one praiseworthy Cincinnati woman did in 1852, women mounted a physical attack on the gendered order that they could not combat legally.[84] If the law would not protect them and men would not represent them under the law, women would subvert law and order themselves. And if the law did not acknowledge them as persons, if the law disembodied them, then they would physically employ their own bodies in a realm outside of it.[85]

The problem of intemperance and the inability of the movement to eradicate it gave feminist reformers an arsenal against the legal subjugation of women. "The law in its *magnanimity* presupposes every woman to have a *male* protector," Anthony told an audience in 1853. But the law as it stood failed to offer a woman the promised protection "when the husband and father becomes a besotted drunkard, and ceases to provide for his family." Far from protecting women, the law "makes [their] condition more hopeless" by confining them to brutal marriages, leaving them without a political voice (even on "domestic" matters like temperance), and making it virtually impossible to be financially independent from men. Bloomer asserted that coverture went against natural law by subjecting some humans to others. Patriarchy was an "unnatural assumption of power"—"Man has degraded woman from her high position in which she was placed as his companion and equal, and made of her a slave to be bought and sold at his pleasure."[86] According to Anthony, the purpose of law was "the weak protected against the strong. ... The law should be his guardian, and those who make the law, the ones to be held responsible and suffer the penalties for crimes and misdemeanors he may perpetrate."[87] By refusing to acknowledge the individuality of each human being within its realm, American law seemed to do just the opposite.

In contrast to the Washingtonian movement, the feminist version of temperance overtly combated the mainstream movement's culture of the self-made man. Feminists employed temperance as a vehicle to achieve and as a venue to discuss the larger agenda of female equality and personhood. In the process, these women articulated a unique version of temperance itself, one that rejected female victimhood and morality and male responsibility and authority. Temperance was less a statement of mastery by self-made men than an admission of poor governance by male dictators and a call for female self-rule.

Of course, women were not the only antebellum Americans denied their individuality. A call for gender equality was inflammatory in itself because it would disrupt some of society's most basic institutions and assumptions. But the issue additionally informed and was informed by those of slavery and racial equality.[88] The subjugation of women and that of blacks bore obvious similarities: Both groups were excluded from citizenship and full legal and social equality. In the dominant temperance discourse, the supposed dependence of both women and blacks bolstered the idea of white male independence and authority. Not surprisingly, then, just as feminists found temperance could aid the cause of women's rights, African Americans and abolitionists saw connections between temperance and racial equality under the law and constructed their own temperance cultures based on this idea.

Frederick Douglass made this connection when he climbed a temperance stage in London on August 4, 1846. The famous black abolitionist had been invited to speak by British activists, and his address came after a sequence of American orators sang the praises of their nation for its leading role in the movement. Douglass's remarks, however, created quite a stir among the American delegation. This was especially true of his declaration that he could not "fully unite with ... their patriotic eulogies of America, and American Temperance Societies" since there were "three millions of the American population, by slavery and prejudice, placed entirely beyond the pale of American Temperance Societies."[89] With these words, cries of "Shame! Shame!" and "Sit down!" arose from the American delegation. Nonetheless, Douglass persisted through the commotion and finished his speech.

After he took his seat, John Kirk of Boston mounted the platform and informed the audience that Douglass had "unintentionally misrepresented the Temperance Societies of America. I am afraid that his remarks have produced the impression on the public mind, that Temperance Societies support slavery."[90] Later, another attendee, Samuel Cox, wrote a letter complaining of Douglass's conduct to the New York *Evangelist*. In his mind, Douglass, "the colored abolition agitator and ultraist," had "lugged anti-slavery or abolition" to the podium with him, "ruin[ing] the influence, almost of all that preceded!"[91] The *Journal of the American Temperance Union* agreed that the incident was "greatly regretted by every friend of good order and true sobriety."[92]

Although Kirk and Cox believed "that the cause of Temperance was not at all responsible for slavery and had no connexion [sic] with it," Douglass clearly saw an intersection between the two reforms, as did other black advocates of temperance.[93] Slavery in the South and racial discrimination everywhere limited blacks' ability to participate in the movement. Southern laws prohibiting the assembly of slaves meant their participation in organizations of any kind, including temperance ones, was impossible. And in the North, whites habitually excluded blacks from their temperance societies. When northern blacks organized their own societies, they at times became the target of white violence.[94] Douglass indicated that he himself had faced discrimination while working for the cause when he contrasted his treatment within the American temperance movement with that during his association with the movement in Ireland, where he undertook a speaking tour in 1845. "How different here, from my treatment at home!" he wrote to William Lloyd Garrison, "In this country, I am welcomed to the temperance platform, side by side with white speakers, and am received as kindly and warmly as though my skin were white."[95]

Douglass saw the obstacles faced by blacks in temperance participation as indicative of "the impediments and absolute barriers thrown in the way of [blacks'] moral and social improvement ... [holding] them in rags and wretchedness, in fetters and chains, left to be devoured by intemperance and kindred vices." Slavery was, of course, the ultimate degradation, as it stripped people of their humanity, individuality, and right to self-improvement and elevation. But racial discrimination could deny even a free black the tools needed to thrive in American society, which included a body of supporters to help him lead a sober life.[96] Douglass believed that racial prejudice originated in the unequal conditions in which blacks and whites lived. "The white man is superior to the black man only when he outstrips him in the race for improvement," he told the readers of the *North Star*, "And the black man is inferior only when he proves himself incapable of doing just what is done by his white brother." To end racial prejudice and discrimination, he concluded, "We must do what white men do," and surpass them in the realms of progress and self-improvement.[97] He left that task up to African Americans themselves. The American system might divest blacks of basic economic, political, and social equality, but it had "not yet been able to take from us the privilege of being honest, industrious, sober, and intelligent." The enemies of equality would love nothing more than to see blacks confirm their own inferiority through poor character and low morals. But if African Americans could exhibit exemplary character, including lives of abstinence from alcohol, prejudice would be "abashed, confused and mortified."[98]

Douglass saw temperance as an important part of an overall moral elevation, and other northern blacks similarly made the connection between total abstinence and black equality. They recognized that the virtue and morality of their own community called attention to the humanity of the slave. "On our conduct, in a great measure, [the slaves'] salvation depends," argued the *Colored American*. "Let us show that we are worthy to be freemen; it will be the strongest appeal to the judgment and conscience of the slave-holder and his abettors." In addition, measures of self-improvement, like temperance, proved that all blacks, slave and free, deserved full civil rights and economic opportunity, "as men and citizens."[99] After its June 1832 meeting in Philadelphia, the Second Annual Convention for the Improvement of the Free People of Color issued a circular that urged blacks to "be righteous, be honest, be just, be economical, be prudent. ... Live in constant pursuit of that moral and intellectual strength which will invigorate your understanding, and render you illustrious in the eyes of a civilized nation." And above all, "beware of that bewitching evil, that bane of society, that curse of the world, that fell destroyer of the best prospects ... *Intemperance*."[100] A sober African American community would be the most upright and industrious and consequently the most effective argument for its own equality. Black leaders supported prohibitory legislation like the Maine Law in order to keep alcohol away from black users, particularly "the very class of our people to whom we are to look as warriors who are to fight ... for our liberty, and our rights." With the grog shop outlawed, the black community elevated, and a sober, black elite in position to lead, "we will see a marked difference in the Colored People of this country, in a political and social point of view."[101] On the other hand, if African Americans did not join the moral reform bandwagon of the antebellum years, "the contrast between our condition and that of our white brethren will be widened."[102]

Like feminists, African Americans viewed temperance as an avenue through which individual equality and identity might be claimed. Temperance was a mark of manhood, in both a human and gendered sense. But for blacks, temperance also became an arena of racial competition, and the stakes were very high. Through temperance, white men made themselves stronger, more virtuous, and more successful. If black men did not similarly fashion themselves, their claim to manhood—any sort of manhood—would become increasingly weak, as the differences between blacks and whites grew more numerous and more obvious. Intemperance acted much like slavery in the destruction of African American humanity and equality. But unlike slavery, intemperance might be defeated by the black community itself, despite white attempts to exclude blacks from the movement.

Temperance highlighted not only the general issue of black equality but the specific issue of slavery's abolition. On an organizational level, a temperance-abolition nexus was well-established from the origin of both movements through the participation of individual reformers. William Goodell, Gerrit Smith, Elizur Wright, Joshua Leavitt, George Cheever, and others chiefly known by the 1850's for anti-slavery work had been deeply, and even primarily, involved in temperance in the 1820's and 1830's. A letter from Henry B. Stanton to Elizur Wright in 1841 provides one example of the overlap between the two reforms. He complained that the "temperance and abolition folks continue to get two or three, and sometimes four or five long speeches a week out of me," and indicated that he supported a plan to "run a ticket in this country this fall—heading 'No slavery! No alcohol!'"[103] The son of an alcoholic, William Lloyd Garrison began his reform career as a temperance man when he took the American Temperance Society pledge in 1826, soon after the organization's founding. Before starting the *Liberator*, Garrison was the editor of the Boston-based *National Philanthropist*, whose motto was "Devotion to the suppression of intemperance and its kindred vices."[104] This latter category included slavery; reformers of Garrison's stripe viewed it and alcohol as twin evils.

The presence of abolitionists within the temperance movement was a constant obstacle for the ATS/ATU as it sought to build a national movement. Although temperance sentiment had always been stronger in the North, the movement showed potential in the South as well. In the 1830's and 1840's, the ATU's organ included many reports of the cause in the

South, and national temperance conventions included delegations from southern states.[105] Still, the South generally lagged behind the North in temperance enthusiasm and activity. For example, though the South contained forty-four percent of the American population, it could claim less than nine percent of its temperance pledges in 1831.[106] Both southern and northern reformers believed that ties between temperance and abolition at least partly accounted for this disparity. At the founding convention of the ATU, there was much discussion over its predecessor's (the ATS) connections to various anti-slavery societies and the ATU's commitment to maintain temperance as its "sole object."[107]

The goal of building a southern movement meant that those members of the ATU who held abolitionist principles would have to make them secondary to those of temperance. The *Journal of the American Temperance Union*—though its editor, John Marsh, had at least moderate anti-slavery leanings—included features that acknowledged the interests of southerners and refrained from criticism of southern slavery. In 1837, the paper printed a letter from a Kentucky hemp farmer who reported great success and productivity after hiring a teetotaling overseer and enforcing strict abstinence among his slaves. He claimed that the effect of his temperance management practices "has been evidently good on their health, cheerfulness and obedience, and no accident whatever occurred." No editorial comment accompanied the letter, and the same issue of the paper included a notice from a temperance society in Natchez, Mississippi asking northerners to subscribe to its newspaper. Here, Marsh added his own plug and reminded the readers that temperance was "a question that should bind together in one solid phalanx every friend of humanity throughout our common country and the world. Let us show our southern brethren that we love them and sympathize with them."[108]

Edward Delavan, an officer of the ATU and the dominant force behind the New York State Temperance Society, took the same negotiated path. Though Delavan was an active member of the Albany Anti-Slavery Society, he kept his reform works segregated. He wrote to his friend Gerrit Smith (a radical abolitionist) in 1837 that he was "not yet convinced that in urging Temperance we should introduce abolition—or that in urging abolition we should introduce Temperance."[109] And given a choice between them, Delavan put temperance first. When the ATU selected a southerner, John Cocke of Virginia, as its president in 1836, Delavan defended the decision: "We want our Southern brethren to like us better than they have lately ... to have their full share in this great work."[110] In 1840, when Smith asked Delavan to consider running for New York Governor on the Liberty Party's ticket, Delavan insisted he had neither the ability nor the inclination to engage in such an endeavor. He sternly replied to Smith, "I have a *decided* objection to anything of the kind; my desires being ... to devote what remains of my life to the best of my ability to persuade my countrymen and the world ... of the duty of abstaining from the use of intoxicating drinks ... in order that intemperance with its long train of evils may cease everywhere."[111] Clearly, for Delavan alcohol was the greater threat to the nation's virtue. By 1851, he was urging Smith to "let the Niggers alone for a little time" and devote himself to other causes.[112]

Gerrit Smith also held both temperance and abolition dear but took the opposite course when he felt compelled to choose between them. By the 1840's, he had resigned his membership in the ATU, though he still supported the Washingtonian movement. Many other radical abolitionists made similar decisions. William Lloyd Garrison, for example, hardly bothered at all with temperance by the 1840's. George Cheever's pet cause by the 1840's and 1850's was definitely abolition, particularly within American churches. The same was true for Lewis and Arthur Tappan, even though the latter had once been on the executive committee of the ATU.[113] But many of these reformers, instead of abandoning temperance altogether, persisted in an attempt to amalgamate it with other, more troublesome reforms like abolition. As the larger political debate over slavery reached a crescendo and the nation stood on the verge of civil war, the intrusion of abolition became exceedingly risky to the temperance movement.[114] If temperance bound northern and southern men together in a common pursuit of authority, abolition ripped through that bond by attacking the basis of southern men's masterhood and threatened not just the movement but the nation.

While moderates struggled to hold their cause together through its isolation, more radical reformers increasingly argued that temperance should be one part of a wholesale eradication of human degradation, whether it came in the form of alcoholism, slavery, gender inequality, or even class exploitation. The career of William Goodell illustrates well how temperance might be configured into such a program. Goodell, an orthodox evangelical Christian and pastor from New York, began his long reform career as editor of a series of temperance newspapers in the late 1820's and 1830's.[115] He was a member of the New York State Temperance Society and an early agitator within the movement for total abstinence; his opposition to communion wine and medical usages of alcohol distinguished him from more moderate temperance men.[116]

A letter to his father-in-law, Josiah Cady, in 1831 demonstrated that even early in his reform work, Goodell departed from the mainstream of the temperance movement. He complained of the moderation of many in the ATS, their refusal to espouse true total abstinence, and their often elitist attitude. His ideal temperance organization—which he called "The People's Temperance Union"—would welcome "*all who will pledge* to abstain from *all* intoxicating drinks, including malt liquors and mixed wines, and traffic in them, whether medicinally or otherwise." All members would share equal access to leadership, which would be based on high character, not social standing. "This would terminate the farce of a luxurious nobility," he wrote. "It would equally secure the work from the blighting influence of those clergy who claim to mould it so as to suit such parishioners and church members as those just described. ... It would be a rallying point for the *real and thorough* friends of the cause." It would be streamlined, both politically and financially, by avoiding alliances with political parties and having no permanent funds.[117]

In his newspaper work, Goodell demonstrated a penchant for branching out from temperance as well. Upon taking over the editorship of the *National Philanthropist* in 1829, he declared his intention to include information on a variety of subjects pertaining to politics and morality, including abolition; in his mind, "a paper exclusively devoted to the cause of temperance is deemed tedious by many readers." And though the paper, and others on which Goodell worked, included the standard temperance fare, it also exhibited links between it and abolition. One article shocked readers with the title, "Slavery in New England," then made an extended analogy between southern slavery and intemperance, ending with a plea to the young men of New England to "rise nobly up and throw off his shackles. ... His name is Rum."[118] He used the same tactic as editor of the *Genius of Temperance* by arguing that "Man is Free" and not meant for slavery or drunkenness.[119]

By the 1840's, Goodell had become increasingly radical, uncompromising, and ever more interested in the cause of equal rights, and he gained prominence as one of the leading figures of the anti-Garrisonian wing of the abolitionist movement.[120] He became a preeminent agitator for abolitionism and general reform within American churches and a leader in the "come outer" movement.[121] In 1843, he accepted the pastorate of a church in Honeoye, New York founded on immediate emancipation, prohibition, and greater democracy within churches (including lay ordination and equal participation by all members). So firmly did he believe in anticlericism that he refused ordination upon assuming the pastorate of the Honeoye church; as a result, other clergymen questioned the legitimacy of the marriages he performed.[122]

Later in the decade, as a co-founder of the Liberty Party with other anti-Garrisonians, including Gerrit Smith, he would apply similar principles to politics.[123] Goodell told Josiah Cady that he and Smith wanted it to be a party of real and total democracy, standing for "*all* the rights of *all* men, as well as for the freedom of the *colored* man." He then related a wish-list of reforms, including the replacement of the tariff system with direct taxation (he called free trade an "inalienable right" and believed the current tax system oppressed the poor), the reduction of government salaries, and an end to executive patronage. The overall aim of the party was "in a word, the conforming of Civil government to its *original business of 'doing justice between a man and his neighbor.'*"[124] He believed government's purpose—as ordained by God—was to protect human rights, which were the basis for morality. All individuals, regardless of race, sex, or class, had a right to "self-ownership," the right to freely pursue industry, improvement, a livelihood and property, and to participate in government.[125] The American government violated these human rights through the protection of slavery, through privileged "class legislation" such as tariffs and the sale of public lands, through the subjugation of women, and through the licensing of the liquor traffic, which ravaged people's self-possession. All of these issues were interrelated, and Goodell abhorred "one idea" organizations, like temperance societies, that picked and chose from reforms that Goodell believed came together in the single goal of human equality. "Such societies," he argued, "not only become opponents of other good objects, but fail of fidelity to their own special trusts." Single-minded reformers failed to see society and its problems as they really were, intricately linked and connected, impossible to alter in part. Goodell thought reform should seek "but the simple restoration and protection of human rights."[126]

As Goodell's vision grew in breadth, temperance remained very much a part of his work. For Goodell, scripture and republican government demanded "a genuine and radical Temperance," total abstinence in one's personal habits and complete dedication in one's political obligations. Intemperance was a "national calamity," and "all public calamities of this sort arise from individual calamities or improvements—there is no way to have a prosperous and solvent community ... without private, individual, family thrift, industry, economy, and prudence." Instead of viewing prohibitory legislation as a restriction of personal freedom, Goodell saw it as a protection of human dignity, much like the abolition of slavery; the alcohol trade produced only "poverty and pauperism and crime."[127] He always put the problem of intemperance within the larger framework of injustice, human degradation, and bad government. The inability or refusal of mainstream temperance reformers to do this frustrated him. He believed this was a major flaw in the movement and the culprit that slowed its momentum by the 1850's. In an 1847 address, he repeatedly attributed the shortcomings of the temperance movement to its myopia, "from the attempt to limit attention and effort within narrower bounds than the case demanded." In fact, Goodell argued, any time reformers worked exclusively for one cause, the effect was to "[divide] ourselves against ourselves ... nullifying our own votes."[128]

Goodell made a significant contribution to radical reformism by incorporating the popular cause of temperance into an all-encompassing vision for the reform of American society that rested, at bottom, on a democratic interpretation of law.[129] In his ideal America, each individual stood equally in all respects, regardless of race, sex, or class. Goodell was unique in his equal pursuit of a variety of reforms, but he joined with the other reformers discussed in making temperance a point of origin for larger purposes. While mainstream reformers continued to view temperance as an emblem of respectable, white, middle-class manhood, reformers like Goodell employed temperance to magnify the weaknesses and failings of a system built around it.

Washingtonian, feminist, African American, and abolitionist temperance cultures revealed the vivacity and complexity of the antebellum temperance movement. These reformers shaped the language and ideas of the popular cause into their own discourses, whether of self-assertion or societal reform. Temperance became a common tongue for multiple cultures and ideas. By the 1850's, however, the dialogue of temperance grew increasingly contentious and momentous as the issues of war and slavery loomed large. The debate within temperance surrounding racial and gender equality entangled it in the mounting conflict between North and South. In 1853, this reality dramatically manifested itself in the events surrounding the World's Temperance Convention in New York City.[130] What was supposed to be a display of the movement's strength and solidarity around the world degenerated into a bitter confrontation over the immediate issue of women delegates and the more general issue of the movement's larger ideological grounding.

The trouble began in May 1853, when temperance reformers met in New York to plan the convention. They included reformers of all kinds—men and women, northerners and southerners, those in the mainstream of the movement and those on its fringes, including abolitionists and feminists. Their differences quickly consumed their common support for temperance. An attempt by the abolitionist Theodore Wentworth Higginson to have the feminist Lucy Stone appointed to a committee threw the meeting into chaos over the issue of female delegates. Having anticipated controversy, Rev. Nathaniel Hewitt, a Congregational minister from Connecticut, rose to deliver a prepared speech, in which he argued that it was "contrary to established usage to have Women take part in Temperance Meetings." Higginson replied that if the reformers present meant to have a World's Convention, "Woman should be represented, otherwise it would be only a Semi-World's Convention." More debate ensued, including both support for the ladies' faithfulness to the cause and criticism for their intention to harm it by blending it with the troublesome issue of women's rights. In the discussion, Susan B. Anthony, Abby Kelley Foster, Emily Clark, and Lucy Stone each tried to speak, but the majority shouted them down. With that, Higginson requested his name be struck from the roll and invited those who resented women's exclusion from the convention to meet that afternoon at Dr. Trall's water-cure establishment. Around a dozen reformers, many of them women, followed him from the gathering.[131]

The exodus resulted in the staging of two temperance conventions the following September and a vigorous, rancorous debate between the two camps in the interim. The *Whole* World's Temperance Convention, which included delegates from the New York State Women's Temperance Society, commenced on September 1, 1853, while the World's Temperance Convention began as originally scheduled on September 6. In their presentations of the immediate and practical issues of temperance, the two conventions differed little. Both advocated the Maine Law, condemned rumsellers and distillers, and portrayed alcohol as a great enemy of the nation. But as the two conventions' names reflected, they offered different versions of temperance, one that related to the authority of white men and one that challenged that authority by asserting the inclusion and equality of women and African Americans.

Most of the dialogue centered on the issue of women's rights, since the question of women's participation in the convention had been the most immediate cause of the division. The Whole World's delegates asserted that male reformers' empty flattery of women's moral authority and the movement's claim to act on behalf of female victimhood merely distracted from gender inequality and the men's failure in their sworn duty to protect dependent women. The Whole World's delegates found it absurd that male reformers called a World's Convention and then "voted [women] as not of the world" by refusing their active participation. "What does this mean?" asked the *Anti-Slavery Bugle,* "Do they consider women appendages to persons? In this latter capacity we suppose they would be glad to have them attend their convention."[132] The convention's speakers boldly argued that woman, the chief victim of intemperance, had been made so by "the laws of this country [which] bound her hand and foot and given her up to the protection of her husband."[133] The evidence clearly showed that protection to be insufficient. Clarina Howard Nichols, one of the numerous women who addressed the convention, claimed she "would not stand here," if "intemperance did not invade our homes and tear them from over our heads ... take from us our clothing, our bread, the means for our own self-development and for the training of our children in respectability and usefulness."[134] For the delegates at the Whole World's Convention, temperance clearly demonstrated that female victims of alcohol needed the removal of male authority, not its strengthening.

In presenting this argument, the Whole World's Convention challenged one of the central tenets of the movement's mainstream and stoked the ire of its members. Delegates to the World's Convention argued that while women's assistance to the cause was important, these particular women had not come to aid the temperance movement but to "subvert the whole order of things" by "undertaking to manage and control in company with mankind, to whom God has given the headship, the great governmental affairs of this world."[135] The movement welcomed the participation of women, "but let them come as *Women* and not as *Men,* just as they come into families, and into Christian assemblies and Christian churches."[136] A woman's usefulness to the movement lay in her "meek and quiet spirit," not in her militant self-assertion. A New York temperance journal echoed this sentiment; woman was powerful because she was "frail, delicate, dependent, limited to a defined and retired sphere. ... From this glorious height the new set would drag woman down and despoil her of all that mighty influence."[137]

The most dramatic confrontation between the two camps was an attempt by Rev. Antoinette Brown to mount the platform of the World's Convention. Her comrade George Clark of Rochester prepared her way by reading a resolution: "That this Convention invite *all* the friends of humanity without respect to age, sex, color or condition, to participate in the deliberations and aid in its glorious work." When delegates responded with angry shouts and hisses, Clark defended himself "as a friend to the cause of Temperance, having been a worker for many years" and insisted he was motivated only by the desire for "the powerful aid of angel woman." He held the floor through "a general hurricane of words," until Brown mounted the platform, inaugurating a firestorm that consumed the remainder of the afternoon session.[138] Brown recalled hearing both virulent attacks, "hissed through the teeth as though coming out of the heart boiling hot," and encouraging words from supporters.[139] One delegate growled that a convention "where *both women and niggers had had their say*" had been held the week prior, and now they should "leave decent white men alone."[140]

This telling comment revealed that the gendered challenge brought by the Whole World's convention had its context in the mounting conflict over slavery and race and in the temperance movement's attempt to maintain national unity. Equally telling was the more surreptitious exclusion of James McCune Smith, a black doctor and reformer. According to Smith, a man stopped him for his credentials at the door, then turned him away "on the ground of informality." An avid temperance supporter for two decades, Smith expressed his dismay that he had been unable to bring information before the delegates regarding the progress of the movement in Africa. His barring proved the convention's sympathies were with only "three quarters of the globe, while the fourth was left to grope in outer darkness of the *Rum Trade* and its twin brother the *Slave Trade*."[141]

Smith's exclusion, like the response to Antoinette Brown, was for the purpose of keeping the World's convention "on message" and promoting temperance as the moderate cause of white men, North and South. In 1853, the temperance movement still had a sizable southern following, but the convention's minutes made clear that maintaining the southern presence was a delicate matter. When George Clark offered his initial resolution, that the convention should be open to all reformers regardless of sex, age, and race, a Virginia delegate complained that southern delegates had come "with the belief that they would ... [be] spared these disgusting embarrassments."[142]

But northern delegates had an interest beyond the comfort of their southern brethren in keeping temperance free of reforms that sought its use for upsetting the racial or gendered status quo. For the majority of male reformers in the temperance movement, their cause was not intended to be a radical reform but one that bolstered white male authority. As one abolitionist paper put it, the actions and words of the majority of the World's delegates revealed their central aim: "They wished to retain supremacy over the people."[143] The convention's supporters described the cause in similarly conservative terms. "Its very name of Temperance is a rebuke to all fanaticism," the *Times* editor wrote. "It ... is wholly alien to that spirit of excitement, of lawlessness, of public and private turbulence." The "prudent" delegates of the World's Convention should be hailed for having "uniformly kept their movements free from the fanatical ultraisms by which other worthy causes have often been so deeply divided."[144] Reformers like Brown or the abolitionist Wendell Phillips, who was also ejected from the World's Convention, were devotees of a greater "fanatical infidelity" that threatened to upset the convention, the movement, and society at large. Dr. Smith also pursued a subversive agenda, his presence "for the purpose, confessedly, of introducing an African element into the ... deliberations."[145]

Ultimately, the temperance debates of 1853 concerned the larger basis of the movement, whether the self-made man, the symbol of male authority and identity, would continue to be the visible image of the movement or whether other reformers who did not fit that mould would employ temperance to assert themselves, both within the reform and in society. In other words, would temperance remain the domain of "decent white men" or would it be a vehicle for people who did not fit that description? The conventions showed that the icon

FIGURE 2.5.1   *The Great Republican Reform Party, Calling on their Candidate* (Currier and Ives, 1856). This political cartoon skewering the Republican Party's association with reformers of various stripes also illustrates moderate temperance reformers' worst fear, that temperance (depicted by the character on the far left, who is asking that alcohol use be made a "capital crime") would be associated with radical feminists (seen here clad in bloomers and smoking a cigar), socialists, free love advocates, abolitionists, and other radical reformers. Library of Congress, Prints and Photographs Division, LC-USZ62–10370.

of the self-made man, rather than serving as a unifying symbol of the movement, proved to be a divisive hazard to its health. This was particularly true given its political context by the 1850's: A vigorous debate over southern slavery and a looming civil war. The World's Temperance Convention controversy displayed how temperance reformers, in discussing the ideological grounding of the movement, entangled it in this broader conflict, as well as how the national crisis informed and provoked a vigorous struggle within temperance. Twelve years after the two-convention show-down, and after the Civil War had come and gone, this debate was largely irrelevant, as was the icon of the self-made man itself.

Notes

1. 26 June 1853, Blackwell Family Papers (microfilm), Library of Congress Manuscripts Division, Washington, DC, reel 63.

2. Jack S. Blocker, *American Temperance Movements: Cycles of Reform* (Boston: Twayne Publishers, 1989), 21–29. The disputes over abstinence mainly concerned the use of wine for communion.

3. Sean Wilentz, *Chants Democratic: New York and the Rise of the American Working Class* (Oxford: Oxford University Press, 1984), 307. Wilentz attributes the success of the movement to the depression, saying that temperance acted as a "balm" (314).

4. Among the six founders were a blacksmith, a wheelwright, a coachmaker, a silverplater, a carpenter and a tailor. Philip S. White and Ezra Stiles Ely, *Vindication of the Order of the Sons of Temperance* (New York: Oliver and Brothers, Publishers, 1848), 20.

5. *Report of the Executive Committee of the American Temperance Union* (New York: American Temperance Union, 1842), 13.

6. Blocker, *American Temperance Movements*, 30–60; Wilentz, *Chants Democratic*, 306–314; Joseph R. Gusfield, *Symbolic Crusade: Status Politics and the American Temperance Movement*, 2nd edition (Urbana: University of Illinois Press, 1986), 44–51; A member of the society, *The Foundation, Progress and Principles of the Washingtonian Temperance Society of Baltimore and the Influence it has had on the Temperance Movements in the United States* (Baltimore: John D. Toy, 1842), 62.

7. Report of the ATU for 1842, *Permanent Temperance Documents of the American Temperance Society* (New York: American Temperance Union, 1843), 9; *Temperance Offering* (Salem, MA), Dec. 1845.

8. *The Washingtonian* (Augusta, ME), 2 June 1841.

9. 30 June 1841; *Michigan Washingtonian* (Jackson, MI), 15 July 1846.

10. *The Washingtonian*, 23 June 1841.

11. Lorenzo Dow Johnson, *Martha Washingtonianism, or History of the Ladies Temperance Benevolent Societies* (New York: Saxton and Miles, 1843), 9.

12. White and Ely, *Vindication*, 20.

13. Although she deals mainly with print culture and Washingtonian narratives were usually spoken, Ann Fabian's analysis of personal narratives in the nineteenth century fits the Washingtonian meetings quite well. She argues that the tellers of such stories asserted a kind of cultural authority that was otherwise beyond their reach. She states, too, that the telling of such stories was "a means of building bonds among people, a means of making visible to themselves and to others the history of those whose voices counted little." *The Unvarnished Truth: Personal Narratives in Nineteenth-Century America* (Berkeley: University of California Press, 2000), quote on p. 7.

14. Quoted in Glenn Hendler, "Bloated Bodies and Sober Sentiments: Masculinity in 1840's Temperance Narratives," in *Sentimental Men: Masculinity and the Politics of Affect in American Culture*, ed. Mary Chapman and Glenn Hendler (Berkeley: University of California Press, 1999), 125.

15. *Foundation, Progress and Principles*, 38.

16. *The Washingtonian*, 28 July 1841. Glenn Hendler argues that working-class Washingtonians constructed gendered spheres much differently than did middle-class Americans due to the lack of separation between domestic and work spaces, leisure and working hours. See "Bloated Bodies and Sober Sentiments," 125–48; Teresa Anne Murphy, *Ten Hours' Labor: Religion, Reform, and Gender in Early New England* (Ithaca: Cornell University Press, 1992); Roy Rosenzweig, *Eight Hours for What We Will: Workers and Leisure in an Industrial City* (Cambridge: Cambridge University Press, 1983); Lawrence W. Levine, *Highbrow/Lowbrow: The Emergence of Cultural Hierarchy in America* (Cambridge, MA: Harvard University Press, 1988). There are striking similarities between the sentimentalized manhood of Washingtonians and that of abolitionists; see Lawrence Friedman, *Gregarious Saints: Self and Community in Antebellum American Abolitionism, 1830–1870* (Cambridge: Cambridge University Press, 1982); Christopher Dixon, "'A True Manly Life:' Abolitionism and the Masculine Ideal," *Mid-America* 77 (1995): 267–90; Lewis Perry, *Childhood, Marriage and Reform: Henry Clarke Wright, 1797–1870* (Chicago: University of Chicago, 1980); Donald Yacovone, "Abolitionists and the Language of Fraternal Love," *Meanings for Manhood: Constructions of Masculinity in Victorian America*, ed. Mark C. Carnes and Clyde Griffen (Chicago: University of Chicago Press, 1990), 85–95.

17. *The Washingtonian*, 9 June 1841, 1 September 1841.

18. W.K. Scott, Address before the Ladies' Temperance Society, Sandy Hill, NY, 21 April 1832, *The American Quarterly Temperance Magazine* (Albany, NY), May 1833; *Worcester County Cataract and Massachusetts Washingtonian* (Worcester, MA), 29 March 1843. The latter did not credit Scott. Also on the issue of working-class gender ideology, see Ruth M. Alexander, "'We Are Engaged as a Band of Sisters:' Class and Domesticity in the Washingtonian Temperance Movement, 1840–1850," *Journal of American History* 75 (1988): 763–87. Also see Barbara Cutter, *Domestic Devils, Battlefield Angels: The Radicalism of American Womanhood, 1830–1865* (DeKalb, IL: Northern Illinois University Press, 2003), who argues that female morality was a concept shared by Americans of all classes and races in the nineteenth century.

19. Ruth Alexander has argued that the Washingtonians attempted to emulate middle-class domesticity, but Barbara Cutter has maintained that the idea of female moral authority pervaded all of American society, not just the white middle-class. See "'We Are Engaged as a Band of Sisters,'" and *Domestic Devils*, respectively.

20. Johnson, *Martha Washingtonianism*, 9.

21. Ibid., 16–17.

22. Ibid., 9.

23. Ibid., 32.

24. Ibid., 28

25. Ibid., 31.

26. Ruth Alexander has identified most of the Martha Washingtonian women as wives of artisans or working-women; "'We are Engaged as a Band of Sisters,'" 765–66.

27. *The Samaritan and Total Abstinence Advocate* (Providence, RI), 25 May 1842.

28. *Michigan Temperance Journal and Washingtonian* (Jackson, MI), 15 July 1847, Microfilm Edition of the Temperance and Prohibition Papers, joint project of the Michigan Historical Collections, Ohio Historical Society, and the Woman's Christian Temperance Union, series I, reel 2; Barbara Cutter, *Domestic Devils*, also bears out this statement.

29. *The Samaritan*, 25 May 1842.

30. This quote comes from a letter from the Directress of the Lady Mt. Vernon Society in New York. Johnson, *Martha Washingtonianism*, 69.

31. *The Fountain, Organ of the Connecticut Washingtonian Total Abstinence Society* (New Haven, CT), 27 March 1841.

32. T.S. Arthur, *Six Nights with the Washingtonians: A Series of Temperance Tales* (Philadelphia: L.A. Godey and Morton McMichael, 1842), 61. Although this account is fictional, it closely mirrors real life incidents. For example, *Cataract*, 22 May 1843.

33. *Cataract*, 5 July 1843.

34. *Chants Democratic*, 309.

35. *Michigan Temperance Journal and Washingtonian*, 15 July 1847; the paper defended itself by saying that often at the stories' ends, the agent of redemption was usually a woman as well.

36. Rev. D.C. Haynes, "The Ungrateful Wife," *The Fountain Organ*, 27 Dec. 1844.

37. On the importance of the saloon to working-class culture in the nineteenth century, see Wilentz, *Chants Democratic*, 306–14; Rosenzweig, *Eight Hours for What We Will*, especially ch. 4; Kingsdale, "The 'Poor Man's Club,'" 485–87. Kingsdale more directly describes the gendered importance of the saloon for working-class men.

38. *Michigan Temperance Journal and Washingtonian*, 15 July 1846. For an examination of the gendered cooperation within working-class temperance, see Murphy, *Ten Hours' Labor*, especially ch. 5; Alexander, "'We are Engaged as a Band of Sisters,'" 763–87.

39. *The Washingtonian*, 24 Nov. 1841.

40. D.C. Bloomer, *The Life and Writings of Amelia Bloomer* (Boston: Arena Publishing, 1895), 20.

41. Ibid., 26.

42. Ibid., 39; *The Lily* (Seneca Falls, NY), 1 Jan. 1849.

43. Ibid.

44. Mary E. Livermore, *The Story of My Life, or Sunshine and Shadow of Seventy Years* (Hartford, CT: A.D. Worthington and Co., Publishers, 1899), 365.

45. Ellen Carol DuBois, ed., *Elizabeth Cady Stanton, Susan B. Anthony: Correspondence, Writings, Speeches* (New York: Schocken Books, 1981), 15–22.

46. Bloomer, *Life and Writings*, 36.

47. Ibid., 20.

48. *Lily*, March 1849.

49. Bloomer, *Life and Writings*, 20.

50. *Lily*, Oct. 1849.

51. Ibid., March 1849.

52. Ibid., Apr. 1850.

53. Ibid., July 1850.

54. Susan B. Anthony to Amelia Bloomer, 26 Aug. 1852, *Stanton, Anthony*, 37–40.

55. Susan B. Anthony, "Expediency," 27 June 1853, Susan B. Anthony Papers (microfilm), Library of Congress Manuscripts Division, Washington, DC, reel 7.

56. Susan B. Anthony to Bloomer, 26 Aug. 1852, *Stanton, Anthony*, 37–40.

57. *Lily*, 2 Jan. 1854.

58. Other historians who have noted a connection between women's work in temperance and women's rights reforms include: Barbara Leslie Epstein, *The Politics of Domesticity: Women, Evangelism and Temperance in Nineteenth-Century America* (Middletown, CT: Wesleyan University Press, 1981); Janet Zollinger Giele, *Two Paths to Women's Equality: Temperance, Suffrage, and the Origins of Liberal Feminism in the United States, 1820–1920* (Cambridge, MA: Harvard University Press, 1996); Ruth Bordin, *Woman and Temperance: The Quest for Power and Liberty, 1873–1900* (Philadelphia: Temple University Press, 1991), 3–14, 156–62; Mary P. Ryan, *Women in Public: Between Banners and Ballots, 1825–1880* (Baltimore: Johns Hopkins University Press, 1990); Nancy Isenberg, *Sex and Citizenship in Antebellum America* (Chapel Hill: University of North Carolina Press, 1998), ch. 6; Paula Baker, *The Moral Frameworks of Public Life: Gender, Politics, and the State in Rural New York, 1870–1930* (New York: Oxford University Press, 1991) and "The Domestication of Politics: Women and American Political Society, 1780–1920," *American Historical Review* 89 (1984): 620–47; Suzanne Marilley, *Woman Suffrage and the Origins of Liberal Feminism in the United States, 1820–1920* (Cambridge, MA: Harvard University Press, 1996), ch. 4; Elizabeth Battelle Clark, "The Politics of God and the Woman's Vote: Religion in the American Suffrage Movement, 1848–95"

(Ph.D. dissertation, Princeton University, 1989); Michael McGerr, "Political Style and Women's Power, 1830–1930," *Journal of American History* 77 (1990): 864–85.

59. *Lily*, 2 Jan. 1854.

60. Amelia Bloomer, "A New Era has Dawned," 7 Feb. 1853, in *Hear Me Patiently: The Reform Speeches of Amelia Jenks Bloomer*, ed. Anne C. Coon (Westport, CT: Greenwood Press, 1994), 41–56.

61. Historians see the blurring of the boundaries between the public and private as an essential step in attacking female subjugation; see Mary P. Ryan, *Women in Public: Between Banners and Ballots, 1825–1880* (Baltimore: Johns Hopkins University Press, 1990); Isenberg, *Sex and Citizenship in Antebellum America*; Ellen Carol DuBois, "The Radicalism of the Woman Suffrage Movement," *Woman Suffrage and Women's Rights* (New York: New York University Press, 1998), 30–42.

62. On Anthony, see DuBois, *Stanton, Anthony*, 15–22; Bloomer, *Life and Writings*, 34.

63. Elizabeth Cady Stanton, Susan B. Anthony et al, *History of Woman's Suffrage*, vol. I (New York: Arno Press, 1969), 76.

64. Ibid., 480–92.

65. Ibid., 118–82.

66. Ibid.

67. *Frederick Douglass Paper* (Rochester, NY), 10 June 1853.

68. 2 Apr. 1852, *Stanton, Anthony*, 54–55.

69. Stanton to Anthony, 20 June 1853, Ibid., 56–57.

70. *Lily*, 1 Nov. 1854.

71. Jane Grey Swisshelm, *Half a Century*, 2nd edition (Chicago: Jansen, McClurg and Co., 1880), 147; *Lily*, June 1849.

72. Ibid., Sept. 1852.

73. Bloomer, "A New Era Has Dawned."

74. *Lily*, June 1849.

75. *Journal of the American Temperance Union* (New York), 1 Sept. 1852.

76. Anthony to Bloomer, 26 Aug. 1852, *Stanton, Anthony*, 37–40.

77. Bloomer concurred with this view, see Bloomer to T.S. Arthur, 1853, *Life and Writings*, 61.

78. Stone to Antoinette Brown, 11 July 1855, Blackwell Family Papers, reel 63; *Anti-Slavery Bugle* (Salem, OH), 10 June 1852 (reprint of a circular by Stanton "To the Women of New York"). Feminist implications drawn from temperance were probably even more disturbing than abolitionist ones. See Kristin Hoganson, "Garrisonian Abolitionists and the Rhetoric of Gender, 1850–1860," *American Quarterly* 45 (1993): 292–329; Michael D. Pierson, *Free Hearts and Free Homes: Gender and American Antislavery Politics* (Chapel Hill: University of North Carolina Press, 2003), 97–114.

79. *Frederick Douglass Paper*, 10 June 1853.

80. Bloomer, "Most Terribly Bereft," *Hear Me Patiently*, 77–82.

81. Bloomer, *Life and Writings*, 55.

82. *Lily,* June 1849.

83. Ibid., June 1849 and 15 March 1854.

84. Ibid., Sept. 1852.

85. Karen Sanchez-Eppler, "Bodily Bonds: The Intersecting Rhetorics of Feminism and Abolition," *Representations* 24 (1988): 28–59.

86. Bloomer, "A New Era has Dawned;" Amelia Bloomer to T.S. Arthur in 1853, in response to his book *Ruling a Wife,* in which he argued that even in unjust conditions, women had the duty of submission; *Life and Writings,* 61. On the similarities between feminism and abolitionism with regard to legal and bodily dispossession, see Karen Sanchez-Eppler, "Bodily Bonds," 28–59; Jennifer Putzi, *Identifying Marks: Race, Gender, and the Marked Body in Nineteenth-Century America* (Athens: University of Georgia Press, 2006).

87. Susan B. Anthony, speech on the Maine Law first delivered in Monroe County, New York on 17 Apr. 1853, Susan B. Anthony Papers, reel 6.

88. For the overlap of feminism and abolition/racial egalitarianism, see Karen Sanchez-Eppler, *Touching Liberty: Abolition, Feminism and the Politics of the Body* (Los Angeles, Oxford: University of California at Berkeley, 1993) and "Bodily Bonds," 28–50; Gretchen Murphy, "Enslaved Bodies: Figurative Slavery in the Temperance Fiction of Harriet Beecher Stowe and Walt Whitman," *Genre* 28 (1995): 95–118; Hoganson, "Garrisonian Abolitionists and the Rhetoric of Gender," 292–329; Dixon, "'A True Manly Life,'" 267–90. On women within the abolitionist movement and the conflict over the women's rights issue within it, see Ira Brown, "'Am I not a Woman and a Sister?' The Anti-Slavery Convention and American Women, 1837–1839," *History of the American Abolitionist Movement,* vol. 4, *Abolitionism and Issues of Race and Gender,* ed. John R. McKivigan (New York: Garland, 1999), 185–203; Donald R. Kennon, "'An Apple of Discord:' The Woman Question at the World's Anti-Slavery Convention of 1840," *Slavery and Abolition* 5 (1984): 244–66; Julie Roy Jeffrey, *The Great Silent Army of Abolitionism: Ordinary Women in the Antislavery Movement* (Chapel Hill: University of North Carolina Press, 1998); Michael Pierson, "Between Antislavery and Abolition: The Politics and Rhetoric of Jane Grey Swisshelm," *Pennsylvania History* 60 (1993): 305–21; Blanche Glassman Hersh, *The Slavery of Sex: Feminist-Abolitionists in America* (Urbana: University of Illinois Press, 1978); Keith Melder, *The Beginnings of Sisterhood: The American Woman's Rights Movement, 1800–1850* (New York: Schocken Books, 1977); Debra Gold Hansen, *Strained Sisterhood: Gender and Class in the Boston Female Anti-Slavery Society* (Amherst: University of Massachusetts Press, 1993); Jean Fagan Yellin, *Women and Sisters: Antislavery Feminists in American Culture* (New Haven: Yale University Press, 1989). Of these, Sanchez-Eppler offers the most unique perspective; she argues that the shared status of women and blacks derived from society's biological categorization of them. Women and slaves (as well as free blacks in many instances) were divested of their very personhood and their individuality on the basis of their physical natures. Race and sex were biological indicators of social, political, and economic function, and the bodies of women

and African Americans marked them for roles of "reproduction and production," not for those of power and domination.

89. Douglass quoted his own speech in a letter to Samuel Cox, 30 Oct. 1846 in *Frederick Douglass: Selected Speeches and Writings,* ed. Philip Foner (Chicago: Lawrence Hill Books, 1975), 40–48.

90. Ibid.

91. Ibid.

92. *Journal of the American Temperance Union,* October 1846.

93. Literature on black abolitionists and northern blacks addresses temperance in part, although no thorough study has been done: James Oliver Horton and Lois E. Horton, *In Hope of Liberty: Culture, Community, and Protest among Northern Free Blacks, 1700–1860* (New York: Oxford University Press, 1997), 221–24; William Gienapp, "Abolitionism and the Nature of Antebellum Reform," *Courage and Conscience: Black and White Abolitionists in Boston,* ed. Donald Jacobs (Bloomington: Indiana University Press, 1993), 21–46; Waldo E. Marton, Jr., *The Mind of Frederick Douglass* (Chapel Hill: University of North Carolina Press, 1984), 139, 166, 174, 185–90; William McFeely, *Frederick Douglass* (New York: Simon and Schuster, 1991); Jane H. Pease and William H. Pease, *They Who Would be Free: Blacks' Search for Freedom, 1830–1860* (New York: Athenaeum, 1974), 56–57, 121, 124–26; Benjamin Quarles, *Black Abolitionists,* 2nd edition (New York: Norton, 1973), 91–100; Patrick Rael, *Black Identity and Protest in the Antebellum North* (Chapel Hill: University of North Carolina Press, 2002), 67–68, 194; Donald Yacovone, "The Transformation of the Black Temperance Movement, 1827–1854: An Interpretation," *Journal of the Early Republic* 8 (1988): 281–97; Frederick Cooper, "Elevating the Race: The Social Thought of Black Leaders, 1827–1850," *American Quarterly* 24 (1972): 604–25.

94. Douglass himself described these occurrences, but also see Robert S. Levine, "Disturbing Boundaries: Temperance, Black Elevation, and Violence in Frank J. Webb's *The Garies and Their Friends,*" *Prospects* 19 (1994): 358; Julie Winch, *Philadelphia's Black Elite: Activism, Accommodation, and the Struggle for Autonomy* (Philadelphia: Temple University Press, 1988), 148–49. Levine offers evidence to suggest that respectability exhibited by blacks in Philadelphia (such as participation in a temperance society) actually heightened racial hostility toward them.

95. Douglass to Garrison from Dublin, September 29, 1845, Frederick Douglass Papers (microfilm), Library of Congress Manuscripts Division, Washington, DC, reel 1.

96. Ibid.; Douglass, "The Right to Criticize American Institutions," before the American Anti-Slavery Society, 11 May 1847, *Frederick Douglass,* 76–83.

97. Editorial in the *North Star,* Jan. 1848, Frederick Douglass Papers, reel 13.

98. Editorial in the *North Star,* July 1848, Ibid.

99. 4 March 1837, in Peter C. Ripley, *Witness for Freedom: African American Voices on Race, Slavery and Emancipation* (Chapel Hill: University of North Carolina Press, 1993), 51–53.

100. "To the Free Colored Inhabitants of These United States," *Witness for Freedom,* 49–51.

101. Essay by Jacob W. White, 24 March 1854, Ibid., 55–56.

102. Editorial by Samuel Cornish, *Colored American* (New York), 4 March 1837.

103. 25 Aug 1841, Elizur Wright Papers, Library of Congress Manuscripts Division, Washington, DC, folio vol. 1. He spoke of the Liberty Party, to be discussed later in this chapter.

104. Henry Mayer, *All on Fire: William Lloyd Garrison and the Abolition of Slavery* (New York: St. Martin's Press, 1998), 49–50. The motto of the paper was printed on the front page of each issue. Garrison edited the paper from 1828 to 1829.

105. Almost every issue during this time period included reports from southern societies. On the presence of southerners at conventions, see for example, September 1841. Ian R. Tyrrell, "Drink and Temperance in the Antebellum South," *Journal of Southern History* 48 (1982): 485–510.

106. Ibid., 485.

107. Ibid., 487.

108. *Journal of the American Temperance Union*, April 1837.

109. Delavan to Smith, 30 Nov. 1837, Gerrit Smith Papers (microfilm), Library of Congress Manuscripts Division, Washington, DC, reel 5.

110. Tyrrell, "Drink and Temperance in the Antebellum South," 487.

111. Delavan to Smith, 23 July 1840, Gerrit Smith Papers, reel 5.

112. 25 March 1851, Ibid.

113. John Stauffer, *The Black Hearts of Men: Radical Abolitionists and the Transformation of Race* (Cambridge, MA: Harvard University Press, 1998), 95; Mayer, *All on Fire*; Bertram Wyatt-Brown, *Lewis Tappan and the Evangelical War Against Slavery* (Cleveland: Case-Western Reserve University Press, 1969); Hugh Davis, *Joshua Leavitt: Evangelical Abolitionist* (Baton Rouge: Louisiana State University Press, 1990).

114. For more on the political climate of the 1850's and the growth of radicalism within the abolitionist movement, see David M. Potter, *The Impending Crisis, 1848–1861* (New York: HarperCollins, 1977); Jane Pease and William Pease, "Confrontation and Abolition in the 1850's," *Journal of American History* 58 (1972): 923–37; Richard Newman, "The Transformation of American Abolition: Tactics, Strategies and the Changing Meanings of Activism, 1780's–1830's," (Ph.D. dissertation, SUNY Buffalo, 1998); Michael Holt, *The Political Crisis of the 1850's* (New York: W.W. Norton, 1983).

115. Including the *Investigator and General Intelligencer* (Providence, Rhode Island); the *National Philanthropist, Investigator and Genius of Temperance*, which had formerly been simply the *National Philanthropist* and edited by William Lloyd Garrison; and the *Genius of Temperance, Philanthropist and People's Advocate* (New York).

116. Paul Goodman, *Of One Blood: Abolitionism and the Origins of Racial Equality* (Berkeley: University of California Press, 1998), ch. 7.

117. Goodell to Josiah Cady, April 1831, William Goodell Family Papers, Historical Collections of Berea College, Berea, KY, box 13, folder 15.

118. Jan 20, 1829 and June 4, 1829.

119. *Genius of Temperance, Philanthropist and People's Advocate*, 1 Jan. 1832.

120. His chief differences (and those of Smith and most others in their circle) with Garrison concerned his belief in the Constitution as an anti-slavery document and in political tactics. The historiography concerning the differences between these two groups of abolitionists is large. Most historians seem to agree that the issue of political reform, not women's rights, was the chief difference. Historians seem to be moving away from the moderate/radical method of categorization, as many anti-Garrisonians were very radical indeed and against what became the "one idea" method of the Liberty Party. Goodell and Smith definitely fit this mould. See Lawrence Friedman, "The Gerrit Smith Circle: Abolitionism in the Burned Over District," *History of the American Abolitionist Movement*, vol. 3, *Abolitionism and American Politics and Government*, ed. John McKivigan (New York: Garland Publishing, 1999), 12–32; Aileen Kraditor, *Means and Ends in American Abolitionism: Garrison and His Critics on Strategy and Tactics* (New York: Random House, 1967); James Brewer Stewart, *Holy Warriors: The Abolitionists and American Slavery*, revised edition (New York: Hill and Wang, 1997), ch. 3–4; Ronald G. Walters, *The Antislavery Appeal: American Abolitionism after 1830* (Baltimore: Johns Hopkins University Press, 1976); William W. Wiecek, *The Sources of Antislavery Constitutionalism in America* (Ithaca: Cornell University Press, 1977); John Stauffer, *The Black Hearts of Men*; Goodman, *Of One Blood*, ch. 7; Lewis Perry, "Versions of Anarchism in the Antislavery Movement," *American Quarterly* 20 (1968): 768–82. For more on the specific constitutional views of Goodell and other anti-Garrisonians, see M. Leon Perkal, "The American Abolition Society: A Viable Alternative to the Republican Party?," *Journal of Negro History* 65 (1980): 57–71 and Randy Barnett, "Was Slavery Unconstitutional Before the Thirteenth Amendment?: Lysander Spooner's Theory of Interpretation," *Pacific Law Journal* 28 (1997): 977–1014. Also see Goodell's own writing on the subject, such as *Views of American constitutional law in its bearing upon American slavery* (Utica, NY: Lawson & Chaplin, 1845).

121. For more on "comeouterism" and the religious side of abolition, see James D. Essig, *The Bonds of Wickedness: American Evangelicals against Slavery, 1770–1808* (Philadelphia: Temple University Press, 1982); Victor B. Howard, *The Evangelical War against Slavery and Caste: The Life and Times of John G. Fee* (Selinsgrove, PA: Susquehanna University Press, 1996); James Brewer Stewart, *Holy Warriors*; Robert H. Abzug, *Cosmos Crumbling: American Reform and the Religious Imagination* (New York: Oxford University Press, 1994); Lawrence Friedman, *Gregarious Saints*; John R. McKivigan, *The War Against Proslavery Religion: Abolitionism and the Northern Churches, 1830–1865* (Ithaca: Cornell University Press, 1984) and "The Antislavery 'Comeouter' Sects: A Neglected Dimension of the Abolitionist Movement," *Civil War History* 26 (1980): 142–60; Anne C. Loveland, "Evangelicalism

and 'Immediate Emancipation' in American Antislavery Thought," *Journal of Southern History* 32 (May 1966): 172–88; Donald G. Mathews, *Slavery and Methodism: A Chapter in American Morality, 1780–1845* (Princeton: Princeton University Press, 1965), 677–695; Douglas Strong, *Perfectionist Politics: Abolitionism and the Religious Tensions of American Democracy* (Syracuse, NY: Syracuse University Press, 1999). Strong gives Goodell much attention as a reformer who led the way in ecclesiastical abolitionism. He sees the Liberty Party as an outgrowth of perfectionist evangelical religion, which stressed the experience of personal sanctification and the belief in human frailty as necessitating human political structures.

122. William Goodell to J. Cady, 6 July 1846, Goodell Family Papers, box 13, folder 16; "In Memoriam. William Goodell" (Chicago: Guilbert and Winchell Printers, 1879), Frederick Douglass Papers, reel 11.

123. Smith's own reform career closely paralleled and intertwined with that of Goodell. His hometown of Peterboro, New York was rife with intemperance, and Smith had been an early temperance proponent. He had been a moderate on that issue and on slavery (he was in favor of colonization), until the late 1830's, when his path turned toward militant abolitionism and other radical reforms. One historian attributed this transition and that made by other reformers to the shock of the financial collapse of 1837. Smith's own fortune suffered, and his ideas seemed markedly affected. Stauffer, *Black Hearts of Men*, 95; Friedman, "The Gerrit Smith Circle."

124. Goodell to J. Cady, 4 April 1846, Goodell Family Papers, box 13, folder 17. For more on the Liberty Party, see Richard H. Sewell, *Ballots for Freedom: Antislavery Politics in the United States, 1837–1860* (New York: Oxford University Press, 1976); Strong, *Perfectionist Politics*. The only thorough history of the Liberty Party is Vernon Volpe's *Forlorn Hope of Freedom: The Liberty Party in the Old Northwest, 1838–1848* (Kent, OH: Kent State University Press, 1990), which views the Liberty Party as the closest thing in American politics to an abolitionist party and an evangelical party. He notes the religious roots of the party; most members were, like Goodell, anti-Garrisonian Protestant Christians, who had been involved in the "comeouter" movements in the major denominations. The Liberty Party's radical egalitarianism, including attacks on the American tax system and the "land monopoly," seems to counter the interpretation of abolitionists as conservatives who reinforced class hegemony. For more on this debate, see David Brion Davis, "Reflections on Abolitionism and Ideological Hegemony," *American Historical Review* 92 (1987): 797–812; Thomas Haskell, "Capitalism and the Origins of Humanitarian Sensibility, Part I," *American Historical Review* 90 (1985): 339–61 and Part 2 *American Historical Review* 90 (1985): 457–566; Betty Fladeland, *Abolitionists and Working-Class Problems in the Age of Industrialization* (Baton Rouge: Louisiana State University Press, 1984); James Brewer Stewart, "The Aims and Impact of Garrisonian Abolitionism, 1840–1860," *Civil War History* 15 (1969): 197–209; Kraditor, *Means and Ends in American Abolitionism*; James L. Huston, "The Experiential Basis of the Northern Antislavery Impulse," *Journal of Southern History* 56 (1990): 192–215.

125. The Liberty Party did not include women's rights in its platform, but subsequent political efforts by Goodell and Gerrit Smith did. The two men went on in 1856 and 1858 to form a New York state equal rights party with an "omnibus" reform platform that featured women's rights more prominently. In addition, John Stauffer has called Smith a "gender radical," and Goodell's anti-clerical stance had feminist ramifications, since the clerical system blocked women's participation in church leadership. See Stauffer, *Black Hearts of Men*, 211; Isenberg, *Sex and Citizenship*, ch. 4; *Gerrit Smith Banner* (New York), 16 and 21 October 1858. In addition, Michael Pierson identifies a "jumble" of gendered views in the Liberty Party, some of them radical; see *Free Hearts and Free Homes*, 20, 25–70.

126. "Address of the Macedon Convention," (Albany: S.W. Green, 1847), quote on 6, 9. With this address, Goodell split from the Liberty Party and formed the Liberty League because he believed the Liberty Party was too single-minded in its pursuit of abolition.

127. "Christian Temperance," delivered in Arcadia, NY in Aug. 1858, Goodell Family Papers, box 8, folder 39; "The Condition and Refuge of our Country," 9 Oct. 1859 at Williamsburg, Ibid., box 8, folder 37.

128. "Address of the Macedon Convention," 6–7.

129. This view is based on an interpretation of liberalism that emphasizes its radical potentials, as expressed in moral reform movements. Abolitionists, feminists, and other radical egalitarians emphasized individualism not for economic self-interest, but on the basis of human rights. See Louis S. Gerteis, *Morality and Utility in American Antislavery Reform* (Chapel Hill: University of North Carolina Press, 1987); Peter F. Walker, *Moral Choices: Memory, Desire, and Imagination in Nineteenth Century American Abolition* (Baton Rouge: Louisiana State University Press, 1978); Isenberg, *Sex and Citizenship*; Linda K. Kerber, *No Constitutional Right to be Ladies: Women and the Obligations of Citizenship* (New York: Hill and Wang, 1998); Amy Dru Stanley, *From Bondage to Contract: Wage Labor, Marriage, and the Market in the Age of Slave Emancipation* (Cambridge: Cambridge University Press, 1998); Sylvia Hoffert, *When Hens Crow: The Woman's Rights Movement in Antebellum America* (Bloomington: Indiana University Press, 1995); Rosemarie Zagarri, "Gender and the New Liberal Synthesis," *American Quarterly* 53 (2001): 123–30; Stauffer, *Black Hearts of Men*; David F. Ericson, *The Debate over Slavery: Antislavery and Pro-slavery Liberalism in Antebellum America* (New York: New York University Press, 2000).

130. For other historical accounts of the events described here, see Elizabeth Cazden, *Antoinette Brown Blackwell: A Biography* (Old Westbury, NY: The Feminist Press, 1983), ch. 2, 3, 5; Isenberg, *Sex and Citizenship*, 99–101; Hoffert, *When Hens Crow*, 20–21.

131. *New York Tribune*, 13 May 1853; *New York Times*, 13 May 1853.

132. *Anti-Slavery Bugle* (Salem, OH), 2 July 1853.

133. *New York Tribune*, 3 Sept. 1853.

134. Ibid.

135. *Journal of the American Temperance Union*, June 1853.
136. Ibid., Oct. 1853.
137. *New York People's Organ, A Family Companion* (New York), 15 Oct. 1853.
138. *New York Tribune*, 7 Sept. 1853.
139. *Una* (Providence, RI), 1 September 1853.
140. *New York Tribune*, 7 Sept. 1853.
141. Ibid., 9 Sept. 1853.
142. Ibid., 7 Sept. 1853.
143. *Anti-Slavery Bugle*, 17 Sept. 1853.
144. *New York Tribune*, 7 Sept. 1853; *New York Times*, 7–8 Sept. 1853.
145. Ibid., 8–10 Sept. 1853.

Bibliography

Manuscript Collections

Susan B. Anthony Papers (microfilm). Manuscripts Division, Library of Congress. Washington, DC.
Blackwell Family Papers (microfilm). Manuscripts Division, Library of Congress. Washington, DC.
Frederick Douglass Papers (microfilm). Manuscripts Division, Library of Congress. Washington, DC.
William Goodell Family Papers. Historical Collections, Berea College. Berea, Kentucky.
Gerrit Smith Papers (microfilm). Manuscripts Division, Library of Congress. Washington, DC.
Elizur Wright Papers. Manuscripts Division, Library of Congress. Washington, DC.

Newspapers and Periodicals

American Quarterly Temperance Magazine (Albany, NY)
Anti-Slavery Bugle (Salem, OH)
The Colored American (New York)
The Fountain, Organ of the Connecticut Washingtonian Total Abstinence Society (New Haven, CT)
Frederick Douglass Paper (Rochester, NY)
Genius of Temperance, Philanthropist and People's Advocate (New York)
Gerrit Smith Banner (New York)
Journal of the American Temperance Union (Philadelphia)
The Lily (Seneca Falls, NY)
Michigan Temperance Journal and Washingtonian (Jackson, MI)
Michigan Washingtonian (Jackson, MI)
National Philanthropist (Boston)
New York People's Organ, A Family Companion (New York)

New York Times

New York Tribune

The Samaritan and Total Abstinence Advocate (Providence, RI)

Temperance Offering (Salem, MA)

The Una (Providence, RI)

The Washingtonian (Augusta, ME)

Worcester County Cataract and Massachusetts Washingtonian (Worcester, MA)

Published Primary Sources

American Temperance Union. *Report of the Executive Committee of the American Temperance Union.* New York: American Temperance Union, 1842.

———. *Permanent Temperance Documents of the American Temperance Society.* New York: American Temperance Union, 1843.

Arthur, T.S. *Six Nights with the Washingtonians: A Series of Temperance Tales.* Philadelphia: L.A. Godey and Morton McMichael, 1842.

Bloomer, D.C. *The Life and Writings of Amelia Bloomer.* Boston: Arena Publishing, 1895.

Coon, Anne C., ed. *Hear Me Patiently: The Reform Speeches of Amelia Jenks Bloomer.* Westport, CT: Greenwood Press, 1994.

DuBois, Ellen Carol, ed. *Elizabeth Cady Stanton, Susan B. Anthony: Correspondence, Writings, Speeches.* New York: Schocken Brooks, 1981.

Foner, Philip, ed. *Frederick Douglass: Selected Speeches and Writings.* Chicago: Lawrence Hill Books, 1975.

Goodell, William. *Views of American constitutional law in its bearing upon American slavery.* Utica, NY: Lawson & Chaplin, 1845.

———. *Address of the Macedon Convention.* Albany, NY: S.W. Green, 1847.

Johnson, Lorenzo Dow. *Martha Washingtonianism, or History of the Ladies Temperance Benevolent Societies.* New York: Saxton and Miles, 1843.

Livermore, Mary A. *The Story of My Life, or The Sunshine and Shadow of Seventy Years.* Hartford, CT: A.D. Worthington and Co., Publishers, 1899.

A member of the society. *The Foundation, Progress and Principles of the Washingtonian Temperance Society of Baltimore and the Influence it has had on the Temperance Movements in the United States.* Baltimore: John D. Troy, 1842.

Ripley, Peter C., ed. *Witness for Freedom: African American Voices on Race, Slavery and Emancipation.* Chapel Hill: University of North Carolina Press, 1993.

Stanton, Elizabeth Cady, Susan B. Anthony et al. *History of Woman Suffrage.* Vol. I. New York: Arno Press, 1969.

Swisshelm, Jane Grey. *Half a Century.* 2nd edition. Chicago: Jansen, McClurg and Co., 1980.

White, Philip S. and Ezra Stiles Ely. *Vindication of the Order of the Sons of Temperance.* New York: Oliver and Brothers, Publishers, 1848.

Published Secondary Sources

Abzug, Robert H. *Cosmos Crumbling: American Reform and the Religious Imagination.* New York: Oxford University Press, 1994.

Alexander, Ruth M. "'We Are Engaged as a Band of Sisters:' Class and Domesticity in the Washingtonian Temperance Movement, 1840–1850." *Journal of American History* 75 (1988): 763–87.

Baker, Paula. "The Domestication of Politics: Women and American Political Society, 1780–1920." *American Historical Review* 89 (1984): 620–47.

———. *The Moral Frameworks of Public Life: Gender, Politics and the State in Rural New York, 1870–1930.* New York: Oxford University Press, 1991.

Barnett, Randy. "Was Slavery Unconstitutional Before the Thirteenth Amendment?: Lysander Spooner's Theory of Interpretation." *Pacific Law Journal* 28 (1997): 977–1014.

Blocker, Jack S., ed. *American Temperance Movements: Cycles of Reform.* Boston: Twayne Publishers, 1989.

Bordin, Ruth. *Woman and Temperance: The Quest for Power and Liberty, 1873–1900.* Philadelphia: Temple University Press, 1981.

Carnes, Mark C. and Clyde Griffen, eds. *Meanings for Manhood: Constructions of Masculinity in Victorian America.* Chicago: Chicago University Press, 1990.

Cazden, Elizabeth. *Antoinette Brown Blackwell: A Biography.* Old Westbury, NY: The Feminist Press, 1983.

Cooper, Frederick. "Elevating the Race: The Social Thought of Black Leaders, 1827–1850." *American Quarterly* 24 (1972): 604–25.

Cutter, Barbara. *Domestic Devils, Battlefield Angels: The Radicalism of American Womanhood, 1830–1865.* DeKalb, IL: Northern Illinois University Press, 2003.

Davis, David Brion. "Reflections on Abolitionism and Ideological Hegemony." *American Historical Review* 92 (1987): 797–812.

Davis, Hugh. *Joshua Leavitt: Evangelical Abolitionist.* Baton Rouge: Louisiana State University Press, 1990.

Dixon, Christopher. "'A True Manly Life:' Abolitionism and the Masculine Ideal." *Mid-America* 77 (1995): 267–90.

———. *Woman Suffrage and Women's Rights.* New York: New York University Press, 1998.

Epstein, Barbara Leslie. *The Politics of Domesticity: Women, Evangelism and Temperance in Nineteenth-Century America.* Middletown, CT: Wesleyan University Press, 1981.

Ericson, David F. *The Debate over Slavery: Antislavery and Proslavery Liberalism in Antebellum America.* New York: New York University Press, 2000.

Essig, James D. *The Bonds of Wickedness: American Evangelicals against Slavery, 1770–1808.* Philadelphia: Temple University Press, 1982.

Fabian, Ann. *The Unvarnished Truth: Personal Narratives in Nineteenth-Century America.* Berkeley: University of California Press, 2000.

Fladeland, Betty. *Abolitionists and Working-Class Problems in the Age of Industrialization.* Baton Rouge: Louisiana State University Press, 1984.

Friedman, Lawrence. *Gregarious Saints: Self and Community in Antebellum American Abolitionism, 1830–1870.* Cambridge: Cambridge University Press, 1982.

Gerteis, Louis S. *Morality and Utility in American Antislavery Reform.* Chapel Hill: University of North Carolina Press, 1987.

Giele, Janet Zollinger. *Two Paths to Women's Equality: Temperance, Suffrage, and the Origins of Liberal Feminism in the United States, 1820–1920.* Cambridge, MA: Harvard University Press, 1996.

Goodman, Paul. *Of One Blood: Abolitionism and the Origins of Racial Equality.* Berkeley: University of California Press, 1998.

Gusfield, Joseph R. *Symbolic Crusade: Status Politics and the American Temperance Movement.* 2nd edition. Urbana: University of Illinois Press, 1986.

Hansen, Debra Gold. *Strained Sisterhood: Gender and Class in the Boston Female Anti-Slavery Society.* Amherst: University of Massachusetts Press, 1993.

Haskell, Thomas. "Capitalism and the Origins of Humanitarian Sensibility, Part I." *American Historical Review* 90 (1985): 339–61.

———. "Capitalism and the Origins of Humanitarian Sensibility, Part II." *American Historical Review* 90 (1985): 457–566.

Hersh, Blanche Glassman. *The Slavery of Sex: Feminist-Abolitionists in America.* Urbana: University of Illinois Press, 1978.

Hoffert, Sylvia. *When Hens Crow: The Women's Rights Movement in Antebellum America.* Bloomington: Indiana University Press, 1995.

Hoganson, Kristin. "Garrisonian Abolitionists and the Rhetoric of Gender, 1850–1860." *American Quarterly* 45 (1993): 292–329.

Holt, Michael. *The Political Crisis of the 1850's.* New York: W.W. Norton, 1983.

Horton, James Oliver and Lois E. Horton. *In Hope of Liberty: Culture, Community, and Protest among Northern Free Blacks, 1700–1860.* New York: Oxford University Press, 1997.

Howard, Victor B. *The Evangelical War against Slavery and Caste: The Life and Times of John G. Fee.* Selinsgrove, PA: Susquehanna University Press, 1996.

Huston, James L. "The Experiential Basis of the Northern Antislavery Impulse." *Journal of Southern History* 56 (1990): 192–215.

———. *Sex and Citizenship in Antebellum America.* Chapel Hill: University of North Carolina Press, 1998.

Jacobs, Donald, ed. *Courage and Conscience: Black and White Abolitionists in Boston*. Bloomington: Indiana University Press, 1993.

Jeffrey, Julie Roy. *The Great Silent Army of Abolitionism: Ordinary Women in the Antislavery Movement*. Chapel Hill: University of North Carolina Press, 1998.

Kennon, Donald R. "'An Apple of Discord:' The Woman Question at the World's Anti-Slavery Convention of 1840." *Slavery and Abolition* 5 (1984): 244–66.

———. *No Constitutional Right to be Ladies: Women and the Obligations of Citizenship*. New York: Hill and Wang, 1998.

Kingsdale, Jon M. "The 'Poor Man's Club:' Social Functions of the Urban Working-Class Saloon." *American Quarterly* 25 (1973): 255–84.

———. *Means and Ends in American Abolitionism: Garrison and His Critics on Strategy and Tactics*. New York: Random House, 1967.

Levine, Lawrence W. *Highbrow/Lowbrow: The Emergence of Cultural Hierarchy in America*. Cambridge, MA: Harvard University Press, 1988.

Levine, Robert S. "Disturbing Boundaries: Temperance, Black Elevation, and Violence in Frank J. Webb's *The Garies and Their Friends*." *Prospects* 19 (1994): 349–74.

Loveland, Anne C. "Evangelicalism and 'Immediate Emancipation' in American Antislavery Thought." *Journal of Southern History* 32 (1966): 172–88.

Marilley, Suzanne. *Woman Suffrage and the Origins of Liberal Feminism in the United States, 1820–1920*. Cambridge, MA: Harvard University Press, 1996.

Marton, Waldo E., Jr. *The Mind of Frederick Douglass*. Chapel Hill: University of North Carolina Press, 1984.

Mathews, Donald G. *Slavery and Methodism: A Chapter in American Morality, 1780–1845*. Princeton: Princeton University Press, 1965.

Mayer, Henry. *All on Fire: William Lloyd Garrison and the Abolition of Slavery*. New York: St. Martin's Press, 1998.

McFeely, William. *Frederick Douglass*. New York: Simon and Schuster, 1991.

McGerr, Michael. "Political Style and Women's Power, 1830–1930." *Journal of American History* 77 (1990): 864–85.

McKivigan, John R. "The Antislavery 'Comeouter' Sects: A Neglected Dimension of the Abolitionist Movement." *Civil War History* 26 (1980): 142–60.

———. *The War Against Proslavery Religion: Abolitionism and the Northern Churches, 1830–1865*. Ithaca: Cornell University Press, 1984.

———, ed. *History of the American Abolitionist Movement*. Vol. 3, *Abolitionism and American Politics and Government*. New York: Garland Publishing, 1999.

———, ed. *History of the American Abolitionist Movement*. Vol. 4, *Abolitionism and Issues of Race and Gender*. New York: Garland Publishing, 1999.

Melder, Keith. *The Beginnings of Sisterhood: The American Women's Rights Movement, 1800–1850.* New York: Schocken Books, 1977.

Murphy, Gretchen. "Enslaved Bodies: Figurative Slavery in the Temperance Fiction of Harriet Beecher Stowe and Walt Whitman." *Genre* 28 (1995): 95–118.

Murphy, Teresa Anne. *Ten Hours' Labor: Religion, Reform, and gender in Early New England.* Ithaca: Cornell University Press, 1992.

Pease, Jane H. and William H. Pease. "Confrontation and Abolition in the 1850's." *Journal of American History* 58 (1972): 923–37.

———. *They Who Would Be Free: Blacks' Search for Freedom, 1830–1860.* New York: Athenaeum, 1974.

Perkal, M. Leon. "The American Abolition Society: A Viable Alternative to the Republican Party?" *Journal of Negro History* 65 (1980): 57–71.

Perry, Lewis. "Versions of Anarchism in the Antislavery Movement." *American Quarterly* 20 (1968): 768–82.

———. *Childhood, Marriage and Reform: Henry Clarke Wright, 1797–1870.* Chicago: University of Chicago Press, 1980.

Pierson, Michael D. "Between Antislavery and Abolition: The Politics and Rhetoric of Jane Grey Swisshelm." *Pennsylvania History* 60 (1993): 305–21.

———. *Free Hearts and Free Homes: Gender and American Antislavery Politics.* Chapel Hill: University of North Carolina Press, 2003.

Potter, David M. *The Impending Crisis, 1848–1861.* New York: Harper Collins, 1977.

Putzi, Jennifer. *Identifying Marks: Race, Gender, and the Marked Body in Nineteenth-Century America.* Athens: University of Georgia Press, 2006.

Quarles, Benjamin. *Black Abolitionists.* New York: W.W. Norton, 1973.

Rael, Patrick. *Black Identity and Protest in the Antebellum North.* Chapel Hill: University of North Carolina Press, 2002.

Rosenzweig, Roy. *Eight Hours for What We Will: Workers and Leisure in an Industrial City, 1870–1920.* Cambridge: Cambridge University Press, 1983.

———. *Women in Public: Between Banners and Ballots, 1825–1880.* Baltimore: Johns Hopkins University Press, 1990.

Sanchez-Eppler, Karen. "Bodily Bonds: The Intersecting Rhetorics of Feminism and Abolition." *Representations* 24 (1988): 28–59.

———. *Touching Liberty: Abolition, Feminism and the Politics of the Body.* Los Angeles: University of California at Berkeley Press, 1993.

Sewell, Richard H. *Ballots for Freedom: Antislavery Politics in the United States, 1837–1860.* New York: Oxford University Press, 1976.

Stanley, Amy Dru. *From Bondage to Contract: Wage Labor, Marriage, and the Market in the Age of Slave Emancipation.* Cambridge: Cambridge University Press, 1998.

Stauffer, John. *The Black Hearts of Men: Radical Abolitionists and the Transformation of Race.* Cambridge, MA: Harvard University Press, 2002.

Stewart, James Brewer. "The Aims and Impact of Garrisonian Abolitionism, 1840–1860." *Civil War History* 15 (1969): 197–209.

———. *Holy Warriors: The Abolitionists and American Slavery.* Revised edition. New York: Hill and Wang, 1997.

Strong, Douglas. *Perfectionist Politics: Abolitionism and the Religious Tensions of American Democracy.* Syracuse, NY: Syracuse University Press, 1999.

———. "Drink and Temperance in the Antebellum South: An Overview and Interpretation." *Journal of Southern History* 48 (1982): 485–510.

Volpe, Vernon. *Forlorn Hope of Freedom: The Liberty Party in the Old Northwest, 1838–1848.* Kent, OH: Kent State University Press, 1990.

Walker, Peter F. *Moral Choices: Memory, Desire, and Imagination in Nineteenth-Century American Abolition.* Baton Rouge: Louisiana State University Press, 1978.

Walters, Ronald G. *The Antislavery Appeal: American Abolitionism after 1830.* Baltimore: Johns Hopkins University Press, 1976.

Wiecek, William W. *The Sources of Antislavery Constitutionalism in America.* Ithaca: Cornell University Press, 1977.

Wilentz, Sean. *Chants Democratic: New York and the Rise of the American Working Working Class.* Oxford and New York: Oxford University Press, 1984.

Winch, Julie. *Philadelphia's Black Elite: Activism, Accommodation, and the Struggle for Autonomy.* Philadelphia: Temple University Press, 1988.

Wyatt-Brown, Bertram. *Lewis Tappan and the Evangelical War Against Slavery.* Cleveland: Case-Western Reserve University Press, 1969.

Yacovone, Donald. "The Transformation of the Black Temperance Movement, 1827–1854: An Interpretation." *Journal of the Early Republic* 8 (1988): 281–97.

Yellin, Jean Fagan. *Women and Sisters: Antislavery Feminists in American Culture.* New Haven: Yale University Press, 1989.

Zagarri, Rosemarie. "Gender and the New Liberal Synthesis." *American Quarterly* 53 (2001): 123–30.

Unpublished Dissertations

Clark, Elizabeth Battelle. "The Politics of God and the Woman's Vote: Religion in the American Suffrage Movement, 1848–1895." Ph.D. dissertation. Princeton University, 1989.

Newman, Richard. "The Transformation of American Abolition: Tactics, Strategies and the Changing Meanings of Activism, 1780's–1830's." Ph.D. dissertation. State University of New York Buffalo, 1998.

Chapter 2: **Critical Thinking Questions**

Directions: Reflect on what you have read and use information from the reading selections as a resource as you respond to the following critical thinking questions.

1. What do you think of the cultural developments in the Americas as indigenous, European, and African people encountered each other in the western hemisphere? Do you agree or disagree that these encounters created a new culture? If so, what are some examples from the readings?

2. In what ways can you identify some weaknesses of cultural developments taking place in the Americas in the late fifteenth through the late nineteenth centuries? How did these changes reflect a struggle for a more inclusive and democratic society by the late nineteenth century?

3. Based on the readings, in what ways did indigenous, African, and European people respond to the way others (outside of their own cultural groups) in their shared sphere viewed changes, such as foodways, epidemics, land use, chattel enslavement, and Christianity? What are some examples from the readings that highlight the consequences of their responses?

4. Reflect on a moment when you were either in a position of power or powerlessness. How did you use your position in relation to those who held either less or more power than you? How did indigenous, African, and European people make use of their positions in the Americas, and how do the readings show the give and take regarding cultural influence in the Americas?

Chapter 3

Broadening the Possibilities

Readings in Western Atlantic Economic Changes from 1492 to 1877

Introduction

In this chapter we explore the colonial economic aims in the Americas and how those objectives shaped the development of the Western Atlantic world as an economic engine that fueled not only the rise of intense economic competition between European empires, but also the rise of an American empire—an empire that came at the expense of indigenous American territory and African labor. Furthermore, the drive of economic competition, fueled largely by a winner-take-all mindset among Europeans, and the commodification of Atlantic world resources resulted in western capitalism.

In this section the selected titles focus on the early economic objectives of the Atlantic world, the intricate connection between enslavement and capitalism, the expansionist motivations of the United States in acquiring territory, the struggle over America's regionally centric political economy during the Civil War, and the economic rebuilding of America's agricultural system in the South after the war. The goal of the chapter is to demonstrate how the Americas and the United States shifted from an indigenous to a Eurocentric to an American style of economy and how these shifts impacted the various populations of the region. It is also feasible for readers to glean how, in spite of the major economic changes occurring from the fifteenth through the nineteenth centuries, groups of people struggled to secure control over their own economic well-being.

The selections in this section also encourage readers to consider the following points.

1. How do the readings shape your understanding of the economic development of the United States?
2. How does America's idea of liberty coincide with economic prosperity in the United States?

Reading 3.1

Expanding Horizons

Anne Gerritsen and Anthony McFarlane

I N THE LATER MIDDLE AGES, EUROPE had two great concentrations of wealth and power: the Italian city-states, which had grown rich from the luxury trades between Asia and Europe ('The Renaissance' in Part IV), and the north German towns of the HANSEATIC LEAGUE, which controlled commerce in the products of northern seas, mines, forests and farms. The southern Netherlands was another region of burgeoning economic activity during the fifteenth century, when its industry and commerce helped the Duchy of Burgundy emerge as a serious rival to the kingdom of France. During the 1500s, however, Europe's economic centre of gravity shifted away from these foundations as medieval patterns of trade were supplemented and surpassed by new routes for commerce, opened by voyages of discovery made from Portugal and Spain during the fifteenth century. Reaching into the Atlantic Ocean from Lisbon and Seville, these routes extended to Africa, Asia and the Americas, hugely expanding European economic, political and cultural horizons and bringing into Western Europe resources that were gradually to transform its economies and societies [...].

Atlantic Explorations

Europeans looked for new trade routes in the later fifteenth century partly because the consolidation of the Islamic Ottoman Empire in the Near East threatened Europe's overland trade with Asia. When Italian and other European merchants began to look beyond the Mediterranean for the sources of their most lucrative trades, they turned to the 'Ocean Sea' (the Atlantic) as a place for exploration, seeking direct maritime routes for the trade in spices from India and access to the rich kingdoms of the 'Great Khan' memorialized in Marco Polo's description of his travels to China ('Europe in 1500' in Part I).

FIGURE 3.1.1   The 'Caravel Redunda', with square and lateen sails, *c.* 1470: 'Classic Sailing Ships' (Web resources).

Their ability to navigate away from European shorelines and into the open sea was closely associated with growing knowledge and improved technology. Late medieval European mariners had adopted the stern-post rudder and square yardarm sails, and in the fifteenth century the combination of square sails with lateen sails on multi-masted caravels made their ships manoeuvrable, able to sail against the wind and capable of long-distance travel (Figure 3.1.1). The compass—possibly brought from China in the thirteenth century—and charts for navigation entered into wider and more systematic use both inside and outside the Mediterranean. Europe was thus well equipped to undertake long-distance maritime exploration and, in its search for silks, spices and other eastern luxuries, had greater commercial incentives than the Arabs, who already traded such commodities, or the Chinese, who in the early fifteenth century had sailed into the Indian Ocean in very large treasure ships, but subsequently abandoned their maritime explorations in preference for defending their vast internal borders ('Beyond Europe *c.* 1500' in Part I).

Although Italians were conspicuous among the mariners and merchants who engaged in Atlantic maritime exploration, the Iberian kingdoms of Portugal and Castile did most to extend the Atlantic frontiers. The former was particularly prominent. Portuguese mariners began to enlarge European knowledge of the Atlantic by pushing southwards down the coast of Africa. One objective was to find the sources of gold and spices that were carried from the African interior by overland caravans into North African territories dominated by Islam; another motive, increasingly important after mid-century, was to take African slaves ('Marginals and Deviants' in Part II; 'Beyond Europe *c.* 1800' in Part VI). Reinforcing the desire for gain were political and religious motives derived from the traditions of crusade against Islam and encapsulated in the myth of a lost Christian kingdom, known as the land of Prester John. Believed to be somewhere to the rear of the great Islamic sphere of influence that extended from Morocco to the Black Sea, the kingdom of Prester John added to the lure of contacts with new lands and new sources of wealth in Africa, for contact with this lost Christian realm offered the possibility of opening a second front in the struggle against Islam (Box 3.1.1).

Inspired by these goals, Portuguese exploration moved in two directions. One led to the two archipelagos of Atlantic islands that lay west from the Moroccan and Saharan coasts. In the 1420s, Prince Henry 'the Navigator' laid claim to the Canary Islands, despite the presence of French and Castilian settlers who had occupied two or three small islands under the auspices of the Castilian monarchy (Russell 2001). This started a long struggle between Portugal and Castile for control of the Atlantic islands, not only for the resources they might offer but also for their strategic positions off the African coast. The other direction lay southwards along the West African coast, where Portuguese traders went in search of gold, tropical commodities and slaves. In 1434, after the rounding of Cape Bojador, the point on the northern coast of the western Sahara long regarded as the impassable limit of exploration, Prince Henry created the Guinea trade that established Portugal as the leader in European trade with Africa. The resources derived from the trade in gold and slaves encouraged the Portuguese to push further south in a more systematic search for the mythical Kingdom of Prester John and, increasingly, for a route which would lead them to the fabled trade of India. In 1488, the second great advance was made, when Bartolomé Dias rounded the Cape of Good Hope, showing a way into the Arab-dominated Indian Ocean that was triumphantly extended by Vasco da Gama's famous voyage to India in 1497–99.

Spaniards were also active in the Atlantic during the later fifteenth century. After many decades of involvement in trade and colonization in the Canary Islands, Castile successfully fought Portugal for their possession in 1475 and secured both an interest in overseas expansion and an advance base from which it might move further into the 'Ocean Sea'. In Spain, too, interest in finding a route to the east intensified during the closing years of the fifteenth century, so that when Columbus prevailed upon the Spanish crown to support a westward voyage to reach the shores of Asia, he received a sympathetic hearing. After his plans had been rejected by Portugal, France and possibly England, Columbus secured support from Isabella of Castile and Ferdinand of Aragon, and in 1492 sailed west across the Atlantic in the belief that he would find a shorter route to China. In so doing, he came across the Caribbean islands and, although he persisted in believing that he had found the shores of Asia, his subsequent voyages and those of other men serving the Spanish monarchy became the points of entry for exploration, conquest and colonization in what was, for Europeans, a 'New World' ('1492': Web resources).

Portugal's expansion took a different route. After landing at Calicut on the west coast of India in 1498, Vasco da Gama began the process whereby Portugal would subsequently create a rich trading empire that stretched far beyond its trading posts in Africa to reach the coasts and islands of South and East Asia. This did not exclude America: in 1500, a fleet under Pedro Alvares Cabral embarked on a second Portuguese voyage to India and, when sailing west in the Atlantic, encountered a land hitherto unknown to Europeans. Cabral called his discovery the 'Land of the Holy Cross' and claimed it for Portugal under the terms of the Treaty of Tordesillas (1494). In the latter, Spain and Portugal had accepted Pope Alexander VI's division of the world beyond Europe into two spheres, with a line of demarcation that reserved new lands to the west for Spain and left Africa and Asia to Portugal. Because Cabral's discovery lay east of that line, which was drawn when the shape and size of the American continent were still unknown, Portugal fortuitously but legitimately acquired rights over the large territory that became known as Brazil.

By the end of the fifteenth century, then, Atlantic exploration had yielded rich results. The sea route to Asia around Africa laid the foundations for the emergence of an expansive Portuguese sea-borne empire in the east, while the westward route allowed Spain to establish bases on which to build a vast territorial empire in the Americas. Expanding commerce and colonization was to enrich the countries that controlled the new circuits of commerce. Both Spain and Portugal saw an unprecedented increase in their economic and political weight within Europe, as their discoveries led to the formation of great empires overseas.

The Spanish and Portuguese Empires

The Spanish American empire was the first and most formidable of the European empires in the western hemisphere. From the Caribbean colonies of Hispaniola and Cuba, Spaniards entered the American continent in pursuit of gold, slaves and new land to conquer. Colonization of the mainlands started on the northern shores of South America in 1509–10, but the crucial feats of conquest were in Mexico and Peru, where small groups of Spaniards defeated large Amerindian states and took possession of lands that were to become Spain's richest colonies ('Beyond Europe *c.* 1500' in Part I). In 1519, Hernán Cortés entered Mexico; by 1521, he had overthrown the Aztec state and, on the ruins of its capital Tenochtitlán, founded Mexico City, later the capital of the Viceroyalty of New Spain. In 1532, Francisco Pizarro penetrated into Peru and, after capturing, ransoming and killing the Inca king Atahualpa, he and his conquistadors entered the Inca capital at Cuzco in 1533, where they established a base for further conquests in South America. By the mid-sixteenth century, waves of Spanish conquerors and settlers had spread from the core areas of conquest into adjoining regions, where they asserted control over many indigenous peoples.

Spanish overseas colonies were concentrated on towns which acted as bases for dominating the Indian countryside (Parry 1963). At first, Spanish colonists sustained and enriched themselves by exploitation of Indian peoples, who were forced to provide settlers with labour, food and other commodities. The primary mechanism for such exploitation was the *encomienda*, which gave individuals (known as *encomenderos*) the legal right to demand payments or services from the Indians. From this practice, some Spaniards acquired a disproportionate share of the rewards of conquest and colonization, and great *encomenderos* came to form wealthy and powerful cliques that royal officials found difficult to control. Gradually, however, the Habsburg monarchy superimposed a system of royal government on the American dominions. At its centre stood the king and his Council of the Indies in Spain, while in the colonies the crown delegated authority to the viceroys of Mexico and Peru, the judges of supreme colonial courts (known as *audiencias*) that were established in all the main colonial regions and, under them, a host of other, lesser officials.

The Spanish crown justified its sovereignty over American lands and indigenous peoples by proclaiming a religious and civilizing mission, but evangelization did little to protect Indians from the dire effects of contact with Europeans. Devastation of Indian communities started in the Caribbean islands where, within two generations of Spanish colonization, native peoples had largely disappeared. When Spanish colonists moved to the mainland, great epidemics of smallpox, measles, diphtheria, influenza and other Old World diseases swept through native populations with catastrophic effect. Perhaps about 80 per cent of the Amerindian population in Spanish America died during the century after Columbus's discovery, cut down by illnesses against which native Americans had little or no immunity (Figure 3.1.2). As the indigenous populations declined, Spain's overseas territories generally became multi-racial societies, formed from the fusion of peoples of

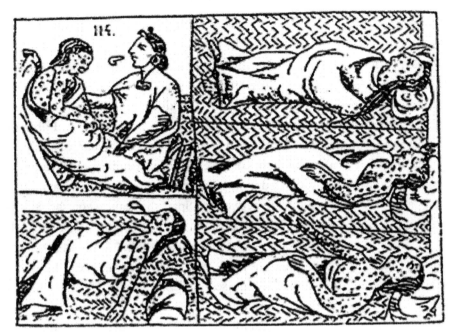

FIGURE 3.1.2   Indians dying of smallpox in the sixteenth century. From *Historia De Las Cosas de Nueva Espana*, vol. 4, book 12: Peabody Museum of Archaeology and Ethnology, Harvard University.

several different origins. People of European descent were a minority; another minority group was that of Africans and their descendants who worked as slaves. The largest elements of colonial populations were made up of Indians and people of mixed race: known as *mestizos* and *mulattos*, they were born from unions between whites, Indians and blacks. This mixture of peoples did not produce integrated societies: whites were regarded as socially superior simply by reason of ethnic origin, while Indians, *mestizos* and blacks were treated as inferiors.

Demographic and social transformation in Spain's American empire was matched by ecological and economic change, as Spanish colonists sought to turn the resources of the New World to their own uses. The principal force for ecological change came from the introduction of European animals, crops and agricultural practices. Cattle and horses, sheep and goats, pigs and chickens, none previously known to the Americas, multiplied rapidly in favourable environments, while European crops like wheat and barley provided new sources of food to supplement or supplant the traditional Indian crops of maize, beans, potatoes and plantains. The 'Columbian exchange', as it has come to be called, also involved the transfer to the Old World of Indian cultigens. Maize (known as 'Indian corn'), potatoes, tomatoes, peppers, squash, common beans and pineapples were among the most notable American crops subsequently cultivated in the Old World, while tobacco became one of the largest American exports across the Atlantic (Crosby 1972).

The discovery of immensely rich deposits of silver in Mexico and Peru was especially important in expanding extra-European trade and shaping the early modern economy. Mexican and Peruvian silver mines provided tremendous wealth for colonists and the Spanish crown. Silver and gold financed the importation of goods from Europe which Spanish colonials regarded as essential to their lifestyle. By the end of the sixteenth century, enormously valuable shipments of silver and European exports were regularly exchanged across the Atlantic, carried in large fleets escorted by naval warships to and from the Spanish port of Seville. This network of Spanish Atlantic commerce was supplemented by another system of trade in the Pacific. In 1564, Spaniards established bases in the Philippines and, with the founding of a colonial base in Manila in 1571, created a rich commerce that circumnavigated the globe. Mexican silver was used to purchase the Chinese silks and porcelains that had become so popular in Europe. The appetite for goods from East Asia that filled the houses of European aristocrats and, increasingly, merchants coincided with a near insatiable demand for silver in China, where all tax duties (previously payable in silks and grain) and labour duties had only recently been commuted to payments in silver. As there was little silver mining in China and only some in Japan, the Chinese economy rapidly grew dependent on the European import of New World silver to keep the wheels of its extensive silverized economy turning (Flynn and Giráldez 2002; Box 3.1.2).

The Portuguese were much slower than the Spaniards to colonize their American lands, where they found neither rich indigenous cultures nor precious metals. By the later sixteenth

---

Box 3.1.2

'[t]here is no gold or silver money in China, but only current weight of gold and silver, and everything is bought and sold by weight; wherefore every man hath a pair of scales and weights in his house, which all are exceedingly perfect. ... For each one laboureth by all means he can to deceive the other, so none do trust the scales and weights of the other, and every one that goeth to buy in the market carrieth a weight and balance and broken silver.'

(From an account of China by the Portuguese Dominican
Gaspar Da Cruz; Boxer 2004, 128–9)

century, however, Brazil had become an important adjunct of European commerce, as it was gradually transformed into Europe's leading source of sugar. Portuguese settlers drew on their previous experience in Madeira to establish sugar plantations and overcame problems with Indian labour by importing African slaves. In 1559, the crown authorized trade in slaves from Africa to Brazil, thus providing a legal basis for the growth of a massive trade in black slaves and for the formation of the world's first great plantation economy. By 1600, Brazil had become the largest sugar-producing area in the western world and its colonial society, resting on black slavery, was on the way to becoming a distinctive Afro-Brazilian culture (Boxer 1969).

The Portuguese placed far greater emphasis on Asia than America, for good reason, since it produced great wealth. The main focus for expansion lay in India and the chain of trading bases that ran from their base at Goa, established in 1510, through Ceylon, Malacca and the Moluccas to the peninsula of Macao in south China. Until they were pushed out by the rather more aggressive Dutch and English traders, the Portuguese controlled most of the Indian Ocean trade, including the coveted trade with China from Macao, where they had established their base from the early sixteenth century. Their initial interest was in black pepper, but they also supplied textiles, LACQUERWARES and porcelains for the European markets. Porcelain had a special appeal, and the first pieces brought back by Vasco da Gama sparked off a European craze that led not only to vast imports but to an ongoing quest for the technology to produce it in Europe. Until specialists at the court of Augustus II (Elector of Saxony and king of Poland) succeeded in producing porcelain in 1708, the Chinese had the monopoly on its manufacture, and European ships transported millions of pieces back to Europe (Finlay 1998; Box 3.1.3).

Box 3.1.3

'The Lusitanian Indian Empire or State, which formerly dominated the whole of the East, ... gave law to thirty-three tributary kingdoms, amazed the whole world with its vast extent, stupendous victories, thriving trade and immense riches, is now ... reduced to ... relics and those but few, of the great body of that State, which our enemies have left us.'

(Boxer 1969, 130)

The Jesuit Manuel Godinho describing the rise and decline of the Portuguese empire in India as he saw it in 1663.

Rival Colonial Powers

While the Portuguese had first embarked on these explorations under the protection of the crown, the English operated under the aegis of the EAST INDIA COMPANY (EIC). Founded in 1600 and built on the principle of a joint-stock organization, the EIC was funded by a large number of merchants and investors and granted a monopoly over Asian trade ('Trading Places': Web resources). Both the Portuguese and the English encountered competition in the form of another joint-stock company: the VEREENIGDE OOSTINDISCHE COMPAGNIE (VOC), established in Amsterdam in 1602 to capitalize on the growing trade in goods from Asia (Figure 3.1.3). The West-Indische Compagnie, founded in 1621, held the Dutch monopoly for trade with North and South America and with Western Africa, coming into direct conflict with Spanish expansion. The VOC, meanwhile, taking advantage of existing trade networks, made its money not just through the import of Asian goods into Europe, but by muscling in on intra-Asian trade. A small investment of (Peruvian) silver brought to Asia could be used to purchase raw silks, exchanged in Japan for copper and gold, which was then used for the purchase of Indian textiles to pay for the coveted cloves, mace and nutmeg bought in the Moluccas, yielding vast profits in the Netherlands (Jacobs 2006, 1). The competition led to frequent and violent clashes in Asia, with the Dutch focusing mostly on the islands in the Indonesian archipelago and the English gradually taking control of India.

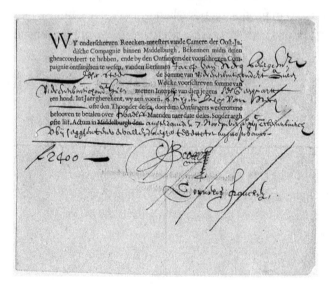

FIGURE 3.1.3   A bond for 2,400 florins issued on 7 November 1623 by the Vereenigde Oostindische Compagnie in its Middelburg chamber, signed in Amsterdam, and now in private ownership. 'Auktionshaus Tschöpe' (Web resources).

The English established their first footholds in Madras (Fort St George was established in 1639), Bombay (Mumbai) in 1661 and Calcutta (Kolkata) in 1702. From those ports, they traded in coffee and textiles and sent ships to China to acquire tea; they also used Indian textiles to fund the trade in African slaves destined for Caribbean plantations. The English advance in India coincided with the collapse of the Mughal state, creating a power vacuum that the East India Company slowly began to fill. Their focus was not on transforming local cultures but on creating a structure to facilitate trade. Throughout the eighteenth century, the English took over more of the governmental functions, leading to the establishment in 1773 of the Bengal governor as governor-general of India.

Meanwhile, in the Americas, the French, Dutch and English were able to set up colonies in the regions not occupied by Spanish colonists. Frenchmen established permanent settlements in Canada and the Lesser Antilles, subsequently turning, like the English, to exploit the absence of Spaniards from the smaller Caribbean islands and the regions along the eastern seaboard of North America. The Dutch made temporary inroads into Brazil, until they were dislodged by Portuguese and Brazilian arms in 1654. While holding islands in the Caribbean and the North American settlement that the English later turned into New York, Dutch interest was more in trade than agrarian settlement and they were much less significant in the Protestant colonization of America than their neighbour and rival, England.

English colonization in the Americas put down firm roots in the early 1600s. Following the foundation of Jamestown in 1607, New England in 1620 and Barbados in 1625, the English gradually built up, between these distant points, an empire that was in most respects quite different from that of the other European powers in the Americas. Compared to the vast extent of Spain's possessions in the American continent, Anglo-America was small, being confined to a few Caribbean islands and a narrow strip on the eastern shores of North America. Unlike the Spaniards, who were drawn deep into the American interior and backlands in their search for native civilizations to conquer and precious metals to exploit, the English remained a fundamentally maritime and rural people. They found neither silver nor great Amerindian peasantries, and their colonies followed other models (Elliott 2006). In North America, the colonies established in New England were based largely on family farms, while Virginia and Maryland came to depend on tobacco plantations worked by indentured labour. In the Caribbean, English colonies took another form: they imitated the sugar plantation powered by African slaves that had been pioneered by the Portuguese in Brazil. So too did the French and other Europeans when they acquired territories in the Caribbean, thereby promoting the tremendous growth of the slave trade that drew West (and later East) Africa into the web of European Atlantic commerce and was to ship millions of Africans across the ocean, with great damage to the African societies that traders plundered for slaves ('Beyond Europe *c.* 1800' in Part VI).

Assessment

The widening of European horizons for settlement and commerce from the early sixteenth century was, then, to have a global impact. It affected not only the European societies such as Spain and Portugal that were in the vanguard of overseas expansion and those which, like the English, Dutch and French, followed in their wake, but also did much to generate or accelerate change in the societies that were exposed to European commerce and colonization. Of these, the Americas were most profoundly affected, because, after being isolated from the rest of the world, their peoples were suddenly forced into contact with Europeans who took their lands, coerced their labour and imposed forms of government, culture and belief that Europeans assumed to be superior. Africans also suffered badly from European expansion. For, although some African rulers and Arab traders grew rich and powerful from the European demand for slaves, the communities that lived within the regions where slavers operated were disrupted, and often devastated, by the losses caused by kidnap and captivity. Asian societies were also adversely affected by the acquisitive violence that accompanied competition for trade in valuable commodities, particularly in the Indonesian islands, where the Portuguese and the Dutch established colonial dominions. On the whole, however, the societies of South and East Asia proved relatively resistant to European political and cultural encroachments, as their states and societies were sufficiently strong to withstand territorial takeover and cultural IMPERIALISM and in some cases to dictate the terms on which trade with Europe was conducted. However, as European states grew stronger from the expansion of their commerce and colonies, those which emerged in the forefront of maritime trade were, during the eighteenth century, to widen and deepen their political dominion over Asia.

Discussion Themes

1. What part did religious ideals play in European expansion in the sixteenth century?
2. Compare the impact of European expansion on Africa and the Americas.
3. Can European expansion in the sixteenth century be regarded as the 'first globalization'?

Bibliography

(A) Sources

Boxer, Charles R. ed. (2004), *South China in the Sixteenth Century, being the narratives of Galeote Pereire, Fr. Gaspar da Cruz, O.P., Fr. Martin de Rada, O.E.S.A. (1550–1575)*, London.

(B) Literature

Boxer, Charles R. (1969), *The Portuguese Seaborne Empire*, London.

Crosby, Alfred W. (1972), *The Columbian Exchange: Biological and Cultural Consequences of 1492*, Westport, Conn.

Elliott, J. H. (2006), *Empires of the Atlantic World: Britain and Spain in America, 1492–1830*, New Haven, Conn.

Fernández-Armesto, Felipe (1987), *Before Columbus: Exploration and Colonization from the Mediterranean to the Atlantic, 1229–1492*, London.

Finlay, Robert (1998), 'The Pilgrim Art: The Culture of Porcelain in World History', *Journal of World History*, 9:2, 141–87.

Flynn, Dennis and Giráldez, Arturo (2002), 'Cycles of Silver: Global Economic Unity through the Mid-Eighteenth Century', *Journal of World History*, 13:2, 391–427.

Jacobs, Els M. (2006), *Merchant in Asia: The Trade of the Dutch East India Company during the Eighteenth Century*, Leiden.

McFarlane, Anthony (1994), *The British in the Americas, 1480–1815*, London.

Parry, J. H. (1963), *The Age of Reconnaissance: Discovery, Exploration and Settlement, 1450–1650*, London.

——— (1966), *The Spanish Seaborne Empire*, London.

Russell, Peter (2001), *Prince Henry 'the Navigator': A Life*, New Haven, Conn.

Wills, John E. (1998), 'Relations with Maritime Europeans' in: *The Cambridge History of China, Vol. 8: The Ming Dynasty, 1368–1644*, ed. F. W. Mote and D. Twitchett, part 2, Cambridge, 333–75.

(C) Web resources

'1492: An Ongoing Voyage' (1993), Library of Congress Exhibition: <http://www.ibiblio.org/expo/1492.exhibit/Intro.html>

'Auktionshaus Tschöpe', auction house for old shares and bonds: <http://www.tschoepe.de/auktion51/auktion51.htm>

'Classic Sailing Ships' (2000), compiled by Colin Munro: <http://website.lineone.net/~dee.ord/Tudors.htm>

'Ferdinand Magellan's Voyage Round the World' (1519–1522), IHSP: <http://www.fordham.edu/halsall/mod/1519magellan.html>

Mandeville, Sir John, 'Prester John' (1366), IHSP: <http://www.fordham.edu/halsall/source/mandeville.html>

'Trading Places', a British Library website on the East India Company: <http://www.bl.uk/learning/histcitizen/trading/tradingplaces.html>

Reading 3.2

Cotton and the US South
A Short History

Sven Beckert

T HE HISTORY OF THE US SOUTH in the nineteenth century is the history of cotton.[1] Cotton growing was the most significant economic activity of Southerners, the American South mattered to the national and global economy because of its cotton, and the greatest political crisis of the United States in the nineteenth century, the Civil War, concerned the social, political, and economic structure that enabled the South's culture of cotton. At the heart of that conflict was the question of whether a cotton-growing regime sustained by slave labor should be able to expand territorially and whether the South's particular form of slave-based capitalism should enjoy the protections of the federal government. When South Carolina Senator and cotton planter James Henry Hammond argued famously on the floor of the Senate in 1858 that "cotton *is* king," he comprehended one of the central dynamics of the Southern and global economy.

So central has cotton become to the image of the American South that many Americans tend to forget that the Southern states came to cotton quite late—toward the end of the eighteenth century—and also quite suddenly, with the invention of the cotton gin in 1793. Cotton's global history is long and complicated, but it was only in the 1790s that aspiring American planters combined European capital, expropriated lands, and enslaved workers of African heritage to begin growing cotton for world markets. It was a move that did more than reshape the Southern countryside from forests, meadows, and swamps into vast cotton farms; it also had a tremendous impact on the larger world, spurring rapid industrialization in western Europe and New England. It enriched merchants throughout the Atlantic world, and the wealth of cities such as New York and Liverpool, Le Havre and Mulhouse, Bremen and Lowell was to a significant degree produced in Southern cotton fields. Merchants in these cities accumulated riches in the global cotton trade, and this capital, in turn, eventually fueled the emergence of other industries and banks. It even transformed the economies of India and the Ottoman Empire, as their position in the global cotton economy shifted in reaction to the rise of a US-fueled European cotton-manufacturing industry. As the supplier of the raw materials for the most dynamic metropolitan industry of the century, the American South was indeed the backbone of the first great phase of capitalist industrialization that began to spread across Europe and the northern United States. It was one of the core connections that explain the North Atlantic's "great divergence," the moment in the late eighteenth and early nineteenth centuries when it became much wealthier than other parts of the world.

"Hashish of the West"

From almost any angle, cotton was important to the mid-nineteenth-century South and vice versa. Unlike rice, tobacco, or sugar cane, which were important though regionally focused industries, cotton stretched from the Atlantic coast to the Mississippi River and beyond. Hundreds of thousands of African American laborers worked the Cotton Kingdom. Indeed, the vast majority of nineteenth-century Southern slaves ultimately labored on cotton plantations. The most significant export of the United States as a whole was Southern-grown cotton, indeed so much so that by 1860, 60 percent of all US exports consisted of cotton. The American South was also, by far, the most important source for the Western world's most crucial raw material. By the late 1850s, the Southern states accounted for nearly 100 percent of the 374 million pounds of cotton used in the United States, a full 77 percent of the 800 million pounds processed in Britain, 90 percent of the 192 million pounds used in France, 60 percent of the 115 million pounds spun in German Zollverein, and as much as 92 percent of the 102 million pounds manufactured in Russia.[2] Cotton had become so central to the prosperity of the Atlantic world that poet John Greenleaf Whittier called it the "Hashish of the West." It was like a drug that created powerful hallucinatory dreams of territorial expansion, of judges who decide that "right is wrong," and of heaven as "a snug plantation" with "angels" as "negro overseers."[3] The importance of Southern cotton to the global economy in the nineteenth century can be compared only to the world's dependence on Middle Eastern oil a century later.

Cotton became important to the American South because this "white gold" had become central to the global economy. Before 1800, producing cotton cloth was mostly a local pursuit. Millions of farmers cultivated small amounts of cotton, which they then spun by hand and finally wove into fabric on simple looms. After 1780, however, with the onset of the Industrial Revolution, production became mechanized, and the geographic distances between cotton growers, spinners, weavers, and consumers increased drastically. For the next hundred years, cotton was so important to the global economy that no other manufacturing industry employed as many people. By inventing the factory as the most efficient way of producing textiles, cotton manufacturers also recast the way humans worked. By searching for ever more hands to staff their factories, English, American, Brazilian, and Japanese cotton manufacturers, among others, encouraged unprecedented movement from the countryside into cities. Likewise, by demanding ever more cotton to feed their hungry factories in Lancashire and elsewhere, manufacturers and merchants stimulated planters to vastly expand cotton lands. And the need for cheap labor to work all that land led to the forced migration of hundreds of thousands of slaves, as well as the colonization of new territories in Asia and Africa. By producing ever more cotton textiles ever more efficiently and selling them to markets throughout the world, these American and European cotton traders inadvertently destroyed less efficient indigenous ways of producing textiles and in the process decisively moved the center of the cotton textile industry from Asia to western Europe and the United States. In their search for labor, capital, land, raw materials, and consumers, these nineteenth-century capitalists brought together different world regions—creating, in fact, one of the earliest globally integrated industries.

During the nineteenth century, cotton was important in numerous places. In Britain, it became a significant manufacturing industry, with raw cotton its biggest import and cloth and yarn a crucial export. In India, shifts within its huge cotton industry—away from spinning and weaving and toward the growing of cotton for export—combined with the loss of its export markets for finished cotton goods created tectonic upheavals in the region's economy. In Continental Europe, cotton became the first mechanized large-scale manufacturing industry. In the United States, raw cotton exports established the young nation's place in the global economy. In Mexico, Egypt, India, and Brazil, the first tentative steps toward domestic industrialization were taken with cotton. Egyptian agriculture was turned into a huge and increasingly monocultural cotton-growing system, focusing on export production. By the late nineteenth and early twentieth centuries, peasants throughout Africa, northern Argentina, Australia, and elsewhere—under pressure from metropolitan governments and capitalists—converted their fields into cotton plantations. Huge profits, meanwhile, were amassed by many merchant and banking families whose names are still familiar today: Baring, Rothschild, Ward, Brown, Rathbone, Volkart, Reinhardt, Knoop, Birla, Tata. Throughout the world, consumer demand for cotton textiles grew too, and especially in areas that came late to cotton, such as Europe, this cotton-manufacturing boom revolutionized how people dressed and how they kept clean. This truly was the era when cotton was king.

Global Networks

The history of cotton in the American South depended on cotton's role in the wider world. For about nine hundred years—between 1000 CE and 1900 CE—cotton was the world's most important manufacturing industry. Originating in South Asia, eastern Africa, and Central America at least five millennia ago, the crop and its manufacture into fabric had spread into most regions of the world by the year 1000 CE. Vibrant artisanal cotton manufacturing complexes emerged, and although they mostly focused on satisfying the need among the growers and producers themselves for yarn and cloth, they also served distant markets. For instance, Indian cottons traveled to Southeast Asia, East Africa, and the Middle East and even showed up in Europe as early as the Roman Empire. Kano, in present day Nigeria, supplied the needs of the people of the Sahara. Aztec cotton goods found their way into what is today the territory of the United States. In the sixteenth century, Europeans, who until this time mostly depended on woolens and linens, began to develop a taste for exotic cotton fabrics and came increasingly to dominate this intercontinental trade. They would export South Asian cotton fabric both to sell to European consumers and to exchange for slaves in Africa. It was at this time, also, that Europeans began to produce cotton textiles themselves, though their share of the global output remained miniscule.

This ancient industry was to undergo a radical shift in the late eighteenth century, as British mechanics invented a fundamentally new way of spinning yarn and—eventually, a few decades later—of weaving cloth. These machines, among them the spinning jenny, the water frame, and the spinning mule, increased human productivity in unprecedented ways. Cotton manufacturing, for the first time, came to be concentrated in Europe.

Such European dominance was the result not just of the mechanical genius of British artisans but also of successful European insertion into and then domination of global networks. The scope of these networks was astonishing. Raw cotton, for example, arrived in huge quantities from distant places, mostly North America but also the West Indies and South America, enabling Europe to overcome its resource constraints by making use of what Kenneth Pomeranz (and the previous chapter) called "ghost acres," that is, land outside of Europe that could be transformed for the production of agricultural commodities for European markets without leading to upheaval in the European countryside itself. The labor that went into the growing of cotton was mostly that of slaves, forcefully deported from yet another part of the world, Africa. Some technologies that were important to the manufacturing process, especially as they related to the crucial dyeing of fabrics, were laboriously copied from Indian artisans. Global networks also affected markets for the finished product, both within Europe and abroad. Domestically, the market for cotton textiles in Europe had expanded as a result of the greater availability of Indian fabrics in the wake of European expansion to that part of the world. And the enormously elastic markets that encouraged British merchants and manufacturers to invest in the fledging new techniques of cotton manufacturing in the first place were largely to be found abroad, first in Africa, Continental Europe, and the Americas, and later in Asia, India primarily. Right from the beginning, global connections, and the ability of European states and capitalists to reshape them, were essential to the emergence of the European cotton textile industry. And one of these connections, a particularly important one, was with the American South.

But how did the US South come to play such a decisive role in the history of cotton? Its arrival to global cotton production is not a straightforward story. Since very little cotton grew in Europe, its young cotton-manufacturing industry depended entirely on its supply of raw materials from non-European sources. At first, in the early eighteenth century, European traders bought cotton from local merchants in the port cities of the Ottoman Empire, especially Izmir, but once demand exploded that supply proved to be insufficient. At the same time, the ability of European capital to recast the Ottoman countryside to facilitate increased production of cotton for export was limited. They found it extremely difficult to persuade peasants to focus their labor on producing cotton for world markets. In fact, in much of the world, European capitalists and statesmen were unable to dispossess rural cultivators from their land or from control over their labor and were incapable of undermining their long-ingrained subsistence strategies. The social power of peasants successfully restricted (but did not preclude) their involvement with production for long-distance markets; state-sponsored coercion was often required to make the transition to world market production possible.

As a result of this difficulty in gaining access to inexpensive cotton from independent peasant producers in the Ottoman Empire, European capitalists turned westward. They looked to new areas of the world—particularly the Americas—and to new methods of labor mobilization—slavery, above all—to slake their demand. At first, cotton growers in the West Indies and Brazil were able to satisfy the rapidly growing hunger of European cotton mills. Planters there applied the lessons they had learned in the growing of tobacco, rice, and, especially, sugar to cotton. Specifically, they applied extraordinary violence to solve the problem of persuading rural cultivators to grow cotton for world markets at ever lower prices. But this Caribbean and Brazilian cotton-growing nexus also soon reached its limits of production, especially in the 1790s when supply was curtailed by slaves rebelling on the Caribbean's most important cotton island, Saint-Domingue, present-day Haiti. When demand for cotton simultaneously shot up in England and France, prices for cotton skyrocketed.

This convergence of factors propelled the United States into the global cotton market. Before 1790, very little US cotton was produced for trade and very little was exported to Britain, indeed so little, that when in 1785 American-grown cotton arrived in the port of Liverpool, the customs authorities confiscated it, saying that it could not possibly be the product of the United States. In very short order, and especially after Eli Whitney invented a new kind of cotton gin in 1793, which allowed for a more efficient removal of seeds of American upland cotton, US cotton was able to capture world markets, dominating them for the next century and beyond. Like the spinning and water frame, which transformed the manufacture of cotton cloth (and other technological breakthroughs studied elsewhere in this book), Whitney's gin overcame a key bottleneck to production, and his easily imitated invention increased productivity by a factor of fifty. Overnight, the invention of Whitney's gin transformed American cotton, triggering what can only be described as a "cotton rush," with land on which cotton grew reputedly trebling in price. The transformation was staggering: in 1800, 25 percent of the cotton unloaded in Liverpool originated from the United States; twenty years later, that number had increased to 59 percent, and, in 1850, a full 72 percent of cotton consumed in Britain was grown in the United States.[4]

Continental Consolidation

Why the United States? What was its competitive advantage? When in the 1790s demand for cotton exploded at the same time West Indian production diminished, the United States was the one area in the world in which emptied lands, plentiful bonded labor, and a politically influential planter class existed. In the areas where cotton was to be grown, no powerful *and* entrenched social structure needed to be dislodged. Instead, indigenous inhabitants were forcefully removed and workers forcefully moved in, leaving planters free to recast nature and reorganize labor as they wished. It is hard, if not impossible, to image that such a transformation of land and labor for the cultivation of cotton could have been effected anywhere else in the world. Indeed, when the British tried to increase cotton production for export in India in the 1820s and 1830s, they largely failed. Production in other parts of the world, such as the West Indies, Brazil, and the Ottoman Empire, also did not expand. The British economist J. T. Danson, in an 1857 article entitled "On the Existing Connection

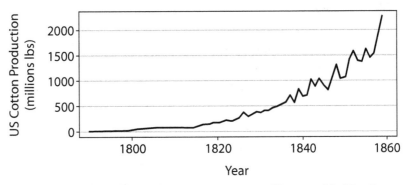

Cotton Production in the United States, 1790–1900 (in million pounds). "Hay, Cotton, Cottonseed, Shorn Wool, and Tobacco—Acreage, Production, and Price: 1790 to 1970—Con.," in *Historical Statistics of the United States, Colonial Times to 1970*, by the US Department of Commerce, part 1 (Washington, DC: Government Printing Office, 1975), 517–518.

between American Slavery and the British Cotton Manufacture" in the *Quarterly Journal of the Statistical Society*, concluded that "there is not, and never has been, any considerable source of supply for cotton, ... which is not obviously and exclusively maintained by slave-labour." Herman Merivale, British colonial bureaucrat, agreed in 1840, finding that Manchester's and Liverpool's "opulence is as really owing to the toil and suffering of the negro, as if his hands had excavated their docks and fabricated their steam-engines."[5]

Central to the global economy and spectacularly profitable, the cotton economy of the American South expanded rapidly throughout the first decades of the nineteenth century. In 1790, three years before Whitney's invention, the United States had produced 1.5 million pounds of cotton; in 1800 that number grew to 36.5 million pounds, and in 1820 to 167.5 million pounds. By 1802 the United States was already the single-most important supplier of cotton to the British market, and by 1857 the United States would produce about as much cotton as China, the world's leading producer until then.[6]

As more and more land was plowed under to plant cotton, a crop that rapidly exhausted the soil, production spread farther west and farther south, facilitated again by newly emptied lands, portable slave labor, and ginning technology that allowed cotton agriculture to be easily transferred to new territories. Unlike the Egyptian, Sea Island, or Pima cotton that grew in the coastal South Atlantic region—where in places it even rivaled the dominion of rice—upland cotton could be grown in diverse locations. All the plant needed was warmth, rainfall, and fertile soil. The cotton belt, sweeping from central South Carolina to east Texas, provided an almost perfect environment for the upland species, and, once the technological issue of separating lint and seed had been resolved, cotton farming spread like a feverish epidemic across the hot and humid Southern landscape.[7]

Agronomists contributed directly to the cotton revolution, crossing plant varieties to produce robust and adaptable plants that yielded high volumes of more readily picked cotton—enslaved workers in the 1830s, for instance, could pick twice the amount of Mexican cotton than older Green Seed varieties. In addition to the superior yield, picking, and disease resistance, the newer varieties had higher lint-to-seed ratios than the plants they replaced, and their widespread introduction was of vital importance to the expansion of the plantation frontier. This happened particularly at times when cotton prices rose. While the price of cotton gradually declined over the first half of the nineteenth century, sharp price upswings—such as in the first half of the 1810s, between 1832 and 1837, and again after the mid-1840s—produced expansionist bursts. In 1811, one-sixteenth of all cotton grown in the United States came from states and territories west of South Carolina and Georgia; by 1820 that share had reached one-third, and, in 1860, three-fourths. New cotton fields sprouted in the sediment-rich lands along the banks of the Mississippi, the upcountry of

Alabama, and the black prairie of Arkansas. So rapid was this move westward that, by the end of the 1830s, Mississippi was producing more cotton than any other Southern state.[8]

Such territorial expansion of cotton agriculture was aided by culture and history. Ever since the first European settlers stepped off their boats, they had been pushing inland. In the late eighteenth century, Native Americans still controlled substantial territories only a few hundred miles inland from the coastal provinces, yet they were unable to stop the white settlers' steady encroachment. The settlers eventually won a bloody and centuries-long war that succeeded in turning the land of Native Americans into land that was legally "empty," a land without most of its people and thus without the entanglements of historically developed social structures. In terms of unencumbered land, the South had no rival in the cotton-growing world.

With the support of Southern politicians, the federal government aggressively secured new territory by acquiring land from foreign powers and from forced cessions of Native Americans. In 1803, the Louisiana Purchase nearly doubled the territory of the United States, in 1819 the United States acquired Florida from Spain, and in 1845 it annexed Texas—all of which contained lands superbly suited to cotton agriculture. While there were many reasons for expansion—cotton being just one—it is difficult to imagine the US rise to world cotton supremacy without these land grabs. Indeed, by 1850, 67 percent of US cotton grew on land that had not been part of the United States half a century earlier.[9]

If the project of continental consolidation provided access to new cotton lands, it also secured major rivers needed to carry the harvested cotton. America's remarkably cheap transportation costs were the direct result of the expansion of its national territory. Most significant was the Mississippi, whose surge of cotton freight turned New Orleans, at the river's mouth, into the key American cotton port. But other rivers—the Red River in Louisiana and the Tombigbee and Mobile in Alabama—mattered as well. The first steamboats appeared on the Mississippi in 1817, cheapening transport costs, and, by the 1830s, railroads connected much of this newly acquired and settled hinterland to rivers and seaports. The Southern style of railroad construction with tracks laid from farm to port, amplified these decisive advantages in transportation infrastructure.[10]

To work these new fields, planters moved thousands of slaves into cotton-producing territories, many from the states of the Upper South, where tobacco agriculture was in a downward spiral. In the 1790s, the slave population of the state of Georgia, for example, nearly doubled, to sixty thousand. In South Carolina, the number of slaves in the upcountry cotton-growing districts grew from twenty-one thousand in 1790 to seventy thousand twenty years later, including fifteen thousand slaves newly deported from Africa.[11] All the way to the Civil War, cotton and slavery would expand in lockstep.

Cotton, until the advent of mechanized harvesting during the 1940s, was a labor-intensive crop. "[T]he true limitation upon the production of cotton," argued the Southern journal *De Bow's Review*, "is labor." And planters in the United States—unlike elsewhere—enjoyed access to large supplies of cheap labor, which the *American Cotton Planter* called in 1853 "the cheapest and most available labor in the world." In the United States, nearly any labor shortage could be fixed with the right amount of money, and the slave markets in New Orleans and elsewhere boomed along with cotton. As significant, hundreds of thousands of slaves already in the United States were available to grow cotton because tobacco production in the states of the Upper South became less profitable after the American Revolution, encouraging slave owners there to sell their human property. As one British observer remarked perceptively in 1811, "[T]he cultivation of tobacco in Virginia and Maryland, has been less of late an object of attention; and the gangs of negroes formerly engaged in it, have been sent into the southern states, where the American cotton planter, thus reinforced, is enabled to commence his operations with increasing vigour." Indeed, by 1830 a full one million people (or one in thirteen Americans) grew cotton in the United States. Most of them were enslaved.[12]

The expansion of cotton production not only led to an enormous shift of slave labor from the Upper to the Lower South, but it also reinvigorated the institution of slavery in North America. In the thirty years after the invention of the cotton gin alone (between 1790 and 1820), a quarter-million slaves were forcefully relocated from other parts of North America; between 1783 and the closing of the international slave trade in 1808, traders imported an estimated 170,000 slaves into the United States, accounting for one-third of all slaves imported into North America since 1619. By 1860, the internal slave trade had moved up to a million slaves forcefully to the Deep South, most to grow cotton.[13]

To be sure, not all cotton in the United States was grown by slaves on large plantations. Free small farmers in the Southern upcountry produced cotton as well, and they did so because it provided ready cash and its cultivation, unlike the growing of sugar or rice, did not require significant capital investments. Yet, despite their efforts, in aggregate they produced only a small share of the total crop. In 1860, for instance, 85 percent of all Southern cotton was grown on farms larger than one hundred acres; the planters who owned those farms owned 91.2 percent of all slaves. The cotton crop was overwhelmingly tended by slaves, and, in areas where large quantities of cotton was grown, there were relatively few white farmers. The larger the farm, the better the planter was able to take advantage of the economies of scale inherent in slave-based cotton production. For instance, only larger farms could afford the gins to remove seeds and presses to compress loose cotton into tightly pressed bales to lower shipping costs. Big operations could also engage in agricultural experiments to wrest more nutrients from cleared soil, and they could buy more slaves to avoid the labor constraints that so limited the expansion of cotton farms elsewhere in the world.[14]

In addition to access to expropriated lands and the violent domination of labor, the nearly complete control of the state by cotton lords also helps explain how the United States gained such a competitive advantage in the emerging global empire of cotton. The Yazoo-Mississippi Delta offers a telling example of how these three factors came together to promote US dominance in the cotton trade, starting with its geography. For millennia, in an area of approximately seven thousand square miles, the mighty Mississippi had offloaded its rich sediments as it flowed to the Gulf of Mexico, creating a seedbed that would become the world's most productive cotton-growing land. In 1859, as many as sixty thousand Delta slaves produced a staggering sixty-six million pounds of cotton, nearly ten times as much as was exported from Saint-Domingue to France during the height of its production in the early 1790s.[15]

For the Delta to become the chief grower of the industrial world's most important commodity—a kind of Saudi Arabia of the early nineteenth century—its land had to be taken from its original inhabitants, and labor, capital, knowledge, and state power had to be mobilized in the service of profit. Between 1820 and 1832, a series of treaties backed by skirmishes and armed confrontations transferred much of the land from the Choctaws—its native inhabitants—to white settlers. Using wagons, rafts, and flatboats, hopeful cotton planters brought slaves from elsewhere in the South to clear that land of its "jungle-like" vegetation and later to hoe the soil, sow seeds, prune the young plants, and then harvest the cotton. The news that the Delta was "the most certain cotton planting area in the world" spread through the South; planters who were able to draw on sufficient capital (mostly in the form of labor since the land itself was cheap) and expertise moved in. The plantations they built became substantial businesses. By 1840, Washington County, in the heart of the Delta, counted more than ten slaves for every white inhabitant. By 1850, each and every white family in the county owned on average more than 80 slaves. The largest Delta planter, Stephen Duncan, owned 1,036 slaves, and the value of his property by the late 1850s was estimated at $1.3 million (the equivalent of $36.5 million in 2014). While not typical cotton farms, which were often much smaller and worked by fewer slaves, plantations in the Delta were highly capitalized businesses—indeed among the very largest in North America—and the investments necessary to operate such plantations were beyond the reach of many Northern industrialists. Wealth, as viewed from the front porches of the lavish and elegantly furnished mansions in the Delta, appeared to flow out of the soil, the result of a strange alchemy that combined emptied lands, slave labor, a supportive state, and, as discussed below, the never ending flow of European capital.[16]

Cotton, Capital, and Slavery

The growing domination of global cotton markets by US planters, in fact, was self-sustaining. As cotton growth expanded in the Southern United States and as British and eventually

Continental European consumers became more and more dependent on that supply, institutional links between the South and Europe—especially Liverpool, Le Havre, and Bremen—deepened. For their part, European merchants based in Charleston, Memphis, and New Orleans built a dense network of shipping connections that integrated the trade in cotton with their other businesses. People engaged in the cotton trade crossed the North Atlantic frequently, forging close business connections, friendships, and even marriages. Such networks, in turn, made transatlantic trade more secure and more predictable and thus lowered costs, giving the United States another decisive advantage over its potential competitors, including India and Brazil.

These networks operated by sending cotton from the United States to Europe and capital in the opposite direction. This capital, more often than not, was secured by mortgages on slaves, giving the owners of these mortgages the right to a particular slave should the debtor default. As historian Bonnie Martin has shown, in Louisiana during the national period, 88 percent of loans secured by mortgages used slaves as (partial) collateral; in South Carolina it was 82 percent. In total, she estimates that hundreds of millions of dollars of capital was secured by human property. Slavery thus not just allowed for the rapid allocation of labor but also for a swift allocation of capital.[17]

With enormous riches gained from expropriated land and labor, planters invested in agricultural improvements, another illustration of how success begot further success. They experimented, for example, with various cotton hybrids, crossing Indian, Ottoman, Central American, and West Indian seeds to create cotton strains adapted to particular local climates and soils. Most significant were the cotton seeds brought from Mexico in 1806 by Natchez planter Walter Burling. This variety produced larger bolls that could be picked by hand more easily and, according to experts, "possessed better fiber quality, especially fiber length, and was resistant to 'rot.' "[18]

Since the expansion of cotton agriculture depended on the advance of credit, often secured by mortgages on slaves and most of which derived from the London money market, plantation patterns began to follow the competitive logic of markets rather than the whimsy of personal aspiration and regional circumstance. The rhythm of industrial production entered the plantation, and capital moved to wherever cotton could be produced in the greatest quantities and at the lowest cost. To the great lament of Southern planters, much of their wealth and power was dependent on merchants—who could sell planters' cotton, supply them with goods, and provide them credit—and on the London money market. But this was not a one-way street: the London money market and the Lancashire manufacturers depended just as much on the planters—as the local experts in the violent expropriation of land and labor—for their wealth and power. The old paternalism of East Coast planters, shielded partially by the mercantilist logic of mutually beneficial and protected exchange between motherland and colony of the greater British imperial economy, had given way to a more competitive and fluid social order mediated by merchant capital.[19]

So important had American cotton become to the Western world that in 1897 a German economist remarked in retrospect that "a disappearance of the American North or West would have been of less significance to the world, than the elimination of the South." Southern planters, convinced of their central role in the global economy, gleefully announced that they held "THE LEVER THAT WIELDS THE DESTINY OF MODERN CIVILIZATION." And their incredible success also served as a self-justification of not merely the necessity but also the rightness of slavery. As cotton became central to ever more manufacturers, a world without slavery became ever less imaginable to cotton industrialists and statesmen. As the *American Cotton Planter* put it in 1853, "[T]he slave-labor of the United States, has hitherto conferred and is still conferring inappreciable blessings on mankind. If these blessings continue, slave-labor must also continue, for it is idle to talk of producing Cotton for the world's supply with free labor. It has never yet been successfully grown by voluntary labor."[20]

This cotton-slavery nexus remained fabulously profitable for many decades. But it also contained within itself tensions that led to its eventual demise. Most important was the fact that slavery was fundamentally unstable. Slavery, after all, relied on violence, and the contest between labor lords and workers could turn at any point, as it did, indeed, in Saint-Domingue in the 1790s. As the cotton industry became increasingly important to European economies, concerns about the stability of its foundation—the institution of slavery—came to the fore. Slavery, manufacturers understood, was at the root of their prosperity, but simultaneously it was a source of constant worry. Saint-Domingue was, after all, in the living memory of many.

Just as potentially disruptive were the emerging political conflicts within the United States itself. The political needs of slave owners, which were directly related to containing the tensions fundamental to the relationship between slaves and masters, increasingly diverged from those of Americans who were profiting from the emerging industrial capitalism in the Northern states of the Union.[21] Eventually, as we all know, this disagreement destabilized the institution of slavery, and with it the world's dominant cotton-producing system came into crisis by the 1860s. The outbreak of Civil War on the North American continent jeopardized future supplies of slave-grown cotton for the factories of Europe. Without slave-grown cotton pouring out of the ports of the US South, Europe's most important industry came to a standstill.

So important was cotton grown in the South that the American Civil War marked, among other things, one of the most important events in the history of global capitalism. The world's first true raw-materials crisis brought to a halt hundreds of factories and hundreds of thousands of workers in the industrial areas of England, France, Germany, Switzerland, and Russia. Workers streamed through the streets of prominent cotton-milling towns such as Oldham, UK, and Mulhouse, France, calling for cotton supplies or relief. The war in North America led to frantic efforts by European governments to secure cotton from different areas of the world. Government bureaucrats and rulers in Paris, Berlin, Moscow, and London poured over maps to figure out who in the world could replace slaves in the American South and might grow cotton for export. And in the South itself the inability to sell the Confederacy's only globally competitive product—cotton—resulted in a severe balance-of-payments crisis, inflation, and a rapid hollowing out of the entire economy of the breakaway region.

Radical Restructuring

One of the most significant results of the war was a radical restructuring of the South's, but also the world's, major industry—cotton. In fact, a key lesson of the Civil War was that labor, more than land, constrained the production of cotton.[22] Emancipation of slaves in the American South, therefore, was recognized as being potentially threatening not only to North American cotton growers but also to the well-being of European industry. With slavery in the world's most important cotton-growing areas abolished, a top question in the offices of European statesmen and capitalists was how to secure cotton without slavery. Emancipation, for them, meant the need to invent a new system of labor to produce cotton. What would that new system be? How could free rural cultivators be organized, mobilized, and motivated to grow the white gold and move it to market, whether in the United States or elsewhere in the world?

At first, pessimism reigned. Antebellum experiences suggested that such a transition would be difficult, since nonslave cotton had arrived only in small quantities in the ports of Liverpool, Bremen, and Le Havre. Cotton manufacturers understood that at prevailing antebellum world market prices, few cultivators in India, Brazil, Africa, or, for that matter, the American South, could produce very much cotton for European markets. Rural cultivators in control of both their labor and land—whether in India, Africa, Egypt, or even the upcountry of the Southern United States—usually had resisted growing cotton for world markets at prices competitive with slave-grown cotton. Moreover, and in singular contrast to emancipation on US sugar cane estates, efforts by cotton planters to rely on wage workers failed, as cultivators the world over refused to work for wages on cotton plantations. As Timothy Mitchell puts it so well, how could rulers make peasants grow crops that "they could not eat, or process to serve local needs?"[23] Indeed, how would global labor be mobilized in an age of freedom? Imperial bureaucrats worked zealously to find ways to reconstruct the worldwide web of cotton production, including what, in the United States, has come to be known as Reconstruction.

Postwar cotton growing can be seen as an example of the global nature of social conflict involving rural cultivators, merchants, imperial statesmen, landowners, and industrialists. Although the specific outcome of this conflict differed from one region of the world to another, the broad contours of the labor system that emerged in cotton growing were similar: nowhere in the world were workers re-enslaved. At the same time, the desire of many rural cultivators, especially in the Southern United States, to turn themselves into landowning farmers who would be able to choose subsistence production over cotton-for-export also failed. Instead, a system of sharecropping and tenant farming evolved, in which cotton growers owned themselves and, sometimes, their tools and, drawing on metropolitan capital, grew cotton for world markets.

In the Southern United States, when efforts failed to turn former slaves into ill-paid wage workers laboring in gangs, sharecropping emerged as an economic compromise secured by a wide variety of laws passed by legislatures that were, in turn, controlled by planters' representatives. Sharecropping gave cultivators a modicum of control over their labor, while keeping them landless. From the perspective of landowners, sharecropping enabled them to retain control over labor and land. This reconstruction of cotton regimes in the US South was informed by and in turn informed such reconstructions of the global cotton-growing countryside elsewhere, from India to western Africa. And that reconstruction of cotton agriculture also allowed the US South to remain an important cotton producer for world markets, even though Southern growers now found themselves in competition with producers in other parts of the world, such as India and Egypt, who had gotten their start during the Civil War and were exerting downward pressure on global cotton prices. Southern producers who had benefited from the largely undifferentiated market in cotton—due to the phenomenal output of the slave-based plantation complex, a compliant state, and unparalleled access to financial credit—now faced rigorous international competition.

Cotton Textiles

During the last decades of the nineteenth century, the South moved beyond cotton farming into the business of cotton textile production. The American South was, in fact, at the vanguard of a global movement that saw the world's cotton industry shift to lower-wage locations. The massive relocation of the cotton industry into the Southern United States had its start at the International Cotton Exposition of 1881 in Atlanta. There, cotton machinery displayed as the *Exposition Cotton Mills* afterward became a functioning mill. What followed was growth so fast that by 1910 the American South was the world's third-largest producer of cotton thread, after Great Britain and the Northern states of the Union. This was an amazing development since at the end of the Civil War there had been hardly any significant cotton manufacturing in the states of the former Confederacy, and as late as 1879 there were seventeen times as many spindles in the North as in the South. By 1919, Southern manufacturers operated 14 million spindles, nearly as many as the 17.5 million spindles turning in the Northern states at that time.[24]

Geography—particularly, proximity to cotton fields—played less of a role in this sudden expansion of cotton manufacturing in the US South than might be expected. Indeed, the slightly lower costs of accessing cotton were offset by the cost of shipping finished goods to Northern markets. The secret of success was plentiful and cheap labor, or, as economist Elijah Helm put it in 1903, "the excessively low labor cost." The destruction of slavery and the attendant transformation of the countryside had created a large and malleable pool of low-wage workers for the cotton factories—at first mostly white rural workers who had once been tenant farmers and, later, African American workers, most of them former share-croppers. As one contemporary observed, Southern cotton growers left the farms "like rats leaving a sinking ship."[25]

Endowed, thus, with huge supplies of cheap labor and aided by supportive local and regional governments, budding local Northern manufacturers opened additional mills in short order. Many of these operations were financed by selling stock to local communities and by securing loans from Northern machine makers seeking markets for their equipment. At the same time lax labor laws, low taxes, low wages, and the absence of trade unions made the South alluring to cotton manufacturers. It was a region of the United States "where the labor agitator is not such a power, and where the manufacturers are not constantly harassed by new and nagging restrictions." As the editor of the *Lynchburg News* put it in 1895, Northern manufacturers moved their milling operations south in an effort "to get away from the meddlesome and restrictive laws enacted at the instigation of 'walking delegates' and lazy agitators."[26]

Low wages characterized these operations, wages depressed in large part because cotton mills could draw on a large number of very young and very cheap workers. In 1905, 23 percent of all workers in Southern cotton mills were younger than sixteen, compared to only 6 percent in the Northern states. Thanks to the absence of national standards, people also worked longer hours in the South—sixty-four hours per week, or even seventy-five hours, were not uncommon. In fact, cotton industrialists' influence over Southern state governments—and the disenfranchisement of large segments of the local working class, especially, but not only, African Americans, that began during the 1880s—allowed for much laxer labor laws than in other states of the union, a defining characteristic of emerging cotton industries throughout the global South. Cotton industrialization, moreover, had strong backing from state governments, whose legislators and governors were vulnerable to the enormous influence and power of organized industrialists.[27]

The American South remained important to the global cotton economy just as cotton continued to be important to the South throughout the nineteenth century. By 1910, the cotton-manufacturing industry of the US South was booming, and the states of the former Confederacy were still, by far, the most important suppliers of raw cotton to global markets. Yet the South's forms of integration had changed. It had morphed from the world's most important producer of raw cotton by slave labor for European factories to a cotton-manufacturing power in its own right based on cheap, but nonbonded, labor, while at the same time still supplying the lion's share of the world cotton industry's raw material, thanks to the labor of millions of sharecroppers and tenant farmers.

A Laboratory of Global Capitalism

The American South—through its relationship with cotton—can be viewed as a giant laboratory of global capitalism. It was not, contrary to many assertions, a backwater of the Industrial Revolution, but instead it was at its very forefront, the location of some of the era's most significant social and economic transformations. Slaveholders and regional commentators considered cotton and slavery to be "structural strengths," and they rejected any fatalistic assumptions that the regional economy faced long-term doom. To be sure, its own industrialization had to await the abolition of slavery and therefore lagged behind other areas of the world, yet the American South was in the vanguard when it came to linking the global Industrial Revolution to the vast expansion of slavery. The American South also showed how the global countryside could be transformed in the wake of slavery's abolition, remaining throughout the nineteenth century at the forefront when it came to the *mise en valeur* (make economically useful) of recently captured territories, setting an example for many European colonialists in Africa and Asia to aspire to with varying degrees of success. And the industrialization of the American South showed the way for the expansion of industry throughout the Global South that would unfold throughout the twentieth century.[28]

This vanguard role of the American South was partly the result of its peculiar political and economic character, which made it both strange and unique. The distinctiveness of the American South in the larger history of the expansion of capitalism was most fundamentally the result of its incorporation into a highly complex polity—the United States of America. Unlike other slave regions of the world, Brazil and the Caribbean among them, the American South was embedded in a nation-state that also contained territories in which people embraced very different ideas, institutions, and political economies. In Massachusetts and New York, in Pennsylvania and Illinois, the order of the day throughout most of the nineteenth century had been the building of an expansive industrial economy, with protected markets, wage labor, and a state committed to the political economy of domestic industrialization. How to incorporate a post–Civil War South into this political economy would stamp the United States in decisive ways to this day, as this conflict left behind a legacy of deep political divisions, splintered labor markets, and racism.

Notes

1. For a fuller exploration of these topics, see Sven Beckert, *Empire of Cotton: A Global History* (New York: Alfred A. Knopf, 2014). This chapter draws on and uses material from *Empire of Cotton*.

2. Sven Beckert, "Emancipation and Empire: Reconstructing the Worldwide Web of Cotton Production in the Age of the American Civil War," *American Historical Review* 109 (December 2004): 1405–1438.

3. John Greenleaf Whittier, "The Hashish," *John Greenleaf Whittier: Selected Poems*, ed. Brenda Wineapple (New York: Library of America, 2004), 43–44.

4. Beckert, *Empire of Cotton*, 102; Sven Beckert, "Slavery and Capitalism," *Chronicle of Higher Education*, December 12, 2014; Beckert, "Emancipation and Empire," 1408.

5. J. T. Danson, "On the Existing Connection between American Slavery and the British Cotton Manufacture," *Journal of the Statistical Society of London* 20 (March 1857): 7. For a similar argument, see Élisée Reclus, "Le coton et la crise américaine," *Revue des Deux Mondes* 37 (January 1862): 176, 187. Herman Merivale, *Lectures on Colonization and Colonies, Delivered before the University of Oxford in 1839, 1840 & 1841* (repr., London: Humphrey Milford, 1928), 301–302.

6. United States Department of Commerce and Bureau of the Census, *Historical Statistics of the United States, Colonial Times to 1970*, Part 1 (Washington, DC: Government Printing Office, 1975), 518; Edward Baines, *History of the Cotton Manufacture in Great Britain* (London: H. Fisher, R. Fisher, and P. Jackson, 1835), 302; Michael M. Edwards, *The Growth of the British Cotton Trade, 1780–1815* (Manchester: Manchester University Press, 1967), 89.

7. Joyce E. Chaplin, *An Anxious Pursuit: Agricultural Innovation and Modernity in the Lower South, 1730–1815* (Chapel Hill: University of North Carolina Press, 1993), 220–226.

8. Stuart W. Bruchey, *Cotton and the Growth of the American Economy, 1790–1860: Sources and Readings* (New York: Harcourt, Brace & World, 1967), 80–81; Alan L. Olmstead and Paul W. Rhode, *Creating Abundance: Biological Innovation and American Agricultural Development* (Cambridge: Cambridge University Press, 2008), 100–114.

9. Beckert, *Empire of Cotton*, 105.

10. This story is related in detail in Adam Rothman, *Slave Country: American Expansion and the Origins of the Deep South* (Cambridge, MA: Harvard University Press, 2005); Lewis Cecil Gray, *History of Agriculture in the Southern United States to 1860*, 2 vols. (Washington, DC: Carnegie Institution of Washington, 1933), 2:709; John Hebron Moore, *The Emergence of the Cotton Kingdom in the Old South West, Mississippi, 1770–1860* (Baton Rouge: Louisiana State University Press, 1988), 6; John

F. Stover, *The Routledge Historical Atlas of the American Railroads* (New York: Routledge, 1999), 15.

11. The numbers are from Rothman, *Slave Country*, 11; John Craig Hammond, "Slavery, Settlement, and Empire: The Expansion and Growth of Slavery in the Interior of the North American Continent, 1770–1820," *Journal of Early Republic* 32 (Summer 2012): 175–206; Allan Kulikoff, "Uprooted People: Black Migrants in the Age of the American Revolution, 1790–1820," in *Slavery and Freedom in the Age of the American Revolution*, ed. Ira Berlin and Ronald Hoffmann (Charlottesville: University Press of Virginia, 1983), 149; Peter A. Coclanis and Lacy K. Ford, "The South Carolina Economy Reconstructed and Reconsidered: Structure, Output, and Performance, 1670–1985," in *Developing Dixie: Modernization in a Traditional Society*, ed. Winfred B. Moore Jr. (New York: Greenwood Press, 1988), 97; Kulikoff, "Uprooted People," 149.

12. *De Bow's Review* 11 (September 1851): 308; see also James Mann, *The Cotton Trade of Great Britain* (London: Simpkin, Marshall, 1860), 53; *American Cotton Planter* 1 (1853): 152; Beckert, *Empire of Cotton*, 108; Charles Mackenzie, *Facts, Relative to the Present State of the British Cotton Colonies and to the Connection of their Interests* (Edinburgh: James Clarke, 1811), 35; "Cotton Cultivation, Manufacture, and Foreign Trade of," letter from the secretary of the treasury, March 4, 1836 (Washington: Blair & Rives, 1836), 16, accessed July 29, 2013, http://catalog.hathitrust.org/Record/011159609.

13. Kulikoff, "Uprooted People," 143; James McMillan, "The Final Victims: The Demography, Atlantic Origins, Merchants, and Nature of the Post-Revolutionary Foreign Slave Trade to North America, 1783–1810" (PhD diss., Duke University, 1999), 40–98; Walter Johnson, introduction to *The Chattel Principle: Internal Slave Trades in the Americas*, ed. Walter Johnson (New Haven, CT: Yale University Press, 2004), 6; James A. B. Scherer, *Cotton as a World Power: A Study in the Economic Interpretation of History* (New York: F. A. Stokes, 1916), 151; Rothman, *Slave Country*, 182–188; Kulikoff, "Uprooted People," 149, 152; Michael Tadman, *Speculators and Slaves: Masters, Traders, and Slaves in the Old South* (Madison: University of Wisconsin Press, 1989), 12.

14. John H. Moore, "Two Cotton Kingdoms," *Agricultural History* 60 (Fall 1986): 1–16; Gavin Wright, *The Political Economy of the Cotton South: Households, Markets, and Wealth in the Nineteenth Century* (New York: W. W. Norton, 1978), 28; Ronald Bailey, "The Other Side of Slavery: Black Labor, Cotton, and Textile Industrialization in Great Britain and the United States," *Agricultural History* 68 (Spring 1994): 38; Wright, *Political Economy of the Cotton South*, 27.

15. At four hundred pounds to the bale. The numbers are from Moore, *Emergence of the Cotton Kingdom*, 129.

16. James C. Cobb, *The Most Southern Place on Earth: The Mississippi Delta and the Roots of Regional Identity* (New York: Oxford University Press, 1992), 8–10.

17. Bonnie Martin, "Slavery's Invisible Engine: Mortgaging Human Property," *Journal of Southern History* 76 (November 2010): 840–841.

18. C. Wayne Smith and J. Tom Cothren, eds., *Cotton: Origin, History, Technology, and Production* (New York: John Wiley & Sons, 1999), 103, 122. On the various origins of American cotton, see also Whitemarsh B. Seabrook, *A Memoir of the Origin, Cultivation and Uses of Cotton* (Charleston, SC: Miller & Browne, 1844), 15.

19. See, for this argument, Philip McMichael, "Slavery in Capitalism: The Rise and Demise of the U.S. Ante-Bellum Cotton Culture," *Theory and Society* 20 (June 1991): 335.

20. Ernst von Halle, *Baumwollproduktion und Pflanzungswirtschaft in den nordamerikanischen Südstaaten*, part 1, *Die Sklavenzeit* (Leipzig: Verlag von Duncker & Humblot, 1897), viii; *Organization of the Cotton Power: Communication of the President* (Macon: Lewis B. Andrews Book and Job Printer, 1858), 7; *American Cotton Planter* 1 (January 1853): 11; Beckert, *Empire of Cotton*, 119.

21. See Sven Beckert, *The Monied Metropolis: New York City and the Consolidation of the American Bourgeoisie, 1850–1896* (Cambridge: Cambridge University Press, 2001).

22. August Etienne, *Die Baumwollzucht im Wirtschaftsprogram der deutschen Übersee-Politik* (Berlin: Verlag von Hermann Paetel, 1902), 28. Labor shortage was also an important subject in discussions on the expansion of Indian cotton production during the US Civil War. See for example *Times of India*, October 18, 1861, 3; February 27, 1863, 6; *Zeitfragen* (May 1, 1911): 1.

23. Kolonial-Wirtschaftliches Komitee, *Deutsch-koloniale Baumwoll-Unternehmungen, Bericht XI* (Spring 1909): 28, in 8224, R 1001, Bundesarchiv Berlin; Thaddeus *Sunseri*, "*Die Baumwollfrage*: Cotton Colonialism in German East Africa," *Central European History* 34 (2001): 46, 48. Peasant resistance against colonial cotton projects in a very different context is also described in Allen Isaacman et al., "'Cotton Is the Mother of Poverty': Peasant Resistance to Forced Cotton Production in Mozambique, 1938–1961," *International Journal of African Historical Studies* 13 (1980): 581–615; Kolonial-Wirtschaftliches Komitee, "Verhandlungen der Baumwoll-Kommission des Kolonial-Wirtschaftlichen Komitees vom 25. April 1912," 169; J. E. Horn, *La crise cotonnière et les textiles indignes* (Paris: Dentu, 1863), 15; Timothy Mitchell, *Rule of Experts: Egypt, Techno-Politics and Modernity* (Berkeley: University of California Press, 2002), 59–60.

24. Mildred Gwin Andrews, *The Men and the Mills: A History of the Southern Textile Industry* (Macon, GA: Mercer University Press, 1987), 1; David L. Carlton and Peter A. Coclanis, "Southern Textiles in Global Context," in *Global Perspectives on Industrial Transformation in the American South*, ed. Susanna Delfino and Michele Gillespie (Columbia: University of Missouri Press, 2005), 160; Alice Galenson, *The Migration of Cotton Textile Workers from New England to the South: 1880–1930* (New York: Garland, 1985), 2.

25. Elijah Helm, "An International of the Cotton Industry," *Quarterly Journal of Economics* 17 (May 1903): 428; Galenson, *Migration of Cotton Textile Workers*, 186; Melvin Thomas Copeland, *The Cotton Manufacturing Industry of the United States* (New York: A. M. Kelley, 1966), 46. See also Steven Hahn, *The Roots of Southern Populism: Yeoman Farmers and the Transformation of the Georgia Upcountry, 1850–1890* (New York: Oxford University Press, 1983); Copeland, *Cotton Manufacturing*

Industry, 40; Gavin Wright, "The Economic Revolution in the American South," *Journal of Economic Perspectives* 1 (Summer 1987): 169. The story of how the transformation of Southern countryside is related to the emergence of wage workers in the American South is told by Barbara Fields, "The Nineteenth-Century American South: History and Theory," *Plantation Society in the Americas* 2 (April 1983): 7–27; Steven Hahn, "Class and State in Postemancipation Societies: Southern Planters in Comparative Perspective," *American Historical Review* 95 (February 1990): 75–88; *Southern and Western Textile Excelsior*, December 11, 1897, as cited in Beth English, "Capital Mobility and the 1890s U.S. Textile Industry," in *Global Perspectives on Industrial Transformation in the American South*, ed. Susanna Delfino and Michele Gillespie (Columbia: University of Missouri Press, 2005), 188.

26. Galenson, *Migration of Cotton Textile Workers*, 189–190; Carlton and Coclanis, "Southern Textiles in Global Context," 155, 156, 158; *Commercial Bulletin*, September 28, 1894, cited in Beth English, *A Common Thread: Labor, Politics, and Capital Mobility in the Textile Industry* (Athens: University of Georgia Press, 2006), 39; *Lynchburg News*, January 18, 1895, cited in English, "Capital Mobility and the 1890s U.S. Textile Industry," 176.

27. Galenson, *Migration of Cotton Textile Workers*, 141; Copeland, *Cotton Manufacturing Industry*, 42; Mary Blewett, "Textile Workers in the American Northeast and South: Shifting Landscapes of Class, Culture, Gender, Race, and Protest," paper presented at Global History of Textile Workers Conference/IISH, November 11–13, 2004, p. 12; See, for example, Katherine Rye Jewell, "Region and Sub-region: Mapping Southern Economic Identity," unpublished paper presented at Social Science History Conference, Boston, November 17–20, 2011.

28. Brian Schoen, *The Fragile Fabric of Union: Cotton, Federal Politics and the Global Origins of the Civil War* (Baltimore: Johns Hopkins University Press, 2009), 157.

Reading 3.3

The Expansionist

Tom Chaffin

T HE FUSE THAT IGNITED THE UNITED States' war with Mexico was lit by Polk's predecessor, John Tyler. On February 28, 1845, four days before Polk took office, Congress, at President Tyler's behest, passed a joint resolution extending the Republic of Texas a long-sought invitation to apply for U.S. annexation. Predictably, Mexican officials condemned Congress' action. They disputed the border claimed by Texas; that republic expansively claimed all land north and east of the Rio Grande, whereas Mexico regarded the more northerly Nueces River as Texas' boundary. Raising tensions still higher, Mexico had never officially recognized Texas' independence—and had vowed that annexation of the contested realm would be regarded as a belligerent act against Mexico.

Disregarding those concerns, Texas, on December 29, 1845—at least in the eyes of officials in Austin and Washington—was formally accorded U.S. statehood. Weeks earlier, in his first annual message to Congress, Polk, wary of European interference in the annexation of Texas, had reached back to President James Monroe's seventh annual message to Congress (1823). Quoting Monroe, Polk—presenting U.S. expansionism in anticolonial language—declared, "The American continents ... are henceforth not to be considered as subjects for future colonization by any European powers." That fall Polk applied to Monroe's admonition the term by which, shorn of the honorific and its possessive form, it has henceforth been known: "Mr. Monroe's doctrine."[1]

Four months later, in April 1846, came an attack on U.S. soldiers by Mexican troops near the mouth of the Rio Grande, in the disputed border region between Texas and Mexico. In May, Congress, at Polk's behest, declared war on Mexico. The president's enemies—antiwar Whigs and Democrats, abolitionists, and assorted opponents of the spread of slavery—were outraged. Three months later, and repeatedly over the next two years, Pennsylvania congressman David

Wilmot, a Democrat, and other members of Congress introduced legislation to ban slavery in any territory won through the war. The measure, soon called the Wilmot Proviso, passed the House several times but never won Senate approval. Much of the support for the Wilmot Proviso, however, arose less from principled opposition to slavery and more from a desire to preserve labor opportunities for white settlers in any new lands won during the war. Wilmot himself accepted a term supporters coined for the measure; they called it a "White Man's Proviso."[2]

Echoing the outrage of other Americans who opposed the Mexican War on moral grounds, abolitionist Frederick Douglass, lecturing in England in September 1846, assayed the morality of a war against a republic that upon its founding in 1821 had outlawed slavery. He condemned the United States for "now seeking to perpetuate and extend the conquests of slavery, and waging a bloody war with Mexico that she may establish slavery on a soil where a semi-barbarous people had the humanity to put an end to it."[3]

For President Polk and his cabinet, however, the war declaration of May 1846 had marked a heady moment. The administration at that time was close to concluding negotiations that would extend Old Glory's dominion to the Pacific Coast. In June 1846, a treaty negotiated by Secretary of State James Buchanan and British minister Sir Richard Pakenham resolved long-simmering geopolitical rivalries between the United States and the United Kingdom over the sprawling Oregon Country. By the pact's terms, Britain retained title to the area now occupied by Canada's province of British Columbia, and Uncle Sam acquired exclusive title to a domain that included all of the area occupied by today's states of Washington, Oregon, and Idaho and the western portions of Montana and Wyoming. Put another way, the two countries agreed to divide the Oregon Country along the forty-ninth parallel, which forms most of the western stretch of today's U.S.-Canadian border.

Emboldened by that outcome, Polk and his supporters, seizing on the April 1846 military clash near the mouth of the Rio Grande but acting on an earlier-contemplated option, settled on war with Mexico as a means by which the United States might secure its claim on Texas and, as policy objectives evolved, the entirety of Mexico's sparsely settled northwestern frontier. That frontier included Mexico's departments of New Mexico and California. Eventually, in February 1848, by the Treaty of Guadalupe Hidalgo between the United States and Mexico, the president secured all of those lands.[4]

In March 1847, looking back on those triumphs, Polk stood at the chronological halfway mark of his four-year presidential term. Most first-term presidents facing that milestone would have been preoccupied with reelection strategies. But not the fifty-one-year-old Tennessean. As a candidate, Polk—matching a promise made by his Whig opponent Clay— had forsworn a second term; if elected, he had promised, his turn in the White House would be for four years, and four years only.

Thus, from one perspective, the new president had begun his administration already a lame duck. In March 1845, when Polk took office, friends, enemies, and rivals alike—Democrats and Whigs—knew, barring unforeseen events, exactly how many days remained in his presidency. Accordingly, as the days passed, they could gage with precision his ostensibly declining powers to reward or punish. But from another vantage, candidate Polk's no-second-term promise gave President Polk a singular advantage: having no need to go back to voters to win a second term, he was free to pursue his policies unburdened by the circumspections that inhibit a president who knows he must again face the electorate.

A glass half full or half empty?

The metaphor ill suits a man of such abstemious habits. Nonetheless, Polk and his cabinet viewed his presidency, at its midpoint, as a half-full glass. That spirit of exaltation propels a letter he wrote in January 1847 to George Bancroft, his ambassador to the Court of St. James:

> For myself, I rejoice that I am under no circumstances to be before the Country for re-election. This determination is irrevocable. Personally—therefore I have no interest, in the question of the succession, but I most ardently desire to maintain the ascendancy of my political principles, and to hand over the Government, at the close of my term, to a successor of my own political faith.[5]

In words and actions, Polk seems to have been emboldened, not hindered, by his one-term pledge. Indeed, if anything, as the missive to Bancroft suggests, the promise added an urgency—and vigor—to his ever-dwindling days in office. Beyond that, the entire body of his correspondence and presidential diary indicate no wavering on his one-term pledge.

Then and now, Polk's diplomatic achievement in Oregon and his military successes in Mexico, actions that won plaudits from leaders both domestic and foreign, have placed an aura of invincibility over his presidency. Conventional wisdom associates that presidency, indeed Polk's very name, with "Manifest Destiny," a locution coined in 1845 by journalist John L. O'Sullivan. Writing in *The United States Magazine and Democratic Review,* a literary and political journal that he co-owned, O'Sullivan, while calling for U.S. annexation of Texas, argued that it is "our manifest destiny to overspread the continent allotted by Providence for the free development of our yearly multiplying millions."[6]

Soon popularized by the era's penny press, the term never received a precise definition. A Procrustean phrase, more often invoked in its day by those selling newspapers than by policymakers, it came to refer to an unbridled, in most cases east-to-west, U.S. expansionism ordained by a Protestant, Anglo-Saxon God. That most of the lands eyed for conquest were home to native peoples and other non-Anglo-Saxon populations mattered little to Manifest Destiny's adherents. Nor, for that matter, did U.S. settlers always proceed from east to west. Often, as with those Texas-bound, many moved from northeast to south-west; in California, with many arrivals coming via the Pacific, newcomers often moved from west to east.

Polk achieved most but not all of the expansionist projects sought by Manifest Destiny's advocates. As a candidate, he had run on a party platform that pledged to fight for a north-ern U.S. border in the Oregon County, which stretched deep into today's British Columbia. "Fifty-four Forty or Fight," the trademark phrase associated with that advocacy—though often linked to Polk's campaign—did not come into use until a year into his term.[7] Those—known as Oregon "ultras"—who invoked the phrase were thus crestfallen when, as president, Polk agreed to the Buchanan-Pakenham treaty that established a border between the two countries at the 49th Parallel, except where it dipped south to accord the United Kingdom title to all of Vamcouver Island. Extending the 49th Parallel border established by earlier treaties, it was the same line that today, stretching westward from Lake of the Woods, Minnesota, demarcates, in those realms, the U.S.–Canada border.

U.S. expansionists who favored acquisition of the entirety of Mexico and the island of Cuba were similarly disappointed. As the war in Mexico neared its end, much of the nation's expansionist penny press—papers such as the *Boston Times* and the *New York Sun*—called for Polk, when negotiating an armistice, to acquire all of Mexico. In 1848, however, the administration—wary of the burdens that such an occupation of the entirety of Mexico would entail—accepted a more modest territorial settlement.

Likewise, the president disappointed supporters of American annexation of Cuba. The idea of U.S. acquisition of Cuba enjoyed a long pedigree in American politics—stretching back to such early advocates as Presidents Thomas Jefferson, James Madison, and James Monroe.[8] During Polk's term in office, invigorated by recent expansionist triumphs, the cause won a new cadre of advocates, whose numbers included South Carolina U.S. senator John C. Calhoun, secretary of state James Buchanan, and journalist and Democratic party activist John O'Sullivan.

Indeed, on May 10, 1848, during the administration's waning months, Polk met with O'Sullivan and Illinois senator Stephen Douglas to discuss the island. The two hoped to persuade the president to support an audacious scheme proposed by the Club de la Habana, a cabal of wealthy Cuban entrepreneurs and planters.

The government of Spain, Cuba's colonial overseer, was heavily indebted to the United Kingdom, and the well-healed Cubans feared that Madrid might, in exchange for London's forgiving of those debts, yield to pressures from British abolitionists and abolish slavery on the island. Thus the Club de la Habana, via O'Sullivan and Douglas, extended a proposal to the president: If Polk would oversee a U.S. purchase of Cuba from Spain, the Cubans would reimburse the U.S. Treasury up to one hundred million dollars.

Polk heard out Douglas and O'Sullivan, but the two left the White House with no inkling of the president's reaction to their proposal. As it happened, the often inscrutable president had already, weeks earlier, made up his mind on Cuba. As Polk confided to his diary mere hours after his meeting with O'Sullivan and Buchanan, "Though I expressed no opinion to them I am decidedly in favor of purchasing Cuba & making it one of the States of [the] Union."

Weeks later, in June 1848, Polk ordered Secretary of State Buchanan to authorize Romulus Saunders, the U.S. minister in Madrid, to offer Spain up to one hundred million dollars for the island. In his instructions to Saunders, Buchanan advised the envoy to, while making the offer, "touch delicately upon the dangers that Spain may lose Cuba by revolution in the Island, or that it might be wrested from her by Great Britain." In the end, however, diplomatic ineptitude by Saunders, combined with reporting by the *New York Herald* on the ostensibly secret overture, embarrassed Spanish officials and the talks were abruptly ended.[9]

In the end, of course, disappointments notwithstanding, Polk did win more than his share of expansionist triumphs. And those victories won wide approval among his supporters. Beyond that, the nation's new status as a continental nation-state soon became enshrined in its self-image—and was celebrated, in often florid language, by its politicians and writers; "I skirt the sierras," rhapsodized Walt Whitman, "my palms cover continents." Henry David Thoreau famously refused to pay a tax because of his opposition to the war, an act that landed him in jail. But over time, poetically if not politically, even the bard of Walden Pond could not resist the spell: "Eastward I go only by force," Thoreau eventually wrote, "but westward I go free."[10]

Indeed, for good or ill, in a broader if poetic sense Polk, Frémont and others of that generation—in their extension of the nation's domain, bequeathing to America its coast-to-coast breadth—gave the country's artists a continental template on which to work, the open road down which American writers, from Jack Kerouac to Robert Pirsig, Mark Twain to Hunter Thompson, John Steinbeck to Woody Guthrie have traveled. Literally and metaphorically, Route 66 runs deep into 1848 Mexican Cession country.

His public aversion to sentimentality notwithstanding, Polk's writings do reveal a gentle side to the president. Letters to family members and those penned as he conducted a brief sentimental journey in May 1847 to his alma mater, the University of North Carolina in Chapel Hill, evoke a softer, even solicitous, side to his personality. However heavily the duties of office occupied his time, family and friends remained important to him. Of the

North Carolina visit's first day, he recorded in his diary, "I have never spent a more pleasant or delightful afternoon & evening."[11]

By the time Polk became president, his mane of once-black hair had faded to gray. Of medium height with a high forehead and a prominent nose, he was an introvert who adapted to the demands of the two professions, trial lawyer and politician, which became his life work. Much like President Richard Nixon, Polk was an introvert in an extrovert's profession.

An assertion, widely repeated by Polk biographers, describes his acumen for public speaking as winning him the accolade "Napoleon of the Stump." But no usage of that sobriquet during Polk's lifetime has been located. Indeed, its earliest located appearance occurs in John S. Jenkins's *Life of James Knox Polk: Late President of the United States,* published in 1850.[12]

Suffice it to say, then, that Polk was not a glad-hander. When he could, particularly as president, he often avoided public events and declined invitations. But when necessity called, he could and did rise to the occasion. After all, he did enjoy success in *both* of his chosen occupations. And as leader of the nation, Polk set aside two evenings each week during which citizens could visit the White House and air concerns to their president.[13]

Tempering his often dour image, contemporary correspondence and accounts of the Polks' life in Washington reveal, by Victorian standards, a tender and equable relationship between him and his wife, Sarah Polk. An able woman, Sarah possessed an advanced education and formidable intelligence. Her counsel, in business and politics, was often sought by her husband. The Polks had no children, but the portrait of their White House life that emerges in the letters is further softened by the retinue of nieces and nephews from Tennessee who stayed for extended visits.[14]

Even so, in most cases, in words and deeds, Polk presented a coldly formal, no-nonsense persona to the world. And that approach, more than sentimental interludes with family and college memories, precluded his adoption of the western fervor of John O'Sullivan and other contemporaries. In fact, so far as we know, Polk never uttered or penned the phrase "Manifest Destiny." Not for this pragmatic politician the bombastic rhetoric that issued from such a gaseous notion. Indeed, Thomas Hart Benton, in his memoirs, published in 1883, insisted that the man whose name is linked to the Mexican War was enamored neither of war—at least for its own sake—nor of romantic nationalism:

> It is impossible to conceive of an administration less warlike, or more intriguing, that that of Mr. Polk. They were men of peace, with objects to be accomplished by means of war; so that war was a necessity and an indispensability to their purpose; but they wanted no more of it than would answer their purposes.

They wanted a small war, just large enough to require a treaty of peace, and not large enough to make military reputations, dangerous for the presidency. Never were men at the head of a government less imbued with military spirit, or more addicted to intrigue.[15]

More to the point, each expansionist project Polk undertook was designed to appeal to specific constituencies—Texas to southern planters and aspirant pioneers from that region; Oregon and California to, among others, mid-Atlantic and New England commercial and maritime interests, as well as aspirant emigrants from that day's "Northwest," today's Midwest.

Privately and publicly, however naively in retrospect, Polk always insisted that whether acquired territories permitted or banned slavery was a separate issue, subordinate to the national interest of expanding the nation's geographic breadth and furthering "the Union." An August 10, 1846, diary entry bears witness to that attitude. The entry concerns the Wilmot Proviso, adopted days earlier by the House of Representatives, which sought to ban slavery in any territory acquired from Mexico. Polk dismisses the amendment as "mischievous & foolish": "What connection slavery had with making peace with Mexico it is difficult to conceive."

Eight months later, he was equally dismissive toward efforts to leave California and Oregon open to slavery. In April 1847, opposing an effort by John C. Calhoun to leave the latter open to the peculiar institution, Polk suspected the South Carolinian of pandering to southern slaveholders to advance presidential aspirations: "He is wholly selfish, & I am satisfied has no patriotism." From Polk's viewpoint, pro- and antislavery partisans alike were exploiting the issue of slavery for political gain: "Both desire to mount slavery as a hobby, and hope to secure the election of their favourite upon it."[16]

Those attitudes notwithstanding, Polk, in his quest for new lands, was also sufficiently aware of political exigencies to, by his lights, balance acquisitions of slave and free territories. And husbanding political capital, he commenced his expansionist initiatives successively, not simultaneously. Far from being unbridled in time and space, each annexation project he undertook was discrete, limited in scope, and bound by considerations of practical politics.[17] As a consequence, readers coming to Polk's writings in search of musings à la Thomas Jefferson on philosophy, the arts, and literature, expressed with the literary flourishes of an eighteenth-century *philosophe*, will come away disappointed. But those who seek the words, however plain spoken, of a Machiavellian political maestro will find, in his private words, precisely those.

James Knox Polk (1795–1849) in an 1846 portrait by George Healy. From 1845 to 1849, Polk served as the eleventh U.S. president. A lawyer and former Tennessee congressman and governor, Polk as president, through war and diplomacy, increased by one-third the area of the United States, giving it a coast-to-coast breadth, thus rendering it a continental nation-state. Though historians often associate his name with the phrase "Manifest Destiny," no record has been located of his ever using the term. (Polk Ancestral Home)

James Knox Polk and his wife, Sarah Childress Polk (1803–1891), in a joint portrait likely taken in 1849 by daguerreotypist Mathew Brady. (Polk Ancestral Home)

An 1844 campaign banner touts that year's Democratic party's ticket of James Polk (left) and vice presidential running mate, former Philadelphia mayor and U.S. senator George Dallas (right). At the Democratic convention, the candidacy of Martin Van Buren, former president and nomination front-runner, faded when opponents implemented a rule that required a two-thirds majority to select a candidate, and the convention deadlocked. Not until its ninth ballot was the nominee, James K. Polk, chosen—an unexpected event, widely believed to have occasioned the first usage in presidential politics of the term "dark horse." The above banner includes one of the sobriquets by which Polk was by then known, "The Young Hickory"—a moniker that alluded to Polk's mentor Andrew Jackson, "Old Hickory." The banner was created by lithographer Nathaniel Currier whose firm, after 1850 when he was joined by a partner, James Ives, became Currier and Ives. (Library of Congress)

HENRY CLAY.

Eleventh President of the United States.

Henry Clay (1777–1852) of Kentucky, the Whig party's 1844 presidential nominee, promised that if he won the presidency, he would serve only one term. Democratic candidate Polk duplicated Clay's pledge. In the November election, Polk defeated Clay by less than two percent in the popular vote, but by a 170 to 105 margin in the Electoral College. Above the optimistic phrase "Eleventh President of the United States" in this campaign lithograph—but illegible in this reproduction—are the words "nominated for." (Library of Congress)

John Tyler (1790–1862), Polk's immediate predecessor as president, in a circa 1860–65 portrait of unknown origin. The Virginian became the tenth U.S. president upon the death of Whig Benjamin Harrison, for whom Tyler had served as vice-president. Though nominally a Whig when he became president, he was soon expelled from that party. It was Tyler who lit the fuse that ignited the U.S. war with Mexico over which Polk would preside. On February 28, 1845, four days before Polk took office, Congress, at Tyler's behest, passed a joint resolution extending the Republic of Texas a long-sought invitation to apply for U.S. annexation. Mexico's government, having never recognized Texas's claimed independence, considered the invitation a belligerent act. (Library of Congress)

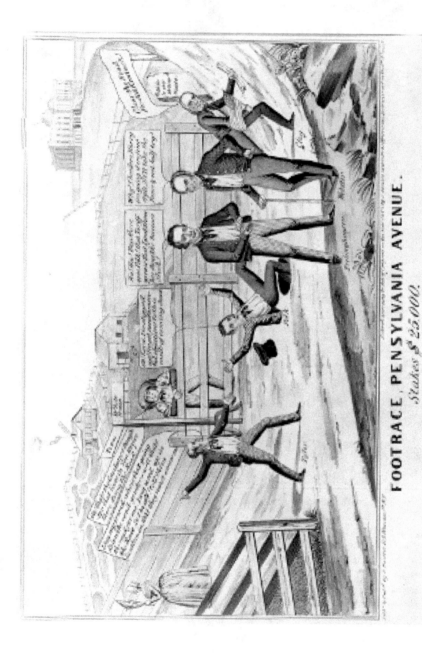

FOOTRACE, PENSYLVANIA AVENUE.
Stakes $ 25,000.

Two political cartoons by H. Bucholzer (above and next page) reflect the vagaries of Polk's road to the presidency. "Footrace, Pennsylvania Avenue" captures the conventional wisdom early in the summer of 1844 that Whig nominee Henry Clay would win the election. "Stakes $25,000" refers to the presidential salary. Whig nominee Clay leads the race, with Polk lagging behind and stumbling in a pothole. Incumbent president John Tyler lags behind Polk. Tyler subsequently withdrew, in August, from the race. In the foreground offering comments are vice presidential candidate Theodore Frelinghuysen, and Whig senator Daniel Webster.

"Texas Coming In," 1844, reflects how the presidential race had changed by the following fall after concerns about Texas had come to dominate the contest, with Polk favoring its annexation and Clay appearing to vacillate on the issue. "Salt River," depicted in the cartoon, was a common metaphor of the era, for failure or embarrassment. Polk, standing ashore, celebrates as Texas patriots (left to right) Stephen Austin and Sam Houston ride a wheeled steamboat-like vehicle across the bridge. Their vehicle is being drawn to the opposite bank by a rope pulled by Clay and other Whigs who otherwise appear helpless in Salt River. (Library of Congress)

Though the likeness of its main subject is unrecognizable—which figure on the platform is the new president?—this engraving from the *Illustrated News of London* purports to depict Polk, on March 4, 1845, amid a stormy downpour, taking the presidential oath, on a platform beside the U.S. capitol's East Portico. U.S. Supreme Court chief justice Roger B. Taney administered the oath. At forty-nine, Polk was then the youngest man to ever attain the presidency, and ten years younger than the average age of earlier presidents. Polk's inaugural address—delivered by that day's custom, *before* the oath of office—reaffirmed campaign promises to aggressively advance U.S. interests in Oregon and Texas. To the platform's left looms a statue, "The Discovery of America," by sculptor Luigi Persico, installed in 1844 and removed in 1958. (Library of Congress)

THE PATRIOTS GETTING THEIR BEANS.

Two cartoons (here and next page)—both by Philadelphia artist Edward Williams Clay (1792–1857)—reflect early and widespread public speculation over the directions that Polk's presidency would take. "The patriots getting their beans," which appeared in 1845, shortly after Polk's election, presents his various Democratic allies and potential beneficiaries of White House patronage promoting their respective causes and personal aspiration as the president-elect sits with hands folded, serenely oblivious to the commotion. (Library of Congress)

Edward Williams Clay's "Polk's Dream," published in 1846, early in the Tennessean's presidency, captures the public's still unsettled view of the new chief of state's intentions: as the president sleeps, assorted figures—ranging from former president Andrew Jackson to the Devil—visit in a dream, each pressing upon Polk his own political wish. (Library of Congress)

James K. Polk and cabinet in a daguerreotype taken by John Plumbe, Jr. in 1846. The image constitutes the earliest known interior photograph of the White House, as well as the first of a President with his cabinet. Standing, left to right: Cave Johnson, George Bancroft; seated, left to right: John Y. Mason, William L. Marcy, President Polk, Robert J. Walker. James Buchanan, secretary of state, is missing. As with all daguerreotypes, this is a mirror image. (Polk Ancestral Home)

War News from Mexico, an 1848 painting by Richard Canton Woodville, captures the public excitement that, in many quarters, greeted U.S. victories in the Mexican War. Note, however, on right, the black man and the little girl—presumably his daughter—both less well dressed than the jubilant men on the porch, and who sit impassively. The victories did not bode well for African Americans—or the Union. (Crystal Bridges Museum of American Art)

Journalist and Democatic party activist John L. O'Sullivan (1813–1895), in an engraving published in *Harper's Weekly* in 1874. Conventional wisdom associates Polk's presidency, indeed his very name, with "Manifest Destiny." But the locution was coined in 1845 by O'Sullivan. Writing in the *United States Magazine and Democratic Review*, a literary and political journal that he co-owned and edited, O'Sullivan, while calling for U.S. annexation of Texas, argued that it is "our manifest destiny to overspread the continent allotted by Providence for the free development of our yearly multiplying millions." Soon popularized by the era's penny press, Manifest Destiny never received a precise definition. A Procrustean phrase, more often invoked in its day by those selling newspapers than by policymakers, it came to refer to an unbridled, in most cases east-to-west, U.S. expansionism ordained by a Protestant, Anglo-Saxon God. That most of the lands eyed for conquest were home to native peoples and other non–Anglo-Saxon populations mattered little to Manifest Destiny's adherents. Nor, for that matter, did U.S. settlers always proceed from east to west. Often, as with those Texas-bound pioneers, many moved from northeast to southwest; in California, with many arrivals coming via the Pacific, newcomers often moved from west to east. (*Harper's Weekly*)

Thomas Hart Benton (1782–1858) in a daguerreotype created by Mathew Brady between 1845 and 1850. Benton served as U.S. senator from Missouri from 1821 to 1851. During his Senate years, he became a principal architect of federal policy in the West. Due to his in-depth knowledge of the region, his prowess in creating policies there often eclipsed contemporary presidents, including Polk. (Library of Congress)

Explorer John Charles Frémont (1813–1890) in a circa mid-nineteenth engraving by T. Knight after a daguerre-otype by Mathew Brady. During the 1840s, Frémont led a series of federally sponsored exploring expeditions into the American West. His published journals proved wildly popular, reshaped popular conceptions of the region and sparked the first mass emigration by U.S. citizens there. Unlike Thomas Jefferson, who, as president, planned explorers Lewis and Clark famous Corps of Discovery expedition (1804–6) into the Far West, Polk played no active role in planning the Frémont expedition conducted during his presidency. The Georgia-born explorer was a son-in-law of Senator Benton, who did play a large role in his career and the shaping of his expeditions. (Library of Congress)

This cartoon—published in December 1848 or early 1849, and possibly drawn by S. Lee Perkins—tapped into fears of designs by foreign states on the gold recently discovered in the new U.S. possession of California. U.S. president Zachary Taylor is depicted as an eagle; and Polk as a snake. Each warns against approaching foreign interlopers—including Queen Victoria of the United Kingdom, French president Louise-Philippe, Spain's Queen Isabella II, and Russian Czar Nicholas I. (Library of Congress)

An 1850 lithograph by J.L. Rogers depicts that year's Whig candidate for president, Zachary Taylor (1784–1850), who succeeded Polk to become the twelfth U.S. president. Taylor had served as the first of Polk's two successive chief generals in the Mexican War. This lithograph—reflecting Taylor's indeterminate party affiliation when he began his presidential campaign—includes the couplet: "About party creeds let party zealots fight/He cant be wrong whose life is in the right." (Library of Congress)

In an 1849 portrait of James Polk by photographer Mathew Brady, the ravages taken on the president by declining health and the duties of office are plainly evident. Months earlier, in a letter to a friend, Polk reflected that, the "country is prosperous in a degree almost without an example, and if the war can be brought to a successful termination, a long course of prosperity is before us, and I shall retire at the close of my term, with the satisfaction of believing I have rendered my country some service." But the future failed to redeem those expectations. Polk's retirement was cruelly brief. Marking the briefest post-presidency retirement in U. S. history, he died in June 1849, three months after leaving the White House. And the legacy of peace and prosperity that he envisioned for the country, which his policies had so enlarged, was also short lived. Within a dozen years of his leaving the White House, a conflict erupted that violently divided the United States. (James K. Polk Ancestral Home)

Notes

1. Polk, "First Annual Message," Dec. 2, 1845, in *A Compilation of the Messages and Papers of the Presidents, 1789–1897*, ed. James D. Richardson (Washington, D.C.: GPO, 1897), 4:398; entry of Oct. 24, 1845, in James K. Polk, *The Diary of James K. Polk during His Presidency, 1845 to 1849*, 4 vols., ed. Milo Milton Quaife (Chicago: A. C. McClurg, 1910) (hereafter cited as Polk, *Diary*, followed by the volume and page number), 1:70. For a discussion of Polk and the Monroe Doctrine, see Jay Sexton, *The Monroe Doctrine: Empire and Nation in Nineteenth-Century America* (New York: Hill & Wang, 2011), 97–118.

2. Eric Foner, *Politics and Ideology in the Age of the Civil War* (New York: Oxford Univ. Press, 1981), 84.

3. Frederick Douglass lecture, Sunderland, England, Sept. 18, 1846, in Frederick Douglass, *The Frederick Douglass Papers*, ser. 1, *Speeches, Debates, and Interviews*, vol. 1, ed. John W. Blassingame (New Haven, Conn.: Yale Univ. Press, 1979), 419.

4. The Treaty of Guadalupe Hidalgo stipulated that, in exchange for abandoning claims to Texas, New Mexico, and California, the Mexican government would be paid fifteen million dollars by the United States. The U.S. government also agreed to pay Mexican debts, relieving Mexico's government of about five million dollars in claims against it by U.S. citizens. The treaty also, in general terms, stipulated anew the boundary between the two nations, with clarifications to be made by a joint U.S.-Mexico commission.

5. For Polk's abstemious habits, see Mark E. Byrnes, *James K. Polk: A Biographical Companion* (Santa Barbara, Calif.: ABC-CLIO, 2001), 171; Polk to Bancroft, Jan. 30, 1847, Polk, *Correspondence* 12:65–66.

6. John L. O'Sullivan, "Annexation," *United States Magazine and Democratic Review* 17 (July–Aug. 1845): 5; Robert D. Sampson, *John L. O'Sullivan and His Times* (Kent, Ohio: Kent State Univ. Press, 2003), 193–207.

7. Walter R. Borneman, *Polk: The Man Who Transformed the Presidency and America* (New York: Random House, 2008), 219.

8. Tom Chaffin, *Fatal Glory: Narciso López and the First Clandestine U.S. War against Cuba* (Charlottesville: Univ. Press of Virginia, 1996; reprint, Baton Rouge: Louisiana State Univ. Press, 2003), 18. For more on U.S. interest in Cuba and on filibusters—clandestine armies, usually from the United States, bent on conquests in foreign, often Latin American, climes—see both Chaffin, *Fatal Glory*, and Robert E. May, *Manifest Destiny's Underworld: Filibustering in Antebellum America* (Chapel Hill: Univ. of North Carolina Press, 2001).

9. For "All Mexico," see Frederick Merk, *Manifest Destiny and Mission in American History* (1963; reprint, Cambridge: Harvard Univ. Press, 1995), 112–13; for Cuba, see Chaffin, *Fatal Glory*, 14–15, 35–36, 41–43; for "expressed no opinion," see entry of May 10, 1848, Polk, *Diary* 3:446. For Saunders, see Chaffin, *Fatal Glory*, 41–43.

10. Walt Whitman, "Song of Myself" (1855), in *Walt Whitman: Complete Poetry and Collected Prose*, ed. Justin Kaplan (New York: Library of America, 1982), 59; Henry David Thoreau, "Walking," in *Henry David Thoreau: Collected Essays and Poems*, ed. Elizabeth Hall Witherell (New York: Library of America, 2001), 234.

11. Entry for May 31, 1847, in Polk, *Diary* 3:45.

12. On Polk's "Napoleon of the Stump" accolade and speaking style, see John S. Jenkins, *The Life of James Knox Polk: Late President of the United States* (Auburn, N.Y.: James M. Alden, 1850), 50–51; see also Sellers, *Polk: Jacksonian*, 275–78. Neither work, however, cites a contemporary usage—a usage during Polk's lifetime—of that epithet.

13. Sellers, *Polk: Continentalist*, 307.

14. For visits by nieces and nephews, see Robert Armstrong to Polk, Jan. 4, 1847, *Correspondence* 12:26; and Polk to Sarah Childress Polk, July 11, 1847, *Correspondence* 12:417.

15. Thomas Hart Benton, *Thirty Years' View; or, A History of the Working of the American Government for Thirty Years, from 1820 to 1850*, vol. 2 (New York: D. Appleton, 1883), 680.

16. For "mischievous" remark, see entry of Aug. 10, 1846, Polk, *Diary* 2:75; for California, Oregon, and Calhoun, see entry of Apr. 6, 1847, Polk, *Diary* 2:457–59.

17. Chaffin, *Fatal Glory*, 26–30; Merk, *Manifest Destiny and Mission*, 61–64.

Bibliography

Published Primary Sources

Benton, Thomas Hart. *Thirty Years' View; or, A History of the Working of the American Government for Thirty Years, from 1820 to 1850*. Vol. 2. New York: D. Appleton, 1883.

Douglass, Frederick. *The Frederick Douglass Papers*. Ser. 1, *Speeches, Debates, and Interviews*, vol. 1. Edited by John W. Blassingame. New Haven, Conn.: Yale Univ. Press, 1979.

Jenkins, John S. *The Life of James Knox Polk: Late President of the United States*. Auburn, N.Y.: James M. Alden, 1850.

O'Sullivan, John L. "Annexation." *United States Magazine and Democratic Review* 17 (July–Aug. 1845): 5–10.

Polk, James K. *Correspondence of James K. Polk: Volume XII, January–July 1847*. Edited by Tom Chaffin and Michael David Cohen. Knoxville: Univ. of Tennessee Press, 2013.

———. *The Diary of James K. Polk during His Presidency, 1845 to 1849*. 4 vols. Edited by Milo Milton Quaife. Chicago: A. C. McClurg, 1910.

Richardson, James D., ed. *A Compilation of the Messages and Papers of the Presidents, 1789–1897*. Vol. 4. Washington, D.C.: GPO, 1897.

Thoreau, Henry David. *Henry David Thoreau: Collected Essays and Poems.* Edited by Elizabeth Hall Witherell. New York: Library of America, 2001.

Whitman, Walt. *Walt Whitman: Complete Poetry and Collected Prose.* Edited by Justin Kaplan. New York: Library of America, 1982.

Secondary Sources

Borneman, Walter R. *Polk: The Man Who Transformed the Presidency and America.* New York: Random House, 2008.

Byrnes, Mark E. *James K. Polk: A Biographical Companion.* Santa Barbara, Calif.: ABC-CLIO, 2001.

Chaffin, Tom. *Fatal Glory: Narciso López and the First Clandestine U.S. War against Cuba.* Charlottesville: Univ. Press of Virginia, 1996. Reprint, Baton Rouge: Louisiana State Univ. Press, 2003.

Foner, Eric. *Politics and Ideology in the Age of the Civil War.* New York: Oxford Univ. Press, 1981.

May, Robert E. *Manifest Destiny's Underworld: Filibustering in Antebellum America.* Chapel Hill: Univ. of North Carolina Press, 2001.

Merk, Frederick. *Manifest Destiny and Mission in American History.* 1963. Reprint, Cambridge: Harvard Univ. Press, 1995.

Sampson, Robert D. *John L. O'Sullivan and His Times.* Kent, Ohio: Kent State Univ. Press, 2003.

Sellers, Charles. *James K. Polk: Continentalist, 1843–1846.* Princeton, N.J.: Princeton Univ. Press, 1966.

———. *James K. Polk: Jacksonian, 1795–1843.* Princeton, N.J.: Princeton Univ. Press, 1957.

Sexton, Jay. *The Monroe Doctrine: Empire and Nation in Nineteenth-Century America.* New York: Hill & Wang, 2011.

Reading 3.4

Civil War and the American Political Economy

Joseph R. Stromberg

T HE TASK BEFORE US IS TO assess in largely material terms the political-economic system arising during and after the American Civil War. Ideological issues existed, certainly, but much evidence suggests that pure idealism had a rather limited run. Antislavery was one of many themes generally serving as the stalking horse for more practical causes. Slavery itself was a colossal background fact constituting, as historian James L. Huston states, the biggest single capital investment in the United States—an enormous material interest uniting millions of people (not just in the South) through ties of interest, commerce, and sentiment. This interest stood athwart the political-economic ambitions of powerful interests in the Northeast.

We may think here of large "forces" at work, each with limits and counter-tendencies. Where slavery is concerned, Americans shirked the job of finding a reasonable solution. Offered one—disunion—some rejected it, after which the blunt instrument of war permitted another solution of sorts. As historian Howard Zinn writes: It was not the moral enormity of slavery but "the antitariff, antibank, anticapitalist aspect of slavery which aroused the united opposition of the only groups in the country with power to make war: the national political leaders and the controllers of the national economy."

Political scientist Thomas Ferguson believes that the goals of money-driven coalitions explain the greater part of American political history. During the mid-nineteenth century, railroads represented the biggest new business opportunity, provided large-scale government subsidies (state and federal) were available. Northern railroad promoters and land speculators, many based in New England, worked both to get subsidies and remove obstacles. On the removal side, some of them, like John Murray Forbes, donated money to John Brown's good works in Kansas apparently to put pressure on southern opponents of internal improvements.

The Republican Party platform of May 1860 stated the minimal program of a historical bloc of northeastern financial and manufacturing interests and Midwestern and western farmers. It began on a high note of egalitarian and republican ideology, aired some Free Soil, antislavery grievances, and thudded to rest with some practical matters: protective tariffs, homesteads (good for votes but rather ambiguous), federally funded improvements of rivers and harbors (Great Lakes subsidies), and a Pacific railroad. In addition,

Railroads presented one of the main opportunities for northern mercantilists to use the Civil War to start or secure their fortunes.

the party's friendliness to central (national) banking was no secret. The Hamiltonian mercantilism of the platform was its central theme, if not quite its only one. Alas for its adherents, they soon found a large bloc of their recent opponents (and potential taxpayers) leaving the Union, beginning with South Carolina in December 1860.

The opposition to northern mercantilism had removed itself from the system. "Why fight to bring it back?" historians Thomas C. Cochran and William Miller ask. Over the Secession Winter of 1860–1861 many northerners asked just that question. Matters were, after all, rather complex. Key New York trading interests were heavily involved with southern cotton—the petroleum of the mid-nineteenth century—and New England manufacturers processed it. If the incoming administration refused to accept secession and used force to retain states allegedly "in rebellion," war would come. Many agreed that, generally speaking, war was never good for business as a whole. For some months hesitation reigned.

It seems clear that the economic interests represented by the Republican Party were ready enough for war, provided other people bore most of the costs.

Ready for War

It seems clear that *key leaders* of the northern "developmental coalition" represented by the Republican Party were ready enough for war, provided other people bore most of the costs. As tax historian Charles Adams writes, "The Wall Street boys and the men of commerce and business were determined to preserve the Union for their economic gains"—a calculation made easier for them after the contrasting U.S. and Confederate tariff schedules were released in early 1861.

With the highest tariff rates at 47 percent (North) and 12 percent (South), a massive shift of English and European trade to Norfolk, Charleston, Mobile, and New Orleans seemed likely. U.S. revenues would plummet, and northern business imagined short-run (or longer) catastrophe. A good many more northern businessmen began to calculate the possible benefits of a war. On cue, hesitating newspapers changed their line. Of course access to the Mississippi River (quite unthreatened in reality), the reluctance of any State apparatus to lose territory, and ideological nationalism played their parts.

War came, and Republican economic operators made the most of it. With so many of their former opponents assembled in another Congress in Montgomery (later Richmond), Republican interest groups conducted what historian Ludwell Johnson calls "a war of economic and political aggrandizement."

To fund and man the actual military struggle, Congress provided numerous excise taxes, inflationary Greenback currency, bond issues (public debt), an unprecedented income tax, tariffs, and mass conscription. Interestingly, most northern enterprisers doing well off the war (like Mellon, Morgan, Armour, and Gould) paid substitutes and never went near a battle. The costs of the war could indeed be shifted. For interests getting vested under cover of the war, there were also tariffs (dual-use, it seems), banking acts, the Homestead Act (1862), the Contract Labor Law (1864), Pacific (and other) subsidized railroad projects complete with land-jobbing, and of course the inevitable rivers and harbors acts. The resulting concentration of capital, active strikebreaking by federal troops in St. Louis and Louisville, and (fairly typical) 50 percent profit rates on U.S. war contracts round out this pretty picture. Transparent loopholes in the Homestead Act ensured that land speculators and mining, timber, and oil companies got far more land than genuine settlers did. In addition, historian Jeffrey Rogers Hummel notes that the Morrill Act of 1862 granted considerable western land to eastern states partly in support of federal military education (more fodder for organized land-jobbers). Intentionally or otherwise, the Fourteenth Amendment (1868) hastened, as historian Arthur A. Ekirch, Jr., writes, "the triumph of national big business under the gospel of the 'due process clause.'"

It follows that a minimal definition of laissez faire as understood by Republicans during and after the war would run as follows: open-ended, active federal assistance for connected businesses through tax money, favorable statutes and legal rulings, and other institutional favors, with no corresponding obligation of these businesses toward society or even the State itself. So assisted, businessmen would make big bucks and accumulate capital, thereby greasing the wheels of progress and development. This was all the common good we need ever expect—a cozy arrangement indeed, despite conflicts and divisions already visible within the Republican machinery.

Historian Clyde Wilson notes that for Republicans "the revolution ... was the point" and finds it odd that scholars fully informed on wartime and postwar corruption "imply that it mysteriously appeared after Lincoln's death, and somehow miss the obvious conclusion that it was implicit in the goals of the Lincoln war party." Lincoln's first secretary of war, Simon Cameron, Pennsylvania iron manufacturer and Republican political boss, oversaw many a dodgy deal. Lincoln himself knew his associates quite well and joked that at least Cameron "wouldn't steal a red-hot stove." Small wonder, then, that Ludwell Johnson finds profiteering and fraud "so pervasive that they seemed to be of the very essence of the Northern war effort."

Johnson sees northern wartime practice with regard to southern property as a policy of "redeeming the South by stealing it." Under vague doctrines of "war powers" and the like, the administration quickly moved to confiscate "rebel" property forfeited for withdrawal of "allegiance" owed. In occupied Confederate territory the U.S. government created special tax districts whose funny auctions of "abandoned" property attracted insider bidders with advance information. The New England Emigrant Aid Company—a land company previously active in Kansas, doing business under a philanthropic veneer—set its sights on conquered parts of Florida. Here it would make money while sharing the bounty of New England civilization. Edward Atkinson, an antislavery textile manufacturer from Massachusetts, took an interest in the Florida project, writing to a colleague, "If he [the former slave] refused to work, let him starve and exterminate himself if he will, and so remove the negro question— still we must grow cotton." (As philanthropy this was perhaps a bit narrow.) And cotton was a hot item—confiscated, stolen, or gotten through trade with the enemy, for which Lincoln personally issued the licenses. Out of $30 million worth of cotton seized under an 1863 law only 10 percent actually reached the U.S. Treasury. Another $70 million in cotton was simply "stolen by Republican appointees," as Wilson notes.

> *One historian found profiteering and fraud "so pervasive that they*
> *seemed to be of the very essence of the Northern war effort."*

In any case, the war was not inexpensive. Claudia D. Goldin and Frank D. Lewis estimate direct war costs in terms of expenditures, lost wages, and more at $3,365,846,000 for the North and $3,285,900,000 for the South. In Georgia alone General Sherman guessed that of $100 million in property destroyed by his forces, 80 percent was "simple waste and destruction" and not a matter of military necessity. For the South as a whole, estimated wealth fell between 1861 and 1865 by about 40 percent—*not* counting the value of slave "property." Hummel gives a figure of 50,000 for civilian deaths in the South, presumably of all races, genders, and conditions. Of southern white males aged 18 to 45, 18–25 percent had been killed.

Reorganized Production

Counting Reconstruction as a political continuation of the war, we may now survey the political-economic structure yielded by the struggle. Here the old debate about whether the war retarded or accelerated American industrialization is of little interest. Mere questions of productivity (or output per square worker) matter less than how production was reorganized and who benefited from any changes. In Hummel's view the wartime illusion of prosperity and full employment cannot survive the fact that wages fell, in real terms, by one-third. In the end, he concludes, the war retarded real growth; indeed, there was a waste of roughly five years' accumulation of wealth. War contracts had not made up for lost southern markets.

In this new economy railroads were both cause and effect. Organized as much for land speculation as for transportation, subsidized railroads gave early signs of having far exceeded demand; in other words, railroads represented massive overinvestment. Yet subsidized transportation was the key lever of the post-1865 American economy. William Appleman Williams writes that the demand for railroad regulation was not socialist, but merely applied "[Adam] Smith's argument against mercantilist joint-stock companies to the railroad corporations of their own time." Railroads particularly required large-scale bureaucratic organization. The modern corporate form served them well, and their short-run success strengthened the corporate form. As Peter N. Carroll and David W. Noble observe, the railroad corporation "patterned itself on the Union army, the first major public bureaucracy."

If there indeed were Robber Barons, they got their start during the war.

Along with increased corporate organization came concentration of capital reinforced by the details of wartime contracts and favored by the tax structure. No less a libertarian than Roy A. Childs, Jr., wrote in 1971 that "much of the concentration of economic power which was apparent during the 1870s was the result of massive state aid immediately before, during, and after the Civil War. ..." Further, in the decades after the war, this led, as Willis J. Ballinger noted in 1946, to an imbalance in favor of savings invested in fixed capital ("oversaving"). (This spawned from the 1880s forward much discussion of "oversaving" and "overproduction," with overseas economic empire as a proposed solution.)

A New Industrial Order

Wartime corruption was only a small part of the story. It is more important that, as Richard F. Kaufman observes, the Civil War brought about a "new industrial order ... composed largely of war profiteers and others who grew rich on government contracts ... and ... were able to influence the economic reconstruction." Further, important and persisting capitalist fortunes arose from wartime contracts: "J. P. Morgan, Philip Armour, Clement Studebaker,

John Wanamaker, Cornelius Vanderbilt, and the du Ponts had all been government contractors. Andrew Carnegie got rich speculating in bridge and rail construction while assistant to the Assistant Secretary of War in charge of military transport." If there indeed were Robber Barons, they got their start in the war.

There were various tensions in the Republican developmental bloc. Some New Englanders, for example, favored lower tariffs and even dared hope that party regulars might steal a little less at a time. According to historian Williams, the Radical wing stood for inflationary currency, high tariffs, and holding the southern states as "a new frontier" for Yankee enterprise.

In political scientist Richard Franklin Bensel's view, a Republican-led northern developmental coalition of capitalists, financiers, and farmers successfully imposed a single market and commercial code on the entire American federation through neomercantilist activism. The war saw the emergence of a powerful new class of financiers in New York City. After 1865 much of their money went into railroads as they worked to remove Greenback currency from circulation from 1870 on. Here they broke with the Radical Republicans. Bankers preferred to control any expansion of credit and wanted their loans repaid in dollars of equal or greater value than those they had lent. Deflation suited them. The Republican capitalist-and-farmer alliance may have lasted as long as it did only because a generous and expanding pension program for Union veterans partly offset what Midwestern and western farmers lost through high tariffs. (A qualified veteran typically got about a third of the average workingman's wages for a year. Here was America's first major welfare program.)

Historian Gabriel Kolko notes rapid expansion and accumulation of capital from 1871 to 1899. Because of recurring upper-class panics over labor organization, "violence was used in America more than in any other country that bothered preserving the façade of democracy"—and the violence was always disproportionate. The Civil War had stimulated manufacturing, railroad investment and building, and mining. Big enterprises rested on family alliances and nepotism. As a result, Kolko writes, the idea of social consensus "wholly obscures the real basis of authority in the United States society since the Civil War—law and the threat of repression." Alas for the members of the ruling class, they so successfully broke "the possibility of opposition [that] they also destroyed as well, social cohesion and community."

In a polemic written in 1937, Texas historian Walter Prescott Webb made a case for the West and South against the North. Railroads, built only in the North between 1860 and 1875, killed off southern river traffic. The North enjoyed major bounties: high tariffs, Union army pensions (seven-eighths of which went to the North—a way of spending the "surplus" raised by high tariffs), northern ownership of most industrial patents, and finally, the modern corporation as such—with 200 majors in 1937, all based in the North. This financial-capitalist "feudalism" was sustained by the Supreme Court's dogma of corporate personhood (1885,

1886, 1889).Anticipating Bensel's analysis by 50 years, Webb noted how Union army pensions ($8 billion, all told) compensated the West for what it lost on the tariff.

Historian C. Vann Woodward notes that, ground down by tariffs and northern business control of most patents, the South remained trapped as an exporter of raw materials. Along with the famous freight-rate differential (which lasted into the 1940s), these levers worked as effectively as the British Board of Trade in reducing the southern economy to colonial status. As Hummel writes, national banking rules "stifled recovery of the South's credit markets." Nor was there cash in small denominations. Here Hummel fills in some gaps in Woodward's argument. (On the orientation of banking law toward the convenience and profit of northeastern financiers, Bensel's *Yankee Leviathan* account reinforces Hummel's *Emancipating Slaves, Enslaving Free Men*.) Further, Hummel notes, southerners were taxed to pay interest on the national debt, nearly all of which went to northern parties and to fund Union army pensions—29 percent of the federal budget by the mid-'70s. Here again was a net outflow northward, while the same southerners paid state taxes for Confederate pensions. Not surprisingly, railroad bonds issued by Republican governments in the South during Reconstruction had been "the occasion of most political fraud below the Mason-Dixon line."

It can be argued that in the end agriculture always *pays* for industrialization. Bensel is quite clear: "The [American] developmental engine left the southern periphery to shoulder almost the entire cost of industrialization. ... The periphery was drained while the core prospered." This means that independence was a serious economic option whose advantages for the South Bensel briefly discusses. But as historian Eugene D. Genovese writes, "Since abolition occurred under Northern guns and under the program of a victorious, predatory outside bourgeoisie, instead of under internal bourgeois auspices, the colonial bondage of the economy was preserved, but the South's political independence was lost."

> *Ground down by tariffs and northern business control of most patents,*
> *the South remained trapped as an exporter of raw materials.*

Under Republican auspices the federal government asserted complete primacy over economic regulation, while advancing a big-business bloc allied to its party. This was in the essential Federalist tradition. "Liberal reform" of the 1870s was partly rooted in bourgeois panic over imaginary Paris Communes about to arise on our shores. One result was attempts *in the North* to disenfranchise "unreliable" voting blocs of workers and immigrants. Here were the beginnings of "de-participation"—the conscious project of removing the people from popular government in favor of permanent bureaucratic management intended to be both effective and inexpensive. Here was America's answer to Benthamism. Our troubles did not begin (or end) with the Progressive Era.

Reading 3.5

Economic Reconstruction and Black Colonization

Edward Royce

D ESPITE THE SCARCITY OF LABOR, SOUTHERN whites in the immediate aftermath of slavery frequently advocated black colonization, the relocation of the black population outside of the South. "If any grand colonization project should be started," a reporter for the *Nation* wrote in 1865, "the Southerners would all favor it, as they say now all they want is 'to get shet of them'; that is, to get them out of the country."[1] Given the prevailing racial ideology in the white South, this was not necessarily a disingenuous or irrational reaction to the abolition of slavery. Many planters fully expected that free black labor would not prove viable anyway and hoped to procure an alternative supply of labor through immigration. In addition, whites throughout the southern states feared that emancipation would inevitably give rise to a race war and regarded the colonization of free blacks as necessary for peace and social order. Whether convinced that free black labor was worthless or concerned about the threat of black insurrection—or whether simply as an expression of a more rudimentary hostility toward black people—southern whites took seriously the possibility of ridding the South of the former slaves and gave strong support to proposals for black colonization. In Virginia, for example, a candidate for Congress in 1865 was expected to receive a "strong vote" in his district because of his outspoken position in favor of "the emigration and colonization of the Negro population."[2]

Planters specifically, however, were understandably equivocal in their support for colonization. In fact, most planters were prepared to accept the continued presence of black people in the South—if they could be made to work and safely relegated to a permanently subordinate position. There would be no need for colonization, planters maintained, if their power to manage the labor force and exercise effective authority over the black race were restored. A Confederate major, shortly after the war, presented a succinct analysis of the "Negro question" that captured precisely the viewpoint of most southern planters: "If you of the North want now to conciliate and settle the South, you must do one of three things: re-establish slavery; give the old masters in some way power to compel the negroes to work; or colonize them out of the country, and help us to bring in white laborers!"[3] To the extent that planters doubted their ability to either "re-establish slavery" or "compel the negroes to work," colonization appeared to be an eminently reasonable policy. The fact that planters advocated colonization as frequently and vociferously as they did is, in itself, a telling indication of the effectiveness of black resistance to the plantation system. Even so, reflecting the difficult situation in which they found themselves, planters remained uncertain about the possibility of black colonization. While they deeply resented the presence of free blacks in the South and hoped to see them deported, planters also had great need for their labor. Planters' ambivalence about the prospect of free black labor is revealingly expressed in the observation that every planter "would be glad to have the entire black race deported—except his own laborers."[4]

Even though the possibility of black colonization typically involved more wishful thinking and tough talk than concrete action, it deserves an important place in the story of economic reconstruction and the rise of share-cropping in the postwar South. What planters had to say about colonization provides valuable evidence regarding their interests, their views on free black labor, and their thoughts on the problem of economic reorganization. An exploration of the possibility of black colonization will illuminate the reasoning and experiences of southern planters and free blacks as they confronted one another with competing visions of a new economic order. Furthermore, as with southern immigration, the historical importance of the possibility of black colonization derives also from its failure; for the defeat of this possibility, and the fact that the southern states were destined to remain the home of millions of black people, made it all the more pressing for planters to make some accommodation with their former slaves.

It is not too surprising that southern whites turned to this possibility in the postwar years, for the idea of black colonization has been a significant presence throughout American history. Proposals for black colonization attracted considerable interest just prior to, and during, the Civil War in particular, when the Lincoln administration and the Republican party played a leading role in the movement to deport freed blacks. The history of the colonization movement prior to the abolition of slavery provides the context necessary for fully appreciating the significance of this possibility in the postwar South.

The Colonization Movement Before the Civil War

Colonization projects in the United States began as early as the 1600s and 1700s, when crimes and rebellious acts committed by blacks were punished by deportation.[5] Proposals for the systematic and large-scale removal of black people, however, were not seriously entertained until the 1770s and 1780s, when colonizationists were motivated, in part, by the desire to Christianize Africa and to obstruct the slave trade by creating a buffer zone along the African west coast. Toward the end of the 1780s and into the 1790s, however, this missionary interest gave way to more pressing domestic concerns. During these years, the upper South, particularly Virginia, experienced a growth, through immigration and manumission, in the population of free blacks. This raised the specter of race war, as most whites assumed that free blacks would neither be granted full equality in America nor submit peacefully to a permanently subordinate status. The resulting potential for violence and insurrection could be removed only by deporting the free black population. This marked a shift in the platform of the colonization movement. After 1787, Winthrop Jordan notes, the primary motive of the colonizationists "was not to get Negroes over to Africa but to get them out of America."[6] As a result of both real and imagined slave insurrections—especially the successful slave revolt in St. Domingue (now Haiti) in the 1790s and the Gabriel Prosser plot in Virginia in 1800—the objective of the colonization movement narrowed even further. After 1800, Jordan argues, "the colonization movement became in much larger measure an effort to free America from the danger of slave insurrection."[7]

The fervor for colonization diminished somewhat in the early 1800s, when the African slave trade closed and antislavery agitation declined.[8] But the founding of the American Colonization Society (ACS) in 1816 and 1817 resurrected the colonization movement. Through its political lobbying and intellectual influence, through the authority of its official publication (the *African Repository*), and through the creation of a black colony along the African west coast (Liberia)—the ACS played the central role in the colonization movement in nineteenth-century America.[9]

The immediate aim of the ACS was to remove free blacks from the United States and relocate them in Africa. Presumably, blacks and whites would both benefit from this separation of the races. Colonizationists believed that it was impossible to eradicate race prejudice, that blacks could never achieve equality in the United States, and that only by settling in another country, apart from whites, could black people hope to better their condition and enjoy the fruits of freedom and liberty. White America would gain from colonization too, for the deportation of free blacks would rid the country of a dangerous presence and a source of national divisiveness.[10]

With respect to the crucial problem of slavery, though, the ACS did not maintain a unified or consistent position, and some members favored avoiding this controversial issue altogether. However, some colonizationists actively supported slavery (indeed, some owned slaves themselves) and regarded the colonization of free blacks as a way of removing a disruptive element and stabilizing the institution of slavery.[11] In contrast, many members of the ACS supported colonization precisely because of their opposition to slavery; they believed that, without some plan for removing free blacks, emancipation would be neither socially desirable nor politically viable. But even when it came out against slavery, the ACS maintained a conciliatory posture and tried to appeal to southern slaveholders with a program combining gradual emancipation and colonization.[12] This greatly underestimated the extent to which planters possessed a specifically economic stake in the preservation of slavery. The strategy adopted by the ACS assumed, incorrectly, that planters' commitment to slavery derived primarily from their apprehension about living alongside a large free black population. But as it turned out, the promise of colonization was not enough to transform planters into abolitionists—although abolition, as we shall see, transformed many planters into colonizationists.

The ACS experienced limited success in recruiting blacks and encouraging settlement in Liberia. Prior to 1860, several thousand free blacks relocated in Africa, although some of these were forced to accept deportation as a condition of manumission.[13] But most free blacks opposed the idea of colonization and expressed hostility toward the American Colonization Society in particular. "On the whole," Louis Mehlinger concludes from an examination of the attitudes of free blacks toward African colonization, "the movement never appealed to a large number of intelligent free people of color."[14]

While trying to gain political support by appealing to all possible groups and interests, the ACS succeeded only in antagonizing nearly everyone—free blacks, slaveholders, and abolitionists alike. Internal conflicts, financial difficulties, and bad press from disillusioned emigrés further contributed to the failure and decline of the ACS in the 1830s and 1840s. In the 1850s, as the conflict over slavery intensified, as fears and expectations of eventual emancipation increased, and as conditions worsened for free blacks in the North, the colonization movement experienced a resurgence—with black people themselves taking much of the initiative.[15] Influenced by a new black nationalism and increasingly impatient with their white allies in the antislavery movement, many free blacks began to reconsider the merits of colonization. Black advocates of emigration still shunned the American Colonization Society, though, and most preferred resettlement somewhere in the Western Hemisphere rather than in Africa. Yet, while growing in appeal during the 1850s, the idea of colonization probably never attracted anything approaching a majority of free blacks; most opted to continue the struggle for equality in the land they considered their rightful home. And with the onset of the Civil War and the renewed hopes it engendered, the momentum of the colonization movement among free blacks was checked.[16]

The Lincoln Administration and Black Colonization

Lincoln's views on emancipation and colonization were consistent with those of the American Colonization Society. He preferred a system of gradual emancipation with compensation to slaveowners and colonization of blacks beyond the borders of the United States. Lincoln's most famous statement in support of colonization was presented in August 1862, before a small gathering of free blacks from the District of Columbia. Lincoln stated that much mutual suffering and divisiveness resulted from two such physically dissimilar races living together. He further argued that even with the abolition of slavery, black people could never hope to attain equality with whites. "It is better for us both, therefore to be separated," Lincoln declared. He acknowledged that most free blacks would probably not see much immediate advantage in colonization, but urged his audience not to take such a "selfish view of the case." If free blacks were willing to make the sacrifice and volunteer for colonization, Lincoln suggested, they might smooth the way for the abolition of slavery. Just as the promise of colonization was used to persuade slaveholders to agree to emancipation, so too did Lincoln use the promise of emancipation to persuade free blacks to agree to colonization. Lincoln concluded his address by describing the virtues of Central America as a possible location for black colonization, emphasizing especially the prospects there for coal mining.[17]

Other rationales for colonization found a hearing in the Lincoln administration. In 1862, the Reverend James Mitchell, subsequently appointed commissioner of emigration, warned that the prospect of an increase in "the mixed breed bastards" posed a threat to the family, to the nation, and to white supremacy. The problem of miscegenation could be avoided, Mitchell argued, only through the colonization of the black population.[18] The 1862 House report on emancipation and colonization also played on white fears of racial "intermixture," defending colonization as serving "the highest interests of the white race."

> Much of the objection to emancipation arises from the opposition of a large portion of our people to the intermixture of the races, and from the association of white and black labor. The committee would do nothing to favor such a policy; apart from the antipathy which nature has ordained, the presence of a race among us who cannot, and ought not to, be admitted to our social and political privileges, will be a perpetual source of injury and inquietude to both. This is a question of color, and is unaffected by the relation of master and slave. The introduction of the negro, whether bond or free, into the same field of labor with the white man, is the opprobrium of the latter; and we cannot believe that the thousands of non-slaveholding citizens in the rebellious States who live by industry are fighting to continue the negro within our limits even in a state of vassalage, but more probably from a vague apprehension that he is to become their competitor in his own right. We wish to disabuse our laboring countrymen, and the whole Caucasian race who may seek a home here, of this error. ... The committee concludes that the highest interests of the white race,

whether Anglo-Saxon, Celt, or Scandinavian, require that the whole country should be held and occupied by those races alone.[19]

The committee on emancipation and colonization extolled the advantages of colonization for the domestic economy as well. The deportation of blacks, the committee report predicted, would encourage immigration from Europe, result in the beneficial substitution of free labor for slave labor, lead to higher wages for white workers, and bring prosperity to previously backward sections of the country.[20] The United States would profit not only from the removal of blacks, but from their resettlement as well. The committee anticipated that the colonization of blacks in Central America would open up new commercial opportunities and would facilitate the creation of a "colonial system" similar to that enjoyed by Great Britain.[21] Black colonization, the committee suggested, would place in Central America a race of people particularly suited to the climate and yet of a sufficient level of civilization to maintain stable governments. In short, the report of the committee presented black colonization as a useful instrument of American colonialism.

> It may therefore be well imagined what would be the result of planting five millions of American negroes ... in a country ... protected by our power and directed by our intelligence, and stimulated to exertion by those motives which the wants of civilization, which they have acquired among us, have never failed to supply. ... If we add to this the certain result of extending our power and influence, through their instrumentality, over the millions of people who already inhabit these regions, we shall be able to form some conception of the value to our commerce which the foundation of such a colony would confer.[22]

Finally, as Wisconsin senator James R. Doolittle declared, the colonization of blacks in Central America was sanctioned also by both Divine Providence and the "natural laws of climate."[23]

All this talk in support of colonization involved more than just idle speculation. The Lincoln administration in the early 1860s undertook two practical experiments in black colonization. The first involved Lincoln with Ambrose W. Thompson and the Chiriqui Improvement Company. Thompson's company controlled several hundred thousand acres of land, ostensibly rich in coal, located in a northern province of Panama. That black emigrés could immediately begin supporting themselves by mining coal especially favored Chiriqui as a site for colonization. During the course of 1861 and 1862, several key members of Lincoln's administration recommended the Chiriqui colonization project. In September of 1862, Thompson and the government signed a provisional contract, and the president appointed Kansas senator Samuel Clark Pomeroy to evaluate the Chiriqui location and oversee the process of colonization. But by late September, most of Lincoln's advisers and cabinet members were becoming distrustful of Thompson and increasingly opposed to the Chiriqui project, though Lincoln persisted. Heated protests against black immigration from the governments of Honduras, Nicaragua, Costa Rica, and other Central American countries finally put an end to the Chiriqui project. In addition, Chiriqui coal was subsequently discovered to be worthless, and Thompson's motives and claim to the land were found to be questionable. The Chiriqui colonization project went down to defeat without a single colony-bound ship leaving harbor.[24]

The second experiment in colonization undertaken by the Lincoln administration resulted in a more disastrous outcome. The proposed site for this colonization project was the island of à Vache, which belonged to the government of Haiti. Initially, the intermediary for this project was businessman Bernard Kock. On December 31, 1862, the government made a contract with Kock to transport five thousand emigrants at fifty dollars a head to the island of à Vache. The contract was annulled when doubts were raised about Kock's honesty and competence. The project proceeded, however, when three New York businessmen, Leonard W. Jerome, Paul S. Forbes, and Charles K. Tuckerman (who turned out to be Kock's associates), came forward to assume the contract. In the spring of 1863, 453 prospective colonists set sail from Fortress Monroe. Kock (back in charge again), drawing on the funds designated to provide food and shelter for the black colonists, purchased "handcuffs and leg-chains" instead and built "stocks for their punishment."[25] In addition, Kock managed to confiscate the money of the colonists, while also refusing to pay them for the labor they performed while on the island. Many colonists died from disease and others fled to Haiti. Less than a year later the government, while trying to avoid embarrassing publicity, sent a relief ship to return the survivors to the United States. So ended Lincoln's second colonization project.[26] That same year Congress repealed all appropriations for black colonization. Whether Lincoln's interest in colonization endured these defeats is an issue of some debate among historians.[27]

The rhetoric in support of black colonization, despite the failure of these projects, served important political purposes for the Republican party. Many northern Republicans hoped that the promise of colonization would not only reduce fears of emancipation in the North, but would also diminish opposition to the abolition of slavery in the South, thus bringing the war to a rapid close.[28] In 1862, for example, Missouri senator Francis P. Blair declared that the war arose not from any "love of slavery," but rather from dread of racial equality. In order to ease fears of "amalgamation," Blair proposed that the races be separated.

> The outbreak, as I have already said, sprang from the convictions in the common
> mind in the disturbed region that the negroes were to be liberated and put

upon an equal footing with the whites. The mere idea of this amalgamation was instrumental in producing the rebellion. … The idea of the separation of the races is a complete antidote to that poison.[29]

The committee on emancipation and colonization, also in 1862, advanced a similar position:

It is believed that the most formidable difficulty which lies in the way of emancipation in most if not in all the slave States is the belief, which obtains especially among those who own no slaves, that if the negroes shall become free, they must still continue in our midst, and so remaining after their liberation, they may in some measure be made equal to the Anglo-Saxon race.[30]

Colonization, Robert Zoellner writes, "was to act as a sugar coating for the bitter pill of emancipation."[31] Lincoln and the Republican party sought to convince both northern and southern whites that—while they were staunchly opposed to slavery, a commitment tempered by respect for property rights—they did not favor social and political equality for blacks. The enemies of slavery were not necessarily the friends of black people.[32]

By speaking out in favor of black colonization, Republican leaders in the North sought to fortify themselves against another politically sensitive issue. The onset of the Civil War and the prospect of emancipation fostered considerable anxiety in the free states, especially in the Midwest, that the North would be overrun by freed blacks emigrating from the South.[33] In order for the Republican party to conduct the war effectively and sell the policy of emancipation, it had to assuage fears of a massive migration of blacks—fears strategically exploited by northern Democrats and southern slaveholders. One strategy adopted by Republicans, demonstrating that their opponents were not the only ones adept at playing on racial prejudice, was to turn the argument around: the abolition of slavery, they countered, would result in a migration into the South of free blacks from the North.[34] But in addition to this rhetorical device, Republican leaders turned to the policy of colonization as a way of further shoring up their position on the impending "Negro question." The need to appease an apprehensive northern constituency became especially pressing with the passage of the Confiscation Acts, with Lincoln's decision to introduce the Emancipation Proclamation, and with increasing evidence that the war was indeed becoming a war against slavery.

With the failure of wartime colonization schemes, northern Republicans hoped that, as a last resort, the freed slaves could be compelled to remain in the South. Accordingly, the Lincoln administration stepped up programs to employ refugee slaves on abandoned plantations and to utilize them for military purposes, e.g., building fortifications. In addition, and more dramatically, the Union army began to enlist blacks as soldiers. According to one historian, this "systematic mobilization of the blacks in the South moderated the racial fears of the Midwest. … No longer was the administration merely relying on climate and sentiment to hold Negroes in the South; it had developed a positive means for containing them there." The policy of "employing and caring" for refugee slaves on abandoned plantations in the South "had effectively sealed the vast majority of them in the region. … In this way, the threat of a great migration was destroyed."[35] This policy, and the value (subsequently demonstrated) of both black laborers and black soldiers, along with Union victories at Gettysburg and Vicksburg and a surging economy in mid-1863, eased the way for northerners to accept the destruction of slavery as a legitimate war goal.[36]

With the end of the Civil War, the issue of black colonization in the North lost some of its political urgency. Northern interest in the deportation of the black race did not disappear entirely though. The American Colonization Society, for example, continued its operation into the postwar era, and even anticipated new opportunities opening up with emancipation.[37] In the aftermath of slavery, however, the primary locus of interest in black colonization shifted to the white South.

White Perspectives on Colonization in the Postwar South

In *The White Savage*, Lawrence J. Friedman identifies two competing racial ideologies in the white South. Adherents of the "proslavery ideology," on the one hand, favored "a social order of integrated subservience." These southern whites, whom I will call integrationists, believed that it was their responsibility to look after, and provide guidance to, the "inferior" black race. Their image of the South made room for black people but envisioned them holding a subordinate status only, a status of tutelage comparable to that of children. Exclusionists, on the other hand, refused to include any place at all for blacks in their vision of the South, even as a permanently subservient laboring class. Instead, they "demanded the expulsion of all blacks from white society" and supported the policy of colonization.[38] As one disgruntled rebel said about the former slaves, outspoken in his support for the exclusionist cause: "They all ought to be drove out of the country."[39]

Embracing the ideology of paternalism, an ideology that denied to black people the capacity for independent agency, integrationists presumed that the fate of the black race rested entirely in white hands. "The Freedmen of the South are a powerful element for good or evil," a Georgia resident proclaimed, "and it is our duty, as the superior race, to educate and direct them."[40] Integrationists thus acknowledged an obligation to oversee the continued "elevation" of the black population and to ensure that it did not "revert to barbarism or utterly perish from the face of the earth." The responsibility of the white race toward the black race did not end with the abolition of slavery. "The negro is among us," a South Carolina planter observed in 1869. "He is here and we cannot help it, and the destiny that placed him here, has placed him here for a wise and good purpose." For this critic of colonization, the black person was "the proper, legitimate and divinely ordained laborer of the South"; he urged his neighbors to comply with the "great duty" of impressing this lesson upon the former slaves.

> Let us teach him that his power lies in his muscles, and that the proper held for its exercise, is in the cotton fields of the South. ... This is our first great duty. We owe it to ourselves, we owe it to the negro, and we owe it to the country.[41]

Black people, integrationists emphasized, were not to blame for the war, and they should not be allowed to die or relapse into savagery. Nor should they be faulted for the adversity and disruption resulting from northern interference. "The negro had no agency in establishing his freedom," explained a North Carolina convention delegate, "and we must not condemn him for that which he made no effort to produce."[42] Neither, integrationists maintained, did the turmoil of Reconstruction justify banishing black people from the South. Rather, as one opponent of colonization stated, the white South must persevere in the "great work" of molding the black race into "effective hirelings."

> The South had already proved itself their greatest benefactor, by rescuing them from barbarism and heathenism and blessing them with the light of a pure Christianity. It now remains to complete the great work by elevating them to the status of intelligent, industrious and effective hirelings. Let us not shrink from this arduous, but benevolent, enterprise.[43]

The integrationist perspective posited a happy fit between altruism, obligation, and economic self-interest. By making freed blacks into industrious workers, and thus facilitating the restoration of the plantation system, southern whites would at the same time fulfill their duty toward the black race and demonstrate their own benevolence. Despite the self-serving features of this ideology, however, integrationism attracted only a minority of the white population in the postwar South.

Instead, the end of the Civil War left most southern whites feeling more bitter than dutiful toward the former slaves. The fear and uncertainty arising from an unprecedented "Negro problem" also stirred up support among white southerners for the ideology of exclusionism and the possibility of black colonization. Hostility toward free blacks inspired much of this interest in colonization, but it was fueled also by the humiliation of defeat and resentment toward northerners. Virginia planters, for example, threatened to do all within their power to drive blacks away and "to make the government odious for freeing them."[44] Such expressions of vindictiveness toward the federal government often accompanied declarations calling for black colonization. Since northern interference created the "Negro problem," it seemed only right that the government assume responsibility for resolving it. "Now that you've got them ruined, take the cursed scoundrels out of the country"—this, one journalist found, was the opinion held by most whites in the interior of Mississippi.[45]

Skepticism about the prospect of ever "elevating" freedpeople to the status of "effective hirelings" gave added support to the possibility of black colonization. The prevailing sentiment among southern whites in the years following the war, according to one report, was "that 'if we cannot have them as slaves, take them away; we don't want them'"[46] Even planters faced with a serious shortage of labor came out in favor of colonization, as John Dennett discovered while reporting from the South in 1865 and 1866.

> Within the past month I have heard a good deal said in favor of colonization, and said by owners of large plantations, who might be expected to desire a crowded labor-market. Speak to them about the vast expense, and other practical difficulties in the way of removing a whole nation from the country in which it has lived for generations, and which it loves, and one will say the Government may have all his share in the public lands to pay it for taking away his niggers; another that he will gladly bear a heavier tax than has yet been imposed on him as part of the expense, and that his acquaintances all say the same thing; and all cite Andrew Jackson's removal of the Indians as a case in point.[47]

During the immediate postwar years, as one historian observed, the "racial antipathy" of planters "warred with their labor force requirements."[48] The motive of "spite, ill-will, and disappointment" frequently took precedence over planters' need for black labor.[49] Despite "the fact that all the planters are complaining about the insufficiency of labor," reported one observer, most southern whites considered free blacks a "nuisance" and "would gladly be rid of his presence, even at the expense of his existence."[50] This widespread desire among southern whites to remove blacks from the South if they could not be retained in bondage was, one black man responded, "really interesting": "If you cannot rob the Negro of his labor and of himself, you will banish him."[51]

Some southern whites favored the colonization of blacks not despite the labor problems that would result from their absence, but because of the troubles caused by their presence. "Blacks have ceased to be producers, and the whites cannot support them," General Alfred Dockery declared in an 1865 speech urging colonization; consequently, he advised, "it would be better for both races that they be separated." As an alternative to the colonization of blacks outside the borders of the country, Dockery recommended that freedpeople, like the Indians, be resettled in segregated reservations.[52] Not everyone in the South, however, was so resistant to acknowledging the inevitable dependence of the southern economy on black labor. The economic wisdom of black colonization was questioned, for example, in an editorial published in the Charleston *Daily Courier*: "Is not the black man still a valuable component of the state? Is not his brawny arm necessary to develop our resources and would not the sudden withdrawal of the entire negro population be an actual calamity?"[53] But even planters desperate for labor had little to gain from the continued existence in the South of the "black man" and his "brawny arm" if the latter refused to work. "The people would rather get rid of them [freedpeople] if there were any possible means of doing so," declared a white Virginian. "They are a nuisance, in the present state of affairs. They will not work."[54] In North Carolina "as everywhere," Sidney Andrews reported hearing the "complaint that the free negro will not work"; and despite the considerable demand for labor, Andrews discovered that "strange as it may seem, the people are warm colonizationists."[55] There was, of course, nothing "strange" about this at all, for if "the free negro will not work," planters had no use for them and their colonization represented no great loss.

The frequent accusation that black people would not work and should therefore be deported drew an angry response from freedpeople. "They have no reason to say we will not work," replied a black soldier opposed to colonization, "for we raised them and sent them to school and bought their land. Now it is as little as they can do to give us some of their land—be it little or much."[56] But like this soldier, most blacks did not want to work for their former masters, but rather intended to farm on land of their own. From the perspective of whites, however, this made them no less suitable as candidates for colonization than if they had refused to work altogether.

While planters were primarily concerned with the problem of labor control, other southern whites favored colonization because they perceived the free black population as a threat to social order. Many were anxious that the continued safety of the white population was in jeopardy; only the separation of the races could ensure its preservation.[57] Slavery was a system of racial domination and control, in addition to being a mode of labor exploitation. More specifically, southern whites commonly believed that the institution of slavery functioned to contain the otherwise barbarian impulses of the black race.[58] With the release of blacks from bondage and their removal from the civilizing influence of white authority, many feared that a war between the races would inevitably erupt. Judge Sylvannum Evans, for example, in a speech given while campaigning for Congress in 1865, charged that "the cause of continued strife and tumult" was the presence of "the vagrant freedmen." "I am sure we do not want the scenes of St. Domingo and Hayti repeated in our midst," Evans warned. "I believe such will be the case if they are not removed. If elected I shall urge the general government the duty of colonizing the negroes."[59] The choice, declared a white Virginian, was for blacks to be either "extirpated" or sent back to Africa.

> These unfortunate creatures thus set at liberty en masse I fear are preparing great trouble as well for the whites as for themselves ... unless the government makes a timely and firm interposition, in a conflict between the two races. Should this be the case, the race must unavoidably be extirpated. ... Africa was the point toward which the whole work tended, and this is the point where it must end if the negro is to be really benefited.[60]

For a New Orleans resident, however, there was no choice at all; the "only way" to deal effectively with the threat of black insurrection, he proposed, was "to kill the niggers off, *and* drive 'em out of the country."[61]

Some southern whites expected that the problem posed by the presence of free blacks would eventually take care of itself; the separation of the races would occur through "natural" processes, rendering any colonization program unnecessary. There was, for example, some anticipation that blacks would depart from the South voluntarily. In his testimony before the Joint Committee on Reconstruction, the Reverend Dr. Robert McMurdy predicted that, upon being placed into competition with white laborers, free blacks would gradually leave the country and immigrate to the West Indies.[62] Similarly, a contributor to *De Bow's Review* from the District of Columbia suggested that the white race, "from their superior capabilities," would multiply faster than the black race and soon acquire ascendancy. Blacks, as a result, "will gradually but certainly tend from the temperate regions of the South to the terras calientas, until the colored race, like a dark fringe, will border the shores of the Southern Atlantic and the Gulf of Mexico."[63]

Especially widespread among southern whites was the belief that blacks, under the rigor of freedom, were doomed to extinction. "The past history of the negro," declared a physician from Alabama, demonstrates that "freed blacks cannot be relied upon as an agricultural population, and that emancipation must ultimately result in their extermination. ... Like the Indian and other inferior races, he may expect to be driven out by the superior intelligence, energy and perseverance of the whites."[64] The *Nation* reported that this was a "nearly unanimous" belief. Southern whites expected that "the colored race is destined to speedy extinction, crowded out of existence by competition with the superior race."[65]

Others believed that, competition from whites aside, the black race would die off from its own natural indolence and from an inability to survive without the supervision and guidance of white authority. "The guardianship of the latter [southern whites] having been withdrawn," wrote the Memphis *Avalanche*, "the former [freed blacks] will rapidly lapse into semi-barbarism and gradually disappear. ... The negro race is doomed."[66] Such ominous predictions were sometimes used to justify the program of black colonization: if they were relocated out of the South, the black race might yet be saved from extermination. "Unless the colored people were removed to Texas, or some South American country," proclaimed one Norfolk resident, "they would surely die out by reason of their laziness and shiftlessness."[67] John Rock, a black critic of colonization writing prior to the war, ridiculed the myth that blacks could not take care of themselves and would be doomed to extinction if set free: "Do you imagine that the Negro can live outside of slavery? Of course, now, they can take care of themselves and their master too; but if you give them their liberty, must they not suffer?"[68]

Besides exclusionism and integrationism, Friedman also refers to a third racial ideology, whose "only prominent proponent," he argues, was William Gannaway Brownlow, the governor of Tennessee during Reconstruction. While sometimes appearing to be a fervent exclusionist, Brownlow, like the integrationists, also maintained a high regard for the paternalistic relationship between blacks and whites that presumably obtained in the antebellum South. According to Friedman, Brownlow's apparent adherence to competing doctrines, rather than signifying any inconsistency, "applied different principles to different Negroes." The ideology of exclusionism applied to "insolent" blacks, while the ideology of integrationism targeted "servile" blacks. This ideological flexibility, Friedman observes, allowed for the "integration of the docile and the exclusion of the defiant."[69]

Yet, rather than being rare, evidence indicates that among planters specifically a variant of the position adopted by Brownlow was quite prevalent in the postwar years. Planters did not necessarily fall into either the exclusionist or integrationist camps exclusively; their position on black colonization was based less on ideology than on practical considerations. On the one hand, to the extent they doubted that integration on the basis of black subordination could be effectively restored, planters favored the option of deporting their former slaves and thus adhered to the ideology of exclusionism. On the other hand, planters seemed willing to forgo demands for colonization if they could somehow reestablish their authority over the black population. That is, to the extent they envisioned the possibility of recreating something approaching the master-slave relationship, planters adhered to the ideology of integrationism.

Many planters, therefore, still held out the possibility that blacks might yet be able to live in the South and make a useful contribution to the southern economy—if, through legislative measures, for example, they were subjected to a strict system of social control. A lawyer from Raleigh, for example, proposed that blacks be placed "under the control of the Legislature," which, he advised,

> ought to provide against vagrancy; adopt measures to require them to fulfill their contracts for labor, and authorize their sale, for a term of years for

breaches of order. Either do that, and so protect us against an intolerable nuisance, or colonize them out of the country.[70]

From this perspective, legislative control over the black population, by repheating certain of the characteristics of slavery, represented an alternative to colonization. Such legislative measures could even be construed as being beneficial to blacks. "The Negro," one southern white explained, "is doomed to undergo extinction. ... The race will first become a pauper and then disappear. Nothing but the most careful legislation will prevent it."[71] A legislative substitute for the authority of the white master might save the black race from extinction. The editors of the *Carolina Times*, similarly, recommended that "the only course to keep the Negro from dying out or relapsing into barbarism" is the enactment by the legislature of "a compulsory code of enforced labor."[72]

For perhaps even most planters then, the paramount consideration in reflecting on the possibility of black colonization was not the ideological conflict between exclusionism and integrationism, but rather the prospect for reestablishing social control: control over a labor force believed to be naturally indolent and incapable of responding to market incentives, and control over a presumably inferior and savage race prepared for insurrection or destined for extinction. Since planters could not be sure how the "Negro question" would finally be resolved, they also expressed equivocation and uncertainty about the desirability of black colonization. From the perspective of most planters, the question of whether or not free blacks should have a future in the South depended upon the resolution of more fundamental issues: whether the preservation of social order was possible given the continuing presence of free blacks, and whether the black population could fulfill the labor force requirements of plantation agriculture. In the final analysis, planters welcomed the continued presence of black people in the South only if they were subjected to a strict system of control.[73]

Black Perspectives on Colonization in the Postwar South

The possibility of black colonization attracted white adherents almost exclusively and thus, to the extent that it depended upon the voluntary emigration of southern blacks, had absolutely no chance for success. Southern blacks after the war were even less inclined than free blacks before and during the war to give their support to any colonization schemes. "I saw none of the negroes," Whitelaw Reid reported, "either residing in Savannah or from the country, who had any desire to be colonized away from their present homes." Freedpeople, he wrote, "utterly revolt" from the idea of being relocated out of the South.[74] "What's the use to give us our freedom," protested one freedman, "if we can't stay where we were raised, and own our houses where we were born, and our little piece of ground?"[75] While many freedpeople certainly wanted to live apart from whites, especially from their former masters, they did not desire racial separation to occur at the expense of a southern homeland.

> Ask them if they would like to live by themselves, and they would generally say "Yes" … but further inquiry would always develop the fact that their idea of "living by themselves" was to have the whites removed from what they consider their own country. … They believe in colonization; but it is in colonization on the lands they have been working.[76]

Thus blacks opposed colonization not from a desire to live alongside southern whites, of course, but rather because they believed they possessed a right to the land on which they had lived and worked for so many generations, and they looked forward to the opportunity to acquire southern homesteads. Freedpeople claimed a positive right to a homeland in the country of their birth. "This is your country, but it is ours too," stated a resolution by a convention of freedpeople in South Carolina in 1865. "You were born here, so were we; your fathers fought for it, but our fathers fed them."[77] In Virginia, also in 1865, a black convention made the following public resolution:

> That as natives of American soil we claim the right to remain upon it, and that any attempt to remove, expatriate, or colonize us in any other land against our will is unjust, for here we were born, and for this country our fathers and brothers have fought, and we hope to remain here in the full employment of enfranchised manhood and its dignities.[78]

In contrast, the idea of colonization looked like a plot to deprive them of their newly won freedom and defraud them of their promised "forty acres and a mule." "If we can get lands here and can work and support ourselves," explained a black man testifying before the Joint Committee on Reconstruction, "I do not see why we should go to any place that we do not want to go."[79] Indeed, the inability of advocates of black colonization after the war to recruit prospective emigrants was due, in part, to the expectation among freedpeople that they would gain possession of the plantations.[80]

Within a decade of the abolition of slavery, however, southern blacks were more seriously entertaining the possibility of emigrating out of the South, if not to a foreign country, at least to the West. The end of Reconstruction and the rise to dominance again of the Democratic party in the South threatened the political and civil rights that black people had won in the years immediately following the war. Their economic situation deteriorated too, as sharecropping continued to evolve into an oppressive debt-peonage system. Thus, later on in the century many blacks, for both political and economic reasons, began reconsidering the possibility of colonization.[81]

Emigration of Southern Whites

One South Carolina planter, "utterly disgusted" with his former slaves, longed to "some day be in a land that is purged of them."[82] This planter hoped for a future in which the free black population would be removed from the South or would disappear through extinction. For some southern whites, however, emigration rather than black colonization appeared to be the most promising route for achieving a homeland "purged" of free blacks.[83] Humiliated by defeat, faced with the loss of their antebellum world, and confronted by an impossible "Negro problem," several thousand white southerners in the years after the war chose to leave the South altogether, and many thousands more gave this possibility serious consideration. "O, what a fall is here," declared the New Orleans *Tribune* in a biting editorial on the white emigration movement. "Has it come to this? Those who but a few years ago were the lords over the poor negroes ... now talk of colonizing elsewhere!"[84]

Even before the war, southern whites had given some thought to expanding southward and extending their domain into the countries of Latin America. With the defeat of the Confederacy and the abolition of slavery, the possibility of white emigration ceased being a matter of mere speculation; southern whites actively began to mobilize around the program of emigration. Emigration agents traveled to destination countries to report on conditions firsthand and make necessary arrangements for resettlement. Southerners with more of an adventurous spirit journeyed to inspect the opportunities for emigration themselves. Prospective emigrants also organized associations, groups, and companies throughout the South. According to one account, every southern state had at least one "society for the promotion of emigration," and in most states numerous such organizations were established.[85] Emigration societies and companies—the Southern Emigration Society of Edgefield, South Carolina, for example—functioned to locate and identify possible sites for relocation, to gather and distribute information, to mobilize support among southern whites, and otherwise to facilitate the process of migration.

Proponents of southern emigration also circulated pamphlets and books advertising the advantages offered by residence in Brazil or Mexico. *The Emigrant's Guide to Brazil,* by Lansford Warren Hastings, *Ho! for Brazil,* by General W. W. Wood of Mississippi, and *Brazil, the Home for Southerners,* written by Ballard S. Dunn, a priest from New Orleans (the latter two both published in 1866) were among the most popular examples of this propaganda literature. Southern whites showed renewed interest in prewar travelers' reports from Latin America as well. The advantages of relocation were also extolled by the first wave of emigrants in personal letters and communications, which were often printed in southern newspapers and periodicals.[86]

Government officials and influential figures in Latin American countries greeted the possibility of southern emigration with considerable enthusiasm. Brazil and Mexico, in particular, actively campaigned to encourage the immigration of southern whites. Both countries advertised in southern newspapers, courted emigration agents, entertained representatives of southern colonization societies, and offered a wide variety of assistance, inducements, and incentives to prospective emigrants. And Americans in both Brazil and Mexico were granted official or quasi-official status in governmental departments concerned with immigration. Authorities in Brazil optimistically predicted that one hundred thousand families from the South would eventually immigrate to that country.[87]

These efforts to promote southern emigration had a significant impact. In 1865, according to an estimate from the New York *Herald*, fifty thousand southerners were ready to emigrate to Brazil alone; many thousands more, anticipating favorable reports, were also preparing to leave; still others wished they could join the movement, but finally lacked the resolve or the financial resources necessary to undertake such a journey.[88] The reality of the emigration movement did not quite match these estimates. Nevertheless, several thousand whites—including a significant number of planters—did in fact leave the South shortly after the war in search of new homes in foreign countries. And many more than this, had they the means, probably would also have gone.[89] For others, moreover, the decision to remain in the South was not an easy one. An Alabama planter told John Trowbridge that he had actually settled on emigrating to Brazil, but in the end he got only as far as Mobile when he decided to remain in the South, despite feeling like a "foreigner" and an "alien."[90]

The motives of those who elected to join the exodus from the South were varied. The political turmoil and uncertainty resulting from the defeat of the Confederacy motivated many southern whites to leave the country. Some were anxious about war reprisals and northern vengeance, while the threat of "Negro domination" or "Yankee rule" drove others away. Many more were motivated by the fear of black insurrection, by the loss of their labor force, and by a general hostility toward free blacks. Major Joseph Abney, president of the Southern Colonization Society established in 1865, gave this explanation for deciding to forsake the South in favor of residence in Brazil:

> The future is enveloped in clouds and darkness ... and now at one fell dash of the pen, to set free the negroes who constituted three fourths of all the property that remained to us, and nearly the whole of the laboring power of the country, and quarter them among us, where they will defy our authority,

remain a subject of continual agitation for fanatics, engender a festering wound in our side, and discourage and utterly hinder the introduction here of a better class of laborers, is enough ... to drive any people to despair and desperation.[91]

Some who chose the possibility of emigration did so because they lacked confidence in free black labor and were attracted by opportunities for reestablishing slavery in a new locale. Brazil and Mexico were especially attractive sites from this perspective, for slavery still existed in Brazil, and labor codes in Mexico appeared to give employers sufficient power to establish something approximating a system of indentured servitude.[92] Matthew Fontaine Maury, for example, an influential proponent of emigration, believed that the "Virginia gentlemen" and the "Southern gentry" were destined to become "hewers of wood and drawers of water to their conquerors" if they remained in the South. The alternative promoted by Maury was to recreate antebellum life in Latin America, to found a "New Virginia" in Mexico.[93]

Despite all the possible motives and apparent advantages for leaving the South, the vast majority of southern whites chose to remain. Those determined to maintain their residence in the South were alarmed by the prospect of white emigration and lobbied hard against the emigration movement. They feared that a further depletion of the white population would only make matters worse, adding to threat of "Negro Domination." The southern press frequently criticized emigration projects and urged whites to remain and make do in the South.[94] *De Bow's Review,* for example, although expressing sympathy for whites choosing to leave the South, nevertheless editorialized against emigration.[95] Critics argued that emigration would only make it more difficult for the native white population to regain control in the South. Northern newspapers also came out against emigration, and the federal government tried more official means for obstructing southern emigration, for example, by prohibiting the operation of emigrant agents from Latin American countries.[96]

Some emigrants left originally with the intention of eventually returning. By the early 1870s, however, even most of those who had intended to relocate permanently had also returned to the South. Economic distress, tropical disease, native hostility, social and political turmoil, and the difficulty of gaining title to land were among the most important reasons for the failure of southern emigration. Economic opportunities in most areas of Latin America, especially the possibilities for recreating the antebellum world, were not great. Emigré planters, for example, found Brazilian slaves no less difficult to control than free blacks.[97] The failure of the possibility of white emigration meant that southern whites were not going to be able to escape the presence of free blacks.

Notes

1. *The Nation* 1 (October 26, 1865): 523.

2. John Richard Dennett, *The South As It Is, 1865–1866* (New York: Viking Press, 1967 [1865–1866]), 76.

3. Whitelaw Reid, *After the War: A Tour of the Southern States, 1865–1866* (New York: Harper & Row, 1965 [1866]), 361.

4. Walter L. Fleming, "Deportation and Colonization: An Attempted Solution of the Race Problem," in *Studies in Southern History and Politics* (New York: Columbia University Press, 1914), 30.

5. Henry N. Sherwood, "Early Negro Deportation Projects," *Mississippi Valley Historical Review* 2 (March 1916): 484–85. On the colonization movement prior to the rise of the American Colonization Society, see also Benjamin Brawley, *A Social History of the American Negro* (New York: Collier, 1971 [1921]), 116–27; Don B. Kates, Jr., "Abolition, Deportation, Integration: Attitudes Toward Slavery in the Early Republic," *Journal of Negro History* 53 (January 1968): 33–47; Winthrop D. Jordan, *White Over Black: American Attitudes Toward the Negro, 1550–1812* (Baltimore: Penguin, 1969), 542–69.

6. Jordan, *White Over Black*, 551.

7. Jordan, *White Over Black*, 561. See also Brawley, *A Social History of the American Negro*, 121–22; Frederic Bancroft, "The Early Antislavery Movement and African Colonization," in *Frederic Bancroft: Historian*, ed. Jacob E. Cooke (Norman: University of Oklahoma Press, 1957), 156.

8. Jordan, White *Over Black*, 565.

9. On the American Colonization Society, see Bancroft, "The Early Antislavery Movement," 156–91; Henry N. Sherwood, "The Formation of the American Colonization Society," *Journal of Negro History* 2 (July 1917): 209–28; Early Lee Fox, *The American Colonization Society, 1817–1840* (Baltimore: Johns Hopkins University Press, series 37, number 3, Johns Hopkins University Studies in Historical and Political Science, 1919); Brainard Dyer, "The Persistence of the Idea of Negro Colonization," *Pacific Historical Review* 12 (March 1943): 53–65; Charles I. Foster, "The Colonization of Free Negroes in Liberia, 1816–35," *Journal of Negro History* 38 (January 1953): 41–66; Willis Dolmond Boyd, *Negro Colonization in The National Crisis, 1860–1870* (Ph.D. diss., University of California at Los Angeles, 1953), especially chapters 1–3; P. J. Staudenraus, *The African Colonization Movement, 1816–1865* (New York: Columbia University Press, 1961).

10. Staudenraus, *The African Colonization Movement*, 15, 19–20, 120–21; Leon Litwack, *North of Slavery: The Negro in the Free States, 1790–1860* (Chicago: University of Chicago Press, 1961), 20–22; George M. Fredrickson, *The Black Image in the White Mind: The Debate on Afro-American Character and Destiny, 1818–1914* (New York: Harper & Row, 1971), 12–24.

11. Jordan, *White Over Black*, 566; Litwack, *North of Slavery*, 254; Bancroft, "The Early Antislavery Movement," 159–62; Ira Berlin, *Slaves Without Masters: The Free Negro in the Antebellum South* (New York: Random House, 1974): 201–2.

12. Fox, *The American Colonization Society*, Staudenraus, *The African Colonization Movement*, 104–06, 120–21.

13. Staudenraus, *The African Colonization Movement*, 251; Fleming, "Deportation and Colonization," 5.

14. Louis Mehlinger, "The Attitude of the Free Negro Toward African Colonization," *Journal of Negro History* 1 (July 1916): 301. On the hostility of free blacks toward African colonization in the prewar period, see also Litwack, *North of Slavery*, 24–26; Berlin, *Slaves Without Masters*, 204–7; Brawley, *A Social History of the American Negro*, 159–64. See especially William Lloyd Garrison, *Thoughts on African Colonization* (New York: Arno Press, 1968 [1832]), part 2, which consists of numerous statements and resolutions by free blacks expressing opposition to colonization schemes generally and to the American Colonization Society specifically.

15. Litwack, *North of Slavery*, 28–29, 252–53; Bancroft, "The Early Antislavery Movement," 187–88; Staudenraus, *The African Colonization Movement*, chapters 17 and 18.

16. On increased support among blacks for colonization during the 1850s, see Litwack, *North of Slavery*, 257–62; Berlin, *Slaves Without Masters*, 356–59; Howard H. Bell, "The Negro Emigration Movement, 1849–1854: A Phase of Negro Nationalism, *Phylon* 20 (1959): 132–42; Eric Foner, *Free Soil, Free Labor, Free Men: The Ideology of the Republican Party Before the Civil War* (New York: Oxford University Press, 1970), 274–75; Richard Blackett, "Martin R. Delany and Robert Campbell: Black Americans in Search of an African Colony," *Journal of Negro History* 62 (January 1977): 217–34. Blackett makes a useful distinction between "nationalist emigrationists," "guided primarily by the desire to develop a black nation," and "antislavery emigrationists," "directed more by their displeasure with the United States as a bastion of slavery." The decade of the 1850s was characterized by a relative increase in sentiment favorable to the "nationalist emigrationists."

17. John G. Nicolay and John Jay, eds., *Complete Works of Abraham Lincoln*, new and enlarged ed. (New York; Lamb Publishing Company, 1905), vol, 8, 1–9. For typical selections from Lincoln on emancipation and colonization, see also ibid., vol. 2, 337–39; vol. 7, 270–74; vol. 8, 117–31. For useful discussions of Lincoln's position on emancipation and colonization, see Kenneth Stampp, *The Era of Reconstruction, 1865–1877* (New York: Random House, 1965), 32–35; Gary R. Planck, "Abraham Lincoln and Black Colonization: Theory and Practice," *Lincoln Herald* 72 (Summer 1970): 61–77; George M. Fredrickson, "A Man but Not a Brother: Abraham Lincoln and Racial Equality," *Journal of Southern History* 41 (February 1975): 30–58. On black reaction, mostly unfavorable, to Lincoln's colonization proposals, see Benjamin Quarles, *Lincoln and the Negro* (New York: Oxford University Press, 1962), 116–19; fames M. McPherson, *The Negro's Civil War: How American Negroes Felt and Acted During the War for the Union* (New York: Random House, 1965), 77–97; McPherson, "Abolitionist and Negro Opposition to Colonization During the Civil War," *Phylon* 26 (1965): 391–99.

18. For Mitchell's views, see Warren A. Beck, "Lincoln and Negro Colonization in Central America," *Abraham Lincoln Quarterly* 6 (September 1950): 172–76.

19. U.S. Congress, House, *Emancipation and Colonization,* Report Number 148, 37th Congress, 2nd Session (Washington, D.C.: Government Printing Office [GPO], 1862), 13–14 (hereafter cited as *Emancipation and Colonization*). See also Robert H. Zoellner, "Negro Colonization: The Cimate of Opinion Surrounding Lincoln, 1860–1865," *Mid-America* 42 (July 1960): 137–41.

20. *Emancipation and Colonization,* 14–18. See also Zoellner, "Negro Colonization," 142–43; Fleming, "Deportation and Colonization," 14.

21. *Emancipation and Colonization,* 19. See also Foner, *Free Soil, Free Labor, Free Men,* 272–74.

22. *Emancipation and Colonization,* 23–24.

23. Zoellner, "Negro Colonization," 139.

24. For the contract between Ambrose Thompson and the U.S. government, see U.S. Congress, House, *Acounts of the Colonization Agent,* Executive Document Number 227, 41st Congress, 2nd Session (Washington, DC.: GPO, 1870), 2–4, For official documents pertaining to the Chiriqui project, see U.S. Congress, Senate, *Message from the President of the United States ... Respecting the Transportation, Settlement, and Colonization of Persons of the African Race.* Executive Document Number 55, 39th Congress, 1st Session (Washington, D.C.: GPO, 1866), 4–11, 13–18 (hereafter cited as *Message from the President, Colonization*). See also Fleming, "Deportation and Colonization, 18–22; Planck, "Abraham Lincoln and Black Colonization," 65–71; Beck, "Lincoln and Negro Colonization," 166–83; Boyd, *Negro Colonization in the National Crisis,* 170–79; Frederic Bancroft, "Schemes to Colonize Negroes in Central America," in *Frederic Bancroft,* ed. Cooke, 203–27; Charles H. Wesley, "Lincoln's Plan for Colonizing the Emancipated Negroes," *Journal of Negro History* 4 (January 1919): 16–17; N, Andrew N. eleven, "Some Plans for Colonizing Liberated Negro Slaves in Hispanic America," *Journal of Negro History* 11 (January 1926): 35–49; Paul J. Schieps, "Lincoln and the Chiriqui Colonization Project, "*Journal of Negro History* 37 (October 1952): 418–53.

25. *Message from the President, Colonization,* 51.

26. For official documents pertaining to the island of à Vache project, see *Message from the President, Colonization,* 11–12, 24–30, 35–37, 40–42, 45–46, 50–52. See also Frederic Bancroft, "The Ile à Vache Experiment in Colonization," in *Frederic Bancroft,* ed. Cooke, 228–58; Boyd, *Negro Colonization in The National Crisis,* 180–208; Fleming, "Deportation and Colonization," 21–26; Planck, "Abraham Lincoln," 72–75; Wesley, "Lincoln's Plan for Colonizing the Emancipated Negroes," 17–19.

27. See especially Schieps, "Lincoln and the Chiriqui Colonization Project," 448–50; G. S. Boritt, "The Voyage to the Colony Linconia: The Sixteenth President, Black Colonization, and the Defense Mechanism of Avoidance," *The Historian* 37 (August 1975): 619–32; Mark E. Neely, Jr., "Abraham Lincoln and Black Colonization: Benjamin Butler's Spurious Testimony," *Civil War History* 25 (March 1979): 77–83.

28. Fleming, "Deportation and Colonization," 11; Zoellner, "Negro Colonization," 137–41; Bancroft, "Schemes to Colonize Negroes," 198–202.

29. U.S. Congress, Senate, *The Congressional Globe*, 37th Congress, 2nd Session (April 11, 1862), vol. 32, part 2, 1633.

30. *Emancipation and Colonization*, 15.

31. Zoellner, "Negro Colonization," 140.

32. Litwack, *North of Slavery*, 275–79; Robert F. Durden, "Ambiguities in the Antislavery Crusade of the Republican Party," in *The Antislavery Vanguard: New Essays on the Abolitionists*, ed. Martin Duberman (Princeton, N.J.: Princeton University Press, 1965), 362–94; Martin Duberman, "The Northern Response to Slavery," in ibid., 395–413; William H. Pease and Jane H. Pease, "Antislavery Ambivalence: Immediatism, Expediency, Race," *American Quarterly* 17 (Winter 1965): 682–95; Lany Gara, "Slavery and the Slave Power: A Crucial Distinction," *Civil War History* 15 (March 1969): 5–18.

33. V. Jacque Voegeli, *Free But Not Equal: The Midwest and the Negro During the Civil War* (Chicago: University of Chicago Press, 1967), 4–9.

34. Voegeli, *Free But Not Equal*, 7, 20, 58; Durden, "Ambiguities in the Antislavery Crusade," 386–88, 393.

35. Voegeli, *Free But Not Equal*, 110–11. See also Fredrickson, *The Black Image in the White Mind*, 166–67; Lawrence N. Powell, *New Masters; Northern Planters During the Civil War and Reconstruction* (New Haven, Conn.: Yale University Press, 1980), 2–3.

36. Voegeli, *Free But Not Equal*, 118–23.

37. Willis Dolmond Boyd, *Negro Colonization in The National Crisis*, chapters 8 and 9; Boyd, "Negro Colonization in the Reconstruction Era, 1865–1870," *Georgia Historical Quarterly* 40 (December 1965): 360–82.

38. Lawrence J. Friedman, *The White Savage: Racial Fantasies in the Postbellum South* (Englewood Cliffs, N.J.: Prentice-Hall, 1970), 26.

39. John T. Trowbridge, *The Desolate South, 1865–1866: A Picture of the Battlefields and of the Devastated Confederacy* (New York: Duell, Sloan and Pierce, 1956 [1866]): 68.

40. *Southern Cultivator* 25 (January 1867): 11.

41. *Southern Cultivator* 27 (February 1869): 50–51.

42. Sidney Andrews, *The South Since the War: As Shown by Fourteen Weeks of Travel and Observation in Georgia and the Carolinas* (Boston: Houghton Mifflin, 1971 (1866)): 157.

43. *De Bow's Review* 1 (January 1866): 73. See also ibid. 1 (January 1866): 59–67; Friedman, *The White Savage*, 23–26.

44. U.S. Congress, House, *Report of the Joint Committee on Reconstruction*, Executive Document Number 30, 39th Congress, 1st Session (Washington, D.C.: GPO, 1866), part 2, 34 (hereafter cited as *Report of the Joint Committee on Reconstruction*).

45. Reid, *After the War*, 417.

46. *Report of the Joint Committee on Reconstruction*, part 2, 128. See also ibid., part 2, 176; U.S. Congress, Senate, *Report of Carl Schurz on the States of South Carolina, Georgia, Alabama, Mississippi, and Louisiana*, by Carl Schurz, Executive Document Number 2, 39th Congress, 1st Session (Washington, D.C.: GPO, 1866), 21 (hereafter cited as *Report of Carl Schurz*); *Southern Cultivator* 26 (November 1868): 328–29; Vernon Lane Wharton, *The Negro in Mississippi, 1865–1890* (New York: Harper & Row, 1965 [1947]), 49–50.

47. Dennett, *The South As It Is*, 171–72.

48. James L. Roark, *Masters Without Slaves: Southern Planters in Civil War and Reconstruction* (New York: W. W. Norton, 1977), 169.

49. *Report of the Joint Committee on Reconstruction*, part 2, 128.

50. Andrews, *The South Since the War*, 28. See also *Report of the Joint Committee on Reconstruction*, part 2, 34; part 3, 16.

51. Herbert Aptheker, ed., *A Documentary History of the Negro People in the United States* (New York: Citadel Press, 1951), 468–69.

52. Andrews, *The South Since the War*. 157.

53. Cited in Thomas Wagstaff, "Call Your Old Master—'Master': Southern Political Leaders and Negro Labor During Presidential Reconstruction," *Labor History* 10 (Slimmer 1969): 336.

54. *Report of the Joint Committee on Reconstruction*, part 2, 76–77. See also ibid., part 2, 29, 32, 207, 244; Dennett, *The South As It Is*, 169.

55. Andrews, *The South Since the War*, 177.

56. Cited in Dorothy Sterling, ed., *The Trouble They Seen: Black People Tell the Story of Reconstruction* (New York: Doubleday, 1976), 43.

57. Andrews, *The South Since the War*, 27, 36, 321; Dennett, *The South As It Is*, 190; Trowbridge, *The Desolate South*, 190; *Report of Carl Schurz*, 32; *The Nation* 1 (July 27, 1865): 107; John Preston McConnell, *Negroes and Their Treatment in Virginia from 1865 to 1867* (New York: Negro Universities Press, 1969 [1910]), 16; Joel Williamson, *After Slavery: The Negro in South Carolina During Reconstruction, 1861–1877* (New York: W. W. Norton, 1975 [1965]), 248–52; Claude H. Nolen, *The Negro's Image in the South: The Anatomy of White Supremacy* (Lexington: University Press of Kentucky, 1967), 40–50, 181–82.

58. Kenneth Stampp, *The Peculiar Institution: Slavery in the Ante-Bellum South* (New York: Vintage, 1956), 11; Stampp, *The Imperiled Union: Essays on the Background of the Civil War* (Oxford: Oxford University Press, 1980), 241–43.

59. *Report of Carl Schurz* (accompanying documents), 65. See also Manual Gottlieb, "The Land Question in Georgia During Reconstruction," *Science and Society* 3 (Summer 1939): 376. The threat of another St. Domingue, even more than a half a century later, was a source of constant worry to southern whites. According to Gottlieb, "The Negro revolution in San Domingo was

to the ruling class of the South what the Bolshevik Revolution is to the present-day bourgeoisie: the sum of all possible horrors.

60. Cited in Boyd, "Negro Colonization in the Reconstruction Era," 363.

61. Trowbridge, *The Desolate South*, 198. Italics added.

62. *Report of the Joint Committee on Reconstruction*, part 2, 93–94.

63. *De Bow's Review* 4 (July 1867): 15–16.

64. *De Bow's Review* 1 (February 1866) 166–67. See also ibid. 1 (March 1866): 269–70; ibid, 2 (September 1866): 285; Dennett, *The South As It Is*, 102–3.

65. *The Nation* 1 (July 27, 1865): 107. In subsequent issues the editors of the *Nation* took issue with the prediction that free blacks were doomed to extinction. See ibid. 1 (September 14, 1865): 325–27; ibid. 1 (September 21, 1865): 362.

66. F. W. Loring and C. F. Atkinson, *Cotton Culture and the South Considered With Reference to Emigration* (Boston: A. Williams and Co., 1869), 20. See also ibid., 5–11; *De Bow's Review* 6 (October 1867): 363; Trowbridge, *The Desolate South*, 47–48, 174, 176–77, 243, 263; Dennett, *The South As It is*, 290, 351; *Report of the Joint Committee on Reconstruction*, part 3, 136; part 4, 131; McConnell, *Negroes and Their Treatment in Virginia*, 47.

67. Dennett, *The South As It Is*, 6. See also *De Bow's Review* 2 (September 1866): 285.

68. Aptheker, ed., *A Documentary History of the Negro People*, 467.

69. Friedman, *The White Savage*, 32, 36.

70. Reid, *After the War*, 44–45. See also Dennett, *The South As It Is*, 163–64.

71. Dennett, *The South As It Is*, 15.

72. Cited in Dennett, *The South As It Is*, 133. On the idea that careful legislation might prevent the extinction of the black race, see also Loring and Atkinson, *Cotton Culture and the South*, 6–7; Reid, *After the War*, 410.

73. Cf. Charles L. Flynn, Jr., *White Land, Black Labor: Caste and Class in Late Nineteenth-Century Georgia* (Baton Rouge: Louisiana State University Press, 1983), 14.

74. Reid, *After the War*. 146–47.

75. *The Nation* 1 (September 28, 1865): 393.

76. Reid, *After the War*, 146–47. See also *Report of the Joint Committee on Reconstruction*, part 2, 248; part 3, 28.

77. Cited in Leon Litwack, *Been in the Storm So Long: The Aftermath of Slavery* (New York: Random House, 1979), 516.

78. Cited in Claude F. Oubre, *Forty Acres and a Mule: The Freedmen's Bureau and Black Land Ownership* (Baton Rouge: Louisiana State University Press, 1978), 6. On black opposition to colonization, see also ibid., 7–8; Andrews, *The South Since the War*, 98; Litwack, *Been in the Storm So Long*, 308, 504, 515–16.

79. *Report of the Joint Committee on Reconstruction*, part 2, 56.

80. Litwack, *North of Slavery*, 262; Boyd, "Negro Colonization in the Reconstruction Era," 378–79.

81. On the growing interest in emigration among blacks in the late and post-Reconstruction period, see Nolen, *The Negro's Image in the South*, 182–88; Walter L. Fleming, "'Pap' Singleton, The Moses of the Colored Exodus," *American Journal of Sociology* 15 (July 1909): 61–82; Fred J. Rippy, "A Negro Colonization Project in Mexico, 1895," *Journal of Negro History* 6 (January 1921): 66–73; John G. Van Deusen, "The Exodus of 1879," *Journal of Negro History* 21 (April 1936): 111–29; Leo Alilunas, "Statutory Means of Impeding Emigration of the Negro," *Journal of Negro History* 22 (April 1937): 148–62; Joseph H. Taylor, "The Great Migration From North Carolina in 1879," *North Carolina Historical Review* 31 (January 1954); 18–33; Frenise A. Logan, "The Movement of Negroes From North Carolina, 1876–1894," *North Carolina Historical Review* 33 (January 1956): 45–65; Nell Irvin Painter, *Exodusters: Black Migration to Kansas After Reconstruction* (New York: Alfred A. Knopf, 1977).

82. Cited in Williamson, *After Slavery*, 252.

83. On the possibility of white emigration from the South after the war, see Roark, *Masters Without Slaves*, 120–31; J. Fred Rippy, "Mexican Projects of the Confederates," *Southwestern Historical Quarterly* 22 (April 1919): 291–317; Lawrence F. Hill, "Confederate Exiles to Brazil," *Hispanic American Historical Review* 7 (May 1927): 192–210; Hill, "The Confederate Exodus to Latin America I," *Southwestern Historical Quarterly* 39 (October 1935); 100–134; Hill, "The Confederate Exodus to Latin America II," *Southwestern Historical Quarterly* 39 (January 1936): 161–99; Hill, "The Confederate Exodus to Latin American III," *Southwestern Historical Quarterly* 39 (April 1936): 309–26; George D. Harmon, "Confederate Migration to Mexico," *Hispanic American Historical Review* 17 (November 1937): 458–87; Blanche Henry Clark Weaver, "Confederate Emigration to Brazil," *Journal of Southern History* 27 (February 1961): 33–53; Andrew F. Rolle, *The Lost Cause: The Confederate Exodus to Mexico* (Norman: University of Oklahoma Press, 1965); Robert E. Shalhope, "Race, Class, Slavery, and the Antebellum Southern Mind," *Journal of Southern History* 37 (November 1971): 556–74; Michael Wayne, *The Reshaping of Plantation Society: The Natchez District, 1860–1880* (Baton Rouge: Louisiana State University Press, 1983), 53–58; Daniel E. Sutherland, "Exiles, Emigrants, and Sojourners: The Post-Civil War Confederate Exodus in Perspective," *Civil War History* 31 (September 1985): 237–56.

84. New Orleans *Tribune*, August 17, 1865.

85. Hill, "The Confederate Exodus to Latin America I," 116–17.

86. Weaver, "Confederate Emigration to Brazil," 33–53; Hill, "Confederate Exiles to Brazil," 193–94; Hill, "The Confederate Exodus to Latin America 1," 114–17; Harmon, "Confederate Migration to Mexico," 458–59. See also Trowbridge, *The Desolate South*, 231; *Report of the Joint Committee on Reconstruction*, part 4, 114, 145.

87. Hill, "Confederate Exiles to Brazil," 192–96; Hill, "The Confederate Exodus to Latin America I," 114; Weaver, "Confederate Emigration to Brazil," 33–53; Harmon, "Confederate Migration to Mexico," 461–65.

88. Hill, "Confederate Exiles to Brazil," 192; Hill, "The Confederate Exodus to Latin American I," 121–22; Dennett, *The South As It Is*, 64; Reid, *After the War*, 211, 374.

89. Sutherland, "Exiles, Emigrants, and Sojourners," 238. Sutherland estimates that approximately 5,000 southerners emigrated to Brazil; 2,500 to Mexico; 1,000 to Honduras; and 500 to Venezuela.

90. Trowbridge, *The Desolate South*, 222.

91. Cited in Hill, "The Confederate Exodus to Latin America I," 110–11.

92. Wayne, *The Reshaping of Plantation Society*, 54–55; Hill, "The Confederate Exodus to Latin America III," 317–18.

93. Cited in Shalhope, "Race, Class, Slavery," 562–64. On the issue of motivation, see Roark, *Masters Without Slaves*, 122–24; Sutherland, "Exiles, Emigrants, and Sojourners," 237–56; Hill, "The Confederate Exodus to Latin America I," 110–13; Powell, *New Masters*, 41–42.

94. Weaver, "Confederate Emigration to Brazil," 37, 45–46; Hill, "Confederate Exiles to Brazil," 193; Harmon, "Confederate Migration to Mexico," 459, 477–79.

95. *De Bow's Review* 1 (January 1866): 108; ibid. 1 (June 1866): 623; ibid., 2 (July 1866): 30–38; ibid. 4 (December 1867): 537–45.

96. Harmon, "Confederate Migration to Mexico," 476–77, 485–86; Roark, *Masters Without Slaves*, 122.

97. Wayne, *The Reshaping of Plantation Society*, 56; Sutherland, "Exiles, Emigrants, and Sojourners," 239, 242–43; Hill, "The Confederate Exodus to Latin America II," 161–99; Hill, "The Confederate Exodus to Latin America III," 309–26; Harmon, "Confederate Migration to Mexico," 473–87; Weaver, "Confederate Emigration to Brazil," 47–53.

Directions: Reflect on what you have read and use information from the reading selections as a resource as you respond to the following critical thinking questions.

1. Do you think that the readings reveal characteristics of American economic development? Why or why not? What examples support your claims?
2. How do the readings illustrate the concepts of race, class, and gender within America's growing economic sovereignty? Can you provide examples?
3. Based on the readings, can you identify some of the strengths and weaknesses of America's economic developments? Can you provide examples? In what ways can you see these developments demonstrating a dilemma over American liberty and economic independence in the United States?